Father Andrew Huu Le Nguyen was born on November 9, 1943 in Vinh Long Province, South Vietnam to a farmer family. He is the youngest of the six siblings.

He studied at Saigon ST. JOSEPH'S Seminary and was ordained into priesthood in 1970. From 1970 to 1975, he served at several parishes in Mekong Delta, South Vietnam.

In 1976, he was arrested by the police under the Communist regime due to his anti-government ideology, and was imprisoned for 13 years in both South and North Vietnam concentration camps. After his release from prison in 1988, he fled to Thailand as a refugee.

In 1990, he was invited by Bishop Dennis Browne, Bishop of Auckland, to New Zealand to look after The Vietnamese Catholic Community. After 30 years in his role as the Vietnamese Chaplain, he is now retired and based in Auckland, New Zealand.

Respectfully to my Motherland, Vietnam.

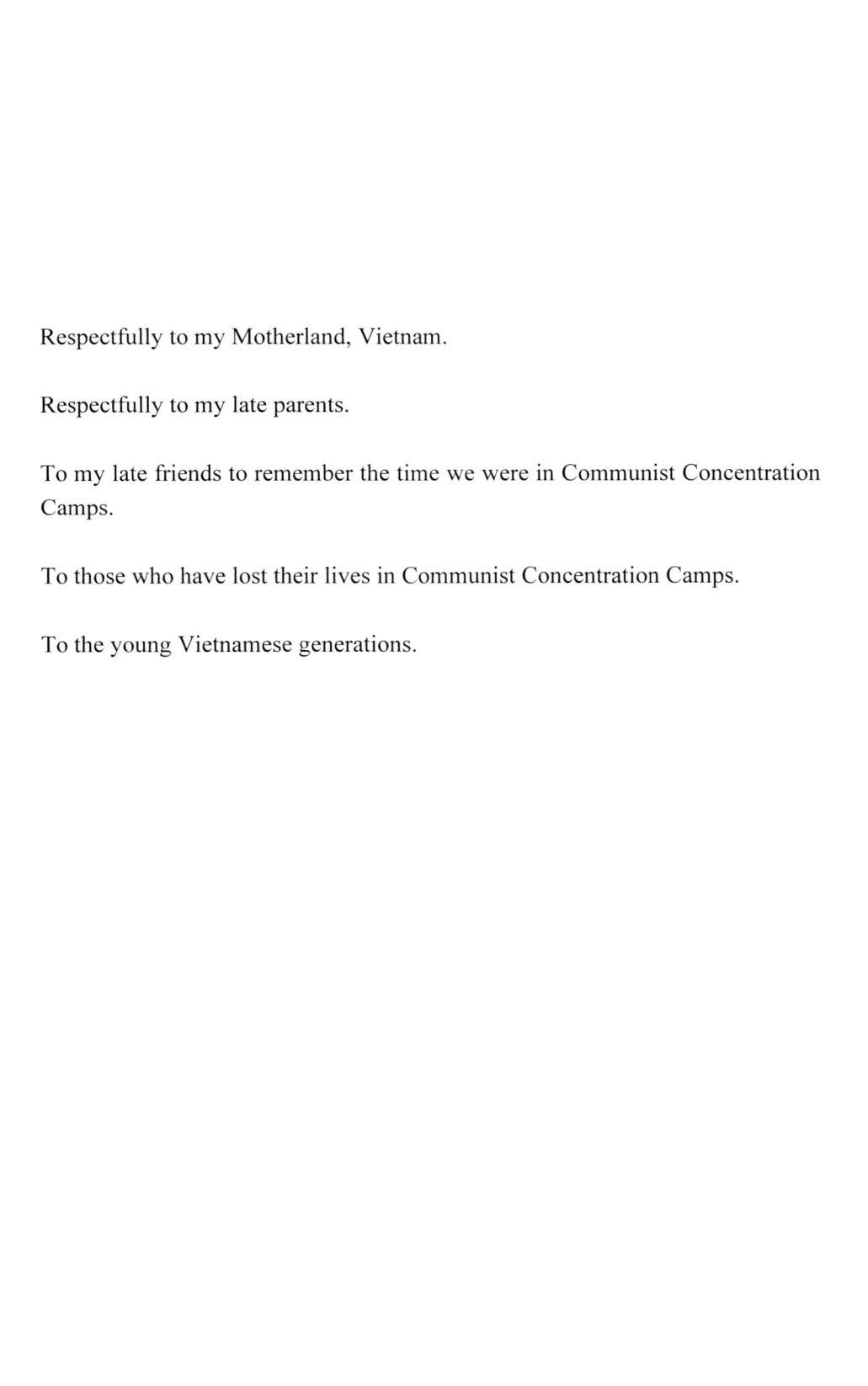

Respectfully to my late parents.

To my late friends to remember the time we were in Communist Concentration Camps.

To those who have lost their lives in Communist Concentration Camps.

To the young Vietnamese generations.

Father Andrew Huu Le Nguyen

"I MUST LIVE!"

The Autobiographical Reflections of a Vietnamese Catholic Priest, in his 13 Years in Communist Concentration Camps.

AUSTIN MACAULEY PUBLISHERS™
LONDON * CAMBRIDGE * NEW YORK * SHARJAH

Copyright © Father Andrew Huu Le Nguyen 2023

The right of Father Andrew Huu Le Nguyen to be identified as author of this work has been asserted by the author in accordance with sections 77 and 78 of the Copyright, Designs and Patents Act 1988.

All rights reserved. No part of this publication may be reproduced, stored in a retrieval system, or transmitted in any form or by any means, electronic, mechanical, photocopying, recording, or otherwise, without the prior permission of the publishers.

Any person who commits any unauthorised act in relation to this publication may be liable to criminal prosecution and civil claims for damages.

All of the events in this memoir are true to the best of the author's memory. The views expressed in this memoir are solely those of the author.

A CIP catalogue record for this title is available from the British Library.

ISBN 9781398493520 (Paperback)
ISBN 9781398493537 (ePub e-book)

www.austinmacauley.com

First Published 2023
Austin Macauley Publishers Ltd®
1 Canada Square
Canary Wharf
London
E14 5AA

First of all, I would like to sincerely thank Ms. Thuy Duong Nguyen (USA) who has cheerfully spent so much time and efforts to translate the memoir into English.

I would also like to thank the following people who have helped me one way or another to make the memoir as perfect as possible.

Sr. Maureen Connolly O.P., New Zealand; Mrs. Margaret Freedman, NZ; Mr Manh van Bui, NZ; Mr Jeff Saunders, NZ; Ms. Louise Trinh and Thomas Pham, NZ; and especially Mrs. Barbara Thomson.

Finally, I would like to offer my big thank you, the Austin Macauley Publishers Ltd. for putting *"I MUST LIVE!"* in readers' hands.

Table of Contents

Introduction	13
Part One: My Life Before Being Imprisoned	21
Chapter 1: My People's Plight	23
Chapter 2: Stepping into the World of War	56
Chapter 3: My Priestly Vocation	95
Chapter 4: The Life-Changing Event	105
Part Two: My Life in the Communist Concentration camps	115
Chapter 5: Life's Turning Point	117
Chapter 6: Prison Camps in the South	133
Chapter 7: Farewell to the South	145
Chapter 8: The Exiled Prisoner	153
Chapter 9: The 'Gateway to Heaven' Camp	172
Chapter 10: From Bad to Worse	201
Chapter 11: For the Sake of Freedom	212
Chapter 12: The Gamble of Life and Death	222
Chapter 13: "I Must Live! I Must Live! I Must Live!"	237
Chapter 14: The Pits of Hell	247
Chapter 15: 'Bình Thanh', The Notorious Bandit	263
Part Three: From Small Concentration camps to a Huge One	279
Chapter 16: Last Leg of the Journey	281

Part Four: Release from Prison   **299**

   Chapter 17: Thinking of the Road Ahead   *301*

Epilogue: In the Pursuit of Freedom Again   **311**

   Supplement 1: Death of Bình Thanh   *313*

   Supplement 2: Pristine Land Beckons Birds   *323*

   Supplement 3: Thankful for a Can of Water   *330*

   Supplement 4: Meeting Bùi Đình Thi Again 15 Years Later   *334*

Map of Vietnam
And The Prison Camps I Was Detained

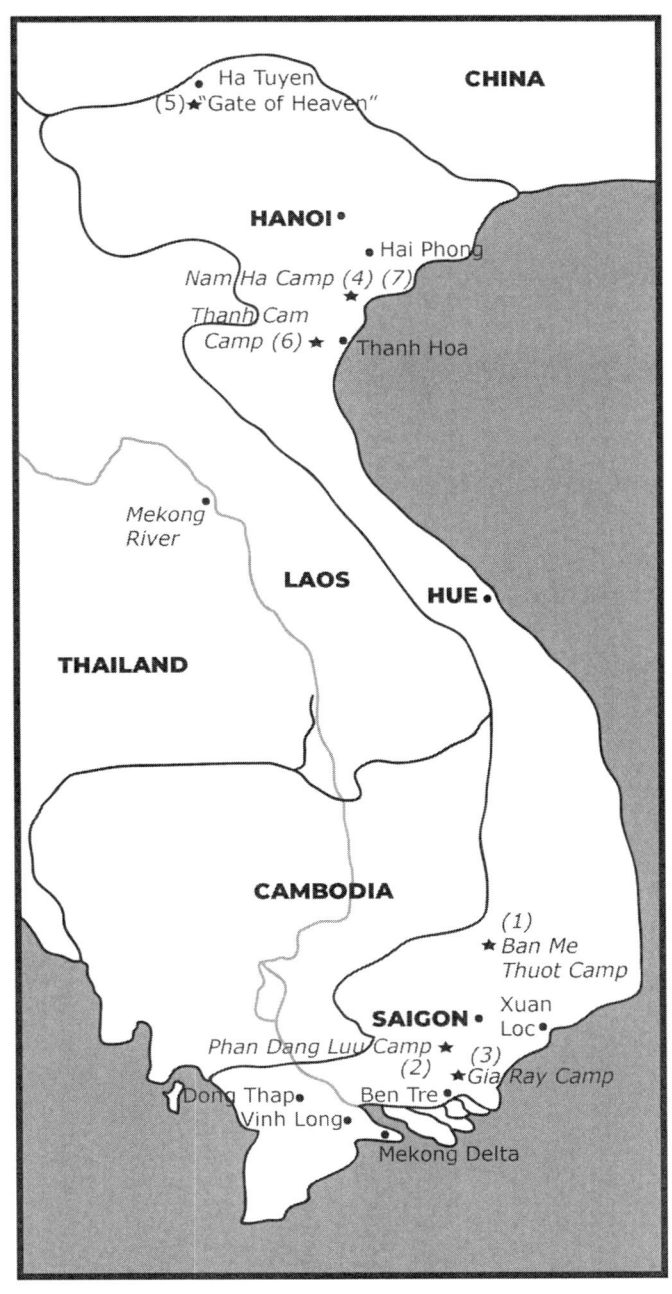

HAMILTON  DIOCESE

P.O. Box 4353
Hamilton East
Hamilton 3247
New Zealand

Bishop's Office

Telephone 0-7-856 6989
Fax 0-7-856 1215
E-mail: bishop@cdh.org.nz

14 February 2009

Anyone who reads "I Must Live!" is due to have a reading experience that is beyond compare.

In his detailed description of life in prison, Father Nguyen Huu Le describes the horrendous ordeals that he and other prisoners endured at the hands of communist overlords. Father Le's story is a story of horrendous inhumanity and relates episodes of events that would have shattered the soul of most people. The fact that Father Le was able to maintain his faith and at the same time uplift the spirits of his fellow prisoners gives testimony to a life of complete dedication to God. As Father Le refers to on many occasions in the text, it was only his faith in God and in his Priesthood that gave him the strength to endure.

Despite his horrendous suffering, both mental and physical, Father Le is able to see the good side of his oppressors. He is also able to write with a degree of poetical brilliance and a delightful sense of humour in what were impossible conditions. One cannot help but be uplifted by such commitment and faith.

As you read these reflections I know that you will thank God for Father Le's safe delivery and for his faith that still flowers very brightly in his life.

✠ Denis Browne
BISHOP OF HAMILTON

Introduction

On a sunny summer day in 1988, a packed bus stopped on the main street in the city of Hanoi. Among the passengers jostling their way out were the three just-released prisoners from *Nam Hà* Prison. Brother *Kỳ*, a former seminarian and a Native of the North Vietnam, whereas *Nguyễn Đức Khuân* and I came from the South. *Khuân* and I were setting foot in Hanoi for the first time. We followed Brother *Kỳ* closely. This was an overwhelming change of environment to us. Just this morning, we had been locked in the silent, almost deserted *Nam Hà* Prison. Now, in the early afternoon, we were in the noisy, bustling Capital city of Vietnam. Although there were not as many automobiles as I remembered in Saigon a decade ago, there were lots of motorcycles and bicycles.

During my eleven years in the Northern concentration camps, I had passed through Hanoi four times, but only in the night, and was always handcuffed. The first time was on April 20, 1977; the Ocean liner *SÔNG HƯƠNG* transported us, prisoners from the South to the port of *Hải Phòng* from there by truck beyond the city to reach *Nam Hà* Camp.

The same day, this warm afternoon, I set foot legally in Hanoi, relishing my new freedom. I use the word *'freedom'* cautiously because I only held an official Release Permit. That precious piece of paper was kept in a makeshift chest-pocket inside of my shirt, secured by two safety pins. There was no way I was going to risk losing my only legal document. Hopefully, it would also help me to avoid any hassle while I was fresh out of prison. I knew I still reeked of captivity. But I did have official identity! Armed with this document, I intended to travel around the North for a while before heading to Saigon, roughly two thousand kilometres to the South.

The Cradle of My People

Now, I relaxed on a park bench, and observed the people of Hanoi as they walked alone or in twos or threes, but always keeping to themselves. It seems to me that all wore solemn, tired expressions. Men and women alike were dressed in similar black pants and white shirts, and I wistfully recalled the *Áo dài*, the traditional modest dress of the women in pre-war days. Many of the men wore *Nón cối* (Military helmets) while the women wore traditional *Nón lá* (Palm leaf hats). I missed the cheerful chatter of Saigon which I left 11 years ago. For generations, folk songs had described the poetic setting of Hanoi's thirty-six *Phố Phường* (Market Streets). Now I was seeing them with my own eyes and was enchanted. This was not a sophisticated city but instead had natural and many beautiful Vietnamese artefacts. I loved it from that first encounter and started to relax.

Brother *Kỳ* had promised to guide us to the Hanoi Diocesan Centre. As I followed him, I became aware that he was still wearing his prison uniform with the mark '*CẢI TẠO*' (Re-education) printed on the back. What if people around us noticed? Might they not imagine that we were escaped prisoners? I wished he had dressed differently. Then I saw Brother *Kỳ's* growing excitement as we neared our destination, and forgot about his appearance.

This cheerful, dark-skinned Brother always showed exactly what he was feeling. A number of his contemporaries were already priests, but because of his strongly held beliefs, he'd been in prison during the time of his ordination and so missed out. Brother *Kỳ* knew most of the Northern clergymen, from the Cardinal down, to two of his classmates, who were working as housekeepers at the Diocesan Centre. As we neared the Diocesan Centre, the prospect of meeting the Cardinal made me feel nervous.

Suddenly a small man blocked our path. "Did you men just get off the train?" he demanded.

I guessed that he was a secret policeman.

"No, we weren't on the train. Why do you ask us that?" I replied as calmly as I could.

"I went to pick up a family member coming from the South." You appear to be Southerners; so I thought I'd ask you so."

"Do we look like escaped prisoners?" I countered.

He looked flustered. "You are wrong, my friend," I continued.

"We were prisoners, but we haven't escaped. We were released from *Nam Hà* Prison just this morning."

But he persisted. "So where are you heading to?"

"I am heading to South, of course, but not today."

"Where do you intend to stay now?"

"Right here, in this building!" I gestured over his shoulder and we marched on, leaving him nonplussed.

Hanoi Diocesan Centre

Hanoi Diocesan Centre consisted of a number of buildings surrounding a shady courtyard. The main two-storied block was opposite the Cathedral bell tower. Walking into that courtyard was like taking a step back in time. Brother *Kỳ* led us up the front steps to the living quarters. There was no one to be seen, but with his assurance as of a family member, he walked straight in. *Khuân* and I set our backpacks on the concrete steps and relax. Soon, *Kỳ* returned along with a tall fair-skinned young man with a flat-topped crew cut, dressed like an office worker, whom he introduced to us Brother *Trác*. After warmly welcoming us, Brother *Trác* said he would announce our arrival to the Cardinal. He accompanied us into the dining hall, and provided us refreshments before excusing himself. After a few minutes, Brother *Trác* returned.

He looked at me and said, "Greetings Father, are you Father *Lễ*?"

I was astonished, "Had we not just been introduced?" I stammered, "Yes…Yes…Eh…"

Before I completed my response, Brother *Kỳ* laughed out loud. "Father! This is Brother *Trạc*, twin brother of the other gentleman, Brother *Trác*!" (He pronounced his first name with a downward inflection, and the other's is with an upward one).

I burst out laughing. "Good heavens! You two are as alike as peas in a pod!" Not only were they identical in looks, but also in dress. They reminded me of the detectives Thompson and Thomson from Paul Hergé's comic series, 'Tintin and Snowy'.

Now Brother *Trạc* asked me seriously, "Father, before arriving at the Diocesan Centre, did you meet anyone asking you any questions?"

I told him of our encounter with the man at the gate.

He sighed, saying, "That's the way it is in Hanoi now. Even an ant couldn't pass through, much less a human. I may ask, do you have any identification papers? I must report to the Police station at our gate."

We dug into our pockets. Brother *Trạc* smiled as he watched my precious Release Permit past its two safety pins. I felt embarrassed, like a peasant woman searching for her hidden change deep in a small hip pouch. "Caution pays", I explained.

"That's how it has to be! Pickpockets in Hanoi are very crafty! Especially on trains or buses, please be careful. They're as quick as squirrels!" Then he glanced through our papers before taking them out of the room.

Soon Brother *Trác* - or *Trạc*? escorted me to my guestroom while *Kỳ* and *Khuân* waited to be taken to a separate area for seminarians. I had expected that we could all be together. However, 'When in Rome, do as the Romans do'. The room provided for me was spacious and well arranged, it is so much different from the crowded cells in concentration camps I lived in last years. The door overlooked the courtyard. Across the street was the City Cultural Centre. I set down my few belongings and stepped into the bathroom. What luxury to have privacy and to use the sweet-smelling toiletries! Then I stretched out on bed and smiled, "Life is worth living!" After 13 years being locked up in prison, the sense of freedom and of having my own room was so sweet, even for a short stay. How my fortunes had changed! However, when going to meet Cardinal *Trịnh Văn Căn*, I again felt uneasy. Until now, I had known the highest-ranking spiritual leader of the Vietnamese Catholic Church, only by name and photos.

The Cardinal

As we entered his large, simply furnished office, the Cardinal warmly welcomed us at the door. This tall, saintly looking man wore the traditional purple-trimmed cassock with Roman collar. I introduced *Khuân* and myself to him respectfully, and then knelt down to kiss his ring. The Cardinal immediately lifted me to my feet and gave me a long hug, saying, "Father *Lễ*! Your return brings great joy. Thanks be to God! Thanks be to God!"

Then he shook hands with *Kỳ* and *Khuân*, who both kissed his ring. I thanked him for sending parcels to prisoner priests. The Cardinal assured me that he had always tried to do all he could for his imprisoned brothers. He also mentioned Archbishop *Nguyễn Văn Thuận* who was then held under house arrest at *Giang Xá*, and he had also sent him gifts. Last time, however, the gifts had been returned, and the Cardinal was worried. He asked me about other clergies still in prison, how the spiritual lives of clergy and people were holding up. I told him that I was the last Southern priest to be set free. However, three Northern priests were still imprisoned, as well as two from *Huế* Archdiocese.

He asked us about our plans. I told him that *Khuân* planned to return to Saigon first. I would remain in the North for two weeks to observe the state of the Catholic Church in the Northern Dioceses after decades being under Communist regime. He approved my ideas and offered any assistance I might need. He added, "Consider this Diocesan Centre as your home while you're here". Then he asked *Khuân* about his family situation and their living conditions while he had been in prison. I saw in Cardinal *Trịnh Văn Căn* all the signs of pastoral care and felt that the Vietnam Catholic Church was blessed with its leader. As we left his office, the Cardinal suggested that we visit Assistant Bishop *Nguyễn Văn Sang*.

The Assistant Bishop

During my time in prison, I'd heard from Father *Lê Đức Triệu* telling stories about Bishop *Nguyễn Văn Sang*, who was originally from the Hanoi Diocese. Both of them, along with large numbers of clergy, had fled to the South after the 1954 Geneva Cease-fire Agreements. However, the then Father *Sang* soon returned north. At the time, I had admired his apparent acceptance the hardship he would encounter under Communism. Later, he was appointed as Assistant Bishop of the Hanoi Archdiocese.

As we entered his untidy office, Bishop *Nguyễn Văn Sang* sat working at his desk. We introduced ourselves to him, explaining that we'd just been released from prison this morning. "Is that so? Thank you, thank you! Please sit down!" He said.

He remained sitting as he gestured towards the chairs against the wall. This rather careless greeting didn't make me feel welcome. To make conversation, I said, "Are you well, Bishop?"

He began to mumble in a disgruntled voice, "I just got back from a holiday at *Đồ Sơn* Beach Resort yesterday, and I'm not feeling too well. Perhaps there was too much sunshine!"

"I had heard that the *Hải Phòng* Diocese had a vacation home at *Đồ Sơn*. Did you stay there?" I continued.

"No, not at all! The Vietnam Fatherland Front (An external organisation of the Communist Party) invited me to stay at their vacation house." Bishop *Sang* rambled about the luxury provided by the State-owned guesthouse. It was obvious that he had no interest in the 'Accommodation' we had been enduring. He showed no sympathy for the three political prisoners who were just released this morning. In fact, he seemed to have no interest at all! We came to pay him a visit, not to listen to the vacation story in *Đồ Sơn* of the Assistant Bishop.

After a long while, he changed the topic and began talking at length about the French Peugeot bicycles, boasting someone in France just sent him a dozen of this marvellous bicycles. I wanted to slip away but there didn't seem to be any polite way of leaving. Suddenly, sensing we were not good listeners, he stopped mid-sentence, looked at his watch, and said, "I have an appointment."

That freed us. We left Bishop *Sang's* office as if being chased by phantoms. I felt depressed by this example of a very indifferent Vietnamese Bishop.

Back in my room, I found an envelope with a sum of money, sufficient for a fare ticket to Saigon by train and a note from the Cardinal; asking me to join him in a stroll on the terrace after supper.

Traditional Way

I entered the dining hall and found it filled with priests and seminarians. It was almost time to eat, but *Khuân* was nowhere to be seen. When I asked *Kỳ* to fetch *Khuân*, he told me that *Khuân* was a lay person, so he was not allowed to dine with us. He would eat the same food as served for us, but alone in the kitchen. I was surprised at this further indication that the Hanoi Diocese still followed out-dated customs.

After the meal, I followed the Cardinal onto the large, brick-paved terrace. As we strolled shoulder by shoulder, he briefed me on the Northern Catholic Church's situation.

Then he asked, "Do you notice anything unusual about the bricks on this terrace?"

Puzzled, I looked down but found nothing.

"You have to look further". The Cardinal continued, "Looking down at your feet won't show you."

Following his suggestion, I looked towards the end of the terrace and noticed a polished oval area. "It looks as though someone's drawn an oval shape," I answered.

The Cardinal said gloomily, "So you see it now. That's not a drawing but a worn-down track in the bricks. Those are the traces of the late Cardinal *Trịnh Như Khuê*. For more than twenty years of house arrest under the Communist regime, the first Cardinal of Vietnam walked around and around on this terrace. Because he walked for so many years, his footsteps wore the oval-shaped groove you're looking at."

It was sad to hear of Cardinal *Trịnh Như Khuê's* long imprisonment for defying the Communists.

Slow Motion Movies

I had trouble with sleep. I went out to the balcony to watch the people in the City Cultural Centre across the street. A live band was playing for couples dancing on the open terrace. They moved rhythmically enough, and yet somehow seemed to be lifeless, almost like robots. I felt pity for this younger generation, suspecting that deep inside their souls was emptiness. I thought back the previous evening and our tearful farewell of friends at the *Nam Hà* Prison. Then to break out of my melancholy mood, I wrote a short letter to my Sister, telling her of my release.

Even then I tossed and turned on my bed recalling the years past. Thirteen years, over a decade of joy and sadness intermingled in the life of a priest and prisoner. I remembered the day I said goodbye to my aged Mother, wiping away my tears as I left. She had been dead eleven years now but I had never looked upon her grave. I remember the *MINH CHÁNH* shuttle bus trip from *Trung Lương* Intersection to Saigon on a sombre evening of May 1976. That vehicle carried me into such a profound turning point in my life.

At the time, I calmed myself by thinking, "I am going into an uncertain future, with no idea of what my life will be like. However, I'm determined to write about my experiences as a play if I would live on. The trip from *Trung Lương* Intersection to Saigon in the sombre evening of May 1976 will be the opening act".

Part One
My Life Before Being Imprisoned

Chapter 1
My Peoples' Plight

After an emotional farewell to my closest friend, Fr. *Nguyễn Văn Thạnh*, I stepped onto the *MINH CHÁNH* shuttle bus at the *Trung Lương* Intersection heading to Saigon, it was towards evening. On Interstate Highway 4 connecting Saigon with western provinces, the road became quieter as twilight approached. Traffic was sparse and our car travelled faster. During this journey, as I sat quietly in the car, fatigue and depression cloaked me and seemed to turn me into a sleepwalker. I quietly looked towards the front. The scenery raced towards us in the opposite direction as the car swiftly swallowed up the road. I observed nothing, neither did I bother about listening to the talking and laughing in the back seats.

Suddenly, I was feeling drowsy as though I just had a glass of spirits, I leaned my head on the back of the seat, turning my body to find a comfortable position in my slot between the two passengers. I closed my eyes and tried to push aside my petty and tangled thoughts which I couldn't easily forget. The past attacked me. The days and months of serving as a parish priest at a small parish in *Bến Tre* Province were not so long ago; so many incidents occurred, from the big events to the small ones, they all combined leading me towards this path.

The noisy conversations between the driver and the women at the back increased in volume. They talked and laughed unceasingly, I couldn't make out what they were talking about. The man beside me, sitting on my left had a miserable look on him. His gaunt face was tanned. He appeared to be more of a peasant than a desk worker. This perception made me feel more comfortable, because these days, I tended to be wary of strangers, especially those who appeared to be 'cadres' (Communist Party member). I had to be even more alert and cautious. This man didn't look like a Communist cadre. He seemed to have no interest in contributing to other people's conversations. I sat silent, remembering the days past...

The Apparition of Our Lady

One year earlier on April 30, 1975, South Vietnam fell into the Communist's hands. To many people, this was a life-changing event. At the time, I was serving at the Cathedral of *Vĩnh Long*. I was appointed as Parish priest of a small parish in *Bến Tre* Province in May 1975. This area, previously called *Bàu Dơi*, was a poverty-stricken area with a small population.

In the early 1950s, a phenomenon happened where the Virgin Mary appeared in this desolate area, making this area more well-known. Gradually, this site became a Pilgrimage Centre. Later, the area became a parish. From what has been told. A woman was hand-catching fish in the river. She found a picture frame with a no longer recognisable picture. Perhaps the picture frame had been in the river for a long time. The finder didn't quite know what to do with it, so she brought it home to wedge into a hole in the wall to block the elements. One day by chance, a Catholic stopped by the area and saw the picture frame. Thinking it could have been an altar image, the visitor asked the fisher to take it home to display on her family altar.

There had been fighting in this area during the war. One day, French soldiers passing through the river in gunboats, opened fire and destroyed many houses along the riverbanks. In the midst of flying bullets, the family with the frame was frightened and hurriedly crawled under the altar to shelter, praying to Jesus and the Virgin Mary for protection. The surprising thing was, after the gunfire stopped; the family emerged and saw the image of Our Lady of Perpetual Help clearly appearing in the frame. This incident was reported to the Church Authorities to certify and keep records. The news spread, believers multiplied. People came to pray and pay respects to the Virgin Mary.

The Church Authorities did not officially recognise the event; however, the devotion of the people to the Virgin Mary was not discouraged. Many people's prayers were answered. Evidence for this is the many engraved '**THANK YOU**' notes on stone slabs were left in the church. The previously desolate *Bàu Dơi* area was now the Mecca for many worshippers from afar. Roads were repaired and people from elsewhere came to settle. Until 1953, pilgrims contributed money to build a small church which was very well-furbished. It also had temporary accommodation for pilgrims' stay. Bishop *Ngô Đình Thục* promoted this place to a Parish, taking the name of the *La Mã* (Rome) Parish, in remembrance of the Holy City of Rome.

In 1960, the Communist-Originated National Front for Liberation of South Vietnam (NFLSV) was born; kick starting a new phase in the political history of the South. The security that people benefitted from in the first few years of the *Ngô Đình Diệm* Government gradually waned. Following the rhythm of activism and forceful growth of the NFLSV, specifically in *Bến Tre* Province, with the name 'Land of Simultaneous Uprising', the area where the NFLSV was operating strongly made the situation increasingly tenser day by day. In the following years, the Nationalist – Communist conflict gradually escalated and expanded to other areas, especially in *Bến Tre* Province in general and particularly at the *La Mã* Parish.

Facing such a situation, a large number of Catholics migrated, almost completely, to other areas. Pilgrims also became scarce and the parish slowly became desolate. The *La Mã* Parish priest also withdrew, leaving behind only two religious nuns. Very few parishioners stayed to the church and its campus. Since then, the priest from *Cái Bông* parish, six kilometres away, had to come to the area to preside mass and nurture the remaining parishioners' spiritual lives.

The image of Our Lady of Perpetual Help to which pilgrims frequently paid respects, was also relocated to *Cái Bông's* Church for safety purposes. During wartime, the *La Mã* Church became the hiding place for Communist cadres because everybody knew the Nationalists wouldn't bomb religious establishments. Therefore, those places were the safe haven for both civilians and Communist cadres during military raids.

To make things legitimate, high-ranking NFLSV cadres in the area asked to be baptised in order to hide behind the robes of priests and religious nuns away from national security agencies. If those cadres were arrested, they would inevitably first run to the priests and nuns for help. Such situation dragged on over many years brought the result to the region of creating close ties among the priests, the nuns, and the NFLSV cadres.

The war of bombs and artillery stopped after April 30, 1975, the wartime migrants in many areas began returning to their homes. It was also the same way at the *La Mã* Parish. The number of parishioners multiplied, and a priest was needed to take responsibilities. I was assigned for this duty and moved to the Parish on May 24, 1975. At that time, the situation had completely changed. Those who hid in the shadows of priests and nuns were currently war victors and held local powers.

When I arrived, the parish still had two nuns and one Parish Council that mostly consisted of Communist cadres or their family members. I came freshly transferred from another province as a new face, a stranger to everyone in the parish and the region. Despite my utmost effort to live in harmony with everyone, I gradually became an isolated and suspected person who was monitored and spied on, even among the ones closest to me.

On the other hand, in the position of a parish priest, I could not remain silent about atheist ideal's principles, a downright anti-religious attitude. I could not ignore their interference into internal religious matters and their offensive religious oppression. Those in power were feverish with the current events. They caused excessive pain, suffering, and distress to those who were displaced from work due to social change. I will never forget the painful experiences of this transitional period. In that context, I encountered difficulty and pressure from various sources and also from people, which was quite understandable.

Mourning My Father's Death

No sooner I moved to the *La Mã* Parish, I learned that my Father had fallen gravely ill. One of my cousins came during the night by motorbike to take me home to see my Father. A few months ago, when I was at the Cathedral of *Vĩnh Long,* my Father had already been very sick; the family had been busy finding ways to treat his illness. When I took over my position at the parish, his state of health somehow improved. However, his state of health suddenly took a turn for the worst in the past few days.

I arrived at home during the night while my Father slumbered in bed, not knowing that I was there. My Sister told me that he had been exhausted during the past few days, lying there motionless without eating anything. Looking at my Father in bed, I felt hopeless, with severe anguish in my heart. My brothers and sisters had taken turns to watch over my Father the past week. They were all so tired; therefore, I took turn to take care for him that night.

I was lying in a hammock close to my Father's bed, quietly praying for him. At dawn, he turned and the blanket dropped on to the floor. I picked it up and gently covered him. Hearing the noise, he opened his eyes and saw me.

Showing his happiness, he muttered, "Is that you, Lẽ? When did you get home?"

I grasped his emaciated hands and replied through my tears, "I learned that you had fallen ill, I just got home a moment ago. How are you feeling now?"

My Father grasped my hands closely and answered me clearly. His response staggered me and yet made me very happy at the same time. He said, "You just help me sit up. I feel good."

I tried to sit him up and put a pillow behind his back so that he could lean on the headboard. He told me to hand him a bowl of congee. I fed him three spoons of congee; when it came to the fourth spoonful, he shook his head. I laid the congee bowl to the side, grabbed a face towel, and soaked it in the warm water to clean his face and his hands. I was feeling quite happy; thinking that he was getting better when he could sit up talking with me, eating some congee.

He was fully awake and didn't look like a sick person. He asked me to sit on his bed facing him. He grasped my hands and asked me about all the activities at the parish. I had a curious feeling; he had never expressed this kind of open emotion with me before. I didn't dare to talk to him about the difficulties and challenges I was facing. I just said that my life was okay. He kept his eyes closed, listening to me quietly and happily while I was telling him that the parishioners were good and they loved me.

When I finished talking, he opened his eyes, told me to my surprise to bow my head, he put his right hand on my head and said, "I don't know how long I will be alive. This is my blessing for you, I wish you well." His right hand stayed on my head for a while. I was so moved that I burst into tears. I grasped his hand and kissed it. His palm was so thin with many small hardened bumps; resulting from the hard work he had endured to support his family. After that moment, he looked at me and quietly advised with these final words, "As a priest, you have to love your parishioners. Remember my advice to never wish anyone ill. You have to wish everyone well." After finishing his words of advice, he lay down quietly and dozed off.

The next morning, I told the family that my Father was awake for a short while during the night and had eaten some congee. I didn't say anything else. On hearing this, my brothers and sister were somewhat relieved as my Father had been almost motionless and had only sipped some water the past few days. At noon, my Father became somewhat alert and had some more congee. That afternoon, I went to the city of *Vĩnh Long*, 30 kilometres away, to get some medication from a doctor of Oriental medicine who had taken care of medication for my Father in the past few months. It seemed to be effective. Unfortunately, this time while I was waiting to get the medication, one of my relatives arrived to let me know that my Father just passed away. I stood up covering my face with both hands and burst into tears. My Father's destiny had come to its end. I thanked the doctor, very grateful for his having helped my Father.

One hour later, when I reached home, my Father's body was laid on a long table in the middle of the house; his eyes were still slightly open. After I stroked his eyes gently, then, my Father's eyes became eternally shut. I didn't know until later on, the fact that my Father suddenly became awake and alert on the night my return was due the resurrection of those people, who had been ill for a long time, before their deaths. It was like an oiled lamp suddenly bursting up with light and then dying down. As for me, I thought my Father had deliberately waited to see me in order to say a few final words before leaving this world. With all the challenges waiting for me at the parish, I would always remember all my Father's final words.

After my Father's funeral, I stayed on for a few days as my Mother became bed-ridden due to exhaustion. Even on the day of my Father's burial, she was too weak to attend. I returned to the parish with a heart full of sorrows and worries due to my Father's death and my Mother's frailty. In my simple life of a priest in a rural parish, I devoted my time to my daily duties towards the parishioners. The *La Mã* Parish had been neglected for a while, so when I moved in, I had a lot of things to revolve during my first few months.

Shadowed Areas

At the time, due to circumstances and changes and life's pressures from all directions, I was very depressed. As a parish priest, on the one hand, I had to readjust the parish activities after years of devastating war. On the other hand, I had to frequently deal with problems caused by an atheist local Authorities. I tried to be patient and tolerant, waiting for the political fever to pass, so that I could concentrate on serving my regional parishioners effectively without outside interference. Besides my primary responsibilities, I found ways to alleviate my sorrows with two hobbies, fishing and learning to play the *Vọng Cổ* (The Southerners' special melody of music played on guitar.)

I was born and raised in the rural areas of the Mekong Delta with many streams and rivers, where fish and prawns were in abundance. So, as a young boy, I loved fishing. Every time I held a fishing rod in my hand, sitting on the riverbank, I forgot all about the events of life. If I could sit on a boat anchored in the middle of a wide river, nothing would be more joyful. The region where I lived was an estuary, so fish and shrimps were plentiful, especially a kind of three-spiked harmful catfish; its two spikes on either side of the head and one on the back. Any careless person could get pricked, and then they could only sit and call for God's help. On days when I caught a lot of fish, I took them to parishioners and acquaintances in the area.

In general, fishing was a pleasant hobby, bothering no one. However, one time; I almost got into trouble caused by fishing. I was sitting in a wooden canoe anchored at a dock near the church to fish. An unfamiliar Communist cadre wearing a fabric hat and a chequered scarf paddled over to my canoe. He abruptly asked me, "Who are you and what are you doing here?" It was strange that he asked me that.

"I am the Parish priest at *La Mã* Church. I am fishing," I replied.

"You're fishing but where is your rod?" The cadre continued.

I was very surprised this guy must be kidding, but the way he said it was very serious. I had not met him before, so I realised he wasn't kidding.

"Why do you ask me that? Don't you see I'm holding a fishing rod in my hand?" I replied.

He seemed astonished; he looked at the fibre fishing rod I was holding for a while. He pointed to the rod and questioned, "Can this kind of contraption with an antenna and a 'sky wire' signal to… a B52?"

I dropped the rod into my canoe. "Good Heavens! Why do you ask me that? What's a B52 business got to do with this?" I called out in surprise.

The cadre stood silent and suspicious. Immediately, I realised that he had never had a chance to see a so-called 'mechanical fishing rod'. In rural areas, people made bamboo stick for fishing rod. Actually, the fishing string went from the spool and reel through the metal rings along a long flexible bamboo stick, and into the river for fishing. I quickly reeled in the line to show him the sinker and hook; at the end that was pierced into the back of a crustacean wiggling its legs and claws - my bait to fish for three-spiked catfish! Only then, did he believe the rod I was holding was not the antenna, a kind of advanced communication device that could call a…B52! Luckily, he asked me directly, if he had secretly reported this kind of contraption to higher authorities and informed them against me that I used it to contact B52 bombers, it would have made my life miserable much earlier.

My second hobby was learning to play instrumental *Vọng Cổ* on guitar. At the time, there was a young non-Catholic blind man, named *Tám Chánh*. Although he was non-Catholic, he would often visit my Church. He had an exceptional talent playing the traditional Vietnamese music *Vọng Cổ*. He taught many people for free. I often invited him to visit the presbytery to perform this kind of traditional music and teach me those skills. Over time, we grew to be good companions. Our friendship grew deep and he wholeheartedly taught me. He was also cheerful and curious; he often asked me many questions about politics, religion, and society. Our friendship grew deep and he wholeheartedly taught me.

Once, I asked him, "Dear brother *Tám*, why is your music so sorrowful and blue? It's so wonderful, wonderful! Why do I seem to play as though I am banging and pounding on a metal barrel? My practice seemingly achieves nothing!"

"If you want to play like me, you must poke out both eyes, and discard them." His answer in one sentence rendered me speechless.

I understood. My blind friend channelled into his music a sorrowful spirit about his unfortunate life. There were times when I went to visit him at his house while everyone was out, Mr *Tám* sat playing alone, unaware of my presence. I passionately preoccupied with his playing; at the time, I spontaneously said to myself, Mr *Tám* was right, no one with normal eyesight could play like his.

I was very fond of *Vọng Cổ*, especially after I was able to play with more skills, some of the pieces that *Tám Chánh* had taught me. Gradually, I realised that most Southerners likewise enjoyed *Vọng Cổ*, I also remembered, at that time, I laboured together with the locals for digging trenches for irrigation. Because the area for trench-digging was a few days' travel away, we brought rice to cook for our meals. We laboured hard in the day time. In the evening, some young people and I gathered in the backyard of a local to cook. Then, we assembled in groups to play and sing *Vọng Cổ* before bedtime. If the moon was out, that made it even more poetic. What a pity! I loved *Vọng Cổ* but I couldn't sing. Despite that, hearing the melodious voices of singers made my eyes brim with tears. I couldn't control my emotions after hearing a few sorrowful songs.

The Political Heat Wave

I moved to this Parish when the political fever was at its height. There were some people, who were beguiled by it, so intensely that they did everything to show that they were 'revolutionaries'. They even tried to topple those people whom they thought were not revolutionaries. In order to prove that they themselves were real revolutionaries. That was the time they picked at each other, found fault with the way people talked, the decorations people had in the house, the clothes people wore, etc... such as the following story in which I was a victim. I once rode a motorbike from *Bến Tre* to the Parish. As I almost reached home, guerrillas blocked the road. One man carried an AK-47 and wore a fabric hat and a chequered scarf. He stepped up, snatched off my cap, and threw it on the ground yelling angrily, "Even now, you still wear that bastard *Kỳ's* cap?"

I did not understand what he was trying to say, so I asked him, "I don't understand what you say. I bought this; it's my cap, so what's about *Kỳ*?"

The guerrilla got upset, pointed at my face, and made threats, "This is the kind of immoral and corrupted cap the bastard *Nguyễn Cao Kỳ* wears, do you understand? Do you want to imitate that S.O.B?"

I suddenly understood, Mr *Nguyễn Cao Kỳ* (Former Vice-president of South Vietnam) once wore a black cap much like this, so now the cap became 'corrupted'. I made no further comment. I simply stood still in a disgusted manner for the guerrilla to insult me for a while before letting me go. After starting my motorbike and hitting the road again, I smiled and thought that I was still lucky; only losing a black cap. If the guerrilla had accused me of wearing '*Kỳ's* pants'; that day, perhaps, I would have been embarrassed to death for having no trousers on, riding to the Parish!

Anything, in life, which went up to the ceiling had to go down sometime. The situational fever in this region also followed that rule. After a while, they started an educational campaign of contributing duties (Which actually meant paying taxes). Anyone who had lands and rice fields had to join this educational campaign. The parish also had some land to grow coconut palms; so, I had no choice but to sign up for this campaign. The situational fever which turned some people into fool a few months earlier; now it became a big freeze after this educational campaign of contributing duties.

After each re-education course, the Revolutionaries gave each family a cut-throat tax quota. That day, the political fever in my area suddenly deflated like a nail-punctured tire. Many revolutionary families were infuriated, cursing anytime and anywhere about the exorbitant 'Dutiful contributions' newly issued, according to the acreage of cultivated fields. Many elderly women, named '*Vietcong* Warriors' Mothers', were furious and directly insulted the authorities. Some women erupted; yelling in public to whomever would listen, "Damn you guys! If I had known this would happen now, I wouldn't have housed and hidden you guys in my home!" Afterwards, I knew that people cursed when they were angry, but they still paid their dues. If they did not pay enough taxes, the revolutionaries would have alternative measures. No one wanted to see those tough alternative measures.

My relationship with the local authorities became tenser as time passed. For that reason, I knew that my presence in the parish at the time was an obstruction, a thorn in many people's eyes, even to those in the Parish before me, namely the two religious nuns.

The People's Court

One Sunday morning, as usual, I went to the church to say prayers and prepare for Mass. After my short prayers, the parishioners began to arrive. However, the two nuns who normally came to assist me in the mass did not show up. I thought maybe they were sick or overslept, so I went to their quarters to enquire. I was surprised as no one answered the door after my long and hard knocking. Noticing that the door was not locked, I opened it and walked inside the dark room. There were several items here and there. I raised my voice to call them but there were no answers. A horrible thought struck me when I thought something sinister may have happened to them last night. Without my knowledge as my quarters were quite far away from theirs.

I rushed to break the news to one of the trusted members of the Parish Council. This man was also a member of the People's Committee of Giồng Trôm District. Knowing that, I was worried, he said, "Don't worry, Father, the two sisters should be okay. They left during the night. It was a long story. You just go back and say Mass. I'll tell you after Mass."

Later on, I was told that the two nuns had quietly moved their belongings to a boat and left during the night. Actually, well before their departure, the two nuns had secretly collected signatures of a group of people to file the letter of petition to the *Hiệp Hưng* village's Committee to accuse me of…robbing the church's orchards. I was also accused of confiscating the fish pond in front of the Parish house and a bed of onions planted by the two sisters. These details were reported to me later by a clerk who worked at the Village's Office.

After having considered the two sisters' application, *Hiệp Hưng* village's People's Committee had decided that on that Sunday, after the Mass, the Committee would gather all parishioners and set up a People's Court in front of the Church so that the two nuns could read the indictment and the people present would decide on my fate. The People's court's scheme which prepared well was virtually unknown to me.

For some unknown reasons, on Saturday afternoon there was an order from *Giồng Trôm* District not to proceed with the court session. The two nuns were disappointed, and knew that eventually I would know about this matter, so they had no choice but to leave quietly during the night. Looking back, I had noticed that since the day I first moved in, the two nuns would come to the Church to prepare for the mass with an attitude of duty more than a show of respect and cheerfulness. However, I did not expect the matter to explode into such a big event. Later on, I was told that before the two nuns left, they did say, "If we can't stay here, Father *Lễ* will not be able to stay here either!"

The Following Time

After I had learned about the story of the two nuns, I understood that my situation at this Parish was rather tense and more serious than I thought. Thanks to a trusted person, I knew that I was a target which was being watched closely. Occasionally, there was a stranger coming to the parish house waffling about some things, wandering from the front to the back of the house, looking around and then would leave. The two young men staying with me were questioned about my daily work, my readings, and what I hung on the walls in my room. At night, when I had to get out of the house occasionally, I often saw a dark shadow lurking near a bush of banana trees or young bamboo trees near my house. Every now and then, someone would come to me with the news, "An unknown Jeep parked at the Village's Office, someone from the province office will come to take you away …"

After a year living in this situation, I found myself at the end of my tether in this Parish. Moreover, at that time my Mother's health was deteriorating. The Bishop approved my request to leave the parish and return home to look after my Mother. I had the order to turn the parish over to Father *Nguyễn Văn Quang* of *Cái Bông* Parish. Father *Nguyễn Văn Quang* had been in control of the *La Mã* Parish before the Communists took over South Vietnam. He was Father *Thạnh's* older brother, *Thạnh* was the closest friend of mine and currently the Parish priest of *Quới Sơn* Parish, part of *Bến Tre* Province. During my difficult time with many tense situations at the parish, *Thạnh* was the only fellow priest who came to see me occasionally.

Thạnh and I were the same age. We immediately became close friends at *Vĩnh Long* Province's Minor Seminary. In 1963, we went to Saigon and studied together for seven years at St. Joseph Seminary. After graduation, *Thạnh* and I were both ordained priesthood in 1970. We both went to serve in our home Diocese of *Vĩnh Long*; *Thạnh* was assigned to be assistant priest at *Vĩnh Long* Cathedral. I was assistant priest in *Sa Đéc*, thirty kilometres away. Occasionally, we went back and forth to visit each other, our friendship was strengthened. Although we were great friends, our lives were very different. *Thạnh* had a gentle manner and a very quiet life. He had a frail figure. In spite of that, life offered him fortune in many ways.

After two years at the Cathedral, he was appointed Parish priest at the *Quới Sơn* Parish in *Bến Tre* Province in early 1973. When the Communists took over South Vietnam in 1975, *Thạnh* was still there. I thought he would stay at that parish for a long time because after the take-over the Communist government boldly interfered with internal religious affairs, not allowing Bishops to exercise their powers to reassign priests. To change any priest, they needed permission from the government. In general, whoever lived in any area would remain there. My position differed greatly from *Thạnh's*. My life was filled with ups and downs, and had undergone a lot of upheavals. It was the destiny of each person. Even non-believers still must believe that in this life, everyone has a fate.

Ironically, after the transfer of the parish to Father *Quang*, the Authorities of *Hiệp Hưng* village refused to give me a travel permit. They didn't allow me to leave the village; citing the reason that after the sixth election of the National Assembly, there was an order to forbid everyone to leave their residence. I understood right away what would happen to me following this explanation. I was well prepared to deal with the worst scenario. The next day I went back to the Village People's committee to request a travel permit one more time to visit my Mother who was seriously ill. Due to my firm and resolute attitude, they relented and gave me a travel permit valid only for three days.

My hometown was *Vĩnh Long*, more than a hundred kilometres away from *Bến Tre*. People had to take two ferries to get there. *Rạch Miễu* Ferry connected *Bến Tre* and *Mỹ Tho*. *Mỹ Thuận* Ferry connected Saigon with the western provinces in Mekong Delta.

Memory Lane

While riding my motorbike on the road from the Parish to *Bến Tre* Province, I felt immense sadness, wondering if I would ever have a chance to ride on this road again. Although this area used to be unfamiliar to me, in the past year or so, since becoming the *La Mã* Parish priest, I took this gravelled, uneven road many times to go home or to visit *Thạnh*. When I was about six kilometres away from *Bến Tre*, I had to take my motorbike onto a motorboat to cross *Chẹt Sậy* River. This riverbranch was pretty big; the water ran swiftly like a waterfall because it was so close to the main river. This bridge sat on the main road connecting *Bến Tre* Province with the counties by the sea. In the past, there was an iron bridge across the river. During the war, bridges across this river didn't last more than a few years. The Communists would sabotage any bridge being built across the river. It was clear that one side put great efforts into building the bridge, while the other side sought to destroy it. Nationalists tried unsuccessfully to keep the bridge in place. *Việt Cộng* (Vietnamese Communist) had tried many ways to destroy the bridge. They carefully calculated every detail, creating a stunning display like the time they wrecked this bridge, not long before the Republic of the South was lost.

I heard the story told like this, the Nationalists knew that sooner or later the bridge would be destroyed. Early in 1975 they increased their military presence to protect this key bridge day and night. There were many preventative measures, such as surveillance over divers laying mines and also explosives being floated along the river camouflaged in water hyacinths. Thanks to those measures, for a long time, the bridge was safe, and the traffic continued to provide conveniences and benefits for the local people. But in life, as we often said: "Diamonds cut Diamonds!" The malicious minds of the Communists came up with schemes to destroy the bridge. Eventually the Nationalists had to yield to the inevitability of its destruction.

When the tidewater began to ebb, the *Chẹt Sậy* River flowed as swiftly as a waterfall out to the main river. The saboteurs took advantages of this. They chopped down large, tall coconut palms grown in *Bến Tre* to make a raft. They hid the raft in the area of their control, waiting for a high tide. They then cut the ropes and released the raft. The raft, made with hundreds of coconut trunks tied together, increased in speed as it ran swiftly down the river. By the time, the Nationalist guards sighted the raft, they just panicked and shouted.

Unfortunately, only heaven above could rescue the pitiful cold steel bridge that braced itself from its fateful destruction. The giant raft still did its work, approaching its target with the terrible speed of…a coconut trunk raft! When it reached the foot of the bridge, it produced a soft and slow crunch-like sound of freshly-baked rice crackers being crushed in one's hand. Then the raft picked up its long steel friend on piggyback, and steadily drifted downstream on the boundless and ever-flowing Mekong River. The inanimate steel bridge rested in peace! The lives of the locals were heavily impacted, as well as mine.

The Ferry Ride

Leaving *Bến Tre* Province, I followed the road to the ferry in *Rạch Miễu*, ten kilometres away. As I walked my motorbike along with the crowd silently boarding the ferry, a strong sense of farewell arose within me, stronger than ever before. I had been on this ferry many times, I recalled many memorable images. Recalling the first time going across, when I was ten years old. My Parish, *Mai Phốp*, organised a pilgrimage to visit the Virgin Mary of *La Mã*. I followed along with my older sister and many parishioners to the place where I later became the Parish priest.

Another recollection of mine was when our automobile fleet crossed on the ferry at dawn. I briefly recall sunken ships not too far in the distance. One had its smoke stack above water; another ship had its masts still in sight. The adults told me that the French ships were bombed and sunk by the Japanese. I listened for the sake of listening, but didn't know who the French and Japanese were, and the reason why they bombed each other in my homeland. Those long-lasting snapshots that remained in my memory were fascinating at the time.

In 1961, when I was eighteen, I went to *Mỹ Tho* city to attend RẠNG ĐÔNG High School for a time. In the evenings, I would walk out to the pier, not too far away from the ferry, to watch people fishing. The sunken ships as they lay still with their smoke stacks challenging the passage of time. Every time I saw this scene, I remembered the ferry from past years that carried me, a little country boy, across this main river to make a pilgrimage to the Virgin Mary of *La Mã*.

Later in life, when returning to this region with complete awareness and judgment, I noted many new and captivating scenes about this ferry. First of all, the modern ferry was a larger and faster with two stories, with many rows of seats. The second new change was the busy scene of people doing business. Some people sold ice cream, fruit, meat sandwiches, and all kinds of foods. Many beggars actively worked in streets, calling for alms from passengers. The majority of the beggars were blind; a few had disabilities or missing limbs. I guessed they were disabled veterans. Some were guided by children, but some were alone. A large part of them carried musical instruments and sang different songs.

Most of those people sang *Vọng Cổ*, a popular kind of traditional music that easily reached the souls of Southern Vietnamese, especially people from the countryside like me. Some people equipped themselves with hand held amplifiers to enhance their voices and the sound quality. Their activities produce an animated atmosphere on the ferry while crossing the river. Having made this crossing so often, I was familiar with this scene; therefore, I knew most of the beggars. I always carried a small change, ready to offer to the unfortunate. Although I didn't bring much, I still felt guilty when I could offer nothing.

My attention turned to a blind man over thirty, perhaps blinded from smallpox. He had many scars on his face from this brutal illness. Through his old loud speaker, he had a highly expressive voice with great quality of sound as he sang and played the guitar in the *Vọng Cổ* style. A little girl about nine or older walked ahead, with a cord tied around her waist. The other end of the cord was looped around the man's waist; his hands were busy playing the guitar. The girl had a cold silent look of a wax statue, trodding along with the man to follow. On her Cinderella face, she never had any expressions, whether happy or sad. I thought it was deliberate.

I didn't know her relation to the man, but her attitude was always indifferent and her face expressionless. It made me think she had put up with this way of life for a long time and became emotionally hardened. Thinking about that, I felt even more sympathy for her. I always gave more change to this particular beggar and this young girl. Besides, my compassion for the plight of these two, I also greatly enjoyed the man's *Vọng Cổ*. Many times, the ferry docked in the middle of one of his songs, I was convinced that the ferry ran too fast.

That particular morning, the ferry had a noisy atmosphere. It seemed as if passengers were walking around more than usual, mostly women with jam-packed heavy straw bags. Around me, people laughed and talked incessantly, sharp noise of hawkers and the sounds of beggars singing in deafening tones mixed with the noise of ferry engines running. All those kinds of noises fused together into a loud cacophony suppressing the beggar's amplified singing voice as the pair were approaching my seat. I had been waiting for the man to come to the ferry crossing because I was used to seeing him on the ferry. I felt great sadness today and longed to hear his much-loved *Vọng Cổ* song. I had twice the usual amount of change ready because I wanted to help him one last time. I was not certain if I would come to this ferry crossing again.

Suddenly, I heard an echoing, strange and irritating voice, not the emotional *Vọng Cổ* I had heard this beggar singing earlier. It surprised me! I listened intently and, in horror, heard a brassy voice from his cranked-up amplifier with a line of *Vọng Cổ* that startled me, "*Is this war…ah…ah…caused by Americans……..and…… South…… Vietnamese quislings…ah…ah…ah?*" All of a sudden, I became furious at the vapour of dirty politics from this kind of *Vọng Cổ*.

I dropped the change back into my pocket and stood up like a machine and hurriedly walked away in order not to hear any of the blind performer's screaming. Walking away, I cursed him in my head, "*You, naïve man, how incredibly stupid… stupid! Mind your own begging business. Why are you promoting the dirty politics of Revolution?*" Disappointed and offended, I went down to the lower level and went out to the bow of the ferry, where there was no roofing. Feeling annoyed and upset, I folded my arms and leaned against the railing looking out into the distance.

I was moved and saddened by their abuse of the *Vọng Cổ* art, a genuine essence of an art style I loved. I heard stories about this musical style being born many decades ago, starting with a piece called '*Dạ Cổ Hoài Lang*' (Missing husband in the night) by the performer *Sáu Lầu*. It expressed the mood of a lady missing her husband in the night. This piece with its special musical style captured many people's hearts. Later on, the nostalgic tunes were adopted by *Vọng Cổ*. This music grew strong for a period in the South, with famous *Cải Lương*, (A traditional musical play by performing groups.) It became a distinguished cultural activity in the South.

During this political upheaval, people were forced to use this lovely musical style to serve a cheap political purpose for an unstable regime. The *Vọng Cổ* style was not created for that job. It was a musical style that stirred up people's love and warmed up the feelings of compatriots. But ironically, it was being used to promote hostility among people. I felt deep pain in my heart when an embedded part of our people's cultural foundation was abused.

Suffering Vietnam

Sometime later, the ferry was passing by *Cồn Phụng,* a Monastery base of the 'Coconut Monk'. It consisted of many buildings with various colours and architectural styles, which attracted so many visitors previously. Nowadays, the structures were still there. However, I heard that The Coconut Monk (Engineer *Nguyễn Thành Nam* by name), was not there anymore. I also heard that he was captured by the Communists, but I was not sure about the truth of the matter. I only knew that since the Communists took over the South, *Cồn Phụng* became totally deserted.

Leaning over the ferry's metal railing, I looked down at the bubbles that the ferry would whisk away into the red alluvium-filled *Tiền Giang* River. One set after another, the bubbles and foam bounced along the ferry reminding me of life's vicissitudes. I wondered where those scattered delightful bubbles shot off to after the ferry passed. What would their lives be like if the ferry had not skimmed by? Suddenly, I visualised the ferry as a giant steel monster, stirring things up, slicing through and causing chaos to the peaceful lives of bubbles which were having a calm rest at the heart of the gentle river.

Thinking aimlessly and endlessly, I considered the plight of my Vietnamese people. They are a kind, hardworking, and diligent by nature, a race of people born on the *Hồng Hà* River Delta in the North. Through many consecutive ages, they had shed so much sweat and tears. Through hard work and perseverance, they gradually moved south on an S-shaped piece of land over the two thousand kilometres alongside the Pacific Ocean rim. That was the formation and structure of my nation on which my people bursting with dynamic energy gathered together. The sweat from the people's hard work poured out like waters of Mekong river bringing alluvium to enrich the farm fields.

Through many periods in history, those peace-loving people were often provoked and broken up like the calm water beneath my feet, being sliced and destroyed by a metal ferry. Since I first realised the significance of these events in my country's history, I had acute awareness of what the war actually had caused so much misery and suffering for my people. Even now, after more than thirty years of my life, I have never seen my people enjoy true happiness, from the time of French colonisation to the Japanese invasion. The cruelty of rivalling political powers and organised crime was included. Even a few priests took advantage of their religious power to lean on the regime to oppress civilians.

The heaviest suffering still was from the war and the artillery which destroyed homes and properties. This caused forced immigration and bloodshed everywhere. This matter did not take into account the direct suffering for participants among rivalling factions. Countless innocent civilians, both old and young, died unjustly and helplessly. Bombs and bullets were indiscriminate, sparing no one.

The dead rested in peace, their lives were now complete. However, many victims survived with their injuries and lived the rest of their lives with disabilities on the fringe of society. I had utmost sympathy for disabled veterans on both sides of the war. The destructive war stripped away parts of their bodies and part of their capabilities.

 Born into turbulent times, they were forced to become fodder for human killing machines and the majority of them did not know why. Therefore, when one bullet or some shrapnels unintentionally injured them, they were turned into malfunctioning machines thrown into a deep pit in society. Having lost their capabilities, they were forgotten. They were even scorned for their handicaps! Many lost the ability to nurture and care for themselves. They had to rely on the other people's compassion. They became regular beggars on ferries, train stations, at shop entrances, and other places where they could easily find compassion from others, also in such places as at temples or church entrances.

My people were like a river constantly rustled up by vessels, they were ephemeral like sea foam. Since I was young, I had lived with war and massacre, with the sounds of bombs and cannons, and with corpses strewn about. Some were beheaded; some were gutted and floated in the river. Recognising cruel reality, I have seen foreigners, white-skinned and dark-skinned roaming round freely in my country with an air of apparent arrogance.

One thing I had noticed quite soon and could not understand, was why in my Vietnam were there people always plotting to kill one another. Why did they kill one another? What benefits did the killing offer? I could not solve those riddles until I was mature enough. I gradually understood that my Vietnamese people killed each other mainly due to a clash of political views; each individual followed a different set of ideals.

Furthermore, there were horrific scenes within the family. Brothers murdered one another; father and son eliminated each other, only because they supported different political doctrines. As a child, I lacked sufficient understanding of international affairs to understand the disastrous forces and monstrous forces, stirring the calm waters of the River of the Vietnamese Nation.

By the time I had acquired enough knowledge, my Nation and my Peoples were divided at the 17th parallel. The Demarcation Line, into North and South Vietnam was at the *Bến Hải* River as a 'Mason-Dixon Line'. The North worshipped Communism; the Nationalist South followed the course of Freedom. Since then, people killed one another in a crazy and feverish manner.

The painful truth is our Vietnamese people did not have the capability to think up of these Communist ideals. Somebody borrowed those ideals from abroad and brought them home as a colossal discovery. The borrowers' delegation took over the control after the seizure of the government and forced every citizen to accept and worship a political ideal with a strange name. Those who fought back or disagreed to these ideals, by the Communist definition, were deemed unpatriotic. There was a slogan from the Communist regime, "Those who do not love their country, do not deserve to live, and do not have the right to live." They have done so.

Even more painful, the unenlightened lenders of those political ideals are so seemingly generous and willing to lend many other things. They lent a confusing manual which was difficult to understand and to explain. They claimed, under Communist ideal, "The world would become Heaven on Earth", by the magic dust of a genie beyond all imagination, it would bring humanity closer to a golden utopian future.

When this kind of political theory dominated all races, people would live and labour in a global community, *from each according to his ability, to each according to his needs"* (Karl Marx). Never would there be exploitation. Doors would not need to be locked. Possessions fallen in the street no one would pick them up. Due to the system's superiority, they insisted humans had to achieve the goal at any cost. If one generation failed, the next generation would pick up and continue. If necessary, the life of the father had to be sacrificed to strengthen the life of the son.

Human Chess Game

Propaganda was used as a subtle means of brainwashing by Political lenders. Incentives were further promoted by a ready supply of bombs, ammunition, firearms, tanks, planes, warships, rockets, and even money. Absolutely everything was provided so that the Vietnamese people had the means to kill one another. Sometimes, they even lent their own people. When both sides were equal in weight and strength, the human chess match began.

The fighting ring was my S-shaped homeland! People with such power played chess without being present on the battlefield. They sat in some safe place, controlling their chess pieces by means of modern communication. Some were big and tall, fair-haired with sharp noses, sitting all the way overseas, in an office draped with the U.S. stars and stripes, in a painted place called the White House. Others were short and wearing Maoist uniforms sitting in offices behind Tiananmen in Beijing, which wasn't too far from Hanoi. And some sat as far as chilly Moscow in an office draped with hammers and sickles on red flags. These chess players drank champagne and smoked cigars as they pitted their wits against each other in a chess game of human lives.

Through the long months and years of war in my homeland, they had proved themselves to be cold-blooded players. They burnt troops without hesitation, partly because they enjoyed a sensation of almost omnipotent strength and also because they knew that the Vietnamese had a high birth rate!

Those fighting years offered once-in-a-lifetime opportunities for foreign weapon engineers to test modern and deadly weapons in my homeland. How painful it was! My people did not have the ability to make a single bullet, not even a lead pellet to shoot birds. However, the body of my Mother Vietnam in many decades had sustained countless tons of ammunition and bombs of all kinds from foreign nations.

In reality, the superpowers were smart enough to test their new weapons in a faraway nation, with a place for free airstrikes. They used the flesh, blood, and lives of my fellow Peoples for their experimentation, to measure the strength of the destruction of their new weapons. Those bombs and shells that killed or maimed millions of my people; the Agent Orange that ripped the leaves from our beautiful jungles and skin from those, who lived off it, were of lesser concern than the fact that their pet-dog had choked on a bone. It pained me to tears and caused a lump in my throat to think about this.

Meanwhile, among the Vietnamese people; it wasn't much better. Foreign bombs and ammunition were inanimate and killed my fellow peoples indiscriminately. It is even more painful and tragic to see Vietnamese killing another Vietnamese without remorse.

When the ghost of Socialism possessed them, many Vietnamese became blood-thirsty beasts to such an extent that they would cut each other's throats, gutted each other's bodies, ate their livers and drank their blood; husband and wife testified against each other, and children testified against their parents. It was even worse when they presented dead bodies of Vietnamese as gifts on the birthday of *Hồ Chí Minh* on May 19th. On that day in the South, many buses and shuttles hit mines on the road, which killed many innocent passengers, who would eventually turn into precious gifts for *Hồ Chí Minh*. I recalled passing the nauseating remains of those blown-up vehicles, with the smell of rotten flesh. I covered my nose with a handkerchief at the smell of my own peoples killed by their own peoples in my home country.

The Blood Banquet

To achieve the goal of foreign totalitarianism, they did not spare any immoral cruel action. They even trampled on the most sacred tradition of our people. I painfully recalled the *Tết Mậu Thân* Offensive in 1968 when *Vietcong* violated armistice convention for *TẾT* (New Year's Day Celebration). The attack on the Southern provinces was totally unexpected. I didn't have the courage to retell the horrific and devastating consequences of the *Tết* Offensive tragedy. I dared not recall the details of the tens of thousands of innocent civilians, tied in groups with electrical wires and buried alive in the ancient capital *Huế*. The image was too much for my tolerance.

Everyone knew there was no humanity in war, but I did not want the act of burying people alive and destroying homes to become a natural consequence of war. I only wished to say that the advocates of the *Tết Mậu Thân* Offensive had violated the most sacred day of the Vietnamese people, which is **TẾT** (New Year's Day). I wish to state this in bold capital letters. They had transformed ***TẾT*** of the People into a day of a **Mass Funeral** for the People. In the thousands of years of Vietnamese history, *TẾT* had been revered as the time of **Great Happiness** for the People. It was only at ***TẾT MẬU THÂN*** 1968, when *Hồ Chí Minh* and the heartless communists had turned it into a day of **Great Catastrophe** for our People! The history of the Vietnamese people will reserve them for one final reckoning.

I wanted to write the following with the blood from my heart: *I hope that 'Tết Mậu Thân 1968 Offensive is the first and last in the history of the Vietnamese people. I hope that from now on, and in many generations to come, my people respect 'TẾT' as a day of great happiness. I hope my people have the insight to understand that any political institution will pass; only the people will be long-lived*. I declared that any regime that abused the sacred spirit of the nation and the inherited values of the Peoples could not bring any good or benefit to the Peoples. As long as an anti-human regime was in power the Peoples would be suffering in misery.

With this thought, and in irritation, I turned back to that blind beggar. Why did he gullibly run after ephemeral nature of politics, chewing on cheap song phrases and driving away many of his appreciating listeners who had helped him in past years? I stood silently looking at the swift-flowing waters of the river. I said to myself, this current political fever has gotten to such a high degree, who knows when it will drop to a lower temperature. It was also because of this current political fever that I stood here, not knowing what things lay ahead.

Standing and looking at the sky and water for a moment, I felt less stressful. The smell of the river water and the light breeze brought cool moisture, which put me at ease. I leaned my head back, took in a long breath of pure air to fill my lungs. I walked back to the stairs to go up to the deck. I sat on a bench close to the stairs, for an easy exit when the ferry docked. At that point I said to myself: "*Be calm before any drastic changes, all shall pass, each activity has its own time*." I recalled my time at the parish. At first, the current political fever came up like a high wave; after a short time, it flattened.

With this thought, I felt secure and suddenly had sympathy for the beggar who had been singing revolutionary *Vọng Cổ*. I figured out that he didn't support the current affairs on purpose; perhaps that type of song helped him make an easier living for himself. Sitting for a while, I spotted shops beginning to appear clearly on the dock on the other side of the river.

Passengers became agitated, standing up when the ferry reduced speed and prepared to dock. I was about to go to the lower level to get my motorbike, when I suddenly realised something I had not done. Alas, I remembered the amount of money I was going to give to the blind beggar, but when I was upset I had put it back in my pocket.

The masses of passengers were pushing and shoving noisily as they prepared to get off the ferry while I was heading back towards the beggar and the little girl. Sadly, I sighted them on an empty bench at the other end. He sang and begged for alms while the ferry was still in transit. Now no one paid attention to him, his voice, or his plight.

I stepped over and looked at both of them with sympathy, especially looking at the almost-empty small reed basket in the girl's hand. There was only some small change in it. I hurriedly dug my hand into my pocket, emptied it, and put the whole amount of money into the basket. The Cinderella girl with big black eyes turned her head and looked at me for a long time. It was the first time I saw a surprised expression on her face. I knew she was not surprised at the large amount, but because of the unusual passenger who gave money when the ferry was coming into the dock.

I didn't feel satisfied with buying off my guilt, so I grabbed my wallet from a back pocket of my pants, took out a large amount of money, and counted it on the spot. I carelessly stood blocking the narrow walkway while passengers were disembarking. A large older woman had been blocked off, and so she elbowed me to the side with a complaint, "Silly man, what are you doing blocking other people's way?" I hurriedly scooted to the side, quickly threw the money into the girl's basket, and then followed the crowd with a smile to myself, "I really am silly, blocking the others' way."

The City of *Mỹ Tho*

The ferry transported more people than I imagined. A while ago, they filled up two levels of the ferry. Now I saw even more people pouring out from the ferry. I knew that most of them were merchants because they carried large filled bags with unknown contents. I was certain that these were varied merchandise, anything that could be bought and sold, especially Western medicine, textiles, and household items. When I was still at the parish, some women and girls of the parish had also sold things in the same way. They told me a thousand-and-one tales on the trade front.

In the first few months after *Vietcong* came into the South, they told of the tactics with which merchants bluffed their way through checkpoints and of the checkpoint guards setting traps to catch merchants. These merchants found ways to pay bribes and get through, but the police found ways to catch them again to make more money. There were hundreds and thousands of types of tricks and cons. People resorted to whatever skills they had. Ironically, it was thanks to these circumstances that the Vietnamese people became clever. Their mind worked nonstop to find ways to deceive and lie in order to survive.

Based on the theory of evolution, then the Vietnamese people under communist regime would eventually develop their malicious and deceptive minds to the maximum potential, which would accumulate and become genetically inherited by later generations. The more I thought of it the more pain I felt for the unfortunate plight of my people. They had fallen into a dark period in history under communist regime, where there was no place for benevolent and honest people to live.

Seeing it was still early, I rode my motorbike around the city of *Mỹ Tho* where I once studied. I went down to the pier and passed the botanical garden, following the road that edged along the river, passing over the metal bridge. The city hadn't changed much after a year under the new regime. The only difference was the city's sad appearance as people quietly moved about with their heads bowed. As I rode through many blocks, I noticed many streets and schools had been changed into strange names! Unfortunately, I didn't have much time to read why these names were chosen and why they would no doubt eventually become a part of the biography of these important Communist heroes.

I rode along *Hùng Vương* Street, passing *Nguyễn Đình Chiểu* High School. I remembered that in 1961 at this exact location, as a student, I was almost arrested by Dr. *Trần Kim Tuyến's* secret service. A friend and I came here to look for a teacher without realising that teacher and students had distributed anti-*Ngô Đình Diệm* fliers that day. My friend was arrested but I luckily managed to escape. I quickly ran home to get my belongings and I immediately fled to *Vĩnh Long* province. I dared not come back for more than a month to see my arrested friend. What a pity! His skin was pale like a banana leaf because he had been tortured over 15 days of confinement at the province police station. At that time, the image of armoured vehicles, together with plain clothes police walking around campus, frightened every student.

The Old Paths

I left *Mỹ Tho* going towards the Highway 4. I followed this paved road with lush plum orchards on both sides. This kind of fruit was juicy and about the size of an egg, with both sour and sweet taste. This region was famous for its unique species of plums as well as the alluvium from Mekong River. Tourists usually stopped to buy some plums, to enjoy the unique and distinctive taste of this local fruit. After riding less than ten kilometres, I reached the *Trung Lương* Intersection located on Highway 4, which connected Saigon with the lush western provinces of Mekong Delta. I turned left towards *Vĩnh Long*. My family lived in a rural village in this province.

It was high noon. I tightened the strap of my nylon hat with my left hand so it wouldn't fly off. It was difficult to wear such a hat while riding a motorbike since the wind easily blew the visor backwards. In the past, I used to wear a light compact newsboy cap while motorcycling because it gripped my head tightly without any need for a chin strap. The cap shielded the wind from blowing directly into my face, and it also prevented direct sunlight into my eyes. However, ever since I was stopped by guerrillas on my way back to the parish, because this cap was considered '*Kỳ's* corrupted cap', my cap was seized and thrown on the ground. I had no choice but to wear this nylon hat. After that experience, I didn't wear anything 'corrupted' to avoid unnecessary problems. This part of my life was, by itself, still full of complications because of this new powerful regime.

I had been on Highway 4 an asphalted road many times. It was also paved with many of my memories…

A few years earlier, the American military engineers had rebuilt the road that connected Saigon and the Western provinces. It was really wide and well-built by an American contractor with the abbreviated name was RMK-BRJ. This company had also rebuilt two important bridges on this road: *Bến Lức* Bridge and *Long An* Bridge which were between Saigon and the *Trung Lương* Intersection.

In the past year, when coming back to preside at the *La Mã* parish, I had the opportunity to take this route many times without noticing its condition. This time, after sinking into a big pothole, I was startled, realising the road had greatly deteriorated. There were occasional deep potholes and a few collapsed areas creating long and short crevices. All of this signalled a worsening condition to come if no maintenance and repairs would be undertaken.

The road suffered a collapse in several areas partly because it was rural land, cleared and flattened to build roads, so the foundation was not as firm as in mountainous areas. Furthermore, during wartime, tanks and other vehicles with chains would drive freely on the highway, which ploughed up the asphalt in many areas. From what I remembered, it had been six or seven years since the U.S. military engineers had made any repairs. Since then, no repairs have been made.

Story of a Bridge

The 150-kilometer stretch of Highway 4 from Saigon to *Vĩnh Long* had three noticeable landmarks that everyone knew. The first two were *Bến Lức* Bridge, *Long An* Bridge between *Trung Lương* and Saigon. From these landmarks, came the term bridge jam because of the congested traffic on both of these bridges. This term bridge jam had existed since the French built both of these steel bridges. The two bridges had similar Eiffel-styled structure, but the *Bến Lức* was much longer. The bridges were narrow and weak at the time, so there was only one lane. Two-way traffic went one way at a time; each direction took turns using the bridge. This resulted in a bridge jam.

The third landmark situated between *Trung Lương* Intersection and the Mekong Delta provinces was the *Mỹ Thuận* Ferry connecting both sides of a very large Mekong River. Because of the vast number of cars and passengers on the ferry, "Ferry jam" became the best descriptive term for this situation. Bridge jams and ferry jams created many inconveniences for passengers, but they benefited the local people. Locals could sell all kinds of foods, fruits and flowers, plums or meat rolls, rice paper, and pork hash in a banana leaf. Beggars could also make a living during the standstills. At *Mỹ Thuận* Ferry docks, nine kilometres away from *Vĩnh Long*, shops were bustling with people and were doing a thriving business. Some people became rich from the ferry jams there. This gave proof of the fact that one person's inconvenience was another person's fortune!

Because of the high volume of traffic on Highway 4, disastrous accidents happened quite often. Before 1970, the *Bến Lức* Bridge was blown up by the *Vietcong*. After this, the traffic was totally chaotic. Once heading towards home from St. Joseph Seminary in Saigon where I had been studying at the time, I took this route and witnessed a disastrous accident involving travellers.

Normally when this longest Eiffel-styled steel bridge was in place, there was a lot of congestion. The *Bến Lức* Bridge had served vehicles and travellers for almost one hundred years. It was an awe-inspiring sight against the backdrop of the sky. However, after the *Vietcong* blew up a section in the middle, the bridge looked so pitiable. It had become as ugly as it had been beautiful, as odd as the mouth of a smiling giant who had his two front teeth missing. The aftershocks of this event lasted for months. The tragic scene of the destruction of *Bến Lức* was like a large funeral for months. Hundreds of different kinds of vehicles and tens of thousands of people stood on the shores in farewell at the bridge's burial.

Childhood in Wartime

On that occasion, I crossed the *Bến Lức* River during a heavy rain. Rainwater up to the ankles muddied the road leading to the river. A few passenger cars had to turn back because they sank in the mud. Their retreat efforts splashed mud over many pedestrians as they headed for the river, only to find more mud. The brush had been stamped into the mud. People jostled and fought for places in motorboats to take them across the river for a hefty price.

In that disorderly setting, I heard a loud crying of a five or six-year-old girl. She sat in a muddy puddle, a distance from the river. I didn't know what she was wearing, but only knew that she was wet like a drowned rat, coated in mud head-to-toe except for her teary eyes. The mother was also soaked, holding a younger boy who was also crying. Perhaps the little girl did not have the strength to carry on so she sat down in the mud without caring.

The upset young mother could not pull her child up, so she bent over and laid her bag in the mud. Out of the bag peaked two quacking ducks. The angry mother slapped the child sitting in the mud, and yanked her arm to pull her up. The little girl was determined to sit there, which made the mother angrier. She pulled the child's arm harder. It looked like the arm was out of its socket. Meanwhile, the stream of people swiftly continued towards the riverbank under the downpour.

I walked my motorbike among the mass of people. Thanks to a raincoat I was not wet, but the splashes of rainwater blurred my eye glasses. Seeing the child's struggle with her mother, I felt pity for her. It was not that she didn't want to go, but it was the heavy rain which made her fall many times, and she didn't have the strength to continue. The more she was hit and pulled up, the more she struggled and was determined to sit there.

Out of instinct, I hurriedly set my motorbike on its kickstand on solid ground, and stepped over to the struggling mother and child. I unbuttoned the top of my raincoat to expose the Roman clergy uniform as I moved forwards. "She must be tired. Let me lend you a hand in taking care of her", I said.

The mother, with her face wet, hair clumped into rolls and muddied to the knees, looked at me wide-eyed in surprise without saying a word. I understood that she was worried, so I continued, "Don't worry, I am a priest. I see you're so busy with two small children, so I just want to help you."

Hearing that I was a priest, she looked at my purposely - exposed collar. Her expression then became calm. She expressed her trust, "Thank you Father, my child cannot go on." I picked up the child and assured her, "Settle down now, don't cry little girl. I will help you." At first, she was afraid of the stranger, then after she looked to her mother for advice she felt comfortable and let me hold her.

I held her muddy shivering body close to me, so she wouldn't be cold, and I stepped over to the standing motorbike under the careful watch of the mother. I set the girl on top of the fuel tank, telling her to hold the handle bars tightly. I kept her stable as I pulled up the kickstand, then I walked the motorbike beside the mother holding the boy and two ducks in a sack. It seemed that animal calls were just as unhappy like the cursing of humans against misery.

By this time, the child had stopped crying but her face was still wet with rainwater and tears. Suddenly I felt compassion for the girl and those children born in war time. These young ones had tasted the misery of adults, grown-ups growled at each other, killed each other, and found ways to make each other suffer. Perhaps she also felt safe because I did nothing to hurt her; I only help her cross the muddy path to the river. This stretch of road was long and difficult even to adults, let alone for a little six-year-old girl in the downpour. I smiled at the thought of the young mother calling me Father. Actually, I wasn't a priest yet. I was only a seminarian, and it would be one or two more years before I would be ordained.

However, a seminarian in the Higher Seminary could also wear the collar and garb of a priest. When I introduced myself as a priest, she called me Father. This was not the time to explain that as yet I was still a seminarian. The important thing was to gain her trust so that I could help her and the little child.

Stopping the motorbike I bent down and asked, "Are you cold?" deeply without a word. For some reason, this brought tears to my eyes which joined the rainwater running down my face and onto my chest I let them flow, and bowed silently.

I continued walking the motorbike, with a shivering muddy girl on the fuel tank, under my care. The mother carrying a sack over her shoulder with two ducks slogged along beside me with difficulty. Occasionally, she adjusted the boy on her arm. The boy had stopped crying and the ducks were quiet. Things had temporarily calmed down, and the rain relented.

By the time we reached the riverbank, the boat had room for only a few more passengers. There was no room for my motorbike. I tried to put the kickstand down but had no success because the ground was not firm enough. I had a man hold the motorbike up. I picked up the girl and placed her beside her mother on the boat. The mother smiled brightly and said, "Thank you, Father."

I stroked the girl's hair and said, "Be a good girl, don't cry anymore." I backed onto the riverbank as the girl nodded again, just as she had done before.

When the motorboat left shore, the woman and the child waved to me. The woman also held the boy's hand up to wave. I felt I was missing something when saying goodbye to these strangers. I was filled with a sense of sadness for this woman and her children. I stood on the shore and waited for the next boat, remembering what she said: "Thank you, Father."

Actually, I should have thanked the mother and her children because this chance encounter helped me get in touch with the reality of wartime, and I felt even more compassion for the plight of my people. I never saw that family again. Even if we would have met again, we wouldn't be able to recognise one another because no one could really see the other's true face under the mixture of mud and rain. The children were too young, and everyone was covered in mud.

I continued along on my motorbike with my thoughts wandering about. It was not long before I approached *Mỹ Thuận* Ferry, gateway to the city of *Vĩnh Long*.

Family Situation

It was still early after the crossing on *Mỹ Thuận* Ferry, so I stopped by a friend's house in *Vĩnh Long* City. It was partly to visit the friend's family, but partly also to discuss a rather important issue with him. It had been a long time since we last met, so we talked for a considerably long time. His family invited me to stay for a meal. After the meal, I said farewell to my friend's family. I then continued to ride on my Honda towards *Trà Vinh* Province, which was more than 60 kilometres from *Vĩnh Long*. My home was in a rural village named *Hiếu Phụng* situated in the middle of the two provinces.

I purposely slowed down a little to enjoy the fresh cool air on the deserted road in the late evening. It was twilight when I got home. I felt really depressed about facing a miserable situation that my family had to deal with. My Father passed away just ten months ago, and my Mother still lay ill and weak in bed. Our family farmland had been almost completely confiscated. The house had deteriorated. One of my older brothers had reported to the new government for *'Re-education'* with his status as an army officer. The other older brother, previously a Master Sergeant in the Navy, with on-base housing in Saigon, was now demobilised, all his possession sequested by the new government. He temporarily brought his family of eight back to our family home and built a hut next to it.

The Communists hadn't taken over the South for very long, before they had *'Liberated!'* our family almost completely. Luckily, we still had some clothes to wear. In these circumstances, I only wanted to take care of my mother for a while, because I knew she wouldn't live much longer. Meanwhile, I looked to my parish for updated information.

On the fourth day, a close friend told me the news that the authorities of *Hiệp Hưng* village had issued a pursuit warrant for me because I was overdue for returning to the parish. The friend told me never return. I was approaching a crossroads, and figured that I had to leave my home for good. Although I didn't know what my destination would be, I still had to leave because I didn't want my mother to witness horrible things about to happen.

That day, I asked someone to get in touch with Father *Thạnh* who was visiting his home in *Trà Vinh* Province. I asked him to stop by to see me on the way back to his parish. Having received my message, he came quickly, despite not planning to return to his parish that day. My family welcomed him warmly, because he was my close friend and often visited my mother and sister. *Thạnh* was treated like a family member. His visits were happy occasions. Meals with *Thạnh* were always full of laughter.

While my sister got a chicken prepared for the meal, I pulled him out to a corner of the yard to tell him about my situation. Over many past months, he was the only one with whom I shared my thoughts and feelings about things at my parish. It was also *Thanh* who came over to support me through those difficult times. He understood well my circumstances, but hearing about my reaching an impasse, he sadly asked me, "Do you mean you will leave for good?"

I shook my head and said, "Think about it, where would I turn back to? I've turned the parish over to Fr. *Quang*, and I'm not registered as an inhabitant at this house. They'd come and look for me in a matter of days. How would I live?"

With that, *Thanh* knew this was a serious matter. He remained quiet for a moment. Still deep in thought, he plucked a pack of cigarettes out of his pocket. Taking out a cigarette, he stuck it between his lips. As he lit up mine, he asked, "Do your mother and your sister know about your situation?"

I took a puff on the fragrant cigarette, tipped my head back to exhale, and shook my head, "Not yet, I wouldn't dare tell Mom and *Chị Hai (First sister)*. Mom is so weak, and *Chị Hai* would worry herself to death if I tell her. What good would it do? I only speak with you. Oh, I almost forgot, on the way home, I stopped to visit *Khánh* in *Vĩnh Long*. He helped get me a fake travel permit, as a forestry worker in *Lâm Đồng*, a highland province, in case I would need to use it."

Thanh generally avoided situations of conflict. He was not used to dealing with challenges and adversities; so, he only listened without making any comments. I had no intention of asking him for anything. I just needed a friend who understood my circumstances. I had a tentative plan in my head. However, I did have another favour to ask of him. *Thanh* asked me in a low voice, "What can I do to help you out?"

I was touched by my close friend's question though I knew there wasn't anything he could do to help me now. However, I had another reason for seeing him. I said it straight up, "The important thing is that when I'm gone, I want you to visit my mother once in a while. She is so frail that I'm afraid she won't live much longer. If I'm not present for her death, take my place to arrange for her funeral and memorial services. That's my only wish, please promise me and put me at ease."

Hearing that, *Thanh* was deeply moved. Without speaking, he turned towards the kerbside and nodded. In place of a thank-you, I squeezed the hand of my closest priest friend.

My sister called us from patio, "Hey! You two *Đực Mẩm* (*Mẩm* Bulls), come in for dinner now! What are you doing whispering out there?"

My *Chị Hai* still called me by an affectionate nickname "*Đực Mẩm*" (*Mẩm* Bull), the name of the largest bull among our water buffalo herd. As a child, I was plump and round like this bull, so she nicknamed me "*Đực Mẩm*" (*Mẩm* Bull). At first, I grumbled and didn't like that name, but I eventually got used to it. Later, when I grew up and became a priest, she continued to call me by that affectionate nickname in the privacy of our home.

Because *Thạnh* was a close friend of mine, she saw him as her another younger brother and also called him '*Đực Mẩm*' for convenience. This was, despite, the fact that he was skinny and looked nothing like the real plump and round buffalo. We both liked the name very much. Many times had I signed my letters to her as "*Đực Mẩm*". While we were eating, we tried to be natural as though nothing was going on. In my mind, I thought this could be my last meal with my mother at the table and perhaps with the rest of the family.

After the meal, I gathered some necessities and stuffed them into a red nylon bag. I said goodbye to my frail mother and my sister, telling them that I was headed to Saigon, and would be back in a matter of days. That was the last time mother and son would see each other in this life.

I sat on *Thạnh's* motorbike and took off straight away, not daring turn my head back and wave goodbye to my mother. At that time, the sun had fallen in the West. We remained quiet on the rough stretch of two kilometres from my house to the inter-city road at *Cầu Vĩ* T-Junction and turned left heading to *Vĩnh Long*. From there, we would take Highway 4 to *Trung Lương* Intersection where we would say good-bye to each other; then, *Thạnh* would return to his parish in *Bến Tre*.

Far from the Comfort Zone

When we approached *Trung Lương* Intersection, it was almost evening. The *Trung Lương* Intersection had many established businesses. It was the gateway from Highway 4 to *Mỹ Tho* and *Bến Tre* Provinces. We stopped in a café to sit down and chat for a while. When it came time to depart, I saw deep sadness on *Thạnh's* face. We sat in silence.

As the *MINH CHÁNH* shuttle bus was approaching from far away, *Thạnh* grabbed the remaining cash from one of his pockets and thrust it into my hand and said in an emotional broken voice, "Take it; I know you'll need it. Let us depart in peace and good fortune. When you have a chance, please remember to contact me. Alright man, go!" He quickly turned away towards his motorbike, forgetting to get my handshake or hear my farewell.

I understood that *Thạnh* turned away to hide his emotion. I stuffed the cash into my pants' pocket and boarded the shuttle that stopped abruptly at the curb. I looked at *Thạnh* and said, "You be well. Pray for me. If I am still alive, we'll see each other again". I boarded the shuttle bus like a robot, heading to Saigon.

This was the first time I departed without an actual destination. Actually, at the time I didn't know where I would live or what I'd do when I got to Saigon. I was approaching the turning point of my life. Suddenly, I felt the enlightenment and weightlessness of a person having removed a heavy burden. I was completely free, unbound by responsibilities unlike before. From here, I could go anywhere and do anything, and I could throw myself into any situation of life.

However, I clearly felt anxious. I felt like a hunted animal, having to run from the dark thick woods, from a safe haven to an unknown destination and was exposed in an open field surrounded by many hunters and traps. I also knew I could encounter death at any time, by any means. In short, everything was possible when I stepped onto the car and left everything of my past behind, an eventful past of 33 years including 6 as a priest.

Suddenly, I thought to myself, from now on, my life is entering into uncertainty. Today is the first day of the journey to be remembered. What does the future hold for my life? Take note of each day and each task. And later on if I am still alive, and then I must write it out like a play, with today's *MINH CHÁNH* shuttle bus as an opening act.

Chapter 2
Stepping into the World of War

As I sat leaning on the back of a seat in *MINH CHÁNH* shuttle bus, with eyes closed, lively scenes from childhood appeared in my mind…

I was born and raised in wartime in a rural area called *Bưng Trường* of *Vĩnh Long* Province in the Mekong Delta. My parents worked as farmers, with five children. The oldest was a girl, followed by four boys and I was the youngest. My oldest sister, whom I called '*Chị Hai*' (First Sister), was fifteen years my senior. Because she was the oldest daughter, she worked very hard to take care of the household and her younger siblings, especially me. Therefore, I was very close to her and loved her very much. I considered her my second mother.

My family had been Catholic for three generations, and we lived in an area close to *Bưng Trường* Church. At the time, *Bưng Trường* was a small parish without a presiding priest, and was under *Mai Phốp* Parish's management, four kilometres from here. At the time, Father *Lê Vĩnh Trình* (Father Felix) was the Parish priest. At the centre of my childhood world was this village church, a place to attend Mass or spend many days of prayer. Outside on the front of the Church, there were many granite rocks left over after the Church was built. Besides, it was an old mango tree with many dry branches. The rocks had been piled up for quite some time; so, grass grew all over them. Green absinthe wormwood carpeted the area with its many yellow flowers. I often picked the numerous sweet-smelling flowers to put on the altar for Our Lady Mary. I would never forget the strong sage scent of the absinthe wormwood flower.

Later in life, the fragrance of wormwood immediately brought back memories of my childhood and the flowers decorating Mary's altar in my home church. In my childhood world, the image of the admirable Sisters of The Congregation of The Lovers of the Holy Cross was engraved in my mind.

There were always two Aunties (Sisters) in that building, tending to the church, and teaching us writing, reading, catechism and the moral principles. These Aunties had the respectful love of my parents and other local elders. We, children, also loved and feared our Aunties, who were as generous in doling out sweets, as they were in doling out punishments.

By the time I had acquired enough knowledge, I was very familiar with the sounds of ammunition, bombs, and pictures of war. The first images were of the French soldiers, mostly white-skinned, some were black. I couldn't understand their languages and didn't know who they were, or why they were here. In conclusion, I had no knowledge about the French at that time. I only knew that they were tall, blue-eyed, and had a prominent nasal bridge. They were much more powerful than the local Vietnamese. I was very frightened every time I saw them, especially the black French soldiers. Though I was still quite young, I already heard the term '*Việt Minh*' (League for the Independence of Vietnam) and was also very frightened of those people. At that young age, I had little knowledge of our nation's current affairs. Hearing the sounds of bullets and bombs, I only knew there was a fierce war.

I saw many dead bodies floating down the river but didn't know who they were or who killed them. As children, we would often run down together to the riverbank behind the Church to look at corpses floating down the river. We called them *"Thằng chổng"* (Buttocks-up!), perhaps because they floated face-down with buttocks up on the water. Throughout my childhood, I had witnessed many *"Thằng chổng"*, flowing down the river current, surrounded by swarms of flies. Some corpses floated alone, some in twos and some had attached themselves to clusters of water hyacinth. Occasionally, there were headless corpses. Many times, I saw corpses with their arms tied behind their backs. Some came with clothes, some were half-naked. There were many styles of terrifying floating corpses. The sun rays burned and darkened them.

In addition to the brick Church, there were only two other structures of brick and stone. One was the stone bridge right behind the home of the Sisters. The other was a large hollow pipe lying across the ground of the gravel road. This pipe's diameter measured perhaps more than one meter. It carried water from the church's dam into the irrigation canal leading to the field.

The wide stone path crossed in front of the church door and went all the way out to the interprovincial highway, two kilometres away. It was a few hundred meters from the path down to the residential area towards the river. On the other side of the path was a field. Some places had been cultivated to grow rice, but much of the land was left wild with overgrown tall grasses and reeds. Although the stone path was wide enough for two cars, I didn't remember seeing cars on the path. However, I do recall French and Vietnamese soldiers coming down the road, in groups. People said they went on *'Ba trui'* (*Ba trui* was the translation of *Patrouille* in French, being on patrol.)

I have many memories from my early childhood, but only from my family and that of my First Sister is the most cherished memory, she lavished so much love and tenderness on me. My Father was very strict and virtuous, a role model for us. My Mother was frail and thin. This resulted from a medical condition that occurred at the time of my birth. Thus, for this reason I loved her even more.

In my family, morning and evening prayers were important, so important that this family ritual was constant, never be broken! As a child, I dreaded these prayer sessions, perhaps they were too long. Or maybe, as a child I was too tired to endure prayer when I was so sleepy. Household duties and care of siblings were my oldest sister's duties. Recalling my past, I realised that, as a child, I used to be spanked more than my siblings. There was actually no pain! My Sister spanked me lightly with her palm like swatting mosquitoes. Despite that, I pretended to yell so she'd be satisfied and believe the punishment was effective. My behaviour resulted in my having to cope with my older sister every day, whether I liked it or not! She had a habit of grabbing my arm while scolding me and would say, "Look! Your face is as dirty as a prisoner's!" Not a single of my bath went by without that 'trade-mark' phrase.

Forced Evacuation

I lived with peaceful memories at *Bưng Trường* Church until 1949 when I turned six years old. That was also the year when my family had to move to *Cầu Đá*, a safety zone near *Mai Phốp,* which was a bigger parish with a president priest named Father *Lê Vĩnh Trình* (Fr. Felix). At that time, I didn't know why we had to evacuate. Up until now, I only remembered being put on a raft made of timber from an old house, and let go along the river for about two kilometres until we reached *Cầu Vĩ* (Grate Bridge). We temporarily stayed there for a while and then followed alongside the highway to a new place called *Cầu Đá* (Stone Bridge), about two kilometres from *Mai Phốp* Church.

During that evacuation, almost all the Catholic families in *Bưng Trường* Parish left the village. Some moved to *Mai Phốp*. This was a bigger village with a larger population, markets, a church, a presiding priest, a church school, and a French military base. A small number, including my family, settled in *Cầu Đá*. This was a small sub-village at the time with a sparse population without any school or market. All the trading and shops were in *Mai Phốp*. At first, I felt lonely and lost in this strange area. Luckily, a few of my relatives' families lived nearby, and so did long-time residents.

I began this new journey of my youth with new neighbours and the family of my Great uncle, not far from my home. Great uncle is a younger brother of my paternal Grandmother, who had recently evacuated to this area. Great uncle had a youngest child named *Hữu*, whom I called Uncle. Uncle *Hữu* was only one year older than me, so we played together since we were little kids. We were often in conflict but we couldn't be without each other.

Cầu Đá (Stone Bridge) got the name from the bridge made of stone across the inlet, which was only ten meters wide, connecting the main river to the inland fields. This tributary was the main source of water for the people's living and plantations, especially for the farmers. People built houses along both sides of the tributary, so did my family. As an irrigation canal, the water level was around your head when the tide was in, and went down to your knees when the tide was out; that was also the time we could roll up our pants and wade across the inlet to the other side.

Although fairly small and shallow, this tributary had an abundance of fish and prawns. When the tide was in, fish from the river moved in to the inlet and the fields to feed. When the tide was out, they moved back to the river, but on their way out, they were caught by anglers and fishermen. In rainy seasons, the water was everywhere, so fish moved in to stay and reproduce in the fields. In dry seasons, fish moved back to the river in abundance. There were some wild fields covered with water, where fish, in large numbers, stayed for years and kept reproducing there. As the water level dropped and flowed to the main river, troupes of people came to either scoop up, trap, net…fish. In rainy seasons, fish followed the water to the vast flooded field where they flourished. Come dry seasons fish retreated back to the river in droves.

Pleasures of Rural Life

I spent my childhood in *Cầu Đá*, with its immense rice fields, and homes of fish every season and everywhere. I not only loved catching birds and mice, but I also learned to catch them effectively and more than anyone else. My techniques in this field constantly improved. In *Cầu Đá*, the world of my childhood expanded greatly. This was partly because I was one more year older and the area was more populated, so I made more friends of the same age. We often teamed up with each other to play all sorts of children's games. We fished during the day, and at night we took lamps to the fields for night-time fishing.

During dry seasons, when the fields began to dry up, the fish began finding their way back to the river, after a year of thriving in the fields. It was this time that fish-lovers, like me, would work most enthusiastically. The quickest and simplest way to capture them was by blocking their usual path and creating a trench. At night, fish travelled to that blocked point, got upset, jumped forward, and dropped right into the trench.

Besides fish, there were two other things which I indulged in passionately: birds and field mice. Mice multiplied quickly and numerously all over the rice fields, especially in the wild undeveloped lands. As a child, life in the rural area was such a great pleasure, creating series of marvellous legendary days for my childhood. Gradually and unintentionally, I became an expert in catching fish, birds, and mice.

Fearing School

I was an avid lover of fish, birds, mice, and children's games. School became somewhat of a torture because it limited my freedom. My negative attitude resulted in a behaviour for which I was frequently punished. I didn't know whether it was fortunate or unfortunate but the fact was that as soon as we had settled down in *Cầu Đá*, Fr. Felix, had a school built on the riverbank directly opposite from my home. We had a view of the school along with a view of '*Cầu khỉ*' (Monkey Bridge) which led to the other riverbank. The bridge was constructed with one slim single trunk of wood with hand rails. The school was large, spacious with tile roofing, renovated from an old house. I clearly remembered the busy scenes of local villagers and buffalos laying down the school foundation, carrying earth, and construction materials. The school's grand opening was very lively with many people attending. There was so much food and drink. The children enjoyed sweet rice.

Both Catholic and non-Catholic local children were brought to school with the Religious Sisters' teachings. The academic program was not clearly set. The children were divided into two classes. The Upper class studied the books of Catechism, math and reading. Lower classes learned reading from the turtle and rabbit textbook. The two classes were in the same hall separated by a wooden divider of the height of a person.

I began in the Lower class when I was seven. Every school-day I clutched my books and crossed the monkey bridge to school. The class also had square poster board with a bamboo frame. It was hung with a narrow wire. The poster board had the large letters of the alphabet to help us recognise and read these letters. The Aunties taught, reprimanded, and punished us but no one minded. The punishments were actually deserved. Some children of my age did not go to school, they had the freedom to run and jump, chase mice, catch birds, and net fish in the immense rice fields. These friends were from poor families, and they stayed home to grow crops and help their family. Some would work as housekeepers for others.

I had five full days of school every week. I labelled my school-calendar each day with a colour according to the tasks of the day. By nature, I was playful and slack, my mood changed throughout the week.

Sunday was green, I had the day off but I had to go to church. Monday mornings, however, I was lethargic without energy. Wednesday evenings after school, I was full of energy and enthusiasm. Thursday was pink. Not having to attend school.

On pink day, I would follow my ather and brother to the fields. In the afternoon, I would herd seven family buffaloes to join dozens of village buffaloes, to graze on open land. The buffalo herders could catch birds, catch fish, and chase mice, this was incomparable happiness. At that time, I thought I had been born to be a buffalo tender, to catch fish, and to chase mice.

The school days were always black. They began with the sound of drumming echoing loudly at 7:30 a.m to announce a school day. After 2 beats of the drum, I started feeling sick. An hour later, a Sister would ring the bell for pupils to go into class. Although I hated school, I didn't dare skip class because it was considered serious crime according to my family's rules: no exception, or even leniency. I didn't have the courage to skip school, so prayed that the

Sister of my class would get sick. With the birth of this idea, I began to include this petition in my nightly prayers with the family. "God, please make Sister Lucy ill, the longer the better. But do not let her die. I only wanted Sister Lucy be ill enough to give me a day off from school".

I even asked Our Lady to help me in this matter. Unfortunately, the more I prayed the healthier and rosier she seemed to become. Once, my prayer was heard. A Chinese physician, a traditional herbalist from *Mai Phố̂p* market, comes to our school. I heard that Sr. Lucy was ill, so she invited the healer to check her pulses and prescribe herbal remedies. I was overjoyed.

That evening, after Mom had gone to visit Sr. Lucy, I asked Mom about Sister's health condition. My bad thoughts were making me feel very guilty. Nevertheless, I almost jumped for joy when hearing Sister was rather seriously ill with a high fever. After having massage treatments until her neck and temples were reddened, she was given herbal concoctions and then covered with a blanket. My Mother said many locals came to visit her, bringing gifts of oranges and eggs, because all of the locals loved Sisters and appreciated what they did. Although my mother didn't say anything more, I guessed that Sr. Lucy wouldn't be able to get up tomorrow. We would have a day off! Believing this, I had a vision of a rosy day, running in the fields to shoot birds, to catch fish, and to chase mice.

Next morning, the school drums still sounded, I guessed it was for the younger class. It would be a day off for the Upper class. This was not meant to be. When it was almost time for school and I hadn't gotten ready, my sister urged me along with the saying, "You, little devil! It's almost time to go to school and you're not even dressed! Why are you sitting there?"

My sister still called me 'The little devil' and my next-older brother was 'The big devil' because we were troublemakers.

I hesitated and answered, "Sr. Lucy is ill today, why have I to go to school?"

My sister raised her voice, "You, lazy boy! Nobody said you had permission not to go to school".

I replied, "She's ill, how can she teach?"

My sister gave order, "Go, go quickly over there. When Sister gives you permission, then come home. You, lazy boy!"

I reluctantly got dressed, and I was sure that Sr. Lucy would let us go home when she couldn't get up, let alone teach. Crossing the monkey bridge, I quietly wished that all other pupils of my class would stay home.

Upon arriving, I was speechless; everyone was present. When the time came, the bell still rang. Pupils said prayers as usual. Then Sr. Liz from the younger class appeared. After prayers and before the roll call, Sr. Liz told us that Sr. Lucy was ill today and she would be teaching two classes at the same time. She advised us to be quiet so that Sr. Lucy could get her rest. Perhaps tomorrow she would be well and resume teaching. I was disappointed. Sr. Liz was far stricter and used the stick more often than Sister Lucy. Since then, I didn't pray for Sr. Lucy to be ill anymore. Only when both Sisters were sick would we get a day off. Surely, God wouldn't allow them both to be ill at the same time!

Moving to a New School

After completing my studies in *Cầu Đá*, I moved to *Mai Phốp* to study at the Catholic school where my older brother had already been attending for a year. This Catholic School had disciplines and a proper syllabus for all classes. We were educated and prepared for entrance exams into middle school. Failing the exam would mean not being accepted to middle school.

Students were taught by the Sisters, under the management and supervision of the influential Parish priest, Father Felix, who was devoted to education. He often came to visit classrooms and openly reprimanded stubborn students.

Although school had disciplines and a proper syllabus for all classes, it was not perfect and is evident from the following story. On one occasion, two of my classmates were ignorant troublemakers. Sister couldn't cope with these two bad boys, so she temporarily transferred them to the fifth grade for a stricter Sister to deal with them. In theory, the two naughty boys would be straightened out after their 'boot camp', they would eventually return to the original class. But! (What a big 'but'!) They remained there permanently! At the end of the year, they took middle school entrance exams a year before the rest of us!

In the evening of school days, after dinner, my Father would put on his glasses and lay down on the swing chair with a Catechism book. He called on my brother and me to recite the lesson he assigned the day before. Anyone who didn't know their material would receive a straight spanking. Therefore, whatever I did I would have to learn a chapter of Catechism. This made me even more tired of learning.

Meanwhile, one of my village friends who was a few years older than I did not have to go to school but worked as a driver's assistant on a passenger bus. His name was *Chín*, and we nick-named him *Chín Ghẻ* (Scabies *Chín*) because for a while his body was covered with scabies. I envied him because his life was full of happiness. He didn't have to go to school, didn't have to stay up late or get up early, wasn't punished, and he could swear and speak obscenities and vulgarities freely. He could frolic like a bird in an endless sky.

There were days I saw 'Scabies *Chín*' wearing a fabric hat with a chin strap and an outfit the colour of giblets soup, his sleeves rolled up as he played on a swing behind a *Vũng Liêm - Vĩnh Long* route bus. It was quite a sight, and I worked out a dream to later become a driver's assistant when I grew up. There would be no greater happiness than to service the route to Saigon, because Saigon at that time was something beyond my imagination.

Fr. Felix had no mercy for those who stole. He would whack them with a rattan rod to leave marks on the body. I was frightened. In my mind, no one could compare to Fr. Felix. He was just under fifty with salt and pepper hair, moderately tall, well-built with an imposing walk.

After Mass, he wore blue shorts with a short-sleeved white shirt tucked in, white fabric shoes and white knee-high stockings. He looked very healthy, elegant, and handsome.

I noticed that everyone feared Fr. Felix, not only the Vietnamese but the French were also humble when dealing with him. He spoke fluent French although I knew no French. It surprised me to see him yelling at French officers on some occasions. I knew that the French were usually more powerful than the Vietnamese. Religious, political, and social positions had built up an influential role for Fr. Felix on every level. As a child, I heard that Fr. Felix could grant clemency to anyone held and charged by the French.

Every morning I saw many people taken away by the soldiers in rows of four to do *corvée* (French word for miscellaneous work). I knew of a location not too far behind *Mai Phốp* market, called *Gò Dương*, where the French colonists would execute *Việt Minh*, although I'd never seen scenes of execution. This brought back images of corpses floating down the river that I'd seen as a child in *Bưng Trường*.

Rogue Act

During these years at school in *Mai Phốp*, I was even more depressed and tired. On school days, I woke up at 4.00 a.m. with the rest of the family. My Father and brother took care of morning prayers and breakfast to prepare for the fieldwork, and I followed the group that walked two kilometres to *Mai Phốp* to attend morning Mass. When Mass finished early, I went to the village market to get breakfast before school. Every day, my Mother gave me 50 cents to buy some breakfast. I was always hungry and craving food, so along with my bad boy cousin, we set up a rogue act.

That year, the government was about to issue a new bank note, and they printed sample photos of the bill in the newspaper. It was very realistic, so the two of us cut them out of the newspaper and folded them in quarters. When Mass was over and it was barely dawn, we carried the fake bill cut out of the newspaper to buy breakfast.

Waiting for the lady hawker to finish wrapping the hominy, I was very nervous; I had never done something so dishonest before. Taking the hominy from the seller, my hands shook and shivered. Then I threw down the fake bill and ran. She was so surprised and quickly examined the money, yelling after us, "Catch him! Catch him!"

I was caught and held back. Seeing I was shaking and scared, the lady hawker had pity on me and let me have some sweet rice because she knew I did this out of hunger, not because I was a professional thief. A seasoned fraudster wouldn't be shaking like that. Luckily, she didn't know where I lived, because if my parents and my sister would have heard about this, I would certainly be punished severely. I knew my Father was strict about such things.

Family Tragedy

In 1953, when I was ten, a family tragedy occurred in the family of my Great uncle. This event matured me beyond my age! This tragedy related to his daughter Aunty *Thiên* and one of his sons, uncle *Vinh*. Aunty *Thiên* was married with three children. After relocating to *Cầu Đá*, uncle *Vinh* was recruited to be a soldier in the French military in the region. My aunty *Thiên's* husband was seldom at home. I was too young so I didn't know where he was, or what he was doing.

One day, uncle *Vinh* was with the patrol team and a communist *Việt Minh* had wandered into their ambush zone. Sensing a trap, the person ran away but uncle *Vinh* and soldiers chased him, shot him and he fell. Suddenly, he heard the person call his name, "Uncle *Vinh*!" My uncle quickly recognised the voice of his brother-in-law. Horrified, my uncle ran over and picked up his brother-in-law, but his injuries were too serious and he was dying. He murmured, "Uncle *Vinh*! I cannot live, so please help your sister to take care of the three children!" When uncle *Bình's* body was brought home, relatives and neighbours swarmed in and out of the house. Suddenly, amidst the crying, I heard a loud wail, "Oh my brother! It was me who killed you! Forgive me, my brother!"

I shoved my way into the house, only to see a crying uncle *Vinh* holding uncle *Bình's* bloody and muddied body. Hearing uncle *Vinh's* wails, everyone let out heart-rending cries. Perhaps I'd cried the last of my tears at the time. I suffered much from this tragedy. Since then, I wondered about many things that did not have an answer. Who were the French? Who were the French soldiers? Who were the *Việt Minh*? Who were the good guys? Who were the bad guys? Why did brothers in the same family kill each other?

Later on, I learned that the river corpses in *Bưng Trường* were people killed by the *Việt Minh*, and I concluded that the *Việt Minh* were the bad guys because they killed others. I thought the French colonists were good people. However, when I came down to *Mai Phốp*, I heard that many political prisoners had been shot at *Gò Dương* by the French, and so, that made the French bad too. I couldn't understand where the French came from nor what was their purpose being in Vietnam.

For this question, I had no answer. However, there was one thing I understood very early, perhaps earlier than many children of my age at the time, was that the Vietnamese were a suffering people. A feeling of Patriotism had blossomed in my heart and with this love for my unfortunate Peoples.

Misdeeds of Youth

In 1955, at the age of twelve, I was in the fourth grade at *Mai Phốp* Parish School. The teacher of my class was Sister Mary. One morning, a woman brought her son into my class. The new student's name was *Quỳ* (Hereinafter Q.). The boy was my age and had a gentle appearance like a girl. He had a tall and slender figure, a long neck, a round head and buzz cut. At first look, Q. was like a young stork in its nest because of his long neck and bald-looking head. The new student spoke little and shyly lingered around Sister's desk; his hands toying with the seam of his white shirt. The way he buttoned his shirt caught my attention because he closed even the button at the neck. He looked very rural and simple; while our kids' gang also wore this kind of shirts, we didn't fasten the very top button, looking stately and 'fashionable'. In short, Q. caught my attention when he first followed his mother into the classroom.

In the following days, Q. became a class phenomenon. He was unusually gentle and exceptionally good at math, really good. That surprised even Sr. Mary. He solved the in-class math problems at ease, while the rest of us struggled. As the worst math student in class, I struggled the most. Since his arrival, every time we did math, Sr. Mary called Q. up to the blackboard. After solving the problems intelligently and quickly, he was told by the Sister to 'teach' the rest of the class. Unintentionally, the new student's intelligence hurt him. Our group of boys altogether gave him an ironic name *'New Blackboard Master'*.

We boys began to detest him because the smarter he was the more our stupidity was revealed, especially me. Every time Sr. Mary complimented Q., everyone else felt nagged at, and we became even more annoyed with him and expressed an obvious boycotting attitude towards him. I had to admit I was the head of the cruel gang that boycotted Q. because he hurt me the most.

In order to isolate the highly intelligent classmate, I formed an evil alliance and permitted no one to talk to him. During break time, we did not allow him to play tennis-ball soccer. Sometimes, I saw him standing quietly all by his lonesome self in the corner of the playground. There were days, I saw him ask the girls to play ball and pick-up-sticks game with them. Seeing that, I felt satisfied and thought, "You frustrate me in class; so, I'll frustrate you outside."

At the time, I knew that Q. suffered and held out for a long time. He said nothing because our group of old devils was quite large. He sustained silently and patiently with our punishments for a while. There was time, I felt sorry for him. Unfortunately, my childish jealousy overcame my sense of compassion.

A Change of Heart

It was at this time that my village had an outbreak of smallpox, a very contagious disease that killed many people quickly. It left permanent scars on the faces of survivors. One day, Q. was absent from class. I felt relief at the absence of the *'New Blackboard Master'*. I didn't bother to wonder. The next day, before prayer time, Sr. Mary asked the class to pray for *Quỳ* who had smallpox.

I was startled and felt guilty because I mistreated Q. out of jealousy. I felt compassion for a gentle classmate, who unfortunately contracted a disease that killed many people in the area at that time. A feeling of remorse choked my throat. I was determined to apologise and treat him more brotherly, and to protect him when he returned.

A week later, we were still missing the gentle new classmate. I worried and felt more compassion towards him. I missed him. We were not allowed to visit him because smallpox was a highly contagious disease. Every day at recess, I went to the Church to pray that he got well. After unreasonably ill-treating Q., I was tortured by remorse.

One morning, during class, I saw Q.'s mother walking in. I felt scared. The poor young mother came to announce that Q. had died the night before. I bowed my head, my tears flowing, and sat crying audibly at the news. And much later on, I still cried when thinking of *Quỳ*, even now after many decades had passed. I still felt remorse when remembering this, and my tears were still flowing.

The MINH ĐỨC Middle School

In 1956, I passed the elementary school's graduation examination at the age of thirteen. That year was the first time my photo was taken for an Exam ID Card. This was an unforgettable experience! I went to the *Tân Tân* Photo Studio at *Mai Phốp* market. The photographer had me sit on a stool in front of a large black machine mounted on tall legs. He adjusted my posture, told me not to blink, and then went back to the camera. He draped a black cloth over his head and shoulders then counted "one, two, three", and clicked the shutters. I was told that I could pick up the photo in 5 days. This experience was a first for me, I was really impressed! I was so eager to see my headshot! I couldn't eat or sleep properly for five days. When I did see my photo, I was so delighted to see myself captured in picture for the first time. I took it to classroom to compare my photo with the rest of the classmates, to see who had the best look. Some kids called me photogenic! I was so delighted to hear that, and grinned from ear to ear.

During that time, the trips with my sister to the market in *Vĩnh Long* City, thirty-three kilometres from home, provided me new experiences and new observations. I was able to observe a different and astonishing way of life in the city. Once a year, my sister went shopping for *Tết* Celebration (Lunar New Year). As she was shopping, I would look after her big straw basket of purchases. After buying all the necessary goods, she would call a cyclo to take us to the nearby bus station to head home. I was truly overwhelmed and delighted with the city's active residents, traffic, and urban crowds. Everything was new, strange, high class and beautiful. At the time, I thought city life was more of a privilege, reserved for a certain social class. My family and I could never have that kind of lifestyle. These trips out of my rural environment exposed my ignorance.

Fortunately, when I finished elementary school, Fr. Felix had opened *MINH ĐỨC* Middle School, a secondary school in the region. By the time I had acquired enough knowledge. This school was the first of its kind in the area. When Fr. Felix opened the doors of the *MINH ĐỨC* School, a door to my future was opened! Previous to the existence of *MINH ĐỨC*, the reality of my family financial situation meant that my future was predictable. Upon finishing elementary school and obtaining my elementary certificate, I figured my schooling would be finished. I would help my family with our fieldwork just as my brothers and the other village children. Moreover, the daily activities of a rural village as well as the wide rice fields, and the associated joys appealed overwhelmingly to children. It never entered my mind to look any further or to question my future.

The building of *MINH ĐỨC* Middle School gave me the opportunity of choice. Other children were not so fortunate. They had to quit school at a young age. Eventually, they became illiterate. Luckily, I was allowed to further my education. Later, I went onto higher levels of learning which I had never dared to dream of. This was a very fortunate event for me.

Fr. Felix had a long three-classroom school building erected behind the Church. Two rooms served as classrooms. The room on the other end was used as an accommodation for the two teachers coming from the North whom he had invited from Saigon to look after the school program. The new school provided a new experience of teachers and friends.

Many students came from as far as *Vũng Liêm* County, 10kms away, some also rode bicycle to attend *MINH ĐỨC* School. Generally, not many people were capable of sending their children to provincial schools. This was the first time I had a male teacher. Strangely, my idiotic mischief suddenly stopped. I developed a love for learning, and studied well. I was not an exceptional student, but I was always among the top three in the English and French languages.

Incredible Event at Fourteen!

In 1957, another great change occurred in my youth. It was my first trip to Saigon, the Capital of South Vietnam. Saigon at that time was dubbed 'The Pearl of the Far East', the symbol of all the beauties of the nation. Saigon was something beyond my imagination to a child born to a peasant family who'd grown up in rural areas during wartime, going to Saigon at the age of fourteen was a distant dream.

I was ecstatic! My feelings were impossible to describe. Every time I recall this unexpected opportunity, I am thankful and grateful to Teacher *Bùi Sinh Quý*, who made my dream of going to visit Saigon came true. Teacher *Bùi Sinh Quý* (Hereinafter TQ.) was the older of the two teachers whom Fr. Felix had invited to come to teach at *MINH ĐỨC* Middle school. My Father asked him to be godfather at my Confirmation, since that event he loved me as a son.

When school was not in session, I would go to his house to help him with various tasks. He often gave me gifts, which were mostly books and pictures. During one of my visits when he was preparing to return to Saigon for a short break for the National Day Celebration on October 26 under the regime of President *Ngô Đình Diệm*, thinking out loud I said to TQ., "I wonder if I will ever have the opportunity to visit Saigon."

This was no more than a wish out loud. I hesitated to ask him to take me, but he suddenly said, "*Lễ*, go home and ask your parents for permission. If it's granted, come here tonight and you will go to Saigon with me."

I could not believe my ears. So I asked him, "Seriously, are you going to let me go with you?"

As he continued to pack his bag, he looked back smiling and said, "Yes! Go home and ask your parents' permission. If they agree, then I will let you go with me!"

This sudden turn of events was unbelievable. It was about mid-afternoon; quickly I hopped on my bike and took off for *Cầu Đá*.

Why did it take so long to get there! The unsealed road was familiar, only two kilometres long. Hunched over my bicycle on the rocky and bumpy road, a hundred worries raced through my head. Would my parents give me permission? Would there be enough time to prepare for this historic journey? What clothes would I wear in Saigon? And shoes! I had never had a pair of real shoes in my entire life, only wooden clogs. In Saigon, I would have to wear shoes, not clogs. My hair was not cut! What bag would I take? And...and...!

Arriving home, I asked Mom first because she was always more easy-going than Dad. To my surprise, she replied, "You need to ask your Father. If he allows it, you will go!"

I felt frustrated. My Father was still working in the rice fields. I ran like the wind to the fields behind the house, following the walkway straight to the field where Dad and my 19-year-old brother were working. I prayed, as I ran, asking God for my Father to give his consent. Dad and my brother saw it as quite unusual that I was running, no doubt surprised and wondering what was going on. Hearing my request, my Father stopped working and sat down on the dyke at the edge of the field. Unaware of how impatient I was to hear his decision, he slowly and steadily hand-rolled a cigarette as usual.

My Father always made the important decisions. After lighting the cigarette, he blew smoke skywards then turned to ask me, "Have you asked Mom yet?"

It thrilled me to hear him ask that question. From experience, I knew that when he asked this question it would be followed by a red seal of "Approval."

I replied, "I've asked Mom already, and she has approved. If you allowed me to go, then that's fine!"

My Father processed the news, and sank into thought. "How long did TQ. say you'd go?"

I replied, "I didn't hear him say, but probably a week because we're out of school for fifteen days."

My Father nodded, "Yes! If Mom allows, go!"

Most Holy Jesus Christ! My life was in such happiness! I felt as if I'd been elevated through nine layers of clouds, looking down on suffering earthlings below. An overwhelmingly huge sense of joy grabbed me, creating a sense of dizziness.

It had only been a few hours since I had received consecutive ground-breaking news, from the words of TQ., to what Mom said, and now to the words of my Father "***Yes! If Mom allows you, go!***" This short 5-word phrase had the miraculous and magical power to transform a small rural boy into the happiest person on earth, within a minute. I hurriedly said, "I thank you, Father."

I was about to run home. However, my 19-year-old brother, working with my Father, ventured over with his hoe to ask, "Where're you going, *Lễ*?"

I replied, "I asked Father to let me go to Saigon!"

He called out in surprise, "Good heavens! Really? You're really going to Saigon, who are you going with?"

I smiled in response, "Teacher *Quý* would allow me go with him."

He asked, "How long will you be gone?"

I answered, "I don't know, probably a week."

My brother grinned upon hearing that, he teasingly said, "This is the story of "Mr Toad" going to Saigon!"

I didn't answer him, but began to run home as he called after me, "Hey! Remember to watch out for traffic!"

I ran, or rather, flew home. I didn't follow my old path, but 'flew' along the riverbank where most of people built their houses. This was a case of a dream coming true! I'd get to go to Saigon.

A truth beyond my ability to imagine. I wondered if there was anyone in the world who was as lucky as I was. I remembered when my older brother called me 'Mr Toad going to Saigon', it was from a play in an old story where the villager Mr Toad went to Saigon for the first time. We let out belly-bursting laughs when hearing of the bumpkin antics of Mr Toad. I didn't think I would be as bad as Mr Toad, since I had already gone to *Vĩnh Long* City a couple of times with my Sister. Mr Toad had lived in the countryside all his life, without ever going out of the boundary of his village.

Passing through the fields, I approached the walkway by residents' homes on the river banks. I took this route although it was a bit farther, since my group of friends lived here. Even though I was in a rush to get home to prepare before going to TQ.'s house tonight, I couldn't help sharing the ground-breaking news with my friends.

I stopped by the home of each friend and said six words to each, "Tomorrow I am going to Saigon." then moving on to another house. If a friend wasn't home, I would say to an adult, "Greetings Sir, please tell *Inh* that tomorrow I am going to Saigon."

I would also have one kid pass along the message to another because I didn't have time to stop by each one's house. There was another friend on the other riverbank, and I said, "Tell *Bầu* for me, I am going to Saigon." I was like a mailman stopping by each of my friends' houses, the more the better.

By the time I got home, an entire neighbourhood in *An Thành* Hamlet knew that I was about to go to Saigon. However, they didn't know who I was going with, or how long I would stay in Saigon. That wasn't important; the important thing was that *'the fellow Lễ is going to Saigon'*.

One thing I knew for sure was that among my friends, and many adults in this hamlet, no one had been to Saigon. Certainly, they coveted the happiness that I had.

I darted into my house dripping with sweat, I saw Mom and *Chị Hai* preparing the vegetables for dinner, and I said, "Mom, Father has already given permission for me to go!"

Suddenly *Chị Hai* put on a serious face, "You're not going anywhere! You stay home!" I froze on the spot. My sister had always been powerful. Even though, I didn't think she could override my Father's decision, her opinion always weighed heavily.

I was worried, wondering what wrong I could have done to be punished by not being allowed to go to Saigon. I was very worried because *Chị Hai* was the one who knew my faults very well. I looked at Mom for help, but she intentionally turned to another direction. Frustrated, I asked, "But…"

My Sister cut in, "No and nor but, you are lazy and dirty. You stay home!"

I was glad, because I guessed that my Mother and Sister had been plotting to psych me out. Being lazy and dirty were hardly factors in whether I could go to Saigon. Was every Saigonian studious and sparkling clean? Perhaps, seeing that was enough spooking. Mom spoke, "Go and get your hair cut, then come home; your sister would help you bathe, so you can have your dinner and go!" I let out a light sigh. It turned out that Mom and sister saw me so excited that they plotted to spook me for fun!

I rushed to Uncle *Vinh's* house to get my haircut. As I sat in his chair, I said, "Please make it look nice, Uncle, because tomorrow I am going to Saigon!"

I was very pleased and proud to hear Uncle *Vinh* surprisingly ask me, "What'd you say? Tomorrow? Saigon? But going with whom?"

I replied, "I'm going with Teacher *Quý*, he allowed me to go with him to Saigon for the National Day Celebration."

Uncle *Vinh* congratulated me, "You are so blessed. I don't know about Saigon, and I will probably never have an opportunity to visit Saigon until I die"

Then, my uncle and I talked about Saigon until he finished my hair cut. I only wished he would cut my hair a bit faster, but he took it slowly with his manual hair clippers which had been sitting in his box, dipped in kerosene for a long time. Every time he squeezed the handle, the manual clippers would yank out a few hair or even a cluster, painfully right from their roots. I had to clench my teeth and bear with it; tears running down my face because he yanked my hair so hard. However, I still asked him to get my hair cut because it was free of charge; whereas I would have to spend some money at the local barber's shop.

After shearing my hair with the clippers, he used a very sharp razor to shave off the edges. I'd hear a scraping sound before he did the shaving. I feared this part greatly because once, either he wasn't paying attention or I was not sitting very steady, he sliced a bit off my ear and I bled profusely! For that reason, I detested haircuts.

While I was getting my hair cut, my Sister prepared some coconut fibres to scrub me. Because she was preparing me for my trip to Saigon, she scrubbed me more thoroughly with fresher tougher fibres, which almost made me bleed. It was very painful but I didn't dare yell because that would earn a slap on the cheek, along with her usual trade-mark scolding. "Look! You're as dirty as a prisoner!"

As my Sister was scrubbing me, two neighbourhood ladies passed by and talked to my Sister. They said they heard some younger children say I was going to Saigon tomorrow. The ladies gave me an impressive and amazing look, because their children were my friends. They seemed impressed that I was going to Saigon. Everyone told me to gather as much detail as I could when I got there, so I could tell them all about Saigon when I was back home. Overjoyed, I smirked and said, "Don't worry, I will remember everything and tell you all about it!"

At that point, I thought, perhaps, they were secretly wishing, I wish their children were as lucky as '*Lễ*'! Their words made me realise even more emphatically how fortunate I was. I was also delighted because I was sure that my good news had spread quickly through the entire *An Thành Tây* neighbourhood.

After the scrubbing, my next older brother took me on his bicycle to *Mai Phốp* Market, to buy a pair of sandals. I chose a pair of red sandals with a clear rubber sole. The sandals smelled like fresh leather or what I thought was genuine leather. They had an unusual and delighted smell. These were the very first pair of sandals I had ever had. Nobody wore sandals out in the rural country. Throughout my childhood, I was always barefoot. At night, I would wash my feet and put on clogs to keep the bedding clean. When I returned home, I packed my stuff into my school bag. I folded my formal clothes: a long-sleeved white shirt and blue slacks and then added gingham scarf, a toothbrush and a chunk of solid toothpaste as round as a limestone pebble, which I used this by wetting the chunk, then I would scrub the toothbrush into it. I packed those into my bag and waited to put them in the car tomorrow.

It's around five in the evening, my brother and I ate dinner. I couldn't eat much! Seeing this, my sister said, "You're not going anywhere without eating!" So, I hurriedly downed a bowl of rice. During the evening, both my mother and my sister took turns counselling me on a litany of topics. They told me to be careful on the street, to watch for traffic, to be respectful to TQ.'s family, and so on, but actually I didn't remember a thing.

Before leaving, I crossed my arms and bowed my head for a formal goodbye to my Mother and Sister. Then my Mother handed me some spending money. My Bother drove me TQ.'s house. I only wore a white button up shirt with elastic-waisted shorts, my feet were bare. It was almost nightfall when we arrived at *Mai Phốp*. My brother headed home.

I carried my bag and walked into the house as the teacher was packing his clothes into a suitcase. I spoke, "Greetings Teacher! My parents have allowed me to go to Saigon, so here I am!"

Teacher *Quý* seemed surprised, giving me a silent look that produced goose bumps. A moment later, he asked, "So you're really going, *Lễ*?"

Heaven and Earth! How could he ask me such a question? Just this afternoon, he invited me to go to Saigon with him. Were there any complications? I was stunned from head to toe, my mouth open. I felt feverish, my pores seemed to dilate. I nearly fainted; so, I stepped closer to him and held onto the bookshelf. In that minute, it was as if the sky was crashing down. If I couldn't go to Saigon, I would die of disappointment and shame after having heralded the news throughout in village and neighbourhood about my upcoming trip. I didn't know if my Teacher understood my thoughts and feelings, even slightly. I gingerly uttered a few words, as if crying, "Teacher! This afternoon you said I could go to Saigon with you!"

After that, I stood and looked at him as he stood in thought. The phrase 'One minute being longer than a century' would be appropriate for this particular minute of waiting for his reply. I was unimaginably full of suspense, since it would mean a world of difference between a shake and a nod. Finally, the Teacher said, "OK! You can sleep on that canvas lounge, we leave early tomorrow. The pick-up time is at 4:00 a.m. Have you eaten yet?"

I promptly replied, "Yes, Teacher, I have eaten."

Even if I hadn't eaten, I would have said that I had. TQ.'s response gave me great relief! Nothing could have made me happier.

Night of Anxious Waiting

Teacher *Quý* lived in a fairly spacious house. I set my bag on a chair and lied down on the lounger. I couldn't sleep a wink that night. My mind focused on Saigon, the fact that I was actually going kept me awake. My excitement was beyond description. I tossed and turned for a long time, perhaps until midnight, occasionally, stepping out to urinate and then returning to lie down. Knowing I couldn't possibly sleep, I sat up and lit a lamp and decided to read a book, waiting for morning. I chose a rather large book from the bookshelf with a black cover and radiant smooth white pages. The title was The Accomplishments of President *Ngô Đình Diệm*. The book had many pictures. I lay down to read and read, hearing the sound of the ODO wall clock every fifteen minutes. The time dragged on, morning seemed not to arrive.

When Teacher *Quý* came to wake me up, he realised I had been awake for quite sometimes. Teacher told me to wash my face and get dressed. The earliest bus from *Trà Vinh* arrived at 4:00 am. I sprang out of bed like a recoiling spring. This was the anticipated moment I had been waiting for. I quickly grabbed my leather bag, looking for the toothbrush and toothpaste, and then headed outside to the washing area. Strangely, I felt dizzy and was off balance when standing up. I almost fell over, perhaps because I stayed up late reading during the night. My head heated up, my body became wobbly and imbalanced.

After washing my face and brushing my teeth, I felt better and at ease as well as awake and alert. I hurried back inside to get changed. I took off my clothes, folded them up, and then pulled out the special pair of clothes for 'Going to Saigon'. These were the unique clothes I wore to Church on

Sundays; so they were always new and fragrant. First, I put on the long-sleeved white shirt then the 'Going to Saigon' pants. In a split second, I realised a tragic mistake! These weren't mine, they belonged to my older brother!

Yesterday, in a big rush and excitement, I put the wrong pants in my leather bag. My mother had the tailor make three pairs of slacks each, of the same blue Sharkskin fabric, different only in measurements. My 19-year-old brother was taller and much bigger than me. He was roughly double my size and height. When I put the pants on, they were loose and baggy. I pulled the waistband up to my nipples and still the pant leg went past my feet like an elephant trunk! I panicked at the sight of this.

I bent over to roll up the pant legs, but the sharkskin fabric was so soft and smooth as well as thick and heavy. It was not a solution, the fabric simply rolled down. I'd rolled it up, but then same thing would happen. It would fall down again. This mistake caused me too much disappointment.

The bus to Saigon was about to come, and I couldn't get back to my home; it was 2 kilometres away. I wouldn't make it there and back in time even going by bicycle. I paced around in panic. Suddenly, I had the urge to urinate again. I panicked even more when TQ. called out to hurry up. "Are you ready, *Lẽ*? Come on, hurry! Otherwise, we'll miss the bus!"

I had a buzzing in my ears when I heard the teacher's words. I had no choice but to say, "I am done, Teacher!"

I hurriedly put on my new sandals, buckling them up carefully. When I stood up with my sandals and picked up my bag, the two pants cuffs unrolled into a pile over my feet. T.Q. turned out the light and stepped out. As we walked forward in darkness, I hunched over the leather bag with my right hand and holding my baggy pant legs with the left. Although it was before dawn and considerably cold, I was blushing with embarrassment at the thought of how I looked.

Struggle with Pants

Just after a few steps, I was tripping uncomfortably. This was the first time I ever wore sandals, so it felt like two lumps of hard clay with straps. Meanwhile, my two baggy formal pant legs were puddling over the sandals several centimetres; too long attached to my feet. I tried to catch up with my Teacher as he walked ahead. When one foot stepped on the pant leg of the other, I grumbled to myself, "Good heavens! This is just terrible! I'm supposed to be excited and joyful, but these two wacky pant legs are screwing me over!"

At that point, I bent over and pulled the pants up by the thighs with my left hand, while my right hand still clutched the leather bag. In that position, I couldn't possibly walk fast enough to catch up to my Teacher. He was a far distance ahead of me. Seeing I was still scuffling along behind, he turned back and rushed me, "Lẽ, walk faster, being late and we will miss the bus, hurry up a bit now!"

At his call, I tried to run after him but I couldn't run fast while hunching over with my hands full. TQ. was probably surprised and wondering why I was so slow. He saw nothing since it was still dark. If he could see such a sight, he'd probably burst out laughing and pity for the rural boy struggling with his pants.

From the Teacher's house to the paved highway was around 300 meters, we had to pass the Church on the way. Arriving at the Church, Teacher stopped to wait for me before continuing. It was only a short distance from the Church to the main road, I suddenly saw bright headlights of a coming vehicle. The earliest bus was approaching, and immediately passed. At that point, my Teacher ran after the bus with his flashlight, aiming it up and down to signal the bus to stop, but it was too late. The bus passed by as we approached the road. We were about 30 seconds late!

I guessed that TQ. wasn't happy; clearly, we missed the earliest bus because of me. However, in life, one person's misfortune is another's fortune. While TQ. was clearly very disappointed, I was luckily saved. If we had got on the bus at day light, what would happen when people saw me wearing an extra-long pants, double the length of my legs?! Teacher showed regret, and he said to me, "Oh well! we've missed the earliest bus, a pity! It passed right by when we just approached there. Let's go home and rest; then, we turned back for the next bus at 6:00 o'clock."

At home, the first order of business was to take off the damned pants and throw them on the lounger. It lay in a long tangle, as cheesy as a jute bag. It was as long as I was tall. It lay looking at me in a sarcastic and mocking pose. I was so angry, I took the leather bag and beat the formal pants a few times, scolding as I did so. "Curse you, damned thing! You caused me a lot of trouble!" In my anger, I hit the pants so forcefully that it caused a loud noise.

Teacher *Quý's* voice rang out, "What's with the noise, *Lẽ*?"

I hurriedly think of a coverup. "It's nothing, Teacher; I was just beating the dust out of the canvas lounger!"

He seemed surprised and said, "Why didn't you do that last night, but now when we're about to leave? It'll be all dusty when we get back anyway!" With that, I just sat silently.

After removing that useless thing, I put back my only pair of elastic-waist shorts on. I felt at ease. Though, they were not appropriate for 'Going to Saigon', there was no other choice. At that point, I thought my life was very lucky since I had fortunately missed the bus. If I hadn't, I would have had to wear those ridiculous pants to Saigon. They were big enough to swim in. I was still deciding how I was going to behave in the broad daylight when it came time to step off the bus.

Folding up those hopeless pants, I stuck them in my bag because I'd have to return them to my brother anyway. Furthermore, I needed something to put in my leather bag, since I couldn't just take an empty bag to Saigon.

When it was almost 6:00 a.m., TQ. called me out to go. This time, I stepped out lightly in my elastic-waist boxers, wearing sandals. Seeing I was so plainly dressed, the Teacher asked, "Huh? *Lễ*, why are you dressed like that? Where are your pants?"

I dodged again, "I am not accustomed to wearing pants, afraid it will be too hot on the bus."

He seemed a little surprised at that but finally, he said, "Oh well that will do!"

We continued walking. This time he didn't have to rush me or stop and wait. As we walked, I figured if he was clever he could figure out why I was so slow last time, I walked more quickly. Sometimes, I even passed him.

The second bus was the *TÂN HOÀ*, it arrived on time. It was the first time I was on the Saigon bus. This had been one of my wishes. Remembering the days of herding buffalo near the paved road, we would play on the road and admired the Saigon buses because they were so attractive and elegant. Now, I was a passenger on this bus.

After passing the city of *Vĩnh Long*, the sky was beginning to show signs of morning. I opened my eyes widely to take in the scenery. This morning, I would leave *Vĩnh Long* City, take the *Mỹ Thuận* Ferry, and continue for 140 kilometres to get to Saigon. What could be happier!

There was so much traffic, our bus had to get in line to wait for available ferry while passengers got off the bus. It was barely morning then, and TQ. told me we'd get some breakfast at a café as we waited for our bus. As we stepped into the café and pulled up chairs to sit down, he asked me, "*Lẽ*, what would you like to eat?"

I didn't know what to say, so I replied, "I don't know, whatever you're having."

Teacher smiled and said in return, "*Bánh bao*, (Meat-filled dumplings) okay?"

"Yes."

"Hot coffee with milk?"

"Yes."

I ate a delicious, very delicious, hot meat-filled dumpling! After that, I craved more, but I didn't think it's proper to ask for another. When the hot coffee was served, I watched and mimicked Teacher's actions because I'd never had a hot coffee with condensed milked before. It looked so good when he drank some, that I also took a sip from my cup. As soon as it went past my throat, I couldn't stand the taste. It was bitter like Chinese herbal medicine, and I became nauseous. Not being able to hold it in, I ran out to the road where I vomited onto the ground. The teacher saw and pitied for me, telling me if I was not accustomed to it; then, I should not drink it. When I apologised to my Teacher, he said there was nothing to be sorry about, since I was just not familiar with coffee.

The New World

We set off from *Mỹ Thuận* Ferry to Saigon. We passed the *Trung Lương* Intersection. From *Trung Lương*, I saw a train running parallel to the road. This was the first time I had ever seen a train. All these sights were strange and new to me. When we arrived at the *Bến Lức* Bridge, there was a biggest jam I had ever seen. The traffic was backed up because we had to wait for cars to cross the bridge from the other side.

Bến Lức was a sanctuary of sweet pineapples. Many local ladies were selling pre-sliced pineapple, with chili salt for dipping. The vendors would use a small utensil made of a pineapple stem, to scrape some chili salt onto the piece of pineapple before handing it to a customer. The woman sitting next to me had purchased a portion of sliced pineapple. While she was eating it with chili salt. The pineapple juice dribbled down her chin. My mouth was watering. I turned and looked in another direction, thinking it would be the greatest thing ever, if TQ. would buy some for me, but I wasn't going to ask him.

As we approached *Chợ Lớn*, the Chinese-dominated City, I was filled with awe. We had finally arrived at the Main Saigon Bus Station. I was truly overwhelmed with this New World! I could not imagine that Saigon could be so big and vibrant. Seeing people, cars, and shops, I asked myself if there was any city on earth bigger and more beautiful than Saigon. When preparing to get off the bus, TQ. advised me to stay by him so I wouldn't get lost.

When I got up, I felt terrible sore in the feet. The straps of new pair of sandals had rubbed some flesh off my heels and turned my smallest toes as soft as a ripe banana. It was bleeding so painfully. I was planning to take off my sandals and put them away in the leather bag. However, one cannot go to Saigon in bare feet, it would not be acceptable. I endured and continued on. My eyes teared up with each step I took forward. Stepping out, I saw someone bring my Teacher's suitcase to a small blue and white car parked nearby. I thought it was a servant bringing a car to pick him up, in my mind, my Teacher would be very wealthy.

During the commute, he showed me the Presidential Palace, the Cathedral of Notre Dame, the Saigon Zoo, and the *Thị Nghè* Bridge. Those were the first four locations I saw in Saigon that was called the Pearl of the Far East. After passing *Thị Nghè* Bridge, the car turned left into St. Sulpice Seminary. We got out of the car; my Teacher took out his wallet and paid the fare. This puzzled me. The Teacher explained it was a taxi. I realised the car is not his own as I previously thought.

After TQ. took care of some business in the Seminary, we went to the Church of Our Lady of Perpetual Help on *Kỳ Đồng* Street to buy books. It was near afternoon when we headed to his sister's house in *Chí Hòa* County. We relaxed at the house to my enjoyment. After a day of walking, my feet were chafed and bleeding from the sandal straps. There was nothing worse than wearing shoes for the first time and travelled a long journey when you were 14 years old. I took off the sandals as soon as we arrived, as if they were shackles which had tortured my feet during the journey.

That evening, we had stir-fried escargot with green banana and herbs. That was the first time I knew of this Northern dish, and it was very delicious. That night, I went into a deep sleep because I had not slept during the previous night, and the journey was tiring. My feet were also aching.

The next morning, I woke with aching and painful feet; the broken skin was covered with a scab. With this painful condition, I knew I couldn't wear sandals; so, I bent over, intending to wrap them up and put them in the bag. I would wear them again when my feet stopped hurting.

Picking up the sandals, oh goodness, I discovered that last night, a naughty mouse had nibbled all the bloody parts of the sandal straps. I looked at my pathetic sandals with the broken straps, I grieved for the shoes, a bit amused, and angry at the mouse as I cursed it, "You miserable mouse! If I get my hands on you, I will break all your teeth!" Such a great pity the short-lived pair of sandals that served me only one time in my historical trip to Saigon.

Teacher *Quý* had a 17-year-old nephew named *Hán*, he was in the ninth grade. He hung out with me during my stay in Saigon, taking me here and there. Fortunately, *Hán* lent me a pair of clogs. I wore them all the days I was here. Thanks to *Hán* as my host, I had the chance to visit many places such as the zoo, the City Market, the Saigon Cathedral of Notre Dame, the Saigon Port, the Racecourse, and many other places. I had the chance to see President *Ngô Đình Diệm* inspecting troops on Vietnam National Day, October 26.

My memories of Saigon Zoo are vivid with many animals I had only seen in books. I enjoyed this very much because I had only seen the elephant once when a snake-oil vendor rode an elephant to the village market to advertise his medicines. Other than that, I never ever saw lions, tigers, bears, panthers, alligators…

First Bowl of *Phở* (Beef Noodles)

Also, during that trip to Saigon, *Hán* took me to eat *Phở* (Beef noodles) for the first time.

I remember that morning, when *Hán* took me on his bicycle to the Church of Our Lady of Perpetual Help in *Kỳ Đồng* Street. After visiting the Church, we went right outside the gate of the Church's fences where a *Phở* vendor cart stood near the curb. Nearby were some small and low tables, with small fish-vendor-style stools no taller than 10 centimetres off the ground.

Hán ordered two bowls of *Phở* that were served with lime, peppers, and herbs such as basil. I smelled a different but enticing aroma for the very first time. My mouth began to water at first smell, while *Hán* helped me with the procedures before eating. He slowly showed off his expertise as he plucked some long coriander, and Thai basil, added some raw bean sprouts on the surface of the steaming *Phở* soup, not forgetting to add a squeeze of lime.

I thought the formalities were over, and my saliva had nearly filled my mouth. My right hand was ready with a pair of bamboo chopsticks, like a knight brandishing his spear and ready for battle. Eyes wide, I watched every little move of *Hán's* fingers. I had lost all the patience of a rural child, who had smelled the irresistible flavours and tastes of a food that I'd never ever tasted, but *Hán* was unaware of my mindset at the time. I was waiting for his cue, "Okay *Lễ*, go ahead and eat."

Conversely, he stopped and looked up, seeing my eyes opened as wide as… the bowl itself, looking at the bowl of *Phở*. He asked, "Do you eat hot chili?"

I didn't pay attention to his question because my attention was busy with something else. I hurriedly answered in a sentence that later embarrassed me, "Are you done? I don't need anything, I can eat it as-is." I fumbled through that sentence, while trying to keep the saliva from dribbling out. *Hán* didn't know that. Perhaps, he thought everyone could be calm before a steaming just-served bowl of *Phở* with its aromatic glow.

After my off-topic answer, I thought the torture was over. Then, he put the lemon wedge on the table top, fished a wrinkled maroon handkerchief from his pocket, and carefully wiped his fingers for lime pulp. He then slowly explained that *Phở* called for some hot chili to make it enjoyable. All the while, he gave me an avid lecture on how to eat *Phở* properly. It went in one ear and out the other.

I glanced at the neighbouring table, where a girl my age sat working on a bowl of steaming *Phở*, although she ordered after us. Occasionally, she drew up her handkerchief to wipe her nose, perhaps, because of hot chili. This made me even more impatient.

At this point, *Hán* still had my bowl of *Phở* imprisoned. It sat parallel to his bowl, not having gone through the procedures of long coriander and Thai basil…I angrily looked at his face in disdain because of his long-windedness. Normally, when going out, he was mute as a clam when it was an appropriate time to explain about Saigon. For some strange reason, he decided to ramble on; finally, he did me a favour when pushing my bowl over in front of me, after carefully tucking his damn handkerchief back in his pants pocket.

I received the bowl with both hands, with a layer of herbs on top that I knew was very delicious before even tasting it. At this point, I didn't pay attention to the surroundings. My whole world had reduced itself to the size of…the bowl of *Phở*. I pulled the low stool closer to the table, lining it up with the table. Not even saying grace, I bent over and sipped a bit of the broth. I fell into a trance as the tip of my tongue came in contact with the strange and delicious broth. Anyone who saw would laugh at me on how I sipped the broth from the edge of the bowl. It was actually not my extreme craving that I did so, but my mouth was full of saliva. The broth excited me.

I started to hold chopsticks into the bowl to eat, suddenly I heard *Hán's* awful voice. "Hey! *Lễ*, you're not ready yet. Slow down a second, hold on! You don't have *Tương* (Hoisin Sauce) yet. Without *Tương* there is no taste."

I was interrupted at the most unexpected time, so I was angry and embarrassed but I had to control my temper. Meanwhile, *Hán* reached the dirty black plastic bottle at the corner of the table. It had a hollow squeeze-tip with a hole the size of a toothpick. I knew it was the bottle of *Tương*. He reached across the table and squirted me some *Tương* as I waited impatiently.

He squeezed…squeezed…and squeezed, but nothing came out of the tip. Finally, there was the sound of swishing of exiting air coming out of the bottle. The bottle had been emptied for some time now. *Hán* seemed disappointed and a bit upset, perhaps because he embarrassed himself in front of me. He turned his resentment towards the vendor lady at her cart, surrounded by customers and said in a high voice, "Vendor! Why leave the empty container here when you are out of *Tương*? Take it away! Give us another bottle."

Hán's voice was clearly rude, lacking respect as if giving an order. The woman seemed not to hear, or pretended not to hear, while her hands scurried with many tasks at the busy *Phở* cart. He wasn't heard, and his voice went a little higher, "Vendor! Any *Tương* left? Give us another container; didn't you hear me?"

The vendor lady still busied herself with the numerous customers as she prepared their bowls of *Phở*. Seeing the situation was uptight, I said to *Hán*, "Let it go, brother, *Phở* without it is just fine! What's a little loss of flavour?"

I poked my chopsticks into the bowl in a tempting motion. *Hán* reached over and stopped my right hand. "No! No! Wait a moment, just a sec. *Phở* without *Tương* is nothing!"

I was forced to stop once more. At this point, I thought it wasn't about whether there was *Tương*, but he wanted to win his battle with the vendor who didn't hear two requests for it. Perhaps because he was sitting down, now *Hán* stood and walked over to the cart to say to the vendor lady, "Vendor, can I get some *Tương*? I asked twice before but you didn't hear me!"

The young woman had her hands full, so she poked gently without turning around, "You just take one from another table. Sir! I am so busy, understand me, please."

Other customers turned and looked disdainfully at *Hán*. Hearing that, he turned and walked back to the table sitting a relaxed girl working with her toothpick. He asked her to pass him the *Tương*, and she smiled as she nodded.

Taking the first bite of *Phở* into my mouth, I thought to myself, Good God! Is there any dish on earth more delicious than this? I then thought of all the past rulers and wealthiest folks in the world who could eat *Phở* all the times. They eat *Phở* for 365 days a year! Strangely enough, while sitting on that fish-vendor stool on that day, it was the best bowl of *Phở* I ever had. I could never again recreate that splendid experience.

The 'Press Conferences'

After a week in Saigon, I returned home by myself while Teacher *Quý* stayed for a few more days. During the ride home, I wore only pair of shorts and the pair of clogs because I left the remains of my once-worn sandals in Saigon. I grieved for that pair of new sandals, but considering my trip to Saigon was so priceless and wonderful; whether or not, I lost a pair of shoes wasn't a great loss. Overall, I wore the shoes for the trip, and anything would suffice on the return trip. Even bare feet would have been okay, because I'd go back to wearing hide in the country-side, the hide of my own two feet!

It went without saying that it was after Vietnam National Day when school resumed again, I became 'the Star of *Mai Phốp*'. The boys and girls in my class would surround me for discussions. I held press conferences for months but there were still things to tell about Saigon. My friends just sat listening with their mouths open, and their attitudes encouraged me even more. I already had these press conferences with my buffalo herding team at *Cầu Đá*. I tried to tell every detail and faithfully retell what I saw and heard in that historical trip.

It was only the Saigon Zoo experience that I exaggerated for fun, with its lions, tigers, and bears that I said were…a bit bigger than their actual size. For example, if a lion were as big as a calf, then I said it was as big as a…small cow. Although a calf and a small cow are the same, it seemed that a small cow sounded bigger than a calf!

I also told my schoolmates that I saw the USS SAINT PAUL, docked at Saigon Port for Vietnam National Day. As President *Ngô Đình Diệm* came to visit, they welcomed him with a 21-gun salute. A girl interrupted to ask, "How big was the ship, *Lễ*?"

Frankly, I didn't know how big it was, looking back and forth before saying, "It's as big as that…Church over there!"

The girl stuck her tongue out in surprise, while I wondered if such a comparison was accurate. Whether an American warship was bigger or smaller, I didn't know. The Church was the biggest thing around for comparison. That was it!

A Tale of Two Priests

Late 1957, Father *Lê Vĩnh Trình* (Fr. Felix) was transferred to *Cái Bông* Parish in *Bến Tre* Province after 17 years at *Mai Phốp*. Upon leaving the Parish, he left behind a very prosperous legacy of *MINH ĐỨC* School: The number of students doubled from previous year. The priest who replaced him was Father *Nguyễn Văn Tỏ* (Fr. James). This unexpected change affected my life considerably, whether by religious or scholarly means.

Father Felix and Father James were different on many fronts. The sharp contrast in my first two priests' personalities and ways of life left me a deep impression. Father Felix was a stately man with a solid frame of a sportsman. He liked playing soccer, had a portly walk, and lived like noble upper class of *bourgeois*. He had closely-cropped salt and pepper hair, parted in the middle.

I saw Mr *Út Thông* come to give Father Felix's haircut every Saturday evening. Because my classroom was right behind the presbytery, I remembered this very routine clearly. All in all, I thought to myself about the barber every time, "What luck this man has, he gets to touch the head of Father Felix, someone I fear the way I fear God."

When not wearing his black outfit, Father Felix wore shorts. He looked very healthy and stately.

Conversely, our new Parish priest, Father *Nguyễn Văn Tỏ* (Fr. James) was thin and frail as a leaf; weak like an unattractive woman, with black hair combed backwards that made him look like he was permanently wearing a black beret. Not only that, he had an abnormal tissue growth inside his nose. Every five minutes or so we would hear a strange noise, four sounds in succession with two in a raw "*khẹt khẹt...khẹt khẹt.*" Then he would whip out a handkerchief and blow his nose noisily for a string.

People nicknamed him *Cha Tò Khẹt* (The sniffing priest) of course, only behind his back. Father James walked quickly with the quiet easy walk of a cat. When not wearing the black robe, he wore a long black shirt and black pants in the style of old time, women in the old city *Huế would* wear.

Father Felix left the Parish with a fleet of cars, with many people's escort. Father James came on a motorcycle to take over the Parish. Moving to the new Parish, Father James brought with him the family of a church caretaker; he and his boys were also as untidy as their boss. The two priests were the physical manifestation of strength and weakness. I was not surprised at the contrast between the lifestyles, conduct, and job performance of the two religious leaders for the Parish. The sharp 'sun-and-moon' contrast of Fr. Felix and Fr. James had a negative impact on the mind of a 14-year-old boy like me.

What surprised me to the end was Fr. James' first Sunday Mass, when he deliberately attacked Father Felix callously, openly and nastily in his sermon. Fr. James accused Fr. Felix had taken all the belongings of the Parish, including the furniture in the presbytery! Father James' voice was very loud and angry, and the series of snuffing "*khẹt khẹt...khẹt khẹt*" increased with his anger. The more he talked the more he became agitated, like a man falling in a fit of epilepsy as he unleashed his enmity and hatred for his predecessor. That was a very forceful sadistic sermon from Father James to promote a hostility and violation of love for humanity.

Some days later, I saw the appearance of hideous chairs made with shabby planks from milk crates. They were nailed together for people to sit on! These field combat chairs had replaced all the nice chairs in the presbytery, as well as the centre rows in the Church that were reserved for the Parish councillors. Many people, who came to visit Fr. James, left with holes in their pants because nails poked out of his trade-mark chairs in the presbytery. I didn't know what went on between the priests, but Father James's actions to topple Father Felix ended up hurting Father James himself, and left a bad impression on me. It had also contributed to nurturing my intention to become a priest.

Disaster!

The following pertains to Father James' visit to my *MINH ĐỨC* School a few days after he began his job as Parish priest and Principal of the school. Knowing that, Father James hated Father Felix, and that the *MINH ĐỨC* School was the legacy of Father Felix's hard work, Teacher *Quý* advised us to be extremely polite and respectful to Father James so he would love and care for the School. He also explained the abnormal tissue growth inside Father James' nose and giving us fair warning about his audible strange chain snuffing *"khẹt khẹt...khẹt khẹt...."* We were to think nothing of it, and most of all we were not to laugh!

At around three in the afternoon, there were more than one hundred students from sixth and seventh grade crowding the large classroom. We were waiting for two teachers to accompany Fr. James. Looking out, I saw Father James wearing a black outfit and slip-on sandals. Two teachers on either side who looked humbled as they showed respect to the new school Principal. We applauded cheerfully when Father James stepped into the classroom. TQ. invited the new Principal to step up onto the platform, two teachers standing below while students standing at their spots. On behalf of the entire school, TQ. welcomed the new Principal and asked him to take good care of the students.

Teacher *Quý* spoke plainly and seriously. When Father James responded, disaster occurred! He hadn't spoken many words when we began hearing a series of loud *"khẹt khẹt...khẹt khẹt."* Even in a serious setting like that, none of us students could resist laughing! I covered my mouth and tried to hold it in, looking around to see many other kids doing the same. Some people bit down strongly on their lower lip, while their shoulders twitched with the impending outburst of laughs.

At that point, TQ. glared at us while the other teacher was also suppressing laughs. Students and teachers all knew that to laugh was to…commit suicide, so we had to swallow it at any cost. Unfortunately, the laughing virus liked to attack during serious settings. Perhaps, the laughing germ had already infiltrated and taken over the nervous systems of more than one hundred students and two teachers.

After the second set of *"khẹt khẹt...khẹt khẹt,"* the entire crowd erupted in laughter. Even TQ., who had originally warned us not to laugh, was also laughing. The other teacher was laughing even more heartily than the rest of us, students. Father James gave a loud indignant yell, *"All right! Enough!"* as he quickly stepped off the platform and left the classroom to go straight back to the presbytery.

Everyone fell silent as Father James went out to the yard. Teachers and students gave stunned look at one another for a moment, and then…laughed some more! This time the laughs were more dynamic, louder, and more relaxed. It seemed that everyone figured it was going to happen anyway, and that we might as well laugh a good spell to drive out the laugh germ that sat in our insides. TQ.'s face was all contorted, taking off his glasses to wipe tears from his eyes. The other Teacher also did so, along with many students as a result of a belly-busting laugh.

It was about 5 minutes later when all the laughing finally stopped. A horrible disaster had just happened, but TQ. couldn't blame us because he laughed too. After we had our fill of laughs, TQ. had us sit still to weigh the situation and find a solution. I felt so sorry for my Teacher at the time because he had to choose five students to form a delegation and apologise to Fr. James. I was chosen among the five, perhaps because I laughed the hardest.

When our delegation almost arrived at the presbytery, my heart drummed not only for what we were going to do, but I was also about to step into the presbytery. During Father Felix's time, I never had the chance to step inside even though I, among other students, carried bricks for them to build the house. We walked up the steps to the house, built on top of a rather high limestone platform. After forming ranks, TQ. picked up the small bell and rang it three times followed by a time so quiet that we could have heard a mosquito passing by. This time around, even with more *"khẹt khẹt…"* we wouldn't laugh. More accurately, we didn't have the energy to laugh again. Father James came out momentarily, the air of anger still lingering. When TQ. voiced an apology, he said, "All right, you can go now, I'm tired and need to rest, *khẹt khẹt…khẹt khẹt…khẹt khẹt!*" Then our delegation left, supposedly empty handed.

The Sombre Evening Market

After that incident, Father James never came to our school, although he was technically the Principal in name. Many months later, Teacher *Quý* said goodbye to us and left for Saigon. Although he didn't say why, I understood his reason for leaving. I was immensely sad to say goodbye to the one who was there from the beginning, and contributed much to the MINH ĐỨC School. In addition, TQ. was my godfather. He loved me very much and left me a great souvenir for life, the memory of my first trip to Saigon. Thanks to TQ., I will always remember that it was him who led me over the threshold to life. He was the first person to give me a perspective that was wider than the narrow one of a rural village, in which I was still enclosed until the age of fourteen.

When Father Felix was transferred, the future of the *MINH ĐỨC* School became bleak. The school became gloomy after that laugh episode. When TQ. left, the school became paralysed because the student enrolment went down by half. A good number of students dropped out, included my next-older brother. Some went on to the Province to higher education. I left to *Vĩnh Long* City to continue half of my eighth-grade year at *NGUYỄN TRƯỜNG TỘ* Diocesan High School.

As for the fate of *MINH ĐỨC* School after TQ. left, the school functioned erratically and sombrely like a village market in the evening. Finally, what had to come had come, like the lamp run out of oil, my beloved *MINH ĐỨC* School officially closed after two schoolyears "56-57" and "57-58". I was studying at *Vĩnh Long* City at that time; so, I missed out to attend the funeral of the school I loved the most of my life!

Although the *MINH ĐỨC* Middle School was short-lived, it helped a number of students take that first step towards their future. A school in a town or city was itself valuable, and there was even more value in a Middle school opened in the country and was considered a blessing. Later on, wherever I was or whatever I did, I always remember the lovely image of the *MINH ĐỨC* School, the efforts of Father Felix, Teacher *Quý*, and the teachers during that youth era. RIP my beloved *MINH ĐỨC* School 1956–1958!

The two priests Fr. Felix and Fr. James left unforgettable impressions in my mind. Outside all their works and personalities, I noticed that both were very powerful and commanded the respect of the people, especially the young crowd at the time. The two would spank the children and made me even more fearful. Father Felix spanked students for offenses such as fruit theft, throwing things at tamarinds, being truant, fighting, or other offenses…while Father James would spank children because of his unstable mental state. I feared but did not respect him. He punished children even when training for altar serving, or when children turned around in Church during prayer time. Father James prohibited children from looking backwards during Mass when there was noise. Many times, we sat in the Church while he deliberately yelled and banged on furniture to test us. Anyone who turned around would be slapped. As for Father

Felix, I must say I feared him unimaginably. Before the eyes of a rural child, he was a god-like. I would avoid him whenever I saw him.

First Step into Town

Once again, my life had been changed with the new environment of *Vĩnh Long* City. NGUYỄN TRƯỜNG TỘ High School where I attended was a private Diocesan school, which had all classes for the high school level. The school had been well established, it had a respectable management and good disciplines. The Directorate and the Board of Teachers were well organised, the school's programs were good and the discipline was very strict. Students wore City fashion uniform: boys were in white shirts tucked in trousers, and shoes. Girls were in *Áo dài* (Long white dresses) and clogs. This was totally different from the way we used to dress and…bare feet were acceptable at MINH ĐỨC School which I had left. NGUYỄN TRƯỜNG TỘ School was an ideal environment for my study, and of course, I felt very proud of going to school wearing shoes. From now on, I could cast off the old image of a countryside boy tending buffaloes and catching birds, to integrate into the townies' life.

At the beginning, I boarded with some classmates from *Mai Phốp*, who came here to study a few months earlier. Thanks to this, I was not so bewildered by life in the Province. Our boarding house was along the bank of Mekong River. Many men fished in nearby and I soon became one of them. When I was in the countryside, I was already hooked on fishing, but just on those small fish in the fields and tributaries. While in *Vĩnh Long*; during the evenings and on holidays, I often joined those men fishing along the wharf or on dinghies along the riverbanks in order to learn how to fish in large rivers. Gradually, I became better, and eventually one of the top rank anglers. After boarding with some classmates for a few months, I moved in to stay with my older brother in the army barracks of the Provincial Security Forces.

And then, my perspective became wider to absorb many new things, including a strange account of Captain *Phạm Ngọc Thảo*, Commander of *Vĩnh Long's* Provincial Security Forces at that time, which really caught my attention. Captain *Phạm Ngọc Thảo* was third in power after Bishop *Ngô Đình Thục* (Older brother of incumbent President *Ngô Đình Diệm*) and Provincial Chief *Khưu Văn Ba*. I was surprised with Captain *Thảo's* manner as an excessively devout Catholic; while most of Officers at this time were seen as playboys.

Many nights, I saw Captain *Phạm Ngọc Thảo* come to each Catholic family in the barrack asking if we had said our prayers yet. Anyone who was careless in this matter would be chastised and made to sit down for prayers. He would sit with them momentarily and moved on to another family. If Captain *Phạm Ngọc Thảo* found any soldier who skipped Sunday Mass, there was not much hope for his blessings. As for his wife, she was also present in every religious club such as the Legion of Mary. As head of the Club, she worked with much passion. During the time of Captain *Phạm Ngọc Thảo*, the entire military barrack ran like a…Church.

I would never forget the way Captain *Phạm Ngọc Thảo* went to Mass at the Cathedral of *Vĩnh Long*. I attended Mass every Sunday, so I usually had the chance to witness the character of Provincial Chief *Khưu Văn Ba* and Captain *Phạm Ngọc Thảo*. Every Sunday morning, the Provincial Chief's family would be driven to Mass in a shiny black 'Traction 15'. They could enter the Church in a serious manner very conscious of the many eyes looking at them. The high-ranking couple looked very smart, and their two sons looked even smarter. The well-regarded group went straight through the open Church's door, filling straight into their reserved seats in front of the altar. All eyes were upon them when they entered.

Meanwhile, Captain *Phạm Ngọc Thảo* also attended Mass at the same Church, but in an entirely different manner. Normally, he came a bit earlier than the noble family. The devout Catholic Captain wore a long black robe and sandals to Church, like the labourers in the countryside often did. Instead of a car, Captain *Phạm Ngọc Thảo* used a rickety bicycle. It was plain with two brake handles and no mudguard. He would lean his bicycle against the tamarind tree trunk and lock it for peace of mind before entering the house of God. Seeing him busy with the lock, I guessed he was just putting on a show because no one had the nerve to "blow" the bicycle of the Province's Commanding Officer. After making sure the lock was secure, Captain *Phạm Ngọc Thảo* stepped lightly like a cat into the Church by its side door and mingled in with the congregation in some pew or another. The people not paying any attention would never know the high rank of this person in the bench next to them.

One day quite accidentally, I heard a story from a member of the Military Band. He apparently heard the following from the Military Band Director, who spoke about the last time the President visited *Vĩnh Long*. Bishop *Ngô Đình*

Thục and the Provincial Delegation, including the Number-two and Number-three in power, who had also come to *Mỹ Thuận* Ferry to welcome the President.

When the Bishop and the President walked past behind him, the Band Director over-heard the Bishop say to the President, "That *Thảo* is very good." He came back and told his fellow soldiers, "Perhaps this time our Captain will be promoted."

He was correct! *Phạm Ngọc Thảo's* premeditated show paid off, he gained the attention and trust of the Bishop. It was not long before he was promoted to Major and assigned to be Provincial Chief for *Kiến Hòa*. The last time I saw *Phạm Ngọc Thảo* was in 1962. At that time, I was studying at *Vĩnh Long* Seminary. He came to the Seminary to visit Father *Nguyễn Văn Tự*, the powerful right-hand man of Bishop *Ngô Đình Thục*. Major *Phạm Ngọc Thảo* was very stately in his black Mercedes with a chauffeur. No one could imagine that this stately Provincial Chief once rode his rickety bicycle to Sunday Mass in *Vĩnh Long*, while still being the Chief of Provincial Security Forces.

Sometime later, I heard his career path went upwards like a kite in the wind. Not long after; he was promoted to Lieutenant Colonel, then Colonel. But when President *Diệm* was assassinated in 1963 in a coup d'état, *Phạm Ngọc Thảo* was demoted and exiled in Washington DC. Not long after that, he came back with some politicians and staged a political coup in Saigon. The coup was a failure. He escaped, was caught, and killed. I didn't pay much attention to those details, but I was surprised to hear that *Phạm Ngọc Thảo* was a stout Communist. He had a brother, who worked as the North Vietnam Ambassador to a Communist nation.

Phạm Ngọc Thảo was a double agent, pretending to surrender to the Nationalists, covered by Bishop *Thục*, to infiltrate the Government of the South. He surrendered to the *Ngô Đình Diệm* Administration through the mediation of Fr. *Nguyễn Ngọc Quang*, Dean of the *Vĩnh Long* Cathedral. Mr *Phạm Ngọc Thảo* found the right channel. I believed he had studied the plan carefully. Bishop *Ngô Đình Thục* trusted *Thảo* and allowed him to teach for a while at *NGUYỄN TRƯỜNG TỘ* High School. After that, he was assimilated as Army Captain and became Commander of the Provincial Security Forces.

I was not certain about the truth of the information regarding *Phạm Ngọc Thảo*, but later on, when I heard about his abnormal activities, I had suspicions about his exaggerated moral attitude in *Vĩnh Long*. All his morals were ostentatious in front of Bishop *Ngô Đình Thục* for the sake of his premeditated political ambitions.

Chapter 3
My Priestly Vocation

After two years at *NGUYỄN TRƯỜNG TỘ* School, I passed the junior High School placement exam in 1960, I went to study at *RẠNG ĐÔNG* school in *Mỹ Tho* because my brother had transferred there. I skipped the tenth grade to take the Baccalaureate Part I. The following year, I completed the Baccalaureate Part II at the age of 19. I was very fortunate to be the first person in my village to complete both baccalaureate studies. Success meant that my future was wide open ahead. I filled out an application for an entry exam to the School of Medicine. During this time, I thought a great deal about which path to consider towards my future. I thought of wanting to become a priest because then, I would have the opportunity to more effectively serve the poor.

My views on the social situation at the time, included the miserable plight of the vulnerable rural villagers, who were greatly oppressed in many ways. The labourers were among those most disadvantaged. They were oppressed by many different forces, from the French colonists, to the local authorities, and even by some of their religious leaders. The rural villagers were under a dual yoke; they did not know to whom to call for help. To avoid further horrendous consequences, their only option was to bow their heads and silently endure sufferings.

I was deeply concerned about what I saw. My compassion for what I witnessed was very real. This compassion became a major influence for the direction of my life. Ultimately, I wanted in some way to address the inequities that I witnessed. As a priest, perhaps, I would have this opportunity. Another motive for this choice was to change the perception of priests as such, their image, and their lifestyles. Of importance was also the need to consider the appropriate attitude of the priest towards the people for whom he was dedicated to serve.

This perspective dominated my decision, if I became a priest, I would be a priest for the poor and the oppressed, for those people who were trampled on and abandoned by society. Religion would be the voice that would give prominence to equality and humanity! I would raise my voice to fight for all forms of social injustice, which was caused by whatever power. I would never forgive those who made my people suffer even if that position would put my life in danger. That was the ideal that determined my choice. My goal was now to become a priest in the future. If I were a priest, I might encounter some people who liked me and some people who hated me, but I was resolved to make sure that no one would fear me, especially the children. Because when I was young, I was terrified by the power of the first two priests of my life. I first told my parents of my desire to become a priest, my Father was surprised but joyful as he said, "Now that you are mature, make your own decision."

Training someone of my age to be a priest at the time was an exception, because anyone who wanted to be a priest had to start young at High School. I came to see Father *Trương Thành Thắng*, Rector of *Vĩnh Long* Seminary, to express my aspirations. He was supportive. He said, "I am very pleased to know your decision, and if you have heard God's calling, then you must follow through."

From there, I began a new stage in my life in the unfamiliar environment of *Vĩnh Long* Seminary. At that time, the Seminary had instructions in French. This, of course, was a challenge which was somewhat of a disadvantage for me. I had to try my best to catch up with my classmates. Father *Trương Thành Thắng* arranged for me to learn Latin and learn more about my vocation to become a priest at the Lower Seminary. I was assigned a priest who taught me Latin every day in the library.

In August 1963, after two years of intensive study and the strict discipline of the *Vĩnh Long* Seminary, I was officially admitted to a seven-year residential program at St. Joseph Seminary in Saigon. That year was also the 100-year anniversary of the Founding Day for this Seminary. More than two months after my studies began, a coup d'état led by Lieutenant-General *Dương Văn Minh* happened on November 1st, 1963. President *Ngô Đình Diệm* and his younger brother *Ngô Đình Nhu* were murdered. The first Republic of Vietnam was ended.

The Coup D'état

The 1963 Coup d'état was a powerful event which had great impact on my life. Through this event, I understood more about the political, religious, and factional matters of my country, which I was not aware of previously. This event helped grow in me a strong feeling for the fate of my people and my country.

I still remembered that afternoon of All Saints Day; while looking down from the third floor of the Seminary dormitory, I saw many soldiers, some running, some climbing fences, some removing their uniforms. These soldiers were from the nearby Marine base. We were uncertain as to what the upheaval was all about. When we went to the chapel for afternoon prayers, we heard the sound of cannon fire nearby. It was followed by the rattle of gunfire. This caused us to cancel prayers. We went to the bunker, a reinforced storage area in the chapel's basement. The radio network repeatedly called for more involvement in the coup by the Military Revolutionary Council, led by Lieutenant-General *Dương Văn Minh*. This news came to us sandwiched in between by upbeat songs.

That night, we stayed awake in the bunk. Via a radio set up in the middle of the room we followed the events of the mutineers. The sounds of explosions from artillery and gunfire were sometimes sparse, sometimes ample. At around midnight, gunfire like *Tết* (New Year's Day) firecrackers went off by the Seminary. We knew that the mutineers were attacking the Republic's citadel, which was separated from the Seminary by *Thống Nhất* Street. When it was almost morning on November 2nd, the gunfire tapered off. Finally, all was silent. I knew the coup was successful. Although I was not concerned about politics, I still prayed for the safety of the President. In the morning of November 2nd, we exited from the bunker and cleaned up the scattered bullets all over the Seminary's courtyard. A great number of heavily armed soldiers swarmed the nearby streets, many people were walking back and forth. The sight was depressing.

The coup was successful, the President Palace was occupied, but the President and his brother were nowhere to be seen. I was most anxious to find out the fate of the President. I didn't have to wait long, because the first Newspaper posted in the Reading room on November 3rd had the latest. On it was a picture of a smeared bloody President *Ngô Đình Diệm.* He was wearing a black shirt in the photo, his head leaning onto a basin to catch the dripping blood. The headline took up the entire width of the page: ***Brothers, Diệm and Nhu, committed suicide!***

There was nothing else to believe, yet we remained sceptical. The news story that President *Ngô Đình Diệm* and his brother had committed suicide lacked credibility. In reality, the two men were escaping to *Chợ Lớn* city and assassinated on November 2nd when they were being transported in an armoured vehicle between the church in *Chợ Lớn* and the General Staff Headquarters. This fact was later verified in documents that were released later.

Many books and Newspapers had been written about the coup in 1963, including the memoirs of a few people directly involved in that incident. Foreign authors, when writing about issues relating to Vietnam, also touched upon this coupe d'état. I've read through a number of those books, observing that the majority of them retold the coup's progression in the same way, only the details were different. One thing nobody mentioned, or purposely left unsaid, was, why was President *Ngô Đình Diệm* killed?

Later, declassified documents pertaining to this coup d'état showed that; the plot was well planned by the Kennedy Administration in Washington DC in an effort to get rid of President *Ngô Đình Diệm*. He was viewed as an obstacle to the American escalated war strategy, whereby Americans to send troops to South Vietnam to resist against the aggressive attack of the North's Communists. President *Ngô Đình Diệm* vehemently rejected that plan. The Kennedy Administration had no choice, they must change the horse in mid-course.

One thing was obvious and certain, the Americans had no prior plans to kill President *Ngô Đình Diệm* after the coup. This was not from a feeling for humanity, but for fear of negative public opinion. The Kennedy Administration knew quite well that no matter how well they hid their actions, everyone would still know that the Americans were behind this coup d'état. Therefore, if President *Ngô Đình Diệm* was killed, the American Government would be found guilty and would have negative consequences.

The rebellious generals, those who had staged the coup could not make decisions outside of the American command. Lieutenant Colonel Lucien Conein was the representative on duty who issued orders and handed out cash rewards. The life of President *Ngô Đình Diệm* was not fair game for the coup organising officers' decisions. So, why was President *Diệm* killed?

Even now, no one has claimed to have killed President *Diệm*. Most documents pointed towards Lieutenant General *Dương Văn Minh*, because he gave orders to his bodyguard, Captain *Nguyễn Văn Nhung* by holding up two fingers of his right hand, meaning kill both of them when this blood thirsty bodyguard followed the convoy to pick up President *Ngô Đình Diệm* at the Church in *Chợ Lớn*. General *Mai Hữu Xuân* led the convoy and it was Captain *Nhung* who killed the brothers *Ngô Đình Diệm* and *Ngô Đình Nhu* inside the armoured tank. About the details of this assassination, there were differences in the documents. Captain *Nguyễn Văn Nhung* was mentioned the most, and he was considered the person who pulled the trigger on *Ngô Đình Diệm* and *Ngô Đình Nhu*. After the coup, he was promoted to Lieutenant Colonel but later secretly executed not long after the coup when General *Nguyễn Khánh* was in power. Those who survived would either keep quiet, or shift the blame back and forth. This kept the death of President *Ngô Đình Diệm* murky.

Death by One's Grandeur

Who among the generals ordered President *Ngô Đình Diệm*'s death on the morning of November 2nd, 1963? I won't discuss this here, but according to my views, this was a rush decision. After President *Ngô Đình Diệm* telephoned to surrender to the group of rebellious Generals at the General Staff Headquarters, the fate of the brothers was sealed. The sudden phone call made for an awkward situation, and the Generals were forced to make a decision. In other words, it was President *Ngô Đình Diệm* who phoned in for his own death penalty and that of his brother. The situation was very unique. The Generals did not fear that President *Ngô Đình Diệm* was planning a trick, to stall for time, so the tables could be turned, such as in the unsuccessful coup in 1960 led by Colonel *Nguyễn Chánh Thi*. Bringing President *Ngô Đình Diệm* back to the General Staff Headquarters was what the Generals feared most. Then how would they speak to, behave towards, and address him? They couldn't bear their guilt, how could they facing a person who had given them everything, including the military power they were using in their disloyalty.

Among them were some people who were cowardly serving the French military first, then serving President *Ngô Đình Diệm* to be promoted to high power. They then directed their troops against him. They did not know how to treat a prisoner whom they respected and feared the most the day before. They did not know how to address the person who had been addressed most respectfully in Vietnamese terms, addressing him as *"Ông Cụ"*, (Great Elder), and referring themselves the humble term, *"Con"*, (Your little child). Furthermore, perhaps *Dương Văn Minh* and the group of seditious Generals feared that grand person, when escorted back to face traitors perhaps, he would point at each person, call each by name and say, "I can't believe you guys, you're bunch of traitors! You're worse than animals. You have used the blessings I have given you, to harm me". From that judgment, I concluded that President *Ngô Đình Diệm* became a victim of his integrity. Perhaps later, the person who ordered his death would be struck by conscience, then quietly pray for forgiveness, "Great Elder, please understand and forgive me, your little child. I didn't want to kill you, but it was you who put me in that position. There was no other choice for this decision."

Political Turmoil

After the death of President *Ngô Đình Diệm*, the South fell into a large political vacuum. It became a serious crisis for the National authority. Succeeding governments were only the necessary interim setups as placeholders, so the country wouldn't fall into chaos. The individuals who succeeded President *Ngô Đình Diệm* lacked the influence and persuasiveness to gain the people's belief and support. The majority of them were warhorses. They obtained power by military force and mutinied under the name of Revolution, Coup d'état, Readjustments, Power play, etc... Some of these individuals had no skills or political experience. The current political situation provided them with the opportunities to grasp a position on the political stage. Public opinion was divided regarding former President *Ngô Đình Diệm*. Whether he was a benefit or a liability to the country, history will have to determine the final verdict. What cannot be questioned is the fact that President *Ngô Đình Diệm* was a prestigious political leader for the country. Successive national leaders never had this kind of charisma.

Ironically, before a bottle of champagne could be finished off, the Generals who negotiated the coup were themselves finished off by General *Nguyễn Khánh*. He flew in from the Central region into Saigon to carry out a readjustment. He imprisoned the four Generals involved in the coup, except National Leader General *Dương Văn Minh*. General *Nguyễn Khánh* acted promptly to fill this vacuum of leadership. He seized control of the Government.

One significant event happened during General *Nguyễn Khánh's* reign of power. At the time, there were a few days when there was no government, and Saigon fell into real turmoil. I painfully recalled some serious conflicts between the two major religions: Buddhism and Catholicism. Saigon developed a fever that fed on the chaos, and the people became even more frenzied with confusing rumours. There was news that Buddhists would attack Bishop's House in Saigon. Other times, there was news that young Catholics from the migrant camps would attack *Viện Hóa Đạo*, a Buddhist Institute. These kinds of rumours increased the already confusing situation which became more intense as days went by. Meanwhile, the respective religious establishments went on organising means of self-protection. This produced a suffocating atmosphere in Saigon as if a holy war was about to burgeon. I didn't know if religious conflicts actually existed. I was totally unaware of how and where they might be occurring. However, I painfully recall this situation at the time.

Crisis of Power

In a situation of war, Vietnam needed leadership to confront a powerful *Hồ Chí Minh* in the North, who was both malicious and scheming. Regretfully, the South lacked that much-needed leadership. The Government of President *Nguyễn Văn Thiệu* took power in 1967. It was seen as the best alternative among the frivolous governments after the coup of November 1963. It provided temporary political stability; however, it did not provide the stability needed. This was particularly serious, the soldiers lacked coherent motivation for soldiers fighting the *Việt Cộng* (Vietnamese Communism). The real strength of the South was not the people's determination to fight, but rather it was the advanced technology of the weapons supplied by Americans, along with the prospect of a miserable life should the South fall into Communist hands. Those two factors came together to create the prominent and famous military history, of the Army of the Republic of South Vietnam (ARSVN).

Unfortunately, the valiant soldiers of the ARSVN were in the most disadvantageous position. They fought bravely on the battlefield to keep a stable front, while irresponsible urban non-combatants freely reaped the benefits. They gave up their blood and bones to put a stop to the enemy's advances so that those in power could make their wealth and buy their status. They used their bodies as shields, in place of sons of the rich who would bribe commanding officers so that their sons could just be soldiers in name only.

Where was the fighting spirit when the valiant soldiers on the battlefield could hear the enemy bombing mixed with the yells of protesters in rallies, declaring the Commander-in-chief was corrupted? Certainly, they knew that an airplane was always ready, in case the Commander-in-chief wanted to flee with his family and his assets. In this setting, the loss of the South was only a matter of time.

My Priestly Life

I was ordained a priest in Saigon on 29 April 1970 at the age of 27. A month later, I became assistant priest at *Hoà Khánh* Parish, in the township of *Sa Đéc* in Mekong Delta. When I began my life as a priest, the Vietnam War had drastically escalated.

Images and news of war were everywhere. War news was pervasive in prints and radio. Civilians retreated into cities because the rural areas were not safe. Meanwhile, the Saigon Capital's life continued as usual, as though nothing of importance was happening. The urbanites only heard of the war, the majority were not eyewitnesses. They did not see a direct threat to their lives and assets, so everyone lived in an easy-going manner.

Battle news became too familiar. The number of battle casualties from both sides became meaningless statistics, not drawing attention from people in secure areas. Occasionally, the *Việt Cộng* would set off mines or fire missiles into the Saigon Capital, or into cities and schools, causing terrors and casualties for a while, and everything went back to the usual routine. People with duties to fight, fought. Those who were fortunate were not involved in battle, living happily in secure areas, reaped the benefits, as they continued making their fortunes.

With the presence of half a million Americans, who had flooded into the South Vietnam after the toppling of President *Ngô Đình Diệm*, and allied troops in the South at the time. A special society of immorality and disorder was the order of the day. This situation provided the advantageous of wealth and hedonism for a few, but great suffering for many! This was the daily scenario of my people, my beloved country, Vietnam.

Meanwhile, the security of suburbs and rural areas gradually became worse. The rural villagers suffered two disadvantages. They were under the control of Nationalists during the daytime, and in the hands of *Việt Cộng* when nightfall came. They paid a portion of taxes to the Nationalist State, and another ten portions to the *Việt Cộng*. Anyone caught evading State taxes would be imprisoned, but anyone who was considered as evading Communist taxes would be beheaded or gutted. **I had witnessed this cruel sight with my own eyes in my own village**. The Communists infiltrated themselves among the civilians, hiding in civilian homes, eating civilian food, using civilian tax money, and using them as human shields during protest rallies against the Nationalist Government. There were many cases where the local Government imprisoned civilians who paid taxes to the Communists, while the Government itself could not protect the civilians from the Communists' bloodied iron hands. Miserable rural villagers had recourse to no one for help, except heaven. But heaven was too far away.

In the countryside of The South, guerrilla warfare raged. The political turmoil and the infamous Government of President *Nguyễn Văn Thiệu*, resulted in the Southerners feeling totally demoralised. National leadership is the most important factor for a nation to be strong especially during wartime. The South totally lacked moral leadership. *Nguyễn Văn Thiệu* Administration's nastiest corruption and bribery were openly exposed. This included the buying and selling of titles, and prominent people taking advantage of their power to buy and sell goods, even prohibited goods. Some people even dared to smuggle firearms to the *Việt Cộng* and then pocket the money! People were even saying that Mr *Nguyễn Văn Thiệu* was totally corrupt. He was labelled a battleship that swallowed national assets and American aid funds.

The anti-corruption movement mobilised by Father *Trần Hữu Thanh*, a Redemptorist priest, released documents accusing President *Nguyễn Văn Thiệu* and some Commanding Officers of corruption by name. This movement gained many favourable responses. Some people seemed to understand the situation. They spoke openly on the price of the office of the Province, the County chief, an office indeed profitable! I was not clear as to the true extent of corruption, but I knew for sure that in the South at the time, anyone fortunate enough to have a high rank in the Government would quickly become wealthy. Of course, the rank of President was certainly the best. Because civil servants were busy raking in their assets, the South had an Administration with no power. There was a President but there wasn't a National leader.

When I began my life as a priest, I also came into encounter with the reality of social injustices. Before, I had only seen and heard of such a reality. What I witnessed showed me the tragedy of one person exploiting another. The innocence of growing up in a rural environment, made me oblivious and ignorant of people controlling one another in such opportunistic and spiteful ways, I had never thought possible. People in various offices, or at least in the ones with which I had been associated were truly tyrants of the people. They controlled, exploited, and raked in what actually belonged to the public. They did this with no remorse. In the first two years of my serving in *Sa Đéc*, I butted heads and confronted squarely the administrative head of the Province. The Social Service official swallowed all building materials that the Social Bureau supplied to the thousands of displaced Vietnamese people, who returned from Cambodia to southern border provinces to escape a vengeful massacre.

There were also religious leaders who undermined the very religious teachings that they preached. The fuzzy merging of religion and state, at the moment turned them into 'Black-robed Lords'. They took advantage of their religious titles to amass private benefits. These sad facts became a reality which I never could have imagined the weakness of the human person.

In 1972, I was transferred to become Assistant priest at *Cái Đôi* Parish in *Trà Vinh* Province, a remote and isolated Parish along the coastal area. Here, I shared the pain and suffering of the locals, as if they were my own. Many locals came to me crying and complaining. There had been coercion, exploitation, corruption, rape of young girls, and heartless suppression of the lower class by the Chief of the County. The people, especially the non-Catholic and those who didn't belong to the parish, could only cry. They did not know where or to whom to take their complaints.

To make the matter worse, the Chief of the County was a good friend of the Parish priest. In those circumstances, I stood by the people and challenged the power of this inhumane Government Official. In the end, the voice of the people won. The wicked official had to leave office and was imprisoned in a military prison. I paid a hefty price for my action, and was demoted by the Bishop and some of my colleagues. However, I didn't consider it a defeat or a sorrow. On the contrary, I felt happy and joyful for having been able to live up to the ideals I had chosen.

In January 1975, I left the *Cái Đôi* Parish for the *Vĩnh Long* City as Assistant to Fr. *Trịnh Công Trọng* at the *Vĩnh Long* Cathedral.

Chapter 4
The Life-Changing Event

Through the early seventies, war escalated even more violently. This caused even more suffering to the Vietnamese people. People in the North had to confront the rains of American bombs. Meanwhile, the Southerners were more heavily threatened by *Việt Cộng's* bombings in the cities, and terrorism out in the countryside. The miserable lives of people in both regions were a never-ending story. The more the war escalated, the more blood and bones of Vietnamese people piled up. Painfully, the fate of my people was being a pawn in the international political chess game.

When American Secretary of State Henry Kissinger arrived at Beijing airport in 1972, world politics changed. The American jet came down with a forceful landing wind that turned the book of Vietnamese history to the next chapter. Over the following days and months, the world had the chance to smile at the sight of a bunch of deaf men discussing the future of Vietnam at a meeting in Paris. Meanwhile, bombs and bullets continued to rain down over my Motherland; and, of course, the Reaper in charge of Vietnam was busy, just like he'd always been in the past few decades.

In January of 1973, the Paris Peace Accords were signed. They contained clauses that sealed the dark fate of the Republic of Vietnam. Until the end of April 1975, the South was on death row as the Chinese-backed Northerners poured into the region. The Southern Government and its armed forces were disorganised in its ranks. Every day was one step closer to the end of the Republic of Vietnam's regime. Finally, what had to come had come, the fateful day came on April 30, 1975 with the unconditional surrender submission broadcasted on the national radio by the president of the Republic of Vietnam *Dương Văn Minh,* (Who was the same person to lead the *Coup d'état* in 1963 to murder President *Ngô Đình Diệm*, and terminate the First Republic of Vietnam.)

April 30, 1975 was the blackest day in the Vietnamese history book. RIP The Republic of Vietnam Regime! I was serving at *Vĩnh Long* Cathedral when the Communists took over the South.

Words are unable to describe the political hurricane that swept away all the people of the South following the doomsday April 30, 1975. The Communist labelled it as Liberation Day! For the petrified Southerners, it was pure terror aptly labelled "Hell Day!"

The society of the South was brutally uprooted. At the beginning of May 1975, the Southerners experienced with horror the herds of guerrillas that came out from the jungles with their strange trademark outfit, black uniforms, with a bucket hat, chequered scarf, AK-47 over one's shoulder. These jungle men actually were the victors. I witnessed with my own eyes all sorts of hellish events that happened at that time, robberies, killings, plundering's, vengeance, beatings, executions, beheadings, and gutting's!

Hundreds of thousand soldiers, officers and officials of the collapsed Government were herded into jails, ironically disguised as Re-Education Camps.

More than a million of Vietnamese people crossed the border to escape the Communists. They were called boat people. Nearly half of that number had lost their lives on the way to freedom. Words wouldn't be enough to describe the so-called Liberation of the South!

Back to Reality

My recollection of these past events drifted through my thoughts throughout this journey. Suddenly, the voice of the driver pulled me back to reality. Due to the lack of space, I heard the driver ask, "Are you feeling squashed, brother? You can scoot towards me a bit. Hang in a little longer, we're almost there!" Perhaps, seeing me sit quietly for a long time, he wanted to start a conversation for fun.

I smiled and replied, "It's okay! I'm very comfortable, you're a great driver! We're almost in Saigon! Eh?"

The cheerful middle-aged driver grinned as if he wanted to return my compliment. Then, he turned to answer a question from a lady at the back. As the car was moving, he cheerfully held conversations with various people who were at the back seats. He had a habit of inserting the F-word into his speech. Out of ten sentences, nine would have the F-word. I sat quietly, and his cursing was quite witty. At times, I would think, if he didn't pad his speech with some F-words, his stories would come out tasteless and dull. I sat quietly by myself and settled into some random thoughts.

Occasionally, I would turn and observe every move of the driver. He had a thick shining black moustache, like two caterpillars facing head-to-head. Every time he laughed, the moustache twitched like caterpillars playing and dodging. It looked quite bizarre. Every time we passed a passenger car in the opposite direction, he would wave to the other driver with a flick of his left hand, his right hand resting lightly on the steering wheel as he spoke and laughed happily. I sat next to him, eagerly following the drivers' way of greeting. His fingers automatically went up then back down, like automatic store entrances that were run by the 'magic eyes' of motion sensors. This fun sight helped me forget the reality of this long journey.

Most of the passengers were average folks. Hearing them talk, I knew they were acquaintances and often took this route to sell their goods. The way they joked with the driver was also a sign that they were his regular passengers. I sat quietly since I stepped into the car, partly because I didn't know anyone and partly because I didn't have anything to talk about. Frankly, I felt as jumbled up as a crumpled silk cord. Questions continued from the back to the front, over my head. Where would I go after I arrive at the *Phú Lâm* station? Suddenly, I became worried and hoped the car would move slower, much slower, the slower the better. That way we would never actually arrive at the station.

A while after we passed *Long An* Bridge, he turned to me and asked, "You're getting off at *Xa Cảng*?"

"Yes, I'm getting off at *Xa Cảng*." The Western Bus Station at *Phú Lâm* was called *Xa Cảng* (Vehicle Station) for short. I didn't give a very enthusiastic response; so the driver was quiet for a while.

Then he looked straight ahead and said, "In the evening, when there's little traffic, we will go fast. We'll be there in a tick. You live in Saigon?"

Normally, I would have made cheerful conversation with the driver, but at that moment, I only gave an indifferent answer.

"Nope, I came to visit relatives."

He continued, "So you live in *Mỹ Tho*?"

"Nope, I live in *Bến Tre*. I work in *Bến Tre*, but my family is in *Vĩnh Long*."

Hearing '*Vĩnh Long*', he cheerfully turned to me as if he had met a companion.

"*Vĩnh Long*, huh? I have a friend in *Vĩnh Long*. He has a motorboat shop at *Cần Thơ* three-way Intersection called…called…"

"I've forgotten his name, in Bishop *Thục's* vicinity." He continued, "Before the Liberation, he was doing very well, now, I don't know how he's doing, it's been a while since I last saw him."

I had a pretty serious 'gut reaction' to hear anyone say *"Giải phóng"*, (Liberation), when referring to April 30, 1975, the day the Communists took over the South. The driver used the word *Liberation* in an unconscious and habitual way, like he used the F-word. With that in mind I did not feel uncomfortable, and cheerfully answered, "I know Bishop *Ngô Đình Thục's* area."

Remaining quiet for a while, and looking straight ahead as if to gather all his memories from faraway days, he tipped his head towards me.

"The city of *Vĩnh Long* is lovely, I used to visit there before the Liberation. Once I visited the county of *Chợ Lách* too. I would go into the orchards and eat the fruit freely! Not to mention the *Vĩnh Long* girls, especially in *Nha Mân* village, who are famously beautiful. Don't you agree?" He winked and gave me a mischievous look.

I corrected him and avoided the subject. "*Nha Mân* belongs to *Sa Đéc* Province now."

The passenger car was running smoothly, as cars were approaching from afar. He didn't seem to notice as he quickly turned to me in surprise, "Huh? I thought *Nha Mân* was part of *Vĩnh Long* Province! I remember once…once… F*ck! We're approaching a checkpoint! Night is here already! And there are still guards on watch!"

He ended our conversation sharply, tilted his head robotically to the rear, alerting everyone, "Hey! It's a checkpoint folks! People, get your papers ready so we can do this quickly! We're here…"

The car came to a rather abrupt stop. Because he was busy talking, he didn't pay attention to the cars in front, so he stopped abruptly which tossed the passengers around. Yells, talking, and curses rang out from the group of female acquaintances in the back.

It was late April of 1976, one year after the Communists took over the South. I didn't understand what economic policies the Vietnamese Communist government enforced, but I did know that people murmured wherever I went, complaining about the travel restrictions.

Routes by both land and sea had too many checkpoints. At first, these checkpoints began popping up everywhere, about a kilometre apart. Later on, there was fewer, but there were still too many. At first, they inspected travel permits, vehicle licensing for motorcycles, purchase invoice for watches and jewellery, etc…; whoever didn't have documentation would have their goods confiscated for consideration. Then there was inspection of merchandise such as peanuts, coconuts, pork, fruits, and other goods. But in life, "For a thick tangerine peel there is a sharp fingernail". The more government inspections increased, the more people found loopholes to get by. As people found more loopholes, the Government put in more inspection points; each side playing an "Economic one-upmanship."

I heard numerous stories about these loopholes and tricks that merchants used to pass inspection points. I would always remember an incident of a poor expectant woman who was selling goods day-by-day to make her living. She smuggled a few kinds of fruit like bananas and coconuts. One day, an economic inspector confiscated her goods. There were other times, she pleaded for pity when they found a few coconuts, some bunches of bananas that weren't worth much.

There was zero tolerance if they found pork, because it was strictly banned. Smuggling a few kilograms of pork past the inspection point would be many times more profitable than smuggling fruit. This pregnant woman continued to smuggle fruit for a considerably long time.

One day, she was smuggling coconut as usual, but that day she unexpectedly had to wait at the inspection station for a long while. Momentarily, the inspector was surprised to see blood all over her feet. He thought the time had come for her to deliver her baby, so he called for a nurse to help her. Although she strongly denied it, who would allow her to deliver it in public?

When they took her away and got her cleaned up, it turned out she wasn't pregnant at all. She had been smuggling pork by tying it very tightly to her belly when passing through inspection. Of course, she was only "pregnant" to get by the inspectors. Although they were very thorough, who would prod at the belly of a pregnant woman? The day she was 'In labour', it was because she was stuck at the check point for too long. The plastic pork bag broke, and pork blood ran down her legs and to her feet which led to her being caught. Hundreds of guilty people blamed the poor quality of their plastic bags. This black plastic bag was made of recycled plastic. After *'Liberation'*! where would you find the transparent and pure variety of a plastic bag?

The car continued to creep along, bumper to bumper in the long fleet of cars passing through the checkpoint. I flinched when passing through inspection points, because experience told me that anything could happen at these points. Every time we passed through checkpoint, I recalled the frightening sight I had witnessed a year earlier on this route. It was May 6, 1975, five days after the Communists took over the South. I was at the *Vĩnh Long* Cathedral and had a business to attend to in Saigon. I went with a group of people in a Church's car.

Highway 4 that day was unusually disordered with big and small vehicles, pedestrians or armed guerrillas. Everyone clogged the highway like a flea market. A few hundred meters away were a few guerrillas. They stopped cars for inspection. I didn't know what they were inspecting. We didn't have weapons, we had all our documents, but the guerrillas were illiterate. Finally, they checked…receipts! Anything without receipts, especially watches, necklaces or rings were seized until the receipts were brought back to claim them. I heard of many unfortunate owners of motorcycles and watches who had to explain to the guerrillas that they never had to carry receipts before. They could explain as much as they wanted, but the business of revolution still went on.

It was early in the morning when we left *Vĩnh Long*. Now it was late afternoon as we approached *Cái Bè*, which was only half of our 130 kms journey from *Vĩnh Long* to Saigon. We had travelled 50 kilometres in …7 hours! The vehicle crept along, stopped for inspections, and continued creeping on, sometimes stopping for guerrilla hitchhikers.

We arrived at another inspection point. This time, a guerrilla acted strangely. He held up a woman's thatch hat and ordered all passengers in the car to throw in all their documents. We gave each other anxious looks after this outrageous order. Without our personal papers, what would happen to us in this chaos? I asked Brother, "If you keep our papers here, what will we do at the next stop?"

The guerrilla replied, "Just say that Big Brother Four in *Cái Bè* was keeping everything!" Good heavens, our personal papers were crucial in the sentence and heated circumstances, and Big Brother Four treated them as potato leaves. But I couldn't explain or argue with him, especially glancing at the black shiny muzzle of the AK-47 on his shoulder. I knew that the best thing to do was throw our papers into the hat. That was also the last time I saw my identification card from the Republic of South Vietnam.

Stripped off our identity papers, I felt so depressed. We began asking each other should we move on or go home. Finally, we decided to continue towards Saigon because our papers were irretrievable. A checkpoint lay ahead as our car approached *Trung Lương* T-junction. An entire fleet of assorted vehicles had stopped among the swarms of people on highway 4. We were asked for ID, but none of us had ID. We said that Big Brother Four in *Cái Bè* had taken them from all of us. Unfortunately, in a disorderly setting with swarms of people, who knew him anyway? We were sent back. With no other choice, we had to turn back after almost a day of slinking along Highway 4. We turned the car around and filed behind a fleet of other vehicles. We waited for the road to clear so we could creep some more. Then we witnessed a fearsome sight.

An Act of 'Liberation'!

I saw a young guerrilla with a bucket hat, black clothes, chequered scarf, AK-47 over one's shoulder, searching the rider of a *Mobilette* motorbike. The motorbike was on its kickstand. The guerrilla was hunched over while emptying the contents of two saddlebags onto the street while the owner stood nearby. I saw some pineapples and some other odds and ends. This was a familiar sight, so I didn't take much notice of it.

Suddenly and without warning, the guerrilla stepped back quickly as he loaded a round into his rifle. He yelled out loudly, in a tone similar to an officer yelling at his troops in the battlefield, "Lie down! Lie down!" He yelled as he backed up further, the AK in a ready position as the muzzle was pointed towards the poor man lying face-down on the ground. "Both arms forward!" The guerrilla yelled his commands, and the man panicked as he followed orders.

I saw the guerrilla move his rifle, while fixing his stance, but the muzzle was still pointed at the lying man. After the muzzle was in the right position towards its victim, then, *bang! bang! bang! bang*! a volley of gunfire rang out.

People from afar dropped to the ground as a reflex response. The victim's body convulsed several times with each gunshot. Blood splattered everywhere and his body convulsed violently before finally lying still. The sight happened too close, we could smell the gun powder. It happened too fast, without time for me to get frightened. I closed my eyes and turned away, quietly saying a prayer for the victim. I had seen human bodies beheaded and gutted by *Vietcong* in wartime before. However, this was the first time I witnessed a guerrilla shooting someone so barbarously, after the South was '*Liberated*'!

The Reluctant Destination

Returning to reality, I realised that our *MINH CHÁNH* shuttle bus had stopped right in front of the armed security officers. I tried to keep a calm facial expression. Meanwhile, the security officers stuck their dark faces in the window to stare curiously into the car, saying nothing. Really, I didn't know what they were inspecting, controlling people, or catching merchant women smuggling goods. Every car had to stop for a moment, then was let go. Ours was the same. They did not ask anything, but they glared at each driver and passenger as if they were searching for a particular face. After seeing nothing suspicious, the officers waved our bye. The driver was sitting with car in gear so as to move on when a security cadre on the curb stopped us. I was a bit worried.

"Stop a minute! Whose red bag is this?" He pointed at the sack at my feet. I felt uneasy, but tried to keep calm, answering as I picked up the bag and untied the drawstring. "What's inside?" He asked.

I put my hand inside and took out my black *Bà ba* (A farmer outfit). "Just some clothes", I replied.

The officer didn't seem to pay much attention to this. He just took a quick glance. I only feared he would ask to search it himself. Besides, a set of clothing on top, I also had a large olive-coloured bath towel and a black nylon hammock with rope on both ends, bound tightly like a rice roll cake. There was also a flashlight, a kind of switchblade that pilots often used; a pouch for a student nib pen that contained toothpaste, toothbrush, and a bit of medicine to treat malaria. If found in a search, these could raise suspicion and that would require a difficult explanation. Actually, it wasn't that much of a worry because the personal papers I carried that can give him a sufficient explanation for these items. A friend of mine had provided me with a photocopy of a certification as verification for my being a forestry worker. This paper was the proof that I was a forestry service worker from *Lâm Đồng* Province.

I didn't care whether the paper was real or fake, it was good enough as long as it had a printed text and a stamp. The security officer looked at it routinely, then he waved us off.

I felt tremendously relieved; however, the driver was even more relieved than I was. Since we were first delayed, he had been visibly fidgety and irritated. The car was in gear but we couldn't go forward. We would creep forward and fall back again, the engine growling like two fighting dogs tied away from each other.

This time, when the officer waved us by, the driver took his foot off the brakes and hit the gas pedal. The car moved forward like a race-horse taking the initial lunge. The female merchants yelled and cursed the driver when they were tossed back and forth. He just grinned in response. The people continued talking and laughing as naturally as they did before, because these inspections were too familiar to them to pay any notice. I sat still and closed my eyes; partly I wanted to rest after a tiring day, partly, I didn't want to continue talking to the cheerful driver. At the same time, within me, I felt a knot of fear and worries: We were almost there!

When the *MINH CHÁNH* shuttle bus stopped at the Westbound Central Vehicle Station at *Phú Lâm*, it was just about dusk. I stepped off the car, said a few words of gratitude to the driver, swung the bag over my shoulder and walked out to the main road.

The sight of the Westbound Central Vehicle Station in the evening was cold and dreary. I stood on the curb finding in my bag for a pack of cigarettes. The smell of smoke was comforting and suddenly I felt more at ease. Previously, I went to the Westbound Central Vehicle Station to catch a shuttle to get to Saigon. This time, I walked along as a habit to catch a ride to continue my journey. At that point, a motorised-cyclo shuttle stopped in front of me.

The driver asked, "Where're you going?"

I was silent for a moment, which surprised him a bit, so he asked me once more, "Are you going to Saigon or *Chợ Lớn*?"

"Take me to *Chánh Hưng*," I said as I stepped on his shuttle. A friend of my family lived in *Chánh Hưng*, the outskirts of Saigon. In the past, I used to stop by for a visit during my trips to Saigon; sometimes I stayed there for a few days. However, this time such a visit would be a hassle to the family friend.

Too many watchful eyes in the neighbourhood who would readily report a stranger to the government.

Part Two
My Life in the Communist Concentration camps

Chapter 5
Life's Turning Point

I will never forget that fateful day, May 28, 1976 when I was arrested in the jungles of the Highlands of Vietnam, three hours' drive north-west of Saigon. Later, I was taken to the *Đức Lập* Police Station in the Province of *Quảng Đức* where I was searched, and my records were carefully scrutinised.

The next day, I was transported by truck to *Ban Mê Thuột* Province along with about thirty other prisoners consisting of men, women, and children. Our group had been detained for several different charges, including crossing the border, speaking against the Revolution, or being a member of a resistance group. There were also some criminals, bandits, thieves, and some deserters or corrupt soldiers. I had already admitted my intention of escaping to Cambodia. But, possibly because of my bogus forestry-worker papers, they did not believe me. I was classified as a member of the resistance. The adults were handcuffed in pairs.

As I watched the scenery fly past, I found that I couldn't focus on a single thought. So, I turned to my fellow cuff-mate prisoner to seek comfort from someone in the same plight. He was about my age, just over 30, having a wife and two small children in Saigon. He was an ex-Army officer. He joined the Resistance Movement rather than to report for 'Re-education' under the new Government. His group of six people had been captured near the Cambodian border five days earlier. Two were shot dead, one had escaped, and the other two had been captured with him. As he sat gazing outside the window, I tried to guess his thoughts. Was he wondering about escaping?

The vehicle bounced over a pothole and brought me back to reality. At the same time, my partner turned and looked at me with sad eyes. I told him about my family situation. My mother was seriously ill.

This vehicle reminded me of a giant snake trying to slit her away into the forest. We were going into a future as murky and unknown as the forested Northwest Highlands. Questions swam in my head like the elusive light of fireflies on the banks of the Mekong River. For the first time in my life, I felt unsure of the future. Although I usually liked adventures, this one promised no light at the end of the tunnel.

Where to Go?

I was 33 years of age, already six years into my priesthood. I realised that I had reached a decisive turning point in my life. During the past week, I had said goodbye to a friend living in the outskirts of Saigon. In order to avoid complications for his family, I declined his hospitality. No one wanted to be the focus of attention of those looking to get merits from the Communists. For a month, I had to stay on the move, not daring to remain in one place for more than a few days, even though I had fake papers to prove that I was a forestry service worker. These papers proved their effectiveness when I was asked to show my ID. However, I knew my luck couldn't last much longer.

I had taken a clear stand against the Communist regime. I didn't accept Communism and vowed to never live in a Communist society. I objected to Communism, not because of its name, but because of its atheistic ideology and dictatorial rules. I believe Communism strips away all basic human rights. It denies freedom of speech and even freedom of thoughts. It prevents any one from traveling freely and forbids any showing of individuality. Denial of these rights precludes any true democracy. From my experience of living under the regime's harsh control, I could not see that it brought any benefits. I firmly believed that this ism' had been foisted on my peoples from outsiders from the North who did not care for our welfare.

The Republican Government in the South had recently fallen. It had lacked any real direction, had relied on foreign strength for its very existence, and was heavily criticised for its manifest corruption and injustice. At the time, I did not grieve for the fallen regime, but I was terrified of the new one! I was determined to oppose the wickedness of this Government, but not to restore the fallen regime. I was determined to join a Resistance group. Together, we would work to bring benefits to the Vietnamese peoples. My role might resemble that of an insignificant creature before the might of the new power. However, that little creature still had a conscience with a thinking brain and emotions. With a group of close friends, I tried my best to contact the Resistance forces in the South. There were rumours about active resistance groups in the Saigon vicinity, but I discovered that there were only a few members scattered in the jungle.

It was rumoured that the former President *Nguyễn Văn Thiệu* was regrouping his troops at the border, and his Vice-President *Nguyễn Cao Kỳ* was hiding with troops in the jungles. Many people believed the rumours, and their gullibility surprised me. Why would former high-ranking leaders, who had cowardly deserted them in the time of crisis, now leave their safe havens in the United States and Europe to go back to Vietnam to rescue their compatriots? Later, I came to understand that living under the hardship of the new regime, the people were desperate for any hope. They reminded me of passengers from a sinking ship who cling to any debris in the hope that it will keep them afloat, even if it's a rotten body of a dog.

Eventually, I met an Evangelical Church Minister from the Montagnard people who told me of a Resistance Force named the *FULRO* fighting effectively in the deepest parts of the jungle, *FULRO* is an abbreviation from a name in French: *Front Unifié pour la Libération des Races Opprimées* (The Unified Front for the Liberation of the Oppressed Races). I knew that *FULRO* was an ethnic resistance movement that had been struggling, even before the Communist take-over to establish self-rule for its people. *FULRO* had now begun working even more vigorously. We tried to contact their leadership, not to collaborate with their activities, but to seek a way to cross the Cambodian border, and to cross over that country to get to Thailand.

My companions and I left Saigon in mid-May 1976. As we entered the jungle by the Vietnam-Cambodia border, we disguised as forestry service workers. After a few days of walking and hiding without any contact with the *FULRO* Headquarters, our group of four decided to head West by ourselves. For security reasons, we had to keep off the zigzag trails and stick to the tracks the Montagnards had made. (Montagnards were darkly tanned ethnic minority group living in the jungles). This slowed us down. We successfully crossed the border into Cambodia. But instead of being free, we were tracked into that country by the Vietnamese Border Patrol Police. Early in the morning of May 28, this armed force emerged from the thick mist, screaming, "Hands up! Hands up!" I felt as if a black pit had opened up before me. We were all wrestled to the ground and beaten with rifle butts. Then, we were herded back to the *Đức Lập* Police Station the next evening.

The Twenty-Fifth Hour

Now, as I was in the truck, I recalled Virgil Gheorghiu's story 'The Twenty-Fifth Hour'. A sensational story translated into the Vietnamese language, which had made a deep and lasting impression on me while I was in Secondary school. It describes the thirteen-year ordeal suffered by the Romanian Johan Moritz. He was mistaken for a Jew during World War II and moved from labour camp to concentration camp, from Hungarian control to Nazi's control, enduring savage torture. Then, for some reason, the Germans mistook him for one of their own. He had his honour restored and wore SS uniform as part of their security forces. After the war, he was brought before the Nuremberg International Tribunal as SS agent. There, he was convicted for war crimes but was eventually rightfully cleared and allowed to re-join his family. Before his leaving, an American officer took a photo of him. He said to Moritz "Smile now, go on, smile!" But poor Moritz could not smile; because he'd forgotten how!

I was not sure whether I recalled all details of the story, but the unfortunate fate of Johan Moritz has been boldly imprinted in my mind. I thought his fate resembled that of a fern tossed about in a whirlpool. Would that happen to me? I sighed and looked at my wrist, tightly cuffed with stainless steel bands, thin, yet strong. I had never had to wear handcuffs before. These were brand new and polished to a shine. Perhaps my partner and I had the honour of being the first to use them. They were stamped Made in USA and the manufacturers' name Smith & Wesson. So, our former friends and allies made them. Now that, I was confined against my will. I began to appreciate the plight of a girl forced to marry against her will. I quietly hummed a popular folk song where the girl says to the man she loves:

"Why did you not propose to me while I was free?
Now I am married, like a caged bird or a hooked fish.
How can a fish get un-hooked?
And when will a caged bird be freed?"

As I mentally chewed on the words, I appreciated their sadness as never before. The evening was closing in, adding to my depression.

The Rendezvous

The prisoners stirred as the truck entered the small township of *Ban Mê Thuột*. Here the majority of people were Montagnard, wearing only loincloths, and carrying garden tools and reed baskets of firewood on their backs. It was as though we were in a different world, and I had to remind myself that these people were my compatriots. My partner said quietly, "It looks like we're almost there!"

"Yes," I agreed. "Have you ever been to this part of our country before?"

"Never," he said, "But I know *Ban Mê Thuột* was the site of a very big battle before the Communists took over Saigon." Once through the town, the truck passed through a rubber tree plantation. Some trees had fallen from the destruction of war, and a large number of smaller trees were being replanted. Suddenly, we reached a large clearing field with a few houses, and in the distance a long row of wooden buildings. I supposed must be the prison camps.

The truck began slowing down, signalled left turn, and crawled onto the dusty, red dirt road. On either side of the road was a large muddy pond. The vehicle finally stopped in a rather large yard. In one corner of the yard, some officers stood next to a watchtower where a guard sitting with a rifle. As our truck went through the gate, I felt my heart race. Ordinarily, I calmed myself by saying, "Be calm, worry will not change the situation!" But this time, it did not help. An officer wearing a Mao Tse-Tung cap, in his thick Northern accent, ordered us into a corner of the yard. The atmosphere was very strained, especially seeing the flashing whites in the eyes of the young Montagnard soldiers with their rifles in ready position, the muzzles pointed straight at us. They seemed to radiate a sense of death.

Our documents were taken away to the office. We were told to leave all our belongings in a corner and then to sit in straight rows for inspection. It was about five in the evening and a cold wind swept in. There were no other prisoners to be seen. However, I heard the singing from inside a building: *"Let's rise up, heroic people of the South; rise up to move forward against the storm, swearing to rescue the nation."* It was the first time I'd heard the Communist victory song, *"Liberating of the South"*.

As I waited to have my personal belongings inspected yet again, I kept a watchful eye on the child-faced guard standing closest to me. He kept restlessly running his index finger along with the trigger of the rifle in a mischievous manner, and sweeping the muzzle back and forth towards the squatting prisoners. Perhaps, he hoped one of us would take a break so that he could practice his lesson.

Despite yesterday evening's extensive inspection in *Đức Lập* District when we were first captured in Cambodia, today's inspection was no less thorough. Yesterday, they had told us that we could keep only our clothing and a few personal belongings such as toothpaste, toothbrush, and cigarettes. However, all money and valuable items such as gold, watches, jewellery, and medicine had to be registered. "No worries, when you are released home, the Revolutionary Government will return these to you." I received a receipt for my watch that read quality is 'Unclear'. I kept that receipt as a souvenir! Once I took the watch off and handed it to the Security officer, I knew I'd never see it again. This evening they confiscated a few more items.

It was cold, with the bone-chilling cold of the mountains. I pulled up the collar of my military shirt, took out my pack of cigarettes, offered my cuff-mate a smoke, and took one for myself. The cigarettes smoke gave me a feeling of warmth and comfort. I took a very long drag, tipped my head back to exhale into the endless sky, and suddenly I smiled, partly because the smoke relaxed me after the day's stressful journey, but mostly because I suddenly accepted my new situation. Nevertheless, I was determined to change it as soon as I could.

Without the chance to finish our cigarettes, we were ordered to line up before being herded into the camp. I picked up my rucksack, now containing only a sweater, change of clothing, some personal items, and a few packs of cigarettes. Looking at the fading figures of the tired people before me, I felt a sudden surge of emotion. The group of women and children caught while escaping across the border. The children were crying, clinging to their mothers as they moved into prison. The Communist takeover was like a giant dragnet cast into the sea, catching all kinds of fish, large and small, not sparing anyone!

A female officer began dividing us into cell groups. As I waited, I glanced around the camp. In the ebbing light, it made a bizarre scene, with the dark prison buildings looming like gravestones in a cemetery. A few lights flickered through the curtain of mist, like incense to commemorate the unfortunate victims in the mass graves before me. A barbed-wire fence surrounded the whole area. The cold made me hungry and tired. Throughout the entire day, we had been given only a lump of pre-salted rice. I hoped we would get into camp quickly; so I could rest for a while before finding something to allay my hunger. I reminded myself, whatever happened, I was and would remain a priest.

In my previous six years as a priest, five had been spent under the Republic and one under Communism. I would continue wholeheartedly to fulfil my duties and responsibilities, even in Communist jail. Although my ten years of Seminary training had not included instructions for living in this kind of environment, I do know that there would be great trials ahead, I did not worry because I strongly believed in God's support and guidance. It was He who was my strength. So, now as I stepped into prison, I silently prayed, "Oh God, please lift me up in my weakness and teach me how to live as a witness to the love of God among my brothers in this prison life." At that point, I remembered a verse from the Bible, *'My grace is enough for you; my great strength is revealed in weakness.'* (2 Cor. 12,9).

Suddenly, I felt the confidence and enthusiasm of an explorer freely choosing to enter the unknown, hazardous territory. I looked up at the wide sky, and the curtain of night was no longer so heavy and gloomy.

Then, a loud voice from the rear called, "You, in the glasses, halt!"

I supposed he was addressing me, as no one else in the group wore glasses, so I turned and asked, "Who, me?"

The officer answered, "Yes, you. Come over here."

As I stepped out of the line, I caught the worried expressions on the faces of my fellow prisoners. The officer pointed to a workbench and said, "You sit here and wait. If you need anything, tell the guard."

I sat there in the open for what seemed hours. I opened a new packet of cigarettes but found I'd used all my matches. The guard was watching my every move. With the cigarette on my lips, I signalled to ask for a light but he motioned back that he had none. So I held the cigarette in my hand, waiting for someone to pass. When an officer did pass, I asked for a light, and also took the liberty to tell him that I had not eaten all day. He was a bit surprised at that and led me to a building further away.

Inside were fifty or sixty prisoners, all shirtless, some sitting, some standing, and some walking back and forth in the room's aisle. Double wooden bunks flanked both sides of the aisle. He asked the room leader about my ration. Then he left, saying he would return after I was finished. Two bowls, one of rice and another of broth, had been set aside, presumably for me. I supposed that I had been assigned to this cell. However, I could not understand why I had been kept outside. The men in the cell all began asking questions at once, so I didn't know who to answer first. Gradually, I learned that most of them had been officers in the Republican army who had reported to the Communist authorities for retraining, as instructed. This turned out to be imprisonment, some for three days, some for much longer periods. They asked me about news from the outside, about the resistance forces, movement across the border struggles against capitalists…

Discovering that I was a Catholic priest, they became more at ease as a good number of them were Catholic. They hugged me and asked for a blessing. I took advantage of this time to give them spiritual encouragement. I spoke of my awareness of beginning a priest's life in prison. It was an emotional and meaningful meeting. But soon came an officer, flanked by two armed guards, signalled me to follow him. We went out the camp gate where a Land Rover was waiting. In the back sat an old woman holding a large basket of vegetables. I sat next to her with the guards across from us. It was 10.00 p.m. I wondered if they were taking me to elsewhere to butcher me. But, if so, why was the old woman with us?

What a Night!

We drove around the sleeping town for a while, and then stopped in the yard of an old brick house. I guessed it was the *Ban Mê Thuột* Prison, as the rear of the house was surrounded by high walls topped with barbed wire, and fronted by a black iron gate. A man carrying a huge cluster of keys, with a toothpick still in his mouth, stepped out. He ordered me out of the vehicle and pushed me through the gateway. After locking the gate again, he led me through a long courtyard lined with old buildings. He told me to wait in front of a chained metal door locked with two bronze padlocks, then shone his flashlight to find the right key and proceeded to open the door. As the padlocks fell away, the chains rattled alarmingly.

The door creaked open, and in the dull glow from the solitary light bulb, I saw a large number of mosquito nets hanging close together along the length of the room. I hesitated, but the jailer grabbed me by the collar and pushed me inside. Losing my balance, I brought down straight on the nearest mosquito net at the entrance. Some liquid splashed on my face as the iron door clanged behind me. My first steps into a Communist prison were certainly…resonant! It was all happening too fast. I didn't know where I was or whose and what water I had spilled.

I stood up awkwardly, my clothes sopping wet. Wet glasses blurred my vision, so I dried them on my shirt. My first sense of being in captivity was the strong odour of urine. Gradually my eyes adjusted to the gloom. I saw that I had spilled a bucket of human urine, soaking myself with its contents as well as wetting the blankets and the pillows of the prisoners sleeping by the door. In this cell there were no bunks, so the inmates had to sleep on mats on the floor inside their mosquito nets.

Strangely, I did not hear a peep from anyone. Even the man I fell on didn't murmur. Surely, everyone there would have heard me and been aware of the stench. A minute passed and still no one stirred. There was something eerie about this silence. I had heard about new arrivals in prison going through an initiation rite, usually with well-seasoned inmates beating up the new prisoner. I wasn't just the new boy but *'the new-boy-who-had-just-knocked-over-the-waste-bucket'!* Surely, this would make my initiation rite more solemn. I waited and still, there was silence.

I could bear it no longer. I picked up the bucket, placing it in the corner, and said softly but clearly, "Hello my new cellmates. I'm new here. Please forgive me for my accident." Then I waited. The man under the collapsed net begun to stir. He slowly lifted the net's edge and peered out. He looked above to the barred window on the door. I now understood that he had been pretending to sleep while waiting for the guard to leave.

I was about to apologise to him for my mistake, but I didn't have the chance to open my mouth. He threw off his net and sprang up; fists clenched and yelled, "F*ck you! Take off your shoes!"

I softly answered, "Sorry, man. I just got here and didn't know your rules." I felt quite frightened when confronted by this robust man. His head was completely shaven and he had a large dragon tattooed on his chest. A number of his front teeth were missing which gave him a very unattractive appearance. I felt he was dangerous.

As I bent down to remove my sneakers, I thought to myself "Well, that's just my luck! Of all the people to fall on, I had to land on this gorilla!"

I looked up to see a large number of faces surrounding me, the majority of them young. No one wore a shirt. But none looked as threatening as the skinhead with the missing teeth. The 'gorilla' poked his index finger in my face, snarling, "What're you in for?"

"I was caught for trying to cross the border," I answered, choosing the most common reason at the time without revealing too much information about my resistance to the Communist government.

How long have you been detained?"

"Since yesterday."

"Where were you caught?"

"In *Đức Lập*, and I was brought here this evening."

A middle-aged man interrupted gently, "Where do you come from originally?"

I said, "I come from *Vĩnh Long* Province in the Western Region."

The gorilla said derisively:

"From the Western side and you came up here to cross the border! Or did you come here on another business? Tell the truth, what are you really doing here?" His tone was similar to that of the border police, which made me suspicious. Was he a stooge of the authorities?

"I came up here to cross the border, and nothing else," I repeated firmly. But he continued his questions, "You came alone. Why? Where are your wife and your children?"

"I don't have a wife and children," I answered. He sneered and put his face up close to mine.

"What'd you say? No wife and children at your age? So, what do you do for a living?"

"I am a Catholic priest," I replied calmly.

Suddenly, his jaw dropped and his eyes widened. Stepping back, he grabbed my shoulders by both hands and said, "So… you're …you're …you're…a Father…?"

"Yes, I am Father Andrew *Nguyễn Hữu Lễ*, from the *Vĩnh Long* Diocese."

Then he wrapped his arms around me in a hug and said, "Oh my God, Father, I'm sorry, I'm sorry, I didn't know, I am a Catholic myself, my name is *Long*, from the *Hà Lan* Parish. Do you know the Parish priest at *Hà Lan*?"

"No, I'm sorry, I don't know him, but I know Bishop *Nguyễn Huy Mai*. In this Diocese I know Father *Nguyễn Tiến Khẩu*, he was in the same St. Joseph Seminary in Saigon with me, he's three years my junior."

"I know Father *Khẩu* too" *Long* exclaimed cheerfully, "I attended his Home Coming Mass." He turned to the rest and called out for everybody to hear, "Father *Lễ* from *Vĩnh Long* has just arrived. Come here, everybody!"

In just a few moments, the situation had turned right around. Everybody gathered around to welcome me. I still had a few packs of cigarettes and began to share them with the roommates. Food and other necessities were normally received from families at the beginning of the month. Now in the fourth week, the cell was running out of tobacco. I felt as if I was bringing rain to a drought-stricken region.

They asked me about many things on the outside. Of the twelve men, seven were Catholic. They had been confined on many different charges, political prisoners, and criminals alike. Bald *Long* was charged with assaulting a serviceman while drunk and had been confined for six months so far. In the middle of the cell were two high-ranking Montagnards from the *FULRO* Armed forces, also the Minister of Defence who lay paralysed in the corner, and the Chief of Staff. Neither was fluent in Vietnamese.

My cellmates told me that this cell used to be a library; which was the reason for its having no bunks or toilets. Twice a day, morning, and evening, the prisoners were released out to a shallow water tank at the end of the compound to bathe, do their dishes, and conduct their sanitary business. At night, they had to use a plastic bucket, the same one I had splashed earlier. As we gathered around smoking, everyone forgot about their troubles for a few moments. Perhaps, this is the only time I could truly claim: "Smoking can be good for your health!"

But then a guard yelled from outside to be quiet as it was past midnight. Everyone quietly crawled back to his place. *Long* whispered, "Tonight, you sleep next to me." He began preparing a sleeping spot for me, mopping up the urine remaining on the mat. We lay still and waited for the guard to pass and then I asked *Long* to sit up with me for a short prayer before sleeping. Afterward, he whispered in embarrassment, "Spending the night next to you, Father, I get to say prayers, but in the past, I was never a praying person!" He rolled a rucksack into a pillow for me.

I soon heard his regular breathing. I envied his sleep, but no matter how I tried, I couldn't relax. Instead, I found myself replaying major changes in my life, like a slow-motion movie. Ever since the South was lost to the Communists over a year ago, I had felt as though I was living in a giant prison, the one called the 'Great Prison of Vietnam'. Tonight, I had landed in a smaller prison. My thoughts flew further back...

The Communist Political Farce

One month after the Communists took over the South, I was appointed as Parish priest of the *La Mã* Parish in *Bến Tre* Province. At that time, my position as a Catholic priest caused me huge troubles by the people intoxicated with the political fever. I couldn't possibly remember all the disruptions during those troubled times. However, there were a few incidents that left a strong, indelible impression, such as the election for the 6th National Assembly. This would be the first post-war election for the entire country, electing representatives to the National Assembly. This voting took place on Sunday, April 26, 1976.

Before Election Day, everyone who was 18 or older was issued a voter card as in any other election. The unusual thing was that the voting process took place in groups. Each group had twelve people under the control of a group leader. There was collective voters' training, where group leaders had to take care of the roll call and guarantee that a total of twelve people showed up for training. This training took place in the school in front of my Church and was done by Provincial cadres.

The content of the lessons was clear-cut and easy to understand. After a lecture about the importance of this election for the National Assembly, the cadre wrote down the candidates' names for *Bến Tre* Province. If I remembered correctly, there were ten candidates' names on the numbered list. The instructing cadre told us to eliminate the last two names of people according to the 'democratic voting method'. The cadre held up a sample ballot for everyone to see, and continued loudly, "Before going into the room to vote, you will each be given a ballot slip (Demonstrates). In the room, there is a ballpoint pen and a ruler (Demonstrates). Use those to cross out the last two names (Demonstrates), then step out of the room, walk over to the ballot box, fold up your ballot slip, and put it into the box like so (Demonstrates). It's that simple, does everybody get it? Anyone has questions?"

From the back of the class came a woman's voice, "I have a question. Can I eliminate any two numbers, or does it have to be the last two?"

The cadre's eyes widened but he responded quickly, "I said everyone is to eliminate the last two, just as I demonstrated."

He continued, "Did you not catch that, or do you have something else in mind?"

"Not at all. I asked you because I didn't understand. Why must I eliminate only the last two names and not any others?" The woman retorted.

The cadre looked impatient, "Those orders are 'From the Superior'. Just carry them out without questions. Trust in the leadership's wisdom of the Party."

On hearing the word *'Party'*, the woman slowly sat down. The entire class fell silent. So quiet you could hear a pin drop.

Finally, the cadre spoke in a different tone of voice, "Now we come to the practice segment. One by one, you will come up take a piece of chalk and ruler and practice voting."

Dozens of voters took turns to practice voting, each holding a ruler and a piece of chalk to cross out the last two names exactly as the cadre instructed, then returned to their seats.

I sat in the middle of the class, sickened and resentful of the regime's foolishness. However, it was just one example of the new harsh reality, and many other foolish activities that had to be accepted, regardless of what we thought. When it was my turn to practice, I took the ruler and stub of chalk in hand. I felt embarrassed as the others. We had been stripped of all basic rights under this regime, including the right to ask questions. We were transformed into a blinkered workhorse, going straight forward according to the directions of the driver wielding the whip, and he was experienced in correcting wild behaviour.

Early on the morning of voting Sunday, the loud speaker called the people to vote. We wore our name tags on our chests and lined up beside the Church for group leaders to take a roll call. A lion dance led the way, followed by a group of the so-called Good Children of Uncle Ho. Some held blue and red flags and others played drums or cymbals, as if for a festival. It was all very superficial. After the group roll calls had guaranteed that no one was missing, we received orders to march forward in line with our group. By now, the sun had come up above the trees. Our group slowly moved forward. It took an hour to reach the voting station, and then I was very surprised to see the voting booths had been set up in my annexed Church, without my knowledge or consent!

Again the group leaders had to guarantee that there were twelve people in each group. Names were called in order 1, 2, 3, 4, …to march forward to the tables and present our registration cards, receive a ballot and step into the nearby curtained booth. I moved forward mechanically. A wave of deep resentment swept through me. I wanted to use this opportunity to show defiance. The candidates' names were all strange to me; except for one man the villagers gossiped about Mr *Đồng Văn Cống*. They remembered how *Đồng Văn Cống* had tended water buffalo in his village. Later, he joined the *Việt Minh* (League for the Independence of Vietnam) and was taken to North Vietnam. After 1975, he returned to the South with the rank of Lieutenant General Commander of Military Zone 7. I knew nothing of his values, had no basis on which to judge his competence. All the other candidates were completely unknown to me. However, I knew the Communist Party had nominated them all.

I was tempted to write, *"Farce"* across the ballot paper, or to cross out any names at random. But I finally scrapped those ideas because I was already under watch and my vote could easily identify. Furthermore, no matter how I voted, the results were already predetermined. I would only bring harm to myself without making any difference. So I obediently crossed out the last two names, double folded the ballot slip, and cast my vote, feeling powerless and humiliated. I forgave myself with the thought "What can I do?" After the election, our village was commended for having a 100% voter turnout. The newly elected *Bến Tre* Representatives won with 99% of the votes. It was a 'democratic election' of unprecedented success and quality! However, the farce didn't stop there.

The following week, thirteen of my fellow villagers were summoned to the People's Committee for 'work' (A euphemism for interrogation). They were asked why they had not voted according to protocol. Why hadn't they followed orders? Did they want to sabotage the election? Were they planning more rebellions? They were all sentenced to three days of heavy labour. The Representative of the Communist Party concluded, "Because this is your first violation, the Party and Revolution are showing you clemency. Did you know that during the puppet era in the South, voters were told for whom to vote?

Worse still, in the voting room, a hole was cut in the ceiling, and a 'microscope-monitored' people's voting procedure. Anyone who didn't vote as instructed was taken away indefinitely."

A few weeks later, one of my parishioners came to me and said, "Did you know that when you voted, three people were placed behind the curtain to monitor your actions? They commended you for voting well."

I only smiled without a word but I felt a chill go down my spine. I tried to be patient and tolerant while waiting for the political fever to pass. I longed to live undisturbed, serving faithfully the people in the region. In the meantime, my relationship with the local authorities worsened as time passed. I knew that I was a thorn in many people's eyes! What I found more tragic was that some priests eagerly sought positions on the Religious Solidarity Committee established by the Communists. This atheistic regime was out to exploit people in the religious sector, to cause division, and to control and paralyse religious activities. The designated Representatives of the Religious Solidarity Committee were given few benefits, benefits which some were proud of and boasted about.

By the end of April 1976, after a year in *La Mã* Parish, it was impossible for me to work there effectively. Furthermore, my Mother was very ill. So, I went to the Bishop to explain my case. He told me to hand over my ministry to Father *Quang* of a nearby Parish and go home to care for my Mother. Unfortunately, I did not have *Hộ khẩu* (Family Registration!) I couldn't live in family. I had to go into the unknown future! I knew that my circumstances didn't make it fitting for me to stop anywhere. I had to stay on the run in Saigon. The policy of family registration had turned me into an illegal visitor at any household.

Like many of my Peoples, I could not sit by and watch the nation be devastated by the poison of the Communist regime. Despite knowing I was an ordinary person, and perhaps I wouldn't succeed, I still thought, "It's better to fail while trying to do something than to do nothing at all." Thereafter, my life took a long road, a road which led me to this prison.

The 'Nuptial Night' in Highlands!

So tonight, I was in the *Ban Mê Thuột* Prison. The cell was hazy under the flickering light of the solitary electric bulb. *Long's* snoring grew louder and louder, and the other cellmates slept soundly. All was silent outside except for the occasional quiet footsteps that stopped outside the cell door before walking off. I instinctively knew it was the armed guard making his nightly rounds. Feeling cold, I rolled closer to *Long* who slept soundly. I gently pulled the edge of his blanket over me to ease the cold. *Long* murmured something, twitched a little, then lay still and breathed evenly.

My new friend lay on his back, his lips separated to reveal a smile with missing front teeth. He didn't look as fearsome as I had thought in my first impression. In contrast, I felt a sense of empathy towards him, a young man from an unknown place, who had suddenly become my male bedmate lying on the floor on nuptial night for my first night in prison. I laughed to myself at the amusing idea of nuptial night! My 'spouse' was a skinhead with missing front teeth and heavy-build like a wrestler. I continued smiling in the dark. Gradually, sleep caught me in her comforting arms and I drifted into dream world.

Chapter 6
Prison Camps in the South

After two months of temporary detainment in *Ban Mê Thuột* Prison, I was transferred to the Interior Security Department in Saigon for further investigation before being sent to *Phan Đăng Lưu* Camp in *Gia Định* Province in late August 1976.

The prison room had concrete platforms 30 centimetres above the floor along the wall which we called the runway. On the left of the door was a two-cube water tank connected to a tap. Adjacent to this was an empty area for washing and laundry. This area was separated from our bedroom by a dividing wall that reached just above the knees, not to conceal the bather but rather to minimise splashing out of the water. Against the back wall was the toilet closet. The roof was of corrugated iron, there were no windows at all, instead of a ceiling, there was a metal grate to foil any escape attempts. Although it was meant to house thirty prisoners, it often held sixty.

As there were so many of us, it was very hot. Everyone went shirtless and wore only boxers for days on end. We took turns bathing during our designated times. That was arranged according to our sleeping spaces. Everyone bathed nude. Because of my sheltered upbringing, I felt very embarrassed about this, so I watched to see how others coped. As each man stepped into the bath space, he dropped his boxers quickly on to the wet floor, swirled them around twice, wrung them out, and hung them on the divider. Almost everyone faced the wall when performing these actions but some faced the audience in an unruffled manner, while they were holding a conversation. Some of the younger men were so addicted to play chess game, they paid attention to nothing else, and continued to debate moves while bathing. If anyone seemed to be taking too long, the next person hurried him along.

We were provided with a plastic helmet to scoop up the water. Each person was allowed three scoops and whoever took more would receive a warning and a reduction for the next bath. No one had the chance to scrub himself, only give his face, and body a quick wipe. Then he would reach for his boxers, shake them twice again, and put them back on. In that heat, the boxers would dry almost instantaneously.

During this season sweat always covered one's body. I did not bathe on the first day, because I was shy about being naked in public. The next day it was so hot; so, I joined the queue. But as my turn neared, I became more and more uneasy. Should I, or should I not, strip? Should I could I act naturally like everyone else? I would be nude before nearly one hundred and twenty eyes. Somehow, I thought that being nude in front of Catholics made my situation even more embarrassing.

The man before me wiped his face, reached for his boxers, and stepped aside to make room for me. I gave a quick glance around to see if anyone was watching me. Some were playing chess, some fixing their pipes for smoking, others in deep conversation. I told myself to act normally. I stepped into the washing area, removed my boxers, used my regulated three scoops of water, and moved aside for the next man. No one had bothered to look at me at all. After that bathing was no problem, just part of the reality of prison life.

After six months at *Phan Đăng Lưu*, I had been transferred to *Gia Ray* Camp some 30 kilometres away from Saigon just on the week prior to the *Tết* (Vietnamese Lunar New Year's Day) in 1977.

The Transitional Camp

The *Gia Ray* Camp was previously the Military headquarters for the 54th Regiment of the former Regime. A number of ex-military prisoners had once been stationed here after undergoing behavioural life changes. It still looked like a military prison with its tin-roofed barracks, built on dusty red ground undermined by many rat tunnels.

There was no running water, not even a well or stream. A tanker delivered the bare minimum of water daily to the staff and prisoners. We were allotted 750 ml. of water at lunchtime and again at supper. Understandably, there were many arguments in the cell about water issues. Many fights took place against the kitchen team about sharing this precious resource, frequently ending in bloody bruises. Sometimes, hundreds of prisoners tried to break into the kitchen to fight for water. They used sticks, rocks and knives to attack the kitchen team, but never got any more water.

The majority of the thousand prisoners had been State employees under the Republic Government of Saigon and a number had been in the Resistance movement. Most were young. A number were charged with fleeing across the border or being anti-revolutionary. A few weeks after my arrival, just a few days before *Tết* of 1977, a group of prisoners were transferred from *Cà Tum* Camp and this raised the population to over 1,200 people, most of them were Catholic.

Our group was broken into teams and housed in separate barracks, with about sixty people in each. I was in the same barrack as Father *Vũ Đức Khâm*. Father *Vũ Đức Khâm* once worked in the Catholic Resistance Force against the *Việt Minh* in North Vietnam. After the 1954 Geneva Agreement, he migrated to Saigon where he was involved in social services.

For the first two days, we were locked in the room day and night. The barracks had a wooden sleeping platform on either side of a central walkway. There was no toilet, only three artillery shells, each a hand-span in diameter and a metre high, standing on end in a small closet. In the mornings, the barracks were unlocked for a few minutes; at this time, the pipes, containing waste, urine and stool, could be hauled out to be emptied. The metal pipe toilet had proved insufficient for the waste needs of sixty prisoners.

Solving the problem of defecation for a group of more than a thousand was not a simple task! When our door was at last unlocked after our first two days, I immediately headed for the shared latrine. I had to pass several barracks and the kitchen, to make my way along a narrow path between two barbed wire fences that surrounded the camp. As I neared the kitchen, I could hear the noise of a large swarm of green flies surrounded the sun drying cabbage on the kitchen roof. My God! Where could so many green flies come from? Then, I realised that the kitchen was beside an open sewer. The flies fought over the cabbage, buzzed about the opening of the sewer, then landed wherever they could, preferably on our food!

Beyond the kitchen, I found myself at the end of a queue of some dozen people, each holding pieces of paper. Immediately more lined up behind me, and the queue quickly grew longer. I didn't see anyone I knew. Some of the men wore pained expressions, no doubt because of their urgent needs. As we inched forward, I saw a large pit about fifteen meters long by ten wide. On the opposite bank were fifteen cubicles, separated from each other by wicker dividers thirty centimetres high. A canvas roof hung above. In front of each cubicle was a plank much like a diving board, leading out over the pit. Each person in turn had to squat on the end of his plank. Here was another wicker screen, just enough to give some privacy as he faced those waiting for their turns.

Waiting in Pain

I noticed that most people were shirtless and wore only boxers. This was surprising as it was a cold morning and many were rubbing their hands to keep warm. Only those of us new to the camp wore shirts and trousers.

Suddenly, a friendly voice advised me, "Father, take off your pants."

I asked in surprise, "Why?"

"The stench is unbearable there. The smell lingers on clothes for many days and there's no water to wash them. Take off your pants and shirt, Father, and I'll take them back to the cell for you."

As the line moved forward slowly, someone yelled, "Why it's taking you so long? Are you going to sleep there?"

The group laughed and others added their comments. One of the sitters called back, "Don't you know this isn't something you can hurry? Anyway, it stinks like hell here, so I don't know why you're in such a hurry!"

As each finished his business, he pulled up his boxer shorts and moved quickly out as if chased by a ghost.

I eventually joined the priority line, facing the strangers in the stalls. The pit was about head height. Below each stall was a container for human waste but the faecal matter had overflowed to fill almost a third of the pit itself. (I later learned that men hauled the waste away daily to fertilise the vegetables, the primary source of food for camp prisoners.) The foul odour was almost suffocating. A mass of flies, like blown wheat husks, congregated at the pit's opening. On the edge were clumps of wriggling maggots. I quickly looked away before I gagged. In a nearby tower, an armed guard sat on watch, looking down at the queue. I felt pity for him, thinking, it drove me crazy just standing here for even a short while, whereas he had to sit there for hours. How could he bear it?

But one gets used to anything. Every day after that, I came in my boxer shorts like everyone else. I lined up and waited, it was always the same pit with its filth and stench, but it never again horrified me as much as the first day. Sometimes heavy rain turned the pit into a slimy pool with the maggots floating on top, a terrible sight. However, the rain did help to lower the stench, and the flies were fewer perhaps for fear of wings being wet. So, over the months this daily ritual became just a part of life.

The Fellow Priest

In the *Gia Ray* Camp, we were divided into different work teams: kitchen, woodworking, metalworking, or vegetable production. I was placed in the land-preparation team, responsible for clearing trees and preparing the land for crops. The work wasn't too arduous, but we worried about the chance of hitting a landmine with our hoes. These land mines were left over from war time. Sadly, some people were blown to bits, others lost a limb. Each strike we took to the ground with our hoes, I felt we were digging our own grave. Beside this hazard, we had the ever-present discomfort of toiling in the blazing sun, with not a drop of water to wash ourselves at the end of the day.

Some days, we pleaded so much that the armed guards let us bathe at a nearby pit. This was the size of an average room, with muddy water that came up to our knees. By the time our team arrived, several hundred people would be standing shirtless around the pit, having already been in the water. By then, the stirred-up mud looked like mortar. There was no sense trying to clean us in that! Sometimes in the evening, we were allowed to bathe in a small spring near the vegetable garden. We saved empty cans to collect a little of this precious water to rinse the dust off our bodies. The runoff went into the rows of vegetables and on into the stream, often carrying floating faeces with it.

As Father *Vũ Đức Khâm* was old, he was charge with cleaning out the barracks and known as the sanitation man. On Sundays or non-labour days, Catholic prisoners often visited Father *Vũ Đức Khâm* and me. To avoid confusion in addressing two of us, I asked them to call Father *Khâm*, '*Cậu Hai*' (Big Uncle) and me, '*Cậu Bảy*' (Uncle Seven). Sometimes, these men came to make their confessions, but more often just to talk. Some of them brought us food and other useful items.

During the *Tết* holidays, most prisoners received visits from their families along with foods. In contrast, we as the new group were not allowed to tell our families of our whereabouts; so, we missed out on the chance to see them and receive gifts. A prisoner named *Bùi Định* had been appointed prisoners'

Representative. He took care of distributing mail and coordinating family visits, and then inspected any gifts received. Our fellow prisoners warned us to be careful when dealing with him. We also had a cellmate named *Đặng Báu* who spied on his fellow prisoners to earn favour. Although I'd already been in captivity for nine months, this was my first contact with the system of prisoners spying on one another, a system we called *'Antennae'*. (Informers. From a usually metallic device for radiating or receiving audio waves).

We lived peacefully for almost a month before a sad event happened. One day a Catholic told me a story relating to Father *Khâm*. A visiting Northern policeman, knowing my informant was a Catholic, asked if he knew "The rascal *Vũ Đức Khâm* who killed my father." This was very disturbing news! I feared for Father *Vũ Đức Khâm's* safety, but I didn't tell him the story, as he was already depressed. However, I did ask him about the work he did in *Phát Diệm*. Father *Khâm* told me that he had worked with Bishop *Lê Hữu Từ* at the autonomous *Phát Diệm* Base, working against the *Việt Minh* (A predecessor of Communist Regime). Later on, others carried on his work. When I enquired about the large scar below his chin, he said it had happened during an assassination attempt on him in the Church early one morning. He had been grazed by a bullet, which left the scar. After that, he no longer had any connection with the *Phát Diệm* Base.

Father *Vũ Đức Khâm* migrated into the South in 1954, then went to the United States where he studied for a doctorate in Sociology. Coming back to Saigon, he was very active in the Young Catholic Students' Movement and opened the first women's hairstylist classes in Saigon. I knew nothing about Father *Khâm's* past, he was from an older generation and more than twenty years my senior.

After thinking again about the situation, I decided that he should be able to prepare himself, rather than face a sudden accusation. So one night I told him what I had heard. He denied having killed anyone. But in any case, we both sensed impending misfortune, so we helped each other prepare spiritually. Even in his time of distress, he instructed me that in any situation, we must live our priesthood worthily and help our fellow prisoners.

That night, as we lay on the wooden bunks, I squeezed his hand and asked, "If something happens to you, what would you want me to do?"

Father *Khâm* remained pensive for a while, then answered, "*Cậu Bảy*, do tell everyone that I've prepared myself for a peaceful death and that I have not done what I was accused of." With that, he turned away.

To Seal *Fr. Khâm's* Fate

One evening in late March 1977, at roll call, we prisoners filed into four rows outside the barracks as usual. Looking up, I saw something unusual. Instead of the familiar cadres on duty, there was a group unknown to us. The camp security officer, Second Lieutenant *Xuân* led them. This man came from the North, and was known to be extremely evil and often acted in sadistic ways.

On this particular evening, *Xuân* came again, accompanied by two armed guards. Intuition told me that there would be some misfortune. Our team leader ordered us to stand at attention, and proceeded to do a headcount as usual. But *Xuân* stopped him. He was here for another reason. After staring at each of us for some minutes, he said coldly, "*Anh Vũ Đức Khâm*, go bring out all your *Nội vụ* (Belongings!)"

Father *Khâm* was trembling. I felt a pain in my heart as the sixty-five year old priest began to move towards the barrack. I could guess his fate! Other prisoners also looked worried, even though they didn't know the seriousness of the situation. *Xuân* remained there, as the two guards followed Father *Khâm* to the barrack door.

Then I stepped out of line to stand in front of *Xuân*. "Reporting to you!" (This was a compulsory expression before you speak to an officer in all circumstances.)

The officer gave me a surprised look and asked, "What's the matter?"

"I shared the same activities with Mr *Vũ Đức Khâm*, and have some of his possessions. Please allow me into the cell so I can return them to him." Actually, this was only an excuse. I had a stronger and more important reason to see Fr. *Khâm* privately. *Xuân* nodded.

"All right. Hurry up!"

Father *Khâm* was in the middle of the barracks. In his panic, he had thrown his belongings in a heap on the floor. When he saw me, his shaking hands grabbed mine and he said brokenly, "*Cậu Bảy*, stay here and good luck. God bless you. Give my farewell and love to the brothers and remember to pray for each other. Keep all of the food. I will take none with me."

Then he sobbed.

I suppressed my own emotions and said *"Cậu Hai*, prepare yourself for an act of contrition. I will grant you absolution. This is why I asked for permission to come here."

Through the open doorway, I saw *Xuân* approaching. Father *Khâm* sat with his back to the door, eyes closed and lips quivering. I knew that he was praying. I said the absolution formula in Latin, softly enough for just the two of us to hear: *"Dominus noster Jesus Christus te absolvat…"*

As I finished, *Xuân* arrived. He ordered: "Anh *Khâm*, hurry! Bring your *nội vụ*."

I watched as Father *Vũ Đức Khâm* hurriedly left with his bundle of personal belongings, followed by the armed guards. My heart was broken! Perhaps Father *Khâm* guessed his likely fate, and that was why he'd lost his composure.

That night after being locked in, the prisoners especially the Catholics visibly expressed their grief. As for me, it was the first time I felt so utterly alone. My tears flowed freely. Later, when reorganising our shared belongings, I saw he'd forgotten to take the leather belt he usually wore and this made me miss him even more.

The next day I got news of Father *Khâm* through a friend who delivered food to the disciplinary Section. He was being kept in shackles twenty-four hours a day. This friend said he could smuggle things to Father. So, I sent his belt and few bananas. We continued doing like this until the old Father sent word that he didn't need any more food, but asked that we would all pray for him. A week later on our way back from work, we saw a blacked-out car leaving the camp. The next day, my friend told me that Father *Khâm* had been transferred to *Chí Hòa* Prison.

(Later on, when I was in a prison in the North, I came to know from a fellow prison mate, Father *Khâm* actually died in that prison). RIP Father *Vũ Đức Khâm.*

The Subtle Trick!

At that time, as we moved around the camp, we noticed a strangely shaped wooden object sitting just inside the gates. It could possibly have been a bookshelf. It was about 6m tall and 50cm wide. Some guessed it was a ladder, with its rungs very close together. Even the leader of the woodworking team didn't know what it was, but claimed that it was built exactly to the measurements he'd been given. Then, in early April 1977, it disappeared overnight; so, we soon forgot about it.

By April 1977, after 3 months in the camp, there were rumours circulating that we'd be transferred to *Đồng Tháp* Province in the Mekong Delta. Hoping for better conditions in another prison, we hope that this rumour might be true. *Đồng Tháp* is a wetland, approximately sixty kilometres to the South of Saigon. So, we wished for a change. Surely, any place would be preferable to *Gia Ray* Camp that lacked everything, even the basic human necessities like water.

At first, no one knew how the rumour began. Then we found out that someone's relatives had brought the news, learning it from a fruit-seller at a stall outside the camp gates. This girl was friendly with a camp guard who told her that he was taking a leave of absence. When she pestered him for the reason, he said, "Don't tell anyone, this is top secret! But I'm going to escort a number of prisoners to *Đồng Tháp*!"

Less than 24 hours later, there was no *Gia Ray* prisoner who did not know this 'top secret' news. We wondered why *Đồng Tháp* and not elsewhere? What would it be like there? Generally, we felt pleased with the news. It eased our worries of being sent to the North Vietnam, some 2,000 km away. To go to the North was the equivalent of going to Death land. Therefore, this fear haunted each one of us. Now that anxiety had been lifted and it was as if we'd dropped a thousand-pound burden. No one knew much about *Đồng Tháp* but everyone had an excited vision of ample water. It was a wetland with many rivers, not to be compared to *Gia Ray* where a drop of water was as valuable as a blood drop. We happily waited for the day of our departure.

One Sunday afternoon in early April 1977, a Catholic from the kitchen team came to see me for confession. Afterwards, he pulled me over to the camp fence for a private talk. He said, "I just want to let you know, next week after Easter there will be a number of transfers to the North. Your name is on the list. Please keep this a secret, because I'll be in danger if you disclose it. Don't ask me how I got the information. Just know that I'm not working for them." This was very bad news, but I hoped it wasn't true.

Meanwhile, fellow prisoners had lively discussions about leaving for *Đồng Tháp*. I kept quiet about my secret news because of my promise. I was very anxious and as soon as Easter was over, I was in suspense every day, waiting for any sign, and frustrated because I couldn't tell anyone. Monday, Tuesday, Wednesday passed without anything happening. Thursday, Friday nothing happened. Saturday morning all was as usual and I rejoiced, thinking that fortunately my kitchen friend was wrong. On Saturday afternoon, we lined up to go to our labour. I felt full of joy because no one had been transferred to the North this week and I wasn't on any list. Why worry?

It was around 5.00 p.m., we lined up in four columns and returned to camp from working in the camp gardens. I was relaxed, thinking of Sunday tomorrow when I could rest and visit with the fellow prisoners. For the entire week, news of being transferred to the North haunted and oppressed me.

I was always fatigued, as if carrying a heavy load. If it had lasted more than a week, I surely would have preferred going to the cemetery instead! I looked at the blue sky and joy flooded me as if I'd narrowly escaped a fatal accident. Taking a deep breath, I prayed, "*Deo gratias*! (Thanks be to God!)"

But… suddenly, I spotted an army convoy stirring up a cloud of dust on the red clay road heading towards the Camp. I almost stopped breathing. So everything I had worried about for the past week was true. Ironically, some of my fellow prisoners applauded, thinking the long-awaited transport to *Đồng Tháp* had arrived.

Before we could get our allowance of food and water, the *'Kleng'* bell sounded. We all gathered, waiting for the Camp Visionary Board's announcement, presumably about our transfer… (and that must be to *Đồng Tháp!*) The Chief Officer announced that in order to create favourable conditions for re-education, as the present camp was overpopulated and could not care for everyone adequately, a number of prisoners would be transferred to a location with more water. The transfers would take place in groups. The first group consisted of a list of three hundred and fifty names. A roll call followed, and I was in the first group.

When we were released to our barracks, everyone happily thought we were going to *Đồng Tháp*, and there was a great of loud chatter. Prisoners said goodbye to one another and divided up food, drink and any useful items. Some people felt left out because they weren't named in the first group, going to where there would be running water, according to the Camp Chief. As the time had at last arrived when I no longer had to keep my secret, I told them that we were being transferred to the North. Many didn't believe me; some thought I was trying to scare them. That night, I stayed up waiting for an opportunity to escape. But there was no opportunity the guards made sure that the security was even tighter than usual.

The next morning was Sunday, and prisoners on the transfer list each received a large bag for their clothes and belongings, blankets and mosquito nets, but were told to take no food or glass bottles. After stuffing his bag and tying the mouth tightly, each person received two tags with identical numbers. One tag would be attached to the bag, while the prisoner kept the other. Each prisoner was allowed to carry with him one small bag for personal items. All that Sunday, we were busy arranging belongings, and when we finished packing, took them to the meeting hall.

In the evening, we were ordered on to the dozens of waiting military trucks where we were handcuffed in pairs. Tarpaulins covered the windows so we no longer saw outside. By the time the vehicles started to travel, it was completely dark. It was dark as ink outside, so I guessed it was about 10.00 p.m. We felt that we were headed for Saigon. Some people kept saying, "Clearly we're heading for *Đồng Tháp*! We're not wrong!" After a long ride, the truck stopped, but we were ordered to remain inside. Eventually, we were allowed off the vehicle, still handcuffed, and discovered we had been taken to *Tân Cảng* (New Port), near the Saigon Bridge.

The port was teeming with armed police and uniformed officers. A large ocean-going vessel named *SÔNG HƯƠNG* was moored at the dock. Under the flickering streetlights, the ship's silhouette was like a gigantic monster emerging from the river. We were surprised to recognise the strange wooden object from *Gia Ray* Camp. The mysterious object that we speculated to be a bookshelf now leaned against the side of *SÔNG HƯƠNG*. It was a gangplank. We filed into rows and waited for transfer procedures. Ironically, some people were still convinced that the ship would take us to *Đồng Tháp*.

I want to explain why the *Đồng Tháp* phenomenon had such a strong effect on us. Once again, we had to admire the Communists' manipulative tactics. They knew that the prisoners greatly feared of being transported to the North. If we guessed that was our fate, we would make trouble. At least, some would find a way to escape while still in the South. The second factor was that *Gia Ray* Camp was overpopulated and lacked many basics, including water that everyone wished to go to anywhere else better. *Đồng Tháp* was the ideal location for deception, situated as it was in the Delta region. So, they made use of the ploy by telling the young girl a 'secret' about our transfer. By telling her that she "must not tell anyone else!" they insured that their false message would soon be spread throughout the Camp. They succeeded in making the prisoners feel excited and hopeful. Now, even as they arrived at the dock to board the ocean liner, many still believed they must have been going to Đồng Tháp and nowhere else! Man's gullibility is sometimes astounding.

We waited a long time, wondering and worrying. For my part, I clearly knew my destiny. I stared out at my beloved South, for I knew it would be a long time, if ever, before I saw it again. Eventually, we received orders, and in pairs ascended the gangplank. We passed along the deck to a square door, which in turn led to an iron stairway down into the hold. At last, our handcuffs were removed so we could descend the staircase one at a time.

Suddenly, I was overcome by emotion, tears running down my face when I turned my head to see my beloved Saigon by night. I was about to say goodbye to Saigon, to my homeland, a place of precious spiritual values. I remembered the saying, "The place where the placenta is buried." My tears still ran as I stepped down the stairway.

The hold was large and dim, lit only by one small electric bulb. The walls were coated with coal dust, and lumps of coal littered the floor. The ship was obviously a coal transporter. In the far corner were wooden crates with metal handles, the toilets for us, prisoners. At first, I thought it was a large space, but by the time all the prisoners arrived the hold became overcrowded. The metal door was shut, chained, and locked with a large bronze padlock. There was utter chaos as everyone claimed his own territory. There were no more officers designated by the Communist cadres, no more team leaders, and so there was no proper organisation. Everyone became equal in that dirty space.

Chapter 7
Farewell to the South

The ship cast off after midnight. We knew it was moving because we saw the stars moving in the opposite direction. At first, we thought we were the only prisoners on board, but when we knocked on the hold's wall we heard answering knocks from other compartments. Gradually, we understood that the ship had gone to the South to pick up human 'Merchandise' from many different prison camps. It was impossible to be accurate about the number of prisoners on board, but according to the dimensions of the hold, we estimated there could be more than a thousand. It was as if many gaggles of geese had been herded into a single cage.

A rumour soon circulated that we were taking part in a prisoner exchange and that this ship was on its way to the exchange point! Some people claimed that they knew from reliable sources on the outside that negotiations were underway between the Governments of Vietnam and the United States. They said that the United States had agreed to pay compensation for Vietnam of three billion dollars. In return, Vietnam would hand over all prisoners in the re-education camps. That meant not just veterans, but everyone in Communist concentration camps! The point of exchange would soon be agreed upon. The current news commentators in prison also seriously told us that the freed prisoners would be taken directly to the United States. That was followed by applause and exclamations. "That's great! Who thought we'd be so lucky; many people in the free society dream of going to America but they can't!"

Sadly, I recalled the words of my friend from the kitchen. I didn't know the origin of the prisoner exchange news, but I suspected it also began from the same source as *Đồng Tháp* rumour. Almost everyone harboured the hope of going to *Đồng Tháp* or to the prisoner exchange point nearby. Yet, we had only to look around to see that preparations had been made for a long trip. There were sacks provided for our '*nội vụ*' (Belongings) and the ship's officers had thick Northern accents. However, I couldn't blame them for grasping even that slim bit of hope. There was nothing else. And, of course, hope was not costly, so, why not indulge in it?

Out of extreme fatigue the majority of prisoners slept like logs on the ship's cold, metal floor. Strangely, I also had a good night's sleep, probably because I had made a firm decision to cautiously attempt freedom. This had hatched the moment I stepped onto the ocean liner.

The next morning sun glittered on the ocean, reflecting on the starboard side of the ship, and so proving that we were sailing to the North. Yet, even now a small number of prisoners insisted the ship was heading to… *Đồng Tháp*! I saw the guards leaning on the railing and looking down at us. It reminded me of visits to the Saigon Zoo where visitors would look down on bears in their enclosure below. At feeding time, the keepers would throw food down to them and a hose from above cleaned their pit. We were in exactly the same position.

For sanitary cleaning, a guard lowered a rope with a metal hook attached on to which, we hooked the toilet crates, the guards then hauled them up. At feeding time, they threw down food, mostly instant noodles, which we caught and divided among ourselves. The guards yelled at us when we were too loud or disorderly. At times, they threatened to shoot us. However, I knew they were only threats, because the number of prisoners to be transported had been agreed upon. Making the stupid mistake of shooting and killing a unit of human 'Merchandise' could mean that a guard would have to take his place.

After cleaning and breakfast were over, the prisoners sat in the hold in groups. The atmosphere was tense, men staring suspiciously at one another, so I visited a few groups to listen to their conversations. I soon had the feeling that something serious was about to happen. At that point, I was the only priest, and more than half of the prisoners were Catholic, so it's not hard to understand why they accepted me.

A few groups were forming alliances, determined to get rid of the hated '*Antennae*' who had reported on them in the camp. It was the ideal opportunity to do so, because of the general disorder. Those who had played '*Antennae*' knew their likely fate and became more fearful, after sensing the angry revenge! The blacklisted ones sat pale-faced in a corner. Whenever another group approached, the men bowed their heads to avoid eye contact. Some people began to migrate towards my spot. A few began showing respect and friendliness towards me with the obvious motive of seeking protection. This made me feel uncomfortable. I convinced the other group to scrap their plan of revenge. It wasn't an easy task because I didn't have influence on every group, but they agreed after I presented them with something more positive to do.

Hazardous Plot of Freedom

I discussed the idea I had formed the previous evening with Mr *Dương Văn Lợi*, a Civil engineer and the team leader from *Gia Ray* kitchen. He was a clever man with many friends on board the ship. Then, I quietly gathered a number of the mostly young men and I revealed my plan to them. I explained to them that under Communist regimes in Russia, China and other countries, those who disagreed with the regime would be executed or put in Concentration Camps, many never returned. Now, it was the same in Vietnam. Therefore, from the time I was captured, I saw escaping as the road to life, and freeing other prisoners from unjust imprisonment was an obligation. The intention of escaping was always in my mind, and I always looked for opportunities to do this, although I knew it was dangerous and might require a high price, the price of my own life. The moment I stepped on the ship, realising that I was being taken to the North, I was even more determined.

Now, I proposed my plan to the group to take over the ship. They sat in silence for a while. Then they unanimously agreed, much to my surprise. The plan was calculated as follows: Taking advantage of the element of surprise, and carefully noting the guards' weak spots, we would overwhelm them. Then, we would take over the ship's navigation. We would not kill anyone, but all cadres and any passengers on deck would become our hostages. Prisoners with experience of sailing would sail the ship to the nearest free country, probably the Philippines. There we would ask for an international organisation to negotiate an exchange of our hostages for the release of all the prisoners on board. We were aware that it was a daring and dangerous plan. But the vision of dying slowly in the Northern concentration camps made it preferable to take the risk in the effort to be free.

Once the plan was agreed upon, we had to work out the details. This must be done quickly because it would not be a lengthy voyage. *Dương Văn Lợi* and I had already discussed possible problems, and had some ideas about solving them. The chain on the door needed to be sawn through, we would need a rope ladder and some sort of weapons. I invited anyone who had been in the Navy to offer information about the ship's structure, its speed, navigation needs, means of communication, etc. *Dương Văn Lợi* would be my assistant and take care of personnel. *Lợi* chose *Hồ Hoàng Khánh*, a former frog-man, would be his deputy.

The plan was as follows: About 6 hours before our attempt (T-Time), we would saw through the chain locking the door above the stairs. At exactly T-Time, a group of twenty-five men, some of whom were skilled at martial arts, would go up the stairs, through the door, and find places to hide on the deck. There, they would take the first opportunity to quietly overcome the guards, binding their arms and legs and stuffing their mouths with rags. Then they would drop the rope ladders down to the rest of us. We considered that a hundred of us would be enough to take over all essential points of the ship.

We understood that if we killed anyone we would lose ground in our future negotiations. But we needed to take as many hostages as possible. The ship would not be sunk, because there were a large number of cadres, passengers, and high-ranking Interior Department officers on board. Up on arrival in the Philippines, we would negotiate the terms with an international organisation for trading the hostages and the guarantee of safe asylum.

We had the necessary tools: Half a metal saw-blade hidden in a sandal of one prisoner, and several men donated pants to make a rope ladder. Some sharpened segments of the sugar cane we received as food could be used as spears. Our preparations had to be kept from the sharp eyes and ears of the '*Antennae*', some were sitting pale and curled up near my sleeping place. They could neither report on us even if they wanted to, nor could they communicate with the guards on deck. We carefully monitored all their actions and movements, but we knew they were also monitoring ours.

The next day, April 19, 1977, there were two important things to be done. First was to practice sawing the chain above the stair, and second, to have the on-deck guards underestimate the prisoners in the hold. To disguise the noise we were making, I organised the men to sing Communist songs loudly while others clapped. The person sawing would continue to work on the chain, unconcerned about anyone hearing his sawing noise. Also, I suggested the men fight over food when it was thrown down into our pit. Some of the prisoners would call for the cadres to come and mediate.

Of course, no cadre was stupid enough to make his way down, but they did stick their heads in to insult and threaten us. Once, I heard one say, "Those guys only know how to fight over food! Just a useless bunch of savages, let them kill themselves!" I laughed to myself, "My prey had entered my trap." The fighting increased, and someone would call for a cadre, but they didn't want to interfere. Now, we were doing the manipulating! All day, we sang, fought over food, fought among ourselves, and called for the cadres to intervene. And so, they were lulled into thinking everything was secure.

On the night of April 18, I invited all plot participants to sit down together. We discussed the serious nature of our actions that could lead to death. I asked everyone to pray for our upcoming action, according to his own beliefs. We asked the Supreme Power to support our cause, and if this act could not be carried out, we asked our Higher Power to intervene so we could avoid danger and massive death.

As I spoke, the fraternal brothers sat eyeing one another silently. I told them we had just over a day to get everything prepared. Our attempt would take place on April 20. Since T-Time was 1.00 a.m., that gave us twenty-seven hours for preparation. Then, on behalf of the entire group, I paid my respects to our twenty-five leaders. The atmosphere was solemn as I said "We are about to do something that affects our lives and the lives of others. But we must do it to be free of the Communist regime's irrational extermination. You twenty-five who face the danger first will perhaps be the ones sacrificed first. Therefore, on behalf of all the fraternal brothers, I ask you to accept one ritual bow. With Heaven's help, if we are successful; you, fraternal brothers will be the first to reap the rewards. If we are unfortunate and fail, we will all die together in a meaningful death, dying for the ideal of freedom. **The price of freedom is high, and we may pay with our own lives**." With that, I knelt and bowed to the twenty-five brave men. All were touched, sitting still with their heads bowed. Some wept. Tensely, the group disbanded and went to their places. As for the planning committee, we remained to discuss details.

On our first day out at sea, the weather was beautiful with gentle winds and a clear blue sky, with only an occasional cloud cluster gliding past. The ship sailed so smoothly that we hardly felt it move. We had a saying *"In March, old women can cross the sea."*

On the morning of the 19th, the early sun was more brilliant and the sky was cloudless. The sea was still calm and the ship sailed smoothly. We continued to organise ourselves like a group of bears in the Saigon Zoo. When it was time to clean the cage, cadres lowered a hook for us to attach the waste crates. They were hauled up and empty ones lowered to their original spots. At the feeding time, the guards still threw instant noodles down. We caught them and divided the food. By this time, there were only instant noodles, nothing else. On previous days, they threw us watermelon and sugarcane. Drinking water was very limited and was lowered to us in a metal container. By now, the hold was dirty and slippery. The toilet containers used by more than three hundred had no lids, so the stench thickened and grew.

The closer we came to our mission, the more nervous we became. Time passed too quickly. The sun began to move west. Although we were exhausted and stressed, we would occasionally sing loudly and clap. We had to keep up this routine, because that night amid the noise, we were to saw the chain locking the hold. I made rounds to encourage everyone, checking our needs at the same time. We'd prepared the rope ladder, and the segments of sugarcane had been set up ready for action.

Out-of-Season Storm

It was around 3.00 p.m., the weather showed signs of change, and I could no longer see the sun's glow on the ship's side. The gentle wind grew colder with a slight sprinkling of rain. At first, I was happy, thinking the sound of the rain would make it easier for us to hide our activities and distract the guards.

Somewhere between 4.00 and 5.00 p.m. the wind grew much stronger and the rain heavier. The ship began to lean, not much, but enough to make some people uncomfortable and seasick. They found places to lie down. But then I received a frightful surprise. A guard up above switched on a motor, and a giant metal roof moved over to cover the hold. It left only a few feet for ventilation! I had been completely unaware of this roof. Now, I understood that if we tried any kind of escape, the guards above would push a button and close off the hold. What would happen to us? Momentarily, the rain began to taper off. I saw the metal cover retract to show a grey sky with many black clouds. Those familiar with this coast told us it was a sign of a tropical storm, an off-season storm that often occurred in the South China Sea.

The wind increased; screaming and flailing against the side of the ship causing it to rock even more. We became lethargic. Some were seasick and vomited on the floor. To make things worse, during cage cleaning that evening, the guard fell and let go of his load, letting the crate dump its contents over us! The ship's hold had no water or any means of cleaning up! Only a small number of people could manage to sit up and eat. The majority lay stretched out like unburied corpses. As night fell, the wind howled even louder. The ship rocked back and forth, the rain began to fall again, and the metal cover was put in place. I lost all hope.

By 10.00 p.m. all was quiet, except for the seasick people tossing and turning. Others slept soundly, and our time for action was only three hours away. Those who tried to walk about, like Mr *Dương Văn Lợi* and myself, wobbled on our feet. I thought to myself, *"Man proposes, God disposes"*. After consulting with the few remaining, I announced that our plan was to be dropped. Although very fatigued from the past two days, I could not close my eyes. I sat up the whole night, listening to the wind howl and the rain rattle, the miserable ship tossed on the sea like an egg boiling in a pot.

What baffled me most was that, just before dawn, the ship stopped swaying as the wind tapered off. At dawn, the wind dropped completely and the sea calmed. The cover retracted to reveal a clear, blue sky as in the first days. No one could explain the sudden and brief storm. But I understood its meaning. I had prayed earnestly, asking God that if our plot could not be carried out, He would intervene to prevent suffering and drastic consequences. I believed the off-season storm to be a personal miracle. This miracle took place through my faith and prayer, to prevent danger that could spill blood. My ignorance of the metal roof meant our plan could not have worked. **From that incident, I strongly understood God's Providence.**

The seasick quickly recovered, and the ship's hold activities resumed. The only change was the dropping of the hijacking plan. The more determined participants, especially the young men, regretted this, and in their regret they became irritable and aggressive. They looked for another outlet for their frustration and energy. That outlet happened to be the '*Antennae*' on board.

The wave of anger against these men had temporarily abated while we concentrated on other issues, but it was difficult to let go of the vengeance issue. Some came to me during plotting discussions and asked if we could set up court to put the '*Antennae*' on trial, once our plan was successful. They even presented a list of the malicious prisoners in *Gia Ray* Camp to be tried for their crimes. I scrapped that idea, and informed them that it was neither our goal nor my job. I mention this, so that those who have never experienced a Communist prison, can sympathise with the suffering and anger of those harmed by the *'Antennae'*. Those lackeys harmed many political prisoners. To me that was the most painful thing in thirteen years of living in Communist concentration camps.

Now, there was nothing to occupy the mind, and the desire to eliminate the *'Antennae'* had resurfaced. There seemed to be no controlling the rising anger. Although I had stopped a number of people, namely the Catholic ones, I could not stop them all. There were some arguments, followed by men chasing and beating each other. It flared like an epidemic, spreading very quickly and fiercely. Those being chased would try to hide, but how could they escape in a crowded hold? Some were severely beaten and bloodied, with hands, long tobacco pipes, or any other objects that could be used as weapons. I remembered two men who walked with canes; their canes became effective weapons for beating the *'Antennae'*.

I was unfamiliar with all the alliances at *Gia Ray* Camp as I had been there such a short time. Usually, the beaten persons would run to me for protection. Although no one wanted to listen, I called for everyone to cease fighting. The tension fell gradually. However, because I had intervened, those beaten later accused me of encouraging their torture. I had to pay a heavy price for this at the Camp where we were heading towards.

It was about 6.00 p.m. on April 20, 1977, the *SÔNG HƯƠNG's* engines stopped running. We knew we had arrived somewhere in the North. Being kept in the hold, we could not locate where we were. After the ship had been anchored for quite a while, we still didn't disembark, even though we heard other prisoners leaving. From the hold, I could see some inmates who had been with me at *Phan Đăng Lưu* Prison, had remained there while I was transferred to the *Gia Ray* Camp. It was already dusk when we disembarked. We discovered we were in *Hải Phòng*, a seaport in the North.

As a child, I had always dreamed of traveling, of becoming a sailor on an ocean liner, sailing over the ocean waves. My greatest wish had been to set foot in strange ports around the world. Although I did not make this dream come true as an adult, I did not lose my passion and my love for the ocean. Now, my dream had become a sort of reality, but ironically my first sea-going experience was not as a free sailor but as a confined prisoner. Now indeed, I had set foot on an unfamiliar port, not in fulfilment of my adventurous dream, but to begin my uncertain future as an exiled prisoner.

Chapter 8
The Exiled Prisoner

Hải Phòng Port was full of bustling activity. The *SÔNG HƯƠNG* had begun to unload its human cargo, and many curious adults and children were watching us from the street. They began pointing and talking noisily among themselves. Their Northern accents sounded strange to me, and on looking at their faces and gestures, perhaps it was better that I couldn't understand.

When we came ashore, we were immediately cuffed in pairs, ordered to board the waiting buses and handed dry bread for the journey. The escorts announced the rules and the convoy got on its way. Twilight fell. Suddenly small stones began to rain against the unglazed windows. I had to use my uncuffed arm to protect my face so that no pebble would damage my glasses or worse blind me. In the midst of this chaos, I heard the shouts of children by the roadside: "F*ck you all, you're a bunch of puppets, you drink blood and eat the liver of man!" Their insulting voices got louder. A guard said, "You see? If the Party hadn't protected you, these people would have killed you!" Some of us had been slightly injured. A stone left a painful lump on my head. I felt depressed, not knowing where they were taking us to.

Can you imagine the plight of an exiled prisoner, powerless to decide his own destination? With no idea of where he's being taken to, what lies ahead, when, nor even if, he'll ever return? To add to the misery, the people surrounding us had accumulated a great deal of vengeance towards us, defeated Southerners. **More accurately, they including the children had been trained to show vengeance.** It was not necessarily their own thoughts they were voicing. Therefore, I felt compassion for them.

The convoy continued through the night on the long road from *Hải Phòng*, past Hanoi. About midnight, we crossed a river on the *Phủ Lý* Ferry, and then drove through a narrow, winding pass into a basin among the mountains.

Towards dawn, we entered an area surrounded by barbed wire. Through dense fog, I glimpsed many low buildings. We drove through a large gateway and finally stopped in a yard. This was the *Nam Hà* Camp, not far from Hanoi.

The Nam Hà Camp

My initial impression was of a military camp, clean and organised, different altogether from the mess at *Gia Ray*. The low buildings had shingled roofs, and surrounding them were brick walls topped with barbed wire that divided the camp into two distinct sections. At the right was a shallow pond, perhaps nine or ten meters in diameter, encircled by a low cement wall. Nearby were some low out houses that, I guessed, were the camp's laundry area. The divided structure of this new camp baffled me.

We were quickly organised into temporary cells to rest. Although it was cold, we were so tired that we slept soundly. The next morning we all felt the freezing cold and damp fog. Coming from the warmer South, we had not adjusted to the North's biting cold. On looking out through the barred window, I was surprised at the view. Surrounding the Camp was a massive body of water, with small-mounded peaks popping through the surface like giant mushrooms. We laughed excitedly, fancifully comparing the mountains to chess pieces left by giants, or perhaps the eggs of a long-extinct giant bird. Further off mountains lined the horizon, enclosing the Camp.

When we joined the *Nam Hà* Camp on April 21, 1977, there were already more than six hundred prisoners from the South. They had arrived in late 1975 or early 1976, lived in the houses to the left side of the gate. This side was called Section A to separate it from the three hundred and fifty new arrivals of Section B on the right side.

After a time, I noticed that the people in Section A were very quiet and kept to themselves. The majority were old or at least middle-aged. Many were fair-skinned and always well groomed, dressed in blue prison uniforms with turtlenecks. When I heard their names, I recognised them as former elected government officials or high-ranking police officers. They included the former Prime Minister, *Nguyễn Văn Lộc*, and some big names of Saigon regime.

Every time I saw these men lining up for the head-count before going out to their assigned labouring tasks, I felt desolate. Each carried a sack containing an aluminium can for drinking water, and poking out of the top would be a tobacco pipe. These once powerful men, now so humiliated, reminded me of the cyclic rule of human life. They always appeared fatigued but never complained aloud perhaps wanting to prove they accepted their condition in order to increase their chances of clemency from the Party. The guards often told us "To re-educate and to labour well, is the shortest path to your family re-union sooner!"

Every one of these men had reported for re-education according to the communiqué from the Military Administration Committee after the Communists seized the South. At that time, the Communists realised that although ordinary citizens were stunned and fearful, yet under the leadership of the Southern officers, they might still fight back. Such a revolt would be a serious impediment when they were trying to enforce their rules. So, they decided to imprison all the remaining officers and government officials. Already a number of cowards had fled the country. But there were a number of brave leaders still in the South. The Communists understood that they could not hunt down each individual target, so they shrewdly set a trap that would catch many at once.

The Bustle Trick!

The Military Administration Committee announced over the radio that all low-ranking military officers from previous Government, and who the Communist labelled as *Nguy'* (Puppet troops), were to report for education according to the policies of the Party and Revolutionary Government. They were told to bring enough food for three days. Despite some suspicion, all knew it would be disastrous not to follow orders. Besides, hadn't they been told to bring food and necessities for three days only? There was still room for hope. So they reported for training, and three days later, they were issued release documents and allowed to go home. This allayed the general fear and suspicion towards the new regime. Therefore, many began to believe in the propaganda of amnesty policies.

Soon afterwards, the Administration Committee broadcast another directive: All military officers and high-ranking government officials must report at designated locations. They were told to bring enough food, money, and personal belongings for one month. The announcement ended with the threat that anyone not following these orders would be prosecuted according to the current law.

Everyone knew that the Communists could take fearful revenge. I remembered the images from the *Việt Cộng* in *Tết* Offensive in 1968, when thousands of innocent civilians in the South were beaten over the head and literally gutted. Many more were tied in groups with electrical wire and buried alive in *Huế*. It would not be safe to defy the order.

Anyway, the Party was instructing "Bring enough personal necessities for one month," and the soldiers who had taken enough for three days had returned home as promised, hadn't they? It would be all right. So, they hoped to get the training over quickly and then be free to live and work legally. Former senior officers hurried to report at the Re-education registration locations that were popping up like fungi. After bidding goodbye to their loved ones and promising to return in a month, they pushed and shoved until they found themselves at the head of the queue. Even though they envisioned the concentration camp they entered, most believed they would go back home in one month.

However...What evil can lie in the word *'However'!*

By the fourth week of their training, the entire group was very excited. Some counted the days until their graduation ceremony that would surely be splendid. Representatives for the re-educated would give speeches to thank the Party for its hard work in re-education. The families would be present at the ceremony to welcome their loved ones. On the thirtieth night, many people could not sleep. They shook hands with comrades who had fought at their side against Communism. But a page in history book had turned over; now they only wished for a peaceful life with their families.

The next morning, exactly one month after entering the Camp, they rose early to pack their belongings before the graduation ceremony. But instead, the *'Kleng'* sounded as usual for everyone to go to daily tasks. The men looked at one another in silent puzzlement. But they could only bow their heads and get in line, reporting their numbers to the guard at the gate before going out to labour as usual.

During that day, someone proposed a likely reason for the delay: There were thirty-one days this month therefore, the month wasn't yet finished! So, the graduation ceremony would take place tomorrow, day number thirty-one. Satisfied, they went to sleep, anticipating the next day's graduation. However, the next day came and went, as did the days that followed. There was nothing different except for the disappointment showing on many faces. The frustrated men kept asking one another, "What's the meaning of this?" but no one could provide an answer.

One day, a courageous man asked a guard: "Reporting to you brother. I have a question."

"What's that? Whatever question you have, let's hear it."

"Reporting to you brother, according to the announcement from the Military Administration Committee, we were to go home after one month. It is now past one month, so why haven't we been allowed to leave?"

The guard gave a sideways grin, shrugged his shoulders, and said, "Who said training would end after one month?"

The prisoner raised his voice. "Reporting to you brother, I remember each word in the Military Administration Committee's announcement; they said to bring along money, food and necessities for one month. I think everyone here heard the same thing."

Before he could finish, other men chimed in, "Hear, hear, yes, yes, within one month."

The guard sneered, "You, stupid bunch! I really can't believe how stupid you all are! The announcement meant that you were to bring money, food and necessities for one month and after that, the Party would provide for you. Do you understand now? Show me where in the announcement it says training lasts only one month. The Party does not deceive you, gentlemen; your stupidity just interfered with your understanding."

Although the guard spoke quietly, it came across as thunder in the 're-educated' ears.

Section A and Section B

I found that the behaviour of the members of the two Sections was completely different. The prisoners in Section A, obeyed camp rules without arguing. On the other hand, the prisoners in Section B, especially the younger ones, lived proudly and spoke bluntly. One day, a guard told a young man *Đặng Hữu Nam*, formerly in the Resistance Movement, to get him a chair. *Nam* pretended to have misunderstood as he said, "Reporting to you, guard, I don't need to sit down."

The guard, unaccustomed to dealing with such an attitude, asked, "What did you say? I told you to get a chair for me. Who gave you permission to sit down? You think you're so tough."

Đặng Hữu Nam calmly replied, "Reporting to you, if you need to sit in a chair, and get it yourself. Why do you ask me to do it? I came here to be re-educated, not to provide chairs for you to sit on."

Our entire group listened silently. The defeated guard could only say, "You're cheeky! You're not allowed to speak to me that way."

Nam retorted quickly, "And I will report this to the Supervisory Board."

The man walked away before *Nam* finished his sentence, spitting a wad of foamy saliva as he left.

The Supervisory Board never let disobedience pass without punishment. Like their Communists bosses, their approach to discipline was "Mould them until you encountered resistance". If you didn't mould yourselves willingly, you were forced into their desired shape.

The respected elders in Section A had never spoke aloud or attempted to escape. Neither did they participate in labour strikes or fasting from food as a protest. Therefore, they must have felt very nervous when some of Section B shouted, "Down with Communists!" This was in the presence of Education Officer *Huy*.

He turned purple in anger, but pretended to be amused. "Oh, you lot! The Party manages the whole country now, so if you don't live with the Party then how and with whom will you live? I know that you're all young and easily angered, so if you have any complaints, please direct them to the Supervisory Board and they will take care of everything." The voice was as sweet as honey, but it came from one with an iron fist.

The tension in Section B was like an over-stretched balloon. Most of the prisoners were Catholic and I was the only priest. The Communists had a special hatred for Catholic priests, seeing us as leaders of resistance. It goes without saying that I was subject to close watch and held responsible for the protests that took place.

The 'Antennae'

In the months before Christmas 1977, there were many cases of protest. These included fasting and making a racket with pots and pans. At that time, Section B began persecuting members of the *'Antennae'* (Informers). They cloaked them in blankets and beat them until they had broken bones and split lips. Then, victims were made to sleep next to me. During my thirteen years as a prisoner of the Communist regime, I saw that such spies could be found in every camp. They spanned every class, age and position, and I regarded their actions as the most dishonourable! Criminals were bad enough, but the *'Antennae'* were stooges of the enemy, harming their own vanquished brothers. The numbers of *'Antennae'* grew, especially since the road to re-education was lengthy, and only those who jumped through hoops had any hope of going home as promised. Being an *'Antenna'* was seen as a profession, so it involved recruiting and training.

I had been invited to do this job when I was still in the *Phan Đăng Lưu* Camp in the South. It was in 1976, not long after I was first imprisoned. This was before we were assigned labouring tasks. In our cell, sixty of us sat talking, playing chess, reading the *Nhân Dân* Newspaper and waiting for the door to open at mealtime. A guard called me out. He escorted me to the office for 'Work', (the camp euphemism for interrogation). The officer lectured me about the importance of my re-education in order to resume my normal life. I began to guess what he wanted of me and wasn't surprised when he suggested that if I wanted to go home early, then I should be a pioneer and report on events in my cell.

I felt such pity for him! He had definitely chosen the wrong person. But I decided to dupe him, and said that I accepted his proposal. He smiled happily. His superiors would probably be very pleased to know that a Catholic priest had agreed to be an *'Antenna'*. Then, he showed me out, grinning from ear to ear, and promised to meet me again, probably thinking complacently, "I can even recruit a priest!"

Some days later I was called to his office for more work. He welcomed me warmly, offering Chinese tea and cigarettes. Then he got to the point. *"Anh Lễ*, I am happy to hear you have made improvement in re-education. So, did you observe any bad phenomena in your cell?"

I answered seriously: "Reporting to you, yes, plenty."

"Tell me everything, *Anh Lễ*, tell me everything, I promise to keep it secret, you don't have to worry."

"Reporting to you, people in the cell say very bad things."

His face brightened. "What did they say?"

"They speak in obscenities that are unimaginable, especially the young men. Every time they open their mouths it's "F*ck you!" (*đụ mẹ*) or " F*ck off! " (*đéo bà*)

The smile died on his face, and he looked disappointed. "Did they say anything anti-revolutionary, such as speaking against the Party or spreading false propaganda? Swearing is not important."

"Reporting to you, I heard them say "F*ck you!" or "F*ck off!" so much, that I didn't hear the things you mention."

That was the first time I reported, and it was also the last, because I was never called again. I wonder if he regretted the fragrant cigarettes and delicious tea.

There were many different promised rewards for *'Antenna'*, the biggest being the promise that the clemency of the Party and Government may grant an early release. None of us had ever had a trial, nor received a sentence. Therefore, no one knew when he would be released, but everyone nurtures hope. I soon found that the promise of clemency was the bait to entice the *'Antennae'*, who hunted with more gusto, betrayed men more often, hurt men more heavily. Some were willing to kill their fellow inmates.

Sometimes their reward was to meet their wives overnight in the 'Happiness Room' of the Visitors' Centre. Many men strived for this. But those who were regarded as poorly re-educated, despite having been away from their wives for up to a decade, were only allowed to sit at a distance and speak of superficial things. At the head of the table would be a guard to 'share the joy' of a husband and wife reunited after a long time. The husband was not allowed to even touch his wife's hands. On the other hand, any wife who was permitted conjugal nights with her husband received a certificate, so that if she became pregnant she could avoid scandal or any complications with her husband's family.

Smaller rewards included not having to go out to labour when the weather was very bad. Instead, they could stay in the cell and stalk the other prisoners. Another reward was to be made Team Leader. Or to be appointed to kitchen duties and so be able to eat well. Even better was to be promoted to a position in the security or medical sections. These were the officers in prison, although not all of these 'officers' were *'Antennae'*.

When I mentioned the *'Antennae'*, everyone showed contempt. However, there was one case where I had to applaud such a man.

One day, a new prisoner was pushed into our cell in the South. He was of a small build and his complexion had a greenish tinge. In the hot cell, he wore only boxer shorts, like the rest of us, so, we could see how skinny his legs were. When the cell leader showed him his sleeping spot and asked his name and age, he answered reluctantly. He showed no effort towards fitting in, but sat in one corner with his back to the wall, his gaze sweeping back and forth. When it was almost mealtime and everyone was moving around, he stood up and spoke loudly. We were all surprised into silence.

He told us that he was a Communist district officer, imprisoned for accepting a bribe. He also told us he'd previously activated two mines to kill a sizable number of people in the *Mỹ Cảnh* Restaurant at the *Bạch Đằng* Wharf years ago. Then he continued in a very serious voice, "Although I am imprisoned, I am still a Communist. I request that everyone in the cell refrain from spreading anti-revolutionary propaganda or speaking ill of the Party, or I will report you!"

With that, he sat down again and kept silent. Of course, everyone in the cell feared him from that moment. Some hated him, especially after learning that he'd set off mines to kill innocent civilians before the 1975 take-over. However, I admired him for being loyal to his Party opinion and giving us fair warning.

For myself, I had accepted everything that might come, including death. What I had asked of God was help to live worthily as a priest, to be a witness to the love of God even here, to bring this love to my fellow prisoners, and give them spiritual strength in times of trial. I knew that Communists saw all religions as their enemy, with Catholicism being enemy number one. My crimes were clear: a reactionary priest, resisting re-education, instigating revolts in prison. With such a chain of crimes, it was easy to guess my fate.

I was called out for questioning many times about my activities on the *SÔNG HƯƠNG*. The Camp's Security Officers examined me, sometimes even meeting high-ranking officers sent by the Interior Department from Hanoi. Once, I was grilled by Lieutenant Colonel *Hoàng Thanh* who'd had the duty of escorting us from the South, about the plot to hijack the ship. Sometimes, these men spoke as sweetly as sugar. At other times, they yelled and foamed at the mouth. Each time, I gave the same reply, "I don't know about this. If anyone reported this, please let me meet him." Usually the interrogation ended after I said this. No way would they let me face my accuser. Although, I didn't know all the *'Antennae'* that reported the *SÔNG HƯƠNG* incident, I knew some of them. Then for some months, I was left in peace. However, it wasn't because this case was closed.

In October of 1977, after I had spent 6 months at *Nam Hà*, the Camp received a large influx of military prisoners from the *Hoàng Liên Sơn* Camp. This brought the total number of prisoners to more than a thousand. This included six hundred prisoners in Section A. Section B prisoners filled five cells, each housing sixty prisoners.

Although I was actually classed as Section B, our cell number 12 housed only twenty people. We were an assorted mix, I'm a Catholic priest, a few Montagnard pastors, former merchants, Resistance workers, former military officers, and an old Chinese man named *Nùng Bá Lâm*. It was said that he had been a leading general who once commanded a division under the Chinese Nationalist President, Chiang Kai-Shek, but had not followed Chiang to Taiwan. Instead, he led his troops across the Burmese border, where they became outlaws. Frankly, I don't know if this was true. I do know that he was incredibly dirty.

Background Statements

One day in November we were told that we would have to make background statements. Four hundred people selected from Section A, and 19 of us from cell No. 12 in Section B were assigned to the group. This didn't sound particularly frightening. However, it became one of my worst experiences in prison. Every time we did background statements, prisoners had to dig the history through three generations of their families and submit their memories in writing to the Party. This family history report was done many times, but without any definite routine.

I didn't understand the purpose of this exercise, but it probably included gauging the prisoners' honesty. The key point was to remember everything from the first background statement and be consistent, not including any more details or leaving anything out. Some people didn't pay attention to this crucial point. They included extra information in successive reports and paid a high price for doing so. I don't remember how many times I had to write my family history during my thirteen years, I lost count.

The background statements usually took place as follows: A number of officers from the central office in Hanoi lectured us about the importance of background statements, teaching the good way to dig family tree out. As background statements were a big brain drain, and at these times we required better nutrition. Because I was not allowed to labour, normally I was rationed nine kilograms of food per month. Those who laboured would be given ration of twelve kilograms per month. However, during background statement times, I was always given the full amount. This didn't necessarily mean kilograms of rice, as there was not enough of that to feed all the prisoners. The substitutes were corn, potatoes, cassava, barley, and sometimes the discarded parts of beans.

The first day, we gathered in the meeting hall to listen to the officer from Hanoi give a speech. It covered the clemency policies of the Government and emphasised that our providing an honest background statement would be the shortest path to be released. Even at that stage we knew these were blatant lies. It was puzzling how the spin-doctors didn't feel any shame.

Subsequent speeches always included guidelines about how best to submit a satisfactory background statement. We were divided into small groups, with one officer supervising each. We were isolated and were not allowed to speak. The officer provided brown paper for rough drafts and white paper for good copies. We each had a pot of ink and dipping pens. If our pen nib failed, we were to tell the officer. This training session lasted two days, and on the first evening one officer would choose a topic and select a prisoner to speak about it on the following evening. All the prisoners were then supposed to discuss his opinion.

We wrote in our home cell or a place of the officer's choosing, and handed each rough pages to the officer to read through as we finished it. He would sign each page that was satisfactory so that we could write the final copy. But if he was not satisfied, the paper would be torn up and redone until it was satisfactory. Some people wrote over and over again. Whoever was tired could request a break, but no socialising was allowed. When rested, the person would return and continue writing.

In the evening, we handed in all scratch and final copies to the officer. A writing session like this could go on for two or three days and for some people it lasted a week. I even heard that some people wrote for a month without finishing. A final 'dissertation' often reached a thousand pages.

We had to write about our family background and our own life story. The first part, besides the usual information, we had to include family name, date and place of birth, place of residence, religious affiliation, family members, schooling, degrees, decoration and medals, we also had to state the names, ages, locations, and occupations of both spouses for our grandparents, parents, aunts and uncles. We were also required to report on our friends and their addresses, whether they were in or out of the country, or even if they were in prison.

However, the bulk of the writing was our personal life story. Each was to write all that he could remember of his entire life, not leaving out any details. Once, with the intention of making a fool of them, I reported that I had a habit of bedwetting as a child. The guard took my rough draft, furrowing his eyebrows in deep thought. He finally said, "Bedwetting is not anti-revolutionary, so you don't need to write that." At least, the Party could see my 'honest' reporting! The guard always tried to force me to acknowledge that I had committed crimes against the people. I argued that I had only offended the Communist Party, not the people. If anything, I had been of service to my people. My profession was to take care of others. I stuck with this viewpoint despite insults and threats of all kinds.

Resolute Proclamation

On that occasion of background statements, I was selected to speak on the topic, 'Are you content with the re-education policies, and why?'. This question was meant to prove our acceptance of all re-education procedures. The mantras quoted by those who hoped for reunification with their families were "Absolute faith in the clemency policy of the Party and Government". The officer instructed me to give the topic some thought overnight so as to express myself well the following day.

That night, I prayed for God's help to know what I should do. I knew they'd set a trap for me. If I stepped up in front of the officers and more than four hundred prisoners, majority of whom were Catholic, to say I am content with the re-education policies, then everyone would look at me in contempt, correctly seeing me as a liar. The Catholic prisoners would feel ashamed. Technically, I would be alive, but effectively my life would be over. On the other hand, if I were to speak my mind, I might have to give up my earthly life. A priest, is still a human being and afraid of death. I tossed and turned as I considered my options. Finally, I decided I would have to say what I believed.

Next evening was blazingly hot and the heat from the surrounding limestone increased. As usual, we lined up two-by-two to enter the hall with its long wooden benches for us prisoners and a mezzanine gallery for the officers. After the usual opening, the guard introduced the topics for discussion and the names of the designated presenters. He advised everyone to listen carefully so as to be able to discuss the opinions afterwards. My ears hummed to the point that I could hardly hear the guard's words. I began shaking and broke into a sweat. My heart beat faster as my face became heated and flushed, breathing became more difficult. I had a sudden urge to rush to the toilet.

Then I heard the guard say, "First, *Anh Nguyễn Hữu Lễ* from cell 12, team 20, will present the topic: 'Are you content with the re-education policies and why'?"

The moment I feared has now come; I stepped steadily into the aisle and up to the podium. From there, I could see both the rows of prisoners sitting below and the panel of officers looking down from above. They seemed to be a million miles away in that solemn atmosphere. Once I reached the podium, I stood quietly for some minutes. I pictured myself standing at the lectern of my former Cathedral in the *Vĩnh Long* Diocese, as if it was a Sunday Mass at which I was going to deliver my homily. It had been three years since I could preach the truth openly. Today God would speak through me.

My fear had melted away. I felt relaxed, even joyful. I gave my fellow prisoners a warm smile. Then I looked at the officers who gazed at me with surprise; perhaps guessing that something unusual was about to happen, but it was too late to stop me. I took a deep breath and spoke freely:

"Greetings to all the Guards, and to my peers. I am very pleased to have the opportunity to say what I believe: I am not content with the re-education policies. I believe I speak on behalf of my prison brothers, many people speak of being content just to please the Party and the Government. They are telling lies."

The entire room went into shock, sitting as still as statues. Looking at the guards, I continued :

"Gentlemen, how can we be content when you've captured our land, our homes have been confiscated, our children have had to leave school to sell newspapers on the street for a living, our families have disintegrated. And I say, with apologies to my friends, that I am aware that some wives have had to prostitute themselves for money to buy food to feed their husbands in prison. And how can we be content when you confiscate Church properties?

I say this openly and take full responsibility for what I am saying. You, gentlemen, go ahead, call the people of the South to verify what I'm saying. I will stand here and wait."

I took a step backwards and looked at the row of guards. They stared back silently. I continued :

"When we were still at the Gia Ray Camp in the South, the Party forced us to clear land by digging up minefields. Many of my brothers, hit by the exploding mines, died or were left disabled. With the feeling that each hoe stroke we were digging our own graves. How could we be content? Therefore, you must show us the reason to be content. Do not coerce us to say we are."

I stopped abruptly and stood there.

Everyone was stunned in silence. The guards seemed frozen. The prisoners were bewildered, joyful, yet worried. No one knew how they should react. Then I heard a single clap from the back of the hall. Surprisingly, it followed with thunder of applause from all prisoners. With more than 400 prisoners voicing their unspoken wishes through this action, I felt as if the hall is about to explode. But I thought to myself, "This is the sound of the firecrackers as they lower my coffin."

After the next day's session, my work was even more meticulously examined. I waited each day to be called for interrogation. A week passed without anything happening. It felt like the calm before a great storm. I was a nervous wreck, every day hoping I would be summoned. I visualised a face-off with officer and prepared an argument to counter his attack. However, I was mistaken. Things did not happen as I had speculated.

A Wolf in Sheep's Clothing

Almost a month later, I was called for interrogation. My cellmates gave me sympathetic glances as I followed the guard out of the cell. In the department, I saw many guards in their yellow shirts. Suddenly, I felt I was so small compared with the huge mechanism of security officers controlling the camp, let alone the much bigger organisation tightly controlling an entire nation. It was so depressing. I was taken to a small room with the re-education officer sitting behind a small table holding a thermos bottle and an old tea set.

Everything was small in this room; even the guard. There was a folder on the table that I guessed contained my personal dossier.

I said the customary, "Reporting to you, Officer."

He pointed to a chair on the opposite side of the table, "*Anh Lễ*, sit down" Then, he began to talk in a cheerful manner as if we were old friends. This surprised me. He asked me about my health, my stay in camp, family matters including whether my parents were healthy and how my family was holding up. This polite behaviour only showed his superficial courtesy that made me uncomfortable. I knew this was all an act, a game of cat and mouse. He offered me tea and a cigarette. Suddenly, he asked me in all seriousness, "*Anh Lễ*, do you know why we have called you here?"

I noticed that he said 'We' rather than 'I'.

I answered, "Reporting to you Officer, I don't know."

He looked at me intensely. "So you don't know?"

"Reporting to you Officer, how can I possibly know about officers' work?"

He fell silent for a moment, turning the pen in his small, clean fingers. As if to add importance to the story, he pointed the blunt end of the pen in my face, "Do you still remember what you presented in the meeting hall?"

Because I had prepared myself, I answered calmly, "Reporting to you Officer, yes, how can I forget that?"

"*Anh Lễ*!" He continued, "I know you are a man with talents, that you only said such things because of personal issues. We don't see that incident as important, and we only hope that you will re-educate well."

Before I could say anything else, he invited me to drink more tea, chatted a little more, and then escorted me to the door. Back in my cell, I thought that it couldn't really be so simple. They didn't call me up just to offer tea and cigarettes. There must be something more serious that they weren't telling me. "*It's the old foxes you have to be well aware of,*" I said to myself.

Holy Night, Silent Night

Everyone knew that the Communists saw religion as their great enemy, so we were not surprised that in the days leading up to Christmas, the Supervisory Board was especially alert. The guards tirelessly searched section B to remove all Christmas decorations, including lanterns, stars, and nativity scenes. Some men had used parts of their cassava rations to sculpt the statue of the baby Jesus in a manger. Defiantly, they sang popular Christmas carols, less from feelings of devotion than to provoke the guards. I was still the only priest in the Camp, so it's easy to understand how I became a target. The *'Antennae'* stuck to me like shadows.

By now, I was sent to do labouring tasks with the others. Our team was sent to dry peanuts. The weather was very cold. At the end of the day, we were plastered with dirt but had only ice-cold water to wash ourselves. That night I developed bronchitis with a fever. The next day I fainted during evening roll call. Our Team leader, *Nguyễn Trọng Ngạn*, had to piggyback me to the infirmary, and I will always be grateful to him for doing this. Even after I had recovered, I was so weak that I had to use a cane. I couldn't go to work with the others.

To make things worse, I received a letter from my sister informing me that our Mother had passed away in August. She wrote that ever since hearing the news of my imprisonment, Mom sat every day in the shade of a palm tree by the roadside, waiting for my return. On her last day, she had no strength to go outside and died that night. Upon reading my Sister's letter, I sat silently, wanting to cry but not able to produce a single tear. The pain had made me as lifeless as a rock.

Many men came to comfort me in my grief. Some brought food and one even brought a precious can of condensed milk. However, not one single detail of these visits got past the hawk eyes of *Đặng Báu*, a fellow Catholic who regularly reported on me. Because of his reports, the security officer informed me to his office on Christmas Eve. When I sat down, he asked me about my visitors in the previous few days. Why did they come, why did they bring me gifts, and who gave the can of milk? Finally, he demanded scornfully, "*Anh Lễ*, tell me about your intention to disturb the camp tonight."

So that was their problem! However, I knew there was no truth in this report.

Angrily, I answered, "Reporting to you, Officer, if you think something is going to happen tonight, and obviously nothing will, because everyone will be scared off. But you're going on a dishonest report. What's more, if I did intend to do anything, you would never know."

I continued, "Sorry Officer, but let me tell you something: You've got rank and position, but not much intellect. Don't even try to dishonour me in this way." With such an unexpected response, the officer seemed confused and turned to another subject.

I realised that the authorities had become very tense. Throughout Christmas Eve, I pondered the incident, I was aware that something unusual would probably happen. Then at 6.00 p.m., after food distribution, Section B received orders to do a cell shuffle. A new prisoner came to my room and a number of our roommates were transferred to other cells.

Wherever they are, Christmas is a special day for all Christians, especially priests. In the past few days, while mingling with other prisoners in camp, I'd heard the individual confessions of a number of my Catholic brothers. We agreed that after the bedtime *'Kleng'* sounded, I would offer Christmas Midnight Mass secretly in my bunk, using a scrap of bread and wine brought in by another prisoner's family member. All the Catholics would turn towards my room, united by our intentions. Although there were a number of Catholics within my room, no one dared to come over to my spot. These days, the *'Antennae'* watched me very closely. The curious thing was that the most zealous one was himself a Catholic! It was around 10.00 p.m. that night, after the *'Kleng'* had signalled lights out, I sat inside my mosquito net and quietly offered Christmas Mass.

When I have just finished Mass, there was a jangling of keys outside the door. Experience told me that whenever the cell door was opened hastily in the night, it always meant bad news. Since I had come to *Nam Hà* more than eight months earlier, too many incidents had been attributed to me. Now in the dim light, I saw a handful of guards in the walkway between our bunks, an indication that something important was about to happen. Then I gathered all my belongings into a cloth bag, and waited.

Suddenly, a guard's voice rang out, "Everyone, sweep up your mosquito nets and stay in your places. When we call your name, bring all your *'Nội vụ'* (Belongings) and quickly step out of the room!" The entire room suddenly came back to life with the sounds of more than sixty prisoners packing their things. Instantly, nets were swept aside and everyone sat waiting in his place. Naturally, my heart pounded heavily. Then, "Nguyễn Hữu Lễ." My name was called.

Although I had expected it, I was still startled. I unfastened my netting, rolled up my bedding with my clothes, and put the rest of my belongings into a bag. These didn't amount much, just an aluminium can for water, a tobacco pipe and a very few other items. There was a commotion outside and many flashlights sweeping the area. Rifle fire rattled and I heard people running back and forth. "*Nguyễn Sỹ Thuyên*!" The guard's voice called another man. I felt comfort in knowing a friend of mine will go with me. "Hurry up! Bring all your '*nội vụ*' and step outside. Hurry up!" The yelling became more intense.

I turned to look at *Thuyên*, a pitiable sight. He was 50 years old, short, and slight, with a head of grey hair making him look older. As he fumbled with his *Nội vụ*, (Belongings) some of it fell back out of the bag. Both our bunks were on the upper level. We held on to the wooden post and climbed down, while others handed down our belongings. Unfamiliar guards were staring at me without a word, as if thinking 'Ah, so you are that rascal, *Nguyễn Hữu Lễ*?' "Hurry up now!" A loud voice demanded. I waved to my cellmates and they looked back at *Thuyên* and me with pity.

All goodbyes come with sadness. This was especially true of prison goodbyes, because deep down we knew we were unlikely to ever see one another again.

I followed *Thuyên*, both of us staggering as we carried our possessions outside. I was worried with fear, not knowing what awaited me under the sinister cloak of night. I had heard stories of people led from their cells in the middle of the night, never coming back. Now, standing alone in the thick shadow and biting cold, I looked back towards the cells in farewell. It was a farewell to more than a thousand prisoners with whom I had shared joys and sufferings for the past eight months.

The darkness gave me the shivers. As my eyes adjusted, the light of the flickering flashlights that allowed me to see large groups of heavily armed guards. There was a jumble of voices and orders, people were running back and forth, rifles knocking against one another and then the jangling sound of shackles. A flashlight beamed straight into my face. Someone ordered me to drop my belongings and a guard cuffed my hands. This was the first time my hands were cuffed behind my back. I felt dizzy and thought I might vomit.

When first stepping into the yard, I thought I would just be changing rooms. But as I saw the confusion of other prisoners I guessed that more was involved. I closed my eyes and quietly bowed my head, praying for my cellmates.

Immediately, a guard with a rifle marched me towards the large yard in the middle of camp, now dotted with people. I glimpsed at some others, their hands were also cuffed behind their backs. We were made to form groups and our shackles were removed. Some of these men had also been involved in the

SÔNG HƯƠNG ship incident. Others had been leaders in camp protests, and others again had been beating the *'Antennae'* over the past months. There were twenty of us. We were ordered on to a truck and then again cuffed, this time in pairs. The guards told us the rules for the journey. It was about 11.00 p.m. when we began to move. Someone spontaneously began singing the popular Christmas carol "Holy Night in Bethlehem". Immediately, we all joined in. I had sung this song many times before, but never with such emotion. It made this a memorable Christmas.

Meanwhile, our truck laboured heavily along a pot-holed road. By the time the carol ended, we were some distance from the Camp. We searched each other's faces for the reassurance and dependability needed in the days and months to follow.

Considering whom my companions were, I had a premonition that we were going to a much more frightening place than the *Nam Hà* Camp we had left behind.

Chapter 9
The 'Gateway to Heaven' Camp

The old and rickety bus carrying prisoners crawled slowly like an old buffalo with a heavy load plodding uphill. Each time the driver stamped his foot on the gas pedal, black smoke sputtered out from the back of the vehicle. The road was hilly and winding like a snake. The slopes were steep. Looking down you could see what appeared to be bottomless pits. The road was appalling and threatening. If the driver made a mistake, that would be the last one!

I really didn't know where this moribund bus would take twenty of us to. The higher it went the more shrieks it exhaled. It cried for compassion. The frame of the bus was pock-marked in various places and in some places paint had also been stripped off as well. There were some parts where screws and bolts had fallen off or turned loose, which resulted in a mixture of bangs when the bus struck potholes along the roads. Occasionally, I feared that the bus might break into pieces while climbing uphill, which would be a terrific disaster for all of us.

The driver only stopped for the prisoners to go to the toilet, and for the bus to take in some water. While travelling in the bus, we were handcuffed two by two so that we could not run away easily. Therefore, when one person had to answer the nature's call; the other person had to witness the unavoidable incident. If you had no partner, you would be handcuffed to the seat, in case you got off the bus, you would be handcuffed to a guard. During this whole time, my mind was constantly tormented by the question of where they were taking us to, and what would be waiting for us when we arrived at our destination.

I had no answers to these questions, so I stopped worrying. In life, what is meant to be will be… After one day and one night of traversing through forests and mountains, the bus finally stopped in a grey and primitive courtyard of a strange and remote camp. It was possibly past midnight, or in the early hours of December 27, 1977. It was bitterly cold. The cold was like sharp blades going through your flesh.

Peering through the darkness, I saw five or six guards, all wearing heavy coats and gloves. The helmets that covered their ears were strapped beneath their chins. Each held a flashlight and a notebook. Immediately, our group from *Nam Hà* Camp was ordered out of the bus, which we did very clumsily because we had been sitting so long and were still encumbered by handcuffs.

Such cold! While still sitting in the bus, I realised, from the guards' clothing and steaming breath, that it would be cold outside; so, I'd wrapped a scarf around my neck. Then, with my one free hand, I'd fastened my collar. This still left my head exposed, and my feet were bare except for the sandals given to us at *Nam Hà*, where the temperature seldom dropped below 8 degrees Celsius. As I stepped down from the bus, I felt as though I'd been hit in the head. This was extreme cold, greater than any I'd ever experienced, so intense that my poor clothing was useless and I might as well have been naked. I tried to open my mouth to say a few words to my cuffed partner but my jaw locked and no sound came out. Then my knees stiffened so that I couldn't move. Every cell in my body seemed to be affected. I had heard of lethal cold, but had thought it was poetic license. Now, I knew what an apt description that was.

In the past twenty-four hours, we had travelled between tall rock faces and dizzyingly deep valleys. Inside the bus, surrounded by twenty prisoners and five guards, I'd felt quite warm and had taken off my cotton sweatshirt, except for the sleeve that was trapped to my arm by the handcuff. Fortunately, as we climbed to higher altitudes, I'd carefully pulled it back over my head. Now, I wanted to put on the rest of my clothing but it was all bagged up together with the others'.

I didn't know where the next camp was; only that it was far in the North, a full day's drive from *Nam Hà*. The way the bus engine had growled through the darkness, needing frequent rests and top-ups of water to prevent it overheating, I knew we were on the way high in the mountains.

We were uncuffed and given our belongings right away before being locked into a nearby cell for what remained of the night. After only 15 minutes or so of standing outside, my face had become as stiff as a slab of ice. I had a splitting headache and both ears felt like crisp rice crackers. I feared that if someone were to flick one, it would break off. My legs were so stiff that I couldn't walk and two prisoners had to drag me into the cell. This was a small room with planks on the floor and a wooden ledge above. We all hurriedly wrapped ourselves in all the clothing we had.

I curled up as small as possible, but parts of my body were still exposed to the cold air. I fancied that the chill was a centipede with its sharp teeth, burrowing through the pores of my skin and into my blood. I wished that I had a thick padded jacket such as the guards were wearing. Everyone was too cold to sleep, despite the tiring journey. So, we drew close to one another, curling in like a litter of puppies.

In the morning we still felt fatigued, partly because of the energy spent resisting the terrible cold, and because we'd had only a few hours rest after the long bumpy ride. In the morning light, I could see that the cell was very dirty and the floorboards were cracked. There were two small barred windows to let in light. The lower sleeping platform was just fifty centimetres from the floor and the upper only a metre above that. This meant that anyone on the lower platform could only sit or crawl with care lest he bump his head on that above.

The 'Gateway to Heaven' Camp

When we woke, a dense fog obstructed much of our vision. We could see traces of a perimeter wall, with a gate leading to a yard, and the thatched roof of the mess hall. All the buildings were ugly and dirty, unlike those of *Nam Hà* Camp. We suspected that the sun was quite high.

Sometime later, we heard a noise outside. Startled, we looked out but didn't see anyone until suddenly a figure loomed through the fog. He looked in through the window while rubbing his hands together and jingling a large set of keys. We called out "Greetings, Officer."

To our surprise, he answered, "I'm not an officer. I'm a *Trật tự viên* (Prisoner enforcer)." His vaporising breath made him look like a smoker.

That was the first time I'd ever heard the term Prisoner enforcer *(Trật tự viên)*, since *Nam Hà* didn't have any. Now that we knew he was also a prisoner, we had confidence to ask questions.

"What camp is this? Where are we?"

Although this *Trật tự viên* wasn't very cheerful, he seemed willing to answer. "You all are in *Quyết Tiến* Camp, also known as *Cổng Trời* (Gateway to Heaven). It's in *Hà Tuyên* Province."

"And where is the location of *Hà Tuyên*?"

"It is very close to the Chinese border, just ten kilometres as the crow flies."

All twenty of us began a barrage of questions. He didn't know whom to answer first. I called out loudly, "So does this camp have Southern political prisoners?"

Before he had a chance to answer, a number of guards appeared and he went silent. I recognised one of them as Second Lieutenant *Lạc* from *Nam Hà* Camp, who had been responsible for escorting us to this Camp. The *Trật tự viên* unlocked the cell door; a guard stepped inside and ordered us to bring all of our "*Nội vụ*" into the yard for inspection. This happened at every camp transfer. We lugged our things into the yard. Again, it was colder than I expected. I shivered as I walked, and although I'd dressed in many more layers, with this kind of cold they made little difference.

The inspection began. According to camp regulations, any money and valuables had to be deposited into camp accounts. We could choose which of our clothing we wanted to keep and to deposit the rest. Any unregistered clothing would be stamped in tar with **CẢI TẠO** (Re-education) on the shirt backs and on trouser-legs. Some prisoners wanted to deposit some clothing in the hope of getting newer garments to wear when they would leave the Camp. But Officer *Lạc* whispered, "It's really cold here. Keep your clothes, you'll need them. There's no reason to deposit them." When the inspection and transfers were over, he came over to speak to us without the guard's notice. "*Nam Hà* is really a very comfortable camp, and you guys gave it away. I don't know what to say! Oh well, try to re-educate, and make sure you stay healthy."

I was moved by his words. I had now been in prison for two years, yet that was the first time I'd experienced a guard's humanity. I think he spoke this way because he knew this camp would probably cause our deaths.

That day, our group of twenty was split into two. Fourteen persons joined the labour group. I was among the six who went to the maximum-security Section.

The Maximum-Security Section

There were already some prisoners housed in this section. It was a long stone building that was poorly lit. Ten cells evenly flanked a narrow central walkway. Each cell, designed for two people, was three meters wide with a wooden platform on each side. There was a barred window at one end of the walkway with a toilet beside it. I shared mine with a young fellow, *Trần Phụng Tiên*, while four others occupied two nearby cells.

In the following days, we learned more about the Camp through conversations with prisoners in other cells and with the night soil carrier who daily emptied out toilet. *Quyết Tiến* Camp was located close to the Chinese border, in *Hà Tuyên* Province. This camp was nicknamed *Cổng Trời* (Gateway to Heaven) for two reasons. The first was obvious: We were 2,500 meters above sea level, the highest mountain peak in Vietnam. The second reason was because the conditions in this Camp were so severe that considered to 'Heaven's Departure Lounge'.

There were also some convicts whose death sentences had been reduced to life terms, and some with sentences ranging from fifteen to twenty years. No one sentenced to less than ten years was ever sent to the 'Gateway to Heaven'. Criminals still had a chance of being released after serving their sentences, but not many survived the harsh conditions. The majority left their bones there.

When we arrived, there were around three hundred and fifty convicts, almost forty Communism Resistance fighters, and five Southern prisoners selected from other camps. Subsequently, seven priests were among the number of prisoners arrived from other camps. We had a final count of forty-eight in the maximum security Section, and later on we came to call ourselves 'Group 48 *Quyết Tiến*'. It seemed we had been picked from different Northern camps for unofficial death sentences. None of us had ever been convicted in any court. We had no idea whether we were picked at random or according to some definite criteria.

We were locked in our cells all day and night in the maximum-security Section, fortunately not shackled like those in the Punishment Section. We suffered most from hunger and cold. We had arrived at 'Gateway to Heaven' in the middle of winter, and the winter anywhere in North Vietnam was something to be feared. But this camp was at such a high altitude that the cold was even more acute.

Our building had walls of stone that at night radiated their cold and turned the cell into a refrigerator. Even worse was the hunger. There was nothing here that was even temporarily filling. Hunger and cold together attempted to annihilate us. The hungrier the person was, the colder he became; and the colder he became, the hungrier he was.

We were fed twice a day, at mid-morning and evening. Each meal consisted of a chunk of toasted bread, about as wide as a wrist and a hand span long. Prisoners on the outside got breakfast as well because they did labouring. The modest ration of bread gave rise to the prison saying: '*You will be hungry if you don't eat; but you will be even hungrier after eating*'. And it was precisely like that. Mealtime stimulated my stomach so that it demanded more food, more food to fill the empty void, something that couldn't be done. After eating the morning meal, I could only lie in wait for the sounds of the *Trật tự viên* coming through the gate to bring us supper. I used to dream of eating…20 servings of bread at once!

Nowadays, I'm embarrassed that I thought so much about food. However, that was the reality at that time. After swallowing the piece of bread at 5.00 o'clock in the evening, I lay under my blanket in temperatures below freezing, waiting seventeen hours for another meal, I finally received something on which my stomach could get to work. During the long wait, I often lay motionless like a hibernating squirrel.

Appearance of a Stranger

One morning, when my cellmate, *Trần Phụng Tiên,* and I still lay under our blankets, we heard tapping on the window set into our cell door. Startled, I threw off the blankets and went to investigate. I found myself facing a short man wearing a baggy top, and a hat that covered most of his face, leaving only his small eyes so small that they looked like two flattened longan fruit seeds. We said, "Greetings Officer."

He nodded without a word, but then asked softly, "Which one's *Nguyễn Hữu Lễ?*"

I put up my hand. He stared at me silently before asking, "Have you had the toilet finished?"

We said we had and he walked away, leaving *Trần Phụng Tiên* and I wondering who he was. We made enquiries from the night-soil carrier. This convicted prisoner was our daily newspaper, providing all our camp news. In return, we gave him a share of our tobacco known in the camp as 'divine medicine'. He told us the man was Captain *Lãng*, the Camp Commander.

The next day I was called out 'To work'. A guard led me between frozen puddles and hoarfrost, then past beds of turnips as big as rice bowls. It was the first time in two weeks that I had left the cell. Exposed to the outside air in inadequate clothing, my face and limbs soon became numb. I was taken to the office of Captain *Lãng*, who was indeed the Camp Commander. Without his hat on, I could see him more clearly. He looked to be late middle-aged and was so short as to seem stunted, about 1.50 meters tall. He had a long face, wrinkled skin and small eyes that again reminded me of polished black beans. He didn't fit my picture of a Camp Commander.

Greeting me with a smile, he invited me to sit down and have a cup of tea. At this point, my arms and legs were frozen stiff, not obeying my orders anymore. I wanted to warm myself up with the tea but my shaking hands couldn't pick up the cup. My teeth chattered so much I couldn't carry on a conversation, even with one hand holding my chin to stop the chattering. Seeing this, he let me sit quietly in the comparatively warm room for some minutes.

Stammering, I at last managed to ask him for a cigarette to warm myself up. Even then it was half an hour before I became able to speak at ease. Then he asked, "*Anh Lễ*, what did you do at *Nam Hà* to be transferred here?"

"Reporting to you, Officer, I don't know. I am sure you must have read my file."

"Of course I did. I see you're a very intelligent and brave man; so I want to help you. You are a priest. That's not much good to you at the moment, but you can't do much about the times religion is now passé. It would be better to promise me to leave the religious path, take a wife, and start a family like other people. I promise to support and promote you."

Before he could go on, I said, "I thank you for your kind intentions, Sir, but you can't possibly understand how I feel about my religion. If you had any other concerns, I'd be happy to address them. But the priesthood is the life I have chosen. I wish to be excused from this discussion."

From that day on, I wasn't called 'To work' anymore.

Each morning, we'd be woken by the sound of the *'Kleng'* calling the ordinary prisoners to labour in the fields. It was one of the few sounds we'd hear in this cold and deserted place. Every day, we did exercises in our cell to keep our blood circulating and to get warm. Then we would cover ourselves with all our pitifully thin blankets. With no distractions, the two of us soon exhausted all topics of conversation. Occasionally, we called out to the inmates in the other cells, especially asking any newcomers for news.

We were always hungry for news, but anything we heard related only to the Camp. We were often bored. One day, I ran my hand under the planks that formed my bunk and felt an indentation. Former prisoners had carved their names and dates underneath the platform. I recognised the name of Father *Nguyễn Văn Vinh*, who'd been the Dean of the Cathedral in Hanoi. I later heard that all those who'd left their names here had died in this Camp and were buried at *Đồi Bà Then* (*Bà Then* Cemetery Hill). There was a current saying in the Camp: '*Going to Đồi Bà Then*', that is, to die. After deciphering all the names, I said a prayer for their souls. Then I used the tip of a safety pin to carve my own name and the year 1977. I wondered if some other unfortunate person would later read my name, and I hoped he would pray for my soul as well.

I already felt that I had stepped into the land of the dead. The harshness of camp life and the severity of the weather would kill me sooner or later. I had literally come to the dead end of my life, with the grinding wheel of the proletarian dictatorship moving slowly but inexorably, crushing me and anyone else in its path. I couldn't see any way out. I let my memory rewind pictures of the ups and downs of the past 34 years of life…

The fateful day came on April 30, 1975. From that day, the Communists made their dominance fell all over Vietnam and everything was changed. For me, personally, that day was a decisive turning point in my life, the point that had led me to this '*Gateway to Heaven*'.

Terrible Food Poisoning

After a month in the maximum-security Section, I joined the rest of the group in the Collective Section named '*Khu O*' (Section O). This happened shortly before the *Tết* of 1978. Being with friends from *Nam Hà* again was great. In this Section, we worked in mixed teams, including political members and criminals, at woodworking tasks. The team leader, *Toàn*, was a Communist soldier who'd committed rape and received a sentence of 20 years that was reduced to less than 10 years. At this Camp, all the team leaders were criminals and had a great deal of power. Besides the abusive freedom to beat team members at his own discretion, the team leader also had a pair of handcuffs that he could use as he wished. **Placing political prisoners and those imprisoned because of their religious beliefs, under the power of murderers, thieves and rapists was a twisted and deliberate policy of the Communist Regime.** Luckily, *Toàn* treated us with considerable respect.

I still remember my first day with this team. It was nearing *Tết*, (Lunar New Year), some of our team members joined the kitchen staff to help prepare holiday food. Our workmates brought back the discarded ends of cassava (Yucca). We boiled and de-fibered them, keeping only the starchy part. Then, we worked them with a mortar and pestle into a fine paste, packed it into a bamboo pipe, then grilled it. The smell was as appealing as that of cinnamon-fried pork roll! That evening, we divided the delicious food with one another and enjoyed it. Those like me who came fresh from the maximum-security Section received bonus larger portions, a very filling meal after a month of hunger.

We all went to bed early because of the cold, hoping for a warm night's sleep with so many cellmates huddled together. Around midnight, I woke to a bad stomach-ache. This rapidly got worse. I did not want to disturb those who were asleep by getting out of bed, so I clenched my teeth and lay holding and rubbing my stomach. But the discomfort increased, making me nauseous. I knew I was soon going to spurt diarrhoea.

The pain became so bad that I thought I was dying. What should I do now? I threw off the covers and meant to head for the toilet, but collapsed on the floor. In doing so, I brought the mosquito netting down. My ears hummed and I felt dazed but I tried my hardest to crawl towards the toilet. At that point, I was surprised to see cellmates crawling like me. There were sounds of groaning and vomiting. "Everyone hang up your netting. We've got cassava food poisoning!" The Team leader yelled alarmingly. Those who could quickly obeyed. Some of the men on the upper level fell down on to the floor. The room was chaotic, with those relatively unaffected helping the serious cases.

There was only one toilet and dozens of us needed to use it simultaneously. We had no choice but to do our vomiting and defecating on the spot. After vomiting onto the floor and defecating in my pants, I was too exhausted to get up. I could only lurch over to lay face-up on the floor, not really caring where I was. That night, over two thirds of the prisoners in our cell suffered from cassava food poisoning. The room stank unimaginably with vomit and human waste everywhere, including the bedding.

This was the first time I'd suffered poisoning from cassava. I had never even heard of it in the South. There were two types of cassava, industrial and regular consumption. Industrial type contains cyanide substance; they were used mainly in products such as starch. Before consumption, however, it must be properly prepared by peeling off the outer layer and soaked in water for 24 hours before cooking. The industrial type was easier to grow, harvesting was plentiful also. Hence, this type of cassava was given to prisoners. We were fighting with hunger, and ate the cassava without the proper preparation. This was our biggest misstep.

Next morning, those of us affected by food poisoning got a break from labour. I made my way out to the well to launder my clothes and wash myself down, my first bath after being at this camp for a month.

Coffin Maker

Our labour team was divided into two groups, one to split the logs and the other to do the actual woodworking. At first, I was in the woodworking group with *Nguyễn Huy Khoan*, a Catholic, as leader. He was kind, soft-spoken, worked well with others. But after a few days *Khoan* saw that I didn't know anything about carpentry, so he transferred me to the relatively unskilled task of making coffins.

I don't know how coffins in the outside world are made, but ours were very simple. We would collect the unwanted cracked or broken planks from the sawing-splitting team, sort them into appropriate sizes, and then nail them together into a rectangular box. This did not have to be well made just so long as the corpse of the dead prisoner didn't fall out. Any opening that was too big we patched up with more wood to prevent the hand of the deceased sticking out. In the end, it was all going to be buried anyway, so we did not bother with unimportant coffin-making details.

I was very glad to work in this team because it did not take many skills, and furthermore, I got to perform the last service for my prison brothers. At first, I thought it would be an easy job, but I was mistaken. At times, we had so many to be buried that we worked until steam shot out of our ears. Even then we often couldn't cope with the Camp's needs in the high season! Sometimes, we had to wait for the sawing team to provide us with wood. Many criminals had become walking skeletons but they still had to work. The skeletons that I saw moving around one day often became our 'customer' on the next.

After we had enclosed the bodies in coffins, a four-person team of criminals was in charge of digging their graves, a task that they jealously guarded. They were tall and healthy guys, different from our group of frail and ghastly prisoners. Before digging a grave, each gravedigger was fed a ration of scorched rice normally reserved for the Camp's pigs. After lowering a coffin into grave, they received a hard-boiled egg and a bowl of rice. This meal was put right on the top of the coffin.

I could never figure out the reason for this custom but perhaps it was to prevent any pangs of conscience of the administrators. While living, the prisoners were not fed, so they received an offering of rice and a hardboiled egg after death, as if to say, "Don't be angry, we're granting you a favour now." Because burying someone meant receiving extra food, these gravediggers often patrolled the infirmary, kicking anyone who wasn't moving and saying "Hurry up and die soon you can do us a favour instead of lying here groaning."

My Sworn Brother

During my time with the woodworking crew, I was befriended by *Đặng Văn Tiếp* and we made an oath to be fraternal brothers for life however long that might be. We had met each other a couple of times in *Vĩnh Long* and Saigon while supporting the anti-corruption movement in 1974. He was also in the woodworking team and was a skilful handyman, producing beautiful furniture. To create a workplace he claimed the table in the far corner where he could get some privacy and peace. Occasionally, I would come over for a smoke or a talk.

Once, I remarked, "Who'd have thought a high-ranking Air Force Officer, a lawyer and Member of Parliament could also know how to use a saw and make furniture! I admire you so much!"

Đặng Văn Tiếp gave me a toothy grin. "I am practicing and someday I will make a henhouse for my wife, if she still pities me and feeds me two meals a day!"

I teased back, "So if I don't get some professional skills, I'll go home and starve?"

He gestured towards my half-built coffin, "You've got some coffin-building skills, dude! What more do you want?"

"Yeah, sure, so ghouls can employ me for my unskilled coffin crafting."

"If you're ever unemployed, you can be a helper in my henhouse factory!"

Our fun and cheerful banter helped us forget for a short time the misery of prison, especially of our hunger and cold. *Tiếp* was an optimistic fellow with a strong sense of humour and enjoyed socialising with different people. But he was careful to hide his private thoughts, especially regarding any plans for escape, sharing these only with me, his confidant. We had to be wary of all the unfriendly eyes and ears around us.

The terrible cold in the mountains so close to the Chinese border had the greatest power to kill. When we arrived at *Quyết Tiến* Camp, we were given a cotton jacket. Before putting on that final layer, I'd wrap myself with strips of cloth like a meat roll. I wore this day and night throughout the winter months. None of us was keen to strip off to wash all over, although there was a well behind the building. In cases when we did have to wash, we would quickly wipe ourselves down with wet rags.

The Lice 'Convention'!

A young fellow *Ngô Đình Thiện* had been with us at *Nam Hà*. He was a little over 20 years old. At *Nam Hà*, he made himself a warm, long-sleeved coat from a Chinese blanket. He wore it underneath other lay of clothes, on the outside he used a rope to tie it close to his torso like a rolled of pork loin. When he was in the cell next to mine in the maximum-security Section, I would often hear about his itchy rash that caused him day and night. He wanted to go for a medical check-up for his supposed allergy of food which caused itching, but while he was in security, this wasn't possible. One could only go to the infirmary for serious illnesses, and trivial cases such as his had to be overcome.

After joining the woodworking team, he was able to seek treatment at the infirmary. Around that time, we were often fed corn and cabbage with fermented shrimp paste. *Thiện* requested his meal without the salty paste, thinking it might be the cause of the rash. But this didn't seem to make any difference. So *Thiện* carried a bamboo stick to tuck under his clothing and scratch his itches. But he seemed to grow paler and greener, thinning faster than many of us.

On the Lunar New Year's Eve of 1978, it was unusually warm and sunny. I thought this was a sign of God's protection, giving us the chance to wash thoroughly and do our laundry to welcome *Tết*. Our team spent the morning sweeping and cleaning up our workshop. Then, we heated water for washing. In the weak winter sunshine, everyone removed almost all his clothes, revealing skinny, bamboo-green bodies.

When *Thiện* took off the woollen blanket he'd been wearing for the past few months, the inside of this garment revealed a thick layer of lice, more than anyone could count. They were as round as sesame seeds and translucent, each showing a black chunk of swallowed blood. The lice scattered all over the ground.

Although in prison we'd witnessed many cases of dirt, this was the first of its kind. When *Thiện* used a bamboo stick to scrape them out onto a piece of paper, they made a package the size of a soupspoon. For those past few months, this massive number of lice had taken turns sucking his blood. This had been the cause of his itching! He quickly soaked the garment in boiling water and more critters floated on the water's surface, like tiny duckweed blossoms in a carp pond!

Although we all suffered from the cold, this was much worse for the prisoners in the Punishment Section. One of our young cellmates was named *Phó Cẩn*. He was caught stealing a lock, and was taken to the stone punishment building to be leg-shackled. Here, each prisoner was allowed just one set of clothing, one thin blanket, and one mat to lie on the stone floor. Since this building was fairly close to ours, we would hear them howling like wolves from cold at night, until they slept from exhaustion. It was amazing that anyone could survive.

About two weeks later, I came back from work to our cell to see a new addition to our group. The new mate seemed old, perhaps over 50, and was busily washing his clothes at the well. I noticed that he already seemed part of the group and was talking to the others. Only after I got a closer look did I realise it was *Phó Cẩn*, returned from Punishment Section! He had been there for only two weeks, but that had been enough to change him almost out of recognition.

During this time a group of us was planning to escape to China. A few prisoners from this Camp had managed to escape and had broadcast their success on the radio. This made us determined to do so as well. Five of us prepared a plan. On the selected Sunday afternoon, we made a pot of sweetened soup to give us strength for the night's action. But before we could drink it, a *'Kleng'* sounded. Guards came in and called out the names of those who were to move to different cells. Our group was broken up, so our plan had to be scrapped. Had the authorities guessed our intentions? Or was it just a routine procedure? I don't know. But this was the second time my preparations had come to nothing, the second coincidence of its kind. The first one was the out-of-season storm on the ocean liner *SÔNG HƯƠNG* I had mentioned in Chapter 7.

Under the Yoke of Criminal

I was transferred to the gardening team. The *Quyết Tiến* region was very suitable for growing cabbage and the Camp provided enough cabbages for the entire Province of *Hà Tuyên*. The heaviest labour involved carrying the night soil to fertilise the plants. My Group Leader was *Cường*, nick named *Cường Béo* (*Chubby Cường*), a criminal who liked to show his authority by strutting around pompously, followed by two of his body guards. He was known as 'The General'. He'd been a Northern soldier and had plotted to steal military trucks. For this, he'd received a 20-year sentence. During our time at the Camp he had only 10 years left. He ruled those under him mercilessly, and they had no redress. But *Cường* never insulted any of us, political prisoners.

On the other hand, Team leader *Phùng* known as 'Mad *Phùng*' was really cruel. He was a convicted murderer and had a death sentence, later reduced to a life term, then to 18 years. He demanded Father *Cao Đức Thuận's* gold cross worn around his neck, but Father refused doing so. For this reason, he allocated the old priest to the heaviest labour involved carrying the night soil to fertilise the plants. *Phùng* waited for him to reach his destination, and kicked his container over, saying it was only partially filled and he'd have to do it again!

One night during a cell meeting, *Phùng* insulted Father *Cao Đức Thuận*, who had accidentally stepped on his sandals that was left in the walkway. Father *Cao Đức Thuận* defended himself by saying, "It's crowded, and you leave your sandals in the way, of course, we'll end up stepping on them at times."

The guy went nuts. He wanted to get back at Father *Thuận* for not giving him his gold cross. So he yelled, "F*ck you! What are your eyes for, huh?"

While he continued his insults, the old priest sat with his head down on his knees.

Phùng demanded, "You f*cking dead old man! Lift your head up! You don't sit like that during a meeting!"

Father *Thuận* stubbornly replied, "What right do you have to tell me not to put my head down?"

Then *Phùng* got really mad and leaped at him. Instantly, I got up and jumped between them, my fists clenched. Other political prisoners from *Nam*

Hà followed my example. He immediately understood the situation and sat down, continuing to mutter insults.

After only a few days with the gardening team, I was ordered to stay back and write reports of my personal background. There were three others with me and we didn't have the complicated procedures of the confessions at *Nam Hà* the previous year. But we still wrote under the supervision of an education officer.

During this time we began to hear news about Vietnam going to war with China. The Vietnam Government's attitude towards China became more insulting every day. During political lectures, the guards spoke about the Chinese imperialist dream of expansion. Many rumours circulated throughout the camp about an impending war. If such a conflict actually happened, we would be affected first because of our proximity to the border only 10 kilometres as the crow flies, and on clear days we could see the Chinese mountain ranges. We were alternately fearful of our country being invaded, and happy that somehow we might be released. I decided to let God guide our fate.

By July 1978, the Vietnamese-Chinese border situation had become extremely tense. We sometimes saw warplanes circling above the Camp. Occasionally, we'd hear cannon fire. When those who worked outside the Camp returned, they told us that the noise was from Chinese military exercises.

On Sundays, we were made to dig a trench, two meters wide and one and half meters deep. One guard explained that the trench was to prevent civilian livestock from destroying the camp's vegetables. Another said it was for defence when the Chinese Army penetrated the border. Deep down, I thought, perhaps, there was another reason. It wasn't judicious to speak about it, as it would have spread panic, but the idea that it was for our own burial always haunted me.

The Day of Grace!

The 2nd of August 1978 was a significant landmark of my life in prison. Early that afternoon a *'Kleng'* gathered us for an unscheduled meeting. We glanced at one another, wondering what was happening. Then, Commander *Lãng*, announced that, in order to create a more convenient environment for re-education, the Interior Department had decided to relocate prisoners to new location. All four hundred prisoners instantaneously leaped off their feet, they all jumped up with joy, shouted and applauded, patting shoulders and shaking hands with their friends. From outside, they looked like a group of four hundred epileptic patients. I sat frozen in joy, saying to myself, "Thanks be to God!"

It was a long time before the guards could restore order. We weren't interested in hearing anything else enough to know that we were getting away from the 'Gateway to Heaven'. When Captain *Lãng* instructed us about the details of our transfer, I didn't pay much attention. In the past three years, I'd switched camps six times and I knew what had to be done. That evening, when the Education Officer collected the dissertations, I told him that I was not finished. He said it didn't have to be submitted.

That last night at the 'Gateway to Heaven', I forgot all my anxieties. Even more strangely, I felt that I was no longer imprisoned. If *Quyết Tiến* Camp had been the synonym for the Land of the Dead, now it would be just another factor in my memory. It had helped me cope with the harshness of nature, the sight of prisoners abusing prisoners, and the shadow of the Master of Death with its black-cloaked, fleshless bones, sickle in hand, approaching step by step.

The next day was warm and sunny, a rare occurrence for this region. Perhaps, Mother Nature felt guilty for our maltreatment in the past eight months. Today, she extended a parting gift to make amends. We didn't mind being handcuffed as we sat packed into the truck. When we began the slow descent from the mountaintop, I looked at clouds draped midway on the mountain, perhaps a thousand meters below. It was an extraordinarily beautiful sight.

I had a new appreciation of the title 'Gateway to Heaven'.

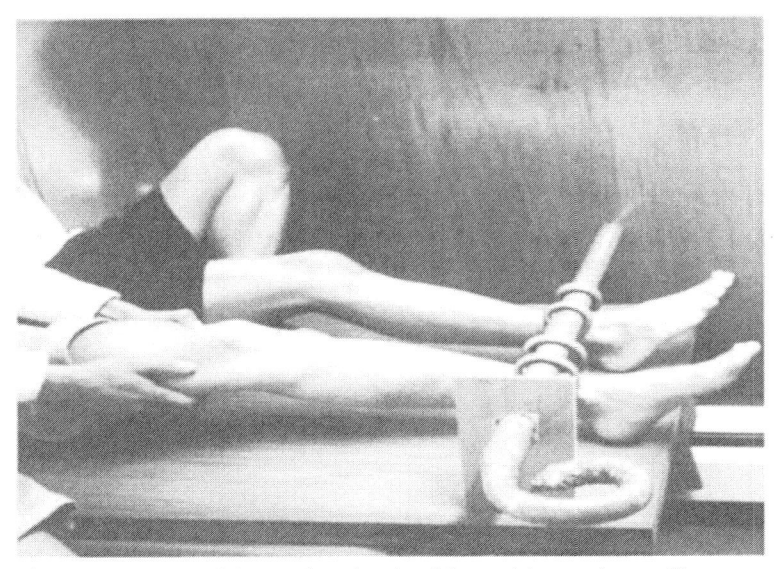

Re-enactment of the author in shackles with another cellmate in Thanh Cẩm prison camp (1979-1982)

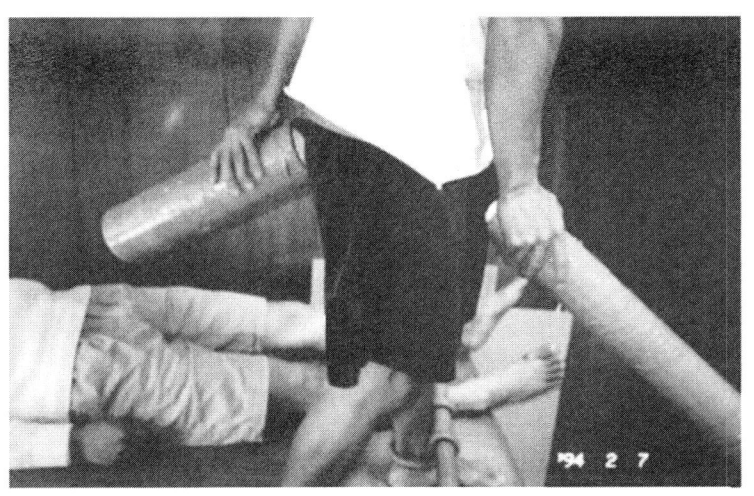

Re-enactment using "bamboo" toilet while standing on the platform

Author (second from left) met Bùi Đình Thi (third from left) in California, 1996

Among Buddhist leaders

Reunion with former inmates

Book signing in San Jose, USA

Book Signing, Germany

Author in Washington, D.C.

Author in Holland

Reunion with English teacher from 1958, Mr Nguyễn Đức Hạnh in Santa Anna

Author on Ordination Day

Book signing in Canada

Author (seat, first from left) with the former President of VN – General Nguyễn Khánh (seated in the middle), in San Francisco

Author offered Mass in Thai Refugee Camp

Author in New Zealand, 2020

Author arrived in New Zealand June 1990

Bishop Brown (right) and author in Auckland 1992

Father Phạm Quý Hòa (left) with Author in New Zealand

Mr Nguyễn Văn Bảy (right) also known as Bảy Chà with author in USA

Mr Nguyễn Văn Lợi (right) with author in Lourdes France

Reunion with Thanh Cầm inmates in California - author middle row first right

Chapter 10
From Bad to Worse

Our group of 48 political prisoners, included fifteen priests, automatically considered to be dangerous rebels, assembled in 'Gateway to Heaven' Camp. Now that China was preparing to attack the Northern border, we were all being moved further to the South. As a result, some of us were able to survive after years in prison.

We made an overnight stop at *Văn Hòa* Camp outside Hanoi. Next morning, after a light breakfast of cassava, we continued on to next Camp. Late in the evening of August 4, 1978, we arrived at *Thanh Cẩm* Camp in teeming rain. No one knew what lay ahead, but we cheerfully told one another, "Any other place will be better than 'Gateway to Heaven'."

Thanh Cẩm Camp was located in an isolated mountainous area about thirty kilometres from the Laotian border in the southern-most province of North Vietnam. It was four hundred meters above sea level, with the large *Mã* River snaking around it. Only one road provided any access. Some scattered villages belonging to the minority *H'mong* ethnic group were just a few kilometres away from Camp, but these people were antagonistic to other Vietnamese. Upon arriving, we encountered the middle-aged officer on duty. He was drunk, tripping over his own feet, waving a cane over his head and creating a noisy racket. Clearly, he wanted to ruffle us.

He was dressed in knee-high gumboots, with filthy khaki pants rolled up to his thighs. Frantically scurrying around him like puppets were two *Trật tự viên* (Prisoner enforcer). The older of these two worked quietly. The younger had a slight leg disability, but his healthy glowing skin contrasted with our own pale, sickly complexions. He tried to act cool, flexing his muscles, shouting orders, his fingers pointing wildly at every direction but he never looked any of us in the eye.

My friend *Nguyễn Sỹ Thuyên* was exhausted. He threw his bag and dirty blankets on to the floor and lay back on them. I was also very tired and sat beside him. After a moment, *Thuyên* nudged me, signalling with his eyes towards the drunken officer. He said quietly into my ear, "That bastard looks like he was dragged up from the sewer!" Before I had a chance to nod along with my agreement, there was a shout from behind, "You two! You're not organising your '*nội vụ*'! What are you doing sitting here chatting? Get on with it." It was the young one whom I'd been wary of from the beginning. I walked away because I knew it was not the time to show my true feelings.

The Hell on Earth

*Thanh Cẩm C*amp was under the authority of a Supervisory Board composed of the Commandant, his deputy and several committees that looked after specialised services like education, security, documents, finance, and provisions. We, prisoners were classified in groups; each headed by a group leader and supervised by a Communist guard or *Cán bộ*, appointed by the Supervisory Board. Every time prisoners left the camp to do outside work, they had to be escorted by two armed guards who took turns on patrol to prevent anyone from escaping.

A number of prisoners considered to be trustworthy were appointed to work in security, health, or education. To be such a *Trật tự viên* (Prisoner enforcer) one had to be physically strong and trusted by the Communist guards. It was tacitly understood that such prisoners were iron fists, enforcers of the security apparatus in the Camp. The *Trật tự viên* in the security Section was very powerful, having the most authorities after the guards. Their duties included accompanying the guard when he checked the nightly locking of prisoners' shackles and unlocking them in the morning, and delivering rations every noon and evening. However, he often did this on his own. Some of these trusted men had become *Trật tự viên* through bribes. Once, they'd attained that position, they didn't have to do hard labour and enjoyed more freedom than the rest of us.

On our second evening, six people from 'Group 48 *Quyết Tiến*' were taken to the maximum-security Section or the Flat House. This was a square building with solid brick walls and a flat concrete roof, hence its name. There were four cells, each with two unglazed windows with thick iron bars, and a concrete sleeping platform about a metre off the floor. A walkway led from the iron door to the toilet. Each cell accommodated five to seven people, crowded in like canned sardines. At night, there was usually one person sleeping on the walkway floor because the bunk was too crowded. This section housed prisoners seen as dangerous and needing to be separated from others.

Although not shackled, we were locked in the cell day and night. We were allowed into the building's central courtyard twice a day for fifteen minutes to receive food and water and use the toilets. Non-security prisoners could bathe and do their laundry once a week in the *Mã* River outside the prison's gate. We had to bathe while being watched by an armed guard if the guards were busy or couldn't be bothered, we could do this only every fortnight or even monthly.

The on-duty guard whom we encountered upon arrival was Captain *Phú*. (Old *Phú*). He was a drunkard and dog meat lover. He was drunk, morning, noon, and night and his face was the colour of a red berry.

Two Prisoner Enforcers

Our *Trật tự viên* was named *Phạm Đình Thăng*. He always looked fierce but was actually fairly reasonable. Although not a Catholic, he showed respect to us, priests. He often helped us with little things, such as giving us a light for our tobacco pipes, or delivering things to other cells.

The younger *Trương Văn Phát*, was part Chinese. He had been a shoemaker and was caught trying to escape from Vietnam. As assistant to *Phạm Đình Thăng,* he was truly evil. I don't know how he behaved with the ordinary prisoners, but every time he came to the Flat House he was very rude, always over reacting. He liked to shout non-stop, "You guys, watch yourselves!"

It was most unusual to have an assistant to *Trật tự viên*. There was a rumour that *Trương Văn Phát* had bribed Old *Phú*. Earlier, *Phát* had had a rich friend who was afraid to hide his cash in case it was found and confiscated, so gave half his money to *Phát* to keep for him. Unexpectedly, they were placed in different camps. *Phát* decided he owned the money entrusted to him. At *Thanh Cẩm*, *Phát* gradually used this money to buy alcohol and dog meat for Old *Phú*. In return, Old *Phú* made him assistant to *Trật tự viên*. To express our contempt for *Phát*, we surreptitiously called him the 'Dog entrée'.

One month later, the camp received three hundred more prisoners, former soldiers of the Saigon regime. A few times while bathing in the river, I recognised old friends. But we dared not say a word, greeting one another with our eyes only. Because I was classified as dangerous, I was prohibited from associating with ordinary prisoners.

A few months after our arrival, *Phạm Đình Thăng* was released. *Trương Văn Phát* temporarily became the boss. He seemed nervous, partly from his youthful inexperience, and partly because the younger prisoners mocked him. The harder he tried to demonstrate his authority, the more he was ridiculed. He became especially autocratic in dealing with prisoners in the maximum-security Section. We didn't like it, but put up with it because we knew he could oppress us in more serious ways, such as not opening our door in time for meals, or not serving us our already meagre cassava portions. Officially we were granted nine kilograms per month, and eating less than that could make us dangerously weak. Knowing our Achilles' heel, he pressed on it even more.

The twice-daily fifteen-minute intervals outside our cells were greatly appreciated. Although each room had a toilet, its door was kept locked in our early days. Instead, we had to urinate into hollowed-out bamboo segments that stood on end in the cell corners. We took turns dumping the contents into the pit by the Black House, the old Punishment Section. At these times, some took the opportunity to quickly scan the guards. If they weren't paying attention, it was possible to wave to friends in the Black House, or quickly hand in a few beads of tobacco. But *Phát* didn't let us enjoy these few minutes. He hurried us back inside, sometimes before our fifteen minutes were up.

One afternoon, it was my turn to dump the pipes. Because they were so full, the contents spilled onto my hands. While I was looking for water to wash them, *Phát* told me to get back in the cell. I pretended not to hear.

He came towards me and yelled, eyes flashing, "I said to get back in the cell! Are you deaf?"

Knowing this guy wanted to stir up trouble, I answered briefly, "I have sh*t on my hands so I have to find water to wash them, see?"

"So wash them in the cell."

I asked, "Where do I get water to wash in the cell?"

He became angry. "Wash with your drinking water!"

"What will I drink?"

Trương Văn Phát stared at me without a word. I went to the water tank by the Black House to get water can to draw water and wash my hands.

Angrily, he said, "You watch yourself! Don't be thinking that nobody will harm you because you're the 'priestly brood'."

The phrase, "A bunch of the priestly brood" was the odd way the Communist guards addressed the Catholic priest prisoners. I silently walked back to the cell, feeling *Phát's* fiery eyes piercing my back.

We referred to ourselves as pigs in a pen, and it was a fitting comparison. All day we sat in the cramped room. We'd talk for a while, but soon ran out of things to talk about. To pass the time, we'd draw squares on pieces of paper for chess, or make dominoes or cards for poker, which we played over and over to pass time between our two meals.

The Education Officer told us that, the entire country has encountered difficulties. Our people have to overcome the consequences left over from the puppets of those Americans!

Depending on the season, our diet consisted of corn, yams, or cassava. Sometimes, we ate nothing but cassava for a month. With churning stomachs, we had no choice but to eat it. What else would keep us alive?

The Main Character

One afternoon in October 1978, a heavy shower left pools of water around the maximum-security Section. In this mountainous area, torrential rain and storms were common. Sometimes, there was hail as big as a man's fist, which the Communist called the 'sky enemy'. After the shower cleared, we sat looking out the window and talking idly when we heard the sound of keys turning in the lock of the fence gate.

Soon, I saw a prisoner carrying a hoe enter the yard. His face was new to me. Our group immediately speculated that perhaps he was the new *Trật tự viên* because no ordinary prisoners were allowed to come into this area. Besides, we knew someone would have to fill *Phạm Đình Thăng's* vacancy. The change of *Trật tự viên* would have a large impact on our lives; so, all six of us pushed our faces against the iron bars to observe him.

The stranger seemed to be in his early forties and strongly built. He ignored us and began to hoe the earth, skilfully digging a drain to clear the puddles outside our building. Whenever he faced our room, I observed him closely. His face was bony with piercing eyes, but the most remarkable feature was his mouth. It seemed to me that his lips were not completely formed because his upper and lower lips did not close together. They looked like two pieces of red meat, always wet with saliva. Sometimes, I saw him move his tongue, licking the white saliva spots that gathered at the edges of his mouth. But I thought it wasn't just his face that made him look different from either *Thăng* or *Phát*.

He was concentrating on his rhythmical hoeing, not paying any attention to the six people just a metre away. Even when he stopped to rest, he didn't look directly at us.

From inside, we tried to show our friendliness by chatting with him but he didn't respond. Eventually, after we'd fired many questions at him, he had no choice but to answer. He told us that he'd been transferred here recently from *Yên Bái* Camp in the far North of Vietnam, and was recently made *Trật tự viên*, taking the place of the out-going *Phạm Đình Thăng*. He was a Catholic from *Hố Nai,* South Vietnam, his family originating from *Hải Phòng* Diocese in the North.

Hearing mention of *Hải Phòng*, Father *Chu Văn Oanh*, an elderly priest sharing my cell, was very pleased. "Really? You're from the *Hải Phòng* Diocese? So am I! Do you know any priests from *Hải Phòng* Diocese?"

"Father *Bình*."

Father *Oanh* was delighted. "Father *Bình* is a good friend of mine, we two were very close!"

After a short silence he admitted, Father *Bình* is my uncle.

"Oh my Goodness!" Father *Oanh* acclaimed.

"That is very lucky. I can't believe I've met the nephew of Father *Bình*. If you ever write to him, do tell him I am Father *Oanh*. Send him my best regards! Eh…eh…What is your name anyway?"

"*Thi!*"

"Your full name?"

He hesitated, seemingly uncomfortable at this old priest's obvious attempt to make a claim on his friendship. However, he finally answered "My name is **Bùi Đình Thi**." (Hereinafter BDT.)

I was ashamed of Father *Oanh*, but also quietly excited that we now had a *Trật tự viên* whose uncle was a priest, and a close friend of Father *Oanh*. Surely, our lives would be better. Father *Oanh* continued to question him but BDT. went to hoe elsewhere.

We immediately called over to the men in the other cells to tell our news. They also thought that from now on we would be more comfortable. Over the last few months, *Phát* had been our only *Trật tự viên* and had caused us quite a lot of trouble. Father *Oanh* laughed and chanted non-stop, "He's a Catholic! We'll win this time! We'll win this time!"

I sat with my back against the wall, feeling guilty about being so prejudiced against the new man just because of his eyes and the shape of his mouth, which he couldn't help. He might be a good guy. He came from an area where the people had a reputation for prayerfulness.

We remained happy until late that afternoon, when the door was opened as usual for us to collect our food and to do our usual jobs. Father *Oanh*, being quite old, had no chores, so he did some stretching exercises. Then he moved to where *Bùi Đình Thi* was distributing food on his first time on duty. Father chattered while BDT. continued his task. Suddenly, we heard BDT. yell loudly **"Get back into your cell, you garrulous old man! And shut up!"**

Father *Oanh* was too shocked to reply to this sudden outburst. Stunned, his mouth hanging open with astonishment, the aged priest shuffled disconsolately back inside. I cannot forget his humiliated expression. Any previous hope we'd had of better conditions disappeared. It was a sombre meal that evening and seeing Father *Oanh* sitting quietly in the corner, I felt sorry for him, and for us as well! My first impression of BDT. had been correct, although I would have preferred to be wrong.

Some days later, we were told by a couple of fellow prisoners that *Bùi Đình Thi* had been like an evil genius while he was 'Prisoner enforcer' (*Trật tự viên*) at the previous camp. Some said he had once declared quite openly, "*I won't have any hesitation in stepping on your corpse for the happiness of my wife and my children.*" Whether he actually did say such a thing, I don't know, but his subsequent behaviour towards us made me think that the story was probably correct.

He became more callous, wanting to prove himself a faithful servant who would do anything for the Communist regime so that he would receive an early release. And the best way to do this was to betray his fellow prisoners. All prisoners, but especially those of us in the maximum-security Section, had to pay a high price for the efforts of the two *Trật tự viên*. They often tried to outdo each other in order to ingratiate themselves, a competition which caused many problems for us.

Taking Side

At the beginning of 1979, we were still not allowed to communicate with our families, something that made our lives very hard in both material and spiritual terms. Because we could not receive gifts of food from them to supplement our meagre rations, we suffered prolonged hunger. Every night by nine o'clock, while the People's Army radio program blasted through the camp loud speaker, I found myself so exhausted that I couldn't sit up and had to lie flat. Next, both my vision and hearing blurred, I would feel feverish and then lose consciousness. Luckily, this lasted only a few seconds before my strength would return, and after sitting up for a while, my fever disappeared.

With the prolonged hunger, the hostile attitude of the guards and the attitudes of the *Trật tự viên*, we felt close to despair, not knowing what our future was going to be like. *Lâm Thành Văn*, a cellmate and friend of mine, had trouble sleeping. In the middle of the night, he and I often sat on the floor in the corner by the toilet, smoking our pipe tobacco. Every time *Lâm Thành Văn* would say sadly, "They're probably gonna keep us in prison until we die with rotten bones!" I will always remember his phrase, "*Die with rotten bones*".

Those of us from 'Group 48 *Quyết Tiến*' were sure the Communist rulers had already determined our fate. If not for the border war, we would have been left to waste away at 'Gateway to Heaven'. Political prisoners were never charged with an offence, but were said to be undergoing Concentration Re-education. Officially, they granted, amnesty, and release to anyone who re-educated well. But although guards always spoke of the Party's humane amnesty, we understood the lying propaganda all too well merely used to lull the gullible prisoners.

Everyone waited to go home. Most lived as passively as they could in the prison environment and left it to fate to take them anywhere it would. Some made efforts to 're-educate' well, or became '*Antennae*', even inventing stories to harm their fellow prisoners. A couple publicly stood on the side of the Communists in the expectation that they would be released early. Others thought about escaping. I was among that group. We realised that *Thanh Cẩm* was pretty much an island, surrounded by mountains with only one path out. To escape wouldn't be an easy task. It was difficult to cross the high mountains, and the local people would trace escapees and inform the police so as to be rewarded with rice or wine. The authorities told us that all who'd made a bid for freedom were caught and brought back. However, we had learned of a few who'd escaped, so it wasn't completely impossible. We knew that if caught, we would be beaten and tortured barbarously, but in our state of hardship I decided to accept all risks.

The 'Great' China!

In early 1979, the war between China and Vietnam peaked. The loud speaker broadcasted news every night. They found ways to insult the Chinese during these broadcasts, wrote offensive dramas and even lyrics to music. I was surprised at the Communist playwrights' ability to develop plays so quickly and skilfully. The old slogans, 'Great China', and 'mountains connected to mountains, rivers connected to rivers' used decades ago by *Hồ Chí Minh* to praise his Chinese Brothers were replaced by the jingle:

> *The national flag a woman's skirt,*
> *The national emblem the chickens coop.*

According to the broadcast, Chinese soldiers plundered from their villagers, taking even the sarongs of women and their chicken coops! I tip my hat in admiration of the Vietnamese Communist Party propagandists' vivid imagination. The saying political farce had no more accurate application than it did here!

Reunited with 'Old Friend'

Life went on monotonously. Then one day at lunchtime in February 1979 a delegation from the Police Department came to see the maximum-security Section. It consisted of five people, wearing non-uniform white shirts tucked into yellow pants, hard hats, and bags on their shoulders, rather like a team of electricians. They moved through the camp, talking with the Camp Commandant, who was pointing out different features. His attitude seemed unusually humble.

We went out as usual for our rations. By this time, we were allowed the use of the cell toilet during the daytime. Usually, we were very happy when the *Trật tự viên* let us outside, often using the opportunity to mix with those from other cells, swapping small articles, and tobacco when nobody was watching. Today, however, with the delegation from the Police Department observing us silently, everything was done correctly. As soon as we had our portions we went inside and BDT. locked the door and placed the iron bar across it.

As we divided the food, I looked out the window and saw a tall man in a police uniform entering the yard. I recognised him as Colonel *Hoàng Thanh*, who had caused me a great deal of trouble years ago. Colonel *Hoàng Thanh* had been head of the Police Department. He had been aboard the ocean liner *SÔNG HƯƠNG* in the delegation of Interior Department from the North to accompany the 'walking' cargo of political prisoners from the South in April 1977 (Chapter 7 of this book).

He is a tall man with fox-liked eyes that never stayed still, always darting around to note any little detail. Even with the best intentions, I couldn't possibly visualise a modicum of honesty in him. I had encountered him many times at *Nam Hà* Camp, before being exiled to 'Gateway to Heaven'. Sometimes, he smiled with his mouth but never with his eyes. His laugh frightened me, it was more like the hiss of viper. In my opinion, *Hoàng Thanh* was born to be a Vietnamese Communist Policeman.

Now *Hoàng Thanh* stood in the yard speaking to the Commandant. Then, the two of them came straight to our room and stood outside the iron door for a moment. Because this door had no grill, I could not tell what they were doing, but I guessed *Hoàng Thanh* was reading the name tags attached to the door. My sixth sense told me that it must be something relating to me, so I tried to prepare myself, knowing that whenever I had encountered him, things never went well. *Hoàng Thanh* returned to the yard and waved the *Trật tự viên* to open the door. We stopped dividing rations and sat in a row on the concrete platform.

The door opened and *Hoàng Thanh* stepped in. We greeted him as required by the camp regulations. He walked slowly along the row, both hands at his back, examining our faces like a general inspecting his troops. The atmosphere had become very tense. Arriving at the end, he turned and headed towards the iron door. I was secretly rejoicing, thinking it was over and nothing was going to happen. But to my dismay, he suddenly turned and pointed straight at me and asked in that familiar raucous voice, "You there in the glasses, sitting in the corner, are you *Nguyễn Hữu Lễ*?"

Although being anxious, I answered clearly: "Reporting to you Officer, correct, it's me, *Nguyễn Hữu Lễ*."

He smirked and said softly, "I intend to invite you for a chat sometime, to talk about the *SÔNG HƯƠNG* Ship incident…eh, *Anh Lễ?*"

Then he walked out the door, without waiting for my reply. I was stunned at the mention of the *SÔNG HƯƠNG*. It seemed that the old fox still had a hold over me.

Chapter 11
For the Sake of Freedom

When I suddenly encountered Colonel *Hoàng Thanh*, I had an uneasy feeling that my future was going to change for the worse. Two years had passed since I had travelled on the *SÔNG HƯƠNG* to the North, but I knew the authorities had not finished investigating the matter. It was my 'Sword of Damocles'! Every time I heard guards talk about it, I worried anew. In my mind, I had prepared answers in case of interrogation. If denial were not possible, I would accept total responsibility and not implicate anyone else. I knew that my punishment would be heavy.

Cell No.1 of Flat House at the time consisted of six inmates:

1. *Nguyễn Sỹ Thuyên*, over fifty and the oldest in the cell. He had taught math at secondary schools in Saigon.
2. *Trịnh Tiếu*, 51, had been a Colonel in the Army of the Republic of South Vietnam and held many important positions including Chief of the Intelligence Service in the 2nd Army Corps, and was the last Chief of *Ban Mê Thuột* Province.
3. *Lâm Thành Văn*, 40, bus driver on the Saigon-*Đà Lạt* route, was caught participating in the Resistance Movement.
4. Father *Nguyễn Công Định*, 45, had been Army Chaplain.
5. *Đặng Văn Tiếp*, 46, a lawyer, had been a Lieutenant Colonel in the Air Force, and later a Representative for Congress.
6. I was the youngest in the cell, at just 36 years of age.

Now, I talked quietly with *Đặng Văn Tiếp* about Colonel *Hoàng Thanh's* remark. *Tiếp* was also worried. We discussed the bleak outlook for both of us as political prisoners, with the authorities killing us gradually through neglect of basic necessities, if not by more drastic methods. Perhaps, this was the time to initiate the plan we'd been hatching for some time. We knew the danger, but there seemed nothing else to do. At 'Gateway to Heaven', we had been ready to escape to China and had decided which tools we would take from the woodworking shop to allow us to break out. But there had been a sudden reshuffling and we went into different cells the very night of our planned escape.

We realised that escaping from this maximum-security Section would be much more difficult than from the general prison. The flat-roofed building was very solidly constructed. We were weak from malnourishment. We had no opportunity to get tools, nor find any metal items that could be used for digging. Moreover, to make us reconsider such action, there was the ever-present sight of the neighbouring Black House, the Punishment Block where we would end up if we were unsuccessful. There were two walls, a lower one topped by two layers of barbed wire surrounding our section, and a five-metre-high stone one that ran around the whole Camp.

We knew the need of everyone's cooperation in the cell was crucial. If anyone was too weak or unwilling to participate, we had to make sure they would not be punished as collaborators after our escape. *Đặng Văn Tiếp* and I tried to assess each man's attitude, testing the waters before actually bringing up the subject. Since we'd all lived together for a considerable time, we thought we could gauge each man's response. We started with those most likely to be sympathetic.

As we expected, *Thuyên* and *Tiếu* agreed on the spot. *Thuyên* said enthusiastically, "I've wanted for this a long time! Thanks for including me."

Văn, who suffered from gastric ulcers, hesitated for a few minutes but then agreed. But Father *Định* proved to be a stumbling block. He was determined not to participate. Father *Định* replied decisively, "I will go home when my name is called. Until then I'm not doing anything that would risk my chance of getting home. Even if that door was wide open, I'd stay here don't even joke about escaping."

"But what you say about if all five of us are going?"

"So you guys just go, I'm staying here by myself!"

"How will you answer to the guards?"

"That's my business!"

I laughed apologetically, "We're not planning anything. I was only teasing!"

Despite this disappointment, we began to secretly formulate possible plans, taking precaution to appear as normal as possible when guards were around. Any accidental slip of the tongue, and everything would fall apart even before we could begin. As well there was Father Định. We didn't think he would report us, but couldn't take any risk.

We planned our escape for the night of May 1st, the Communist Labour Day. To celebrate this holiday the guards were served alcohol. We hoped they'd drink enough to be careless while patrolling that night.

Because we were never sent to labour with the general prisoners, we had plenty of time to make plans and to ponder all possible scenarios. What was the best way to break out of the cell? We decided the latrine would be our area of escape. Behind its closed door, we would be hidden from sight. Could we make a hole in its brick walls? Remove the mortar and then the bricks? This would require a strong spade that we didn't have, nor did there seem to be any loose metal in the cell.

I studied our surroundings ever more closely. Then I noticed the fastening on the latrine door a steel hasp, hinged at one end and slipped over a U-bolt at the other. Whenever this door was unlocked, this bar hung unused. I thought, "Why not use this godsend piece to escape?" The eighteen-centimetre piece of flat steel would surely work as a spade. At times a padlock was slipped through the U-bolt, locking the latrine door. If we could only get the hasp off, a thick nail had been driven through one end into the wooden door and the tip had been flattened over like a rivet.

Our first task was to straighten the tip of the nail, then work it out. But straightening a nail the width of a chopstick was not a simple matter. It was time to bring out our treasures. I had an aluminium spoon I'd managed to hide during the many inspections. But aluminium was too soft to be of much use. Then *Lâm Thành Văn* showed us the handle for a water can that he had made by untangling spike of barbed wire.

This was what we used to drill through the wood beneath the doornail. Then, we bent the two ends into a ring, and used this to gradually lever the nail straight. After that, it was quite easy to remove the steel bar. We took it in turns to sharpen it by rubbing it against the concrete sleeping shelf. Its newly burnished appearance would have given us away, so we rubbed it with soot, and rehung it as if it had never been moved.

Of course, this had to be done without the guards or Father Định noticing.

We told each other that if we were suddenly shuffled into other cells, we'd act as though we had no plans to escape. Our preparations would be abandoned. If by chance a guard or *Trật tự viên* ever discovered that the hasp had been removed and sharpened, we would pretend ignorance. After all, we weren't the only people who'd ever lived in this cell. For the moment, we could relax. Besides, we had the spoon and it might help although it was of only aluminium.

We knew that a tunnel used as a sewer ran under the cells and into a cesspit that had a stout wooden outside door. This pit was just big enough for a prisoner to go into each day to collect excrement. We asked the prisoner charged with this duty about the shape of the tunnel and the time that the door was locked. He told us that the door was open during the daytime and locked during evening roll call. So, we decided that after breaking through the brick wall, we'd crawl through the tunnel to the cesspool, pry the door off its hinges, and watch the guards for our chance to make our way to the foot of the section wall. Once getting over this wall, there'd still be the five-metre-high granite wall with an additional metre of barbed wire on top. The only break in this wall was the camp gate itself, guarded twenty-four hours a day. These guards even had their living quarters at the gate, so there was always someone present there.

We drew diagrams, using charcoal on the concrete shelf, and then quickly obliterated them in case a guard noticed. We tried to cover every detail, every contingency. So as not to arouse curiosity about these discussions, we always had a small group enthusiastically playing chess. Our cell was only big enough for six people to lie down side by side, so it was difficult to hide anything. We had to make every action, word, and glance look innocent.

Tiếp and I got into the habit of discussing details while waiting for our turn to bathe in the river. Or we would wait for Father Định to fall asleep, and then talk in the latrine with the door closed. We always asked the others for any criticism of our plans.

Hatching an Escaping Plot

These were finally narrowed down to two plans. Plan A: It depended on our getting out before midnight, in case we got it, we would run towards the jungle, head west towards the Laotian border thirty kilometres away, from there, we'd find our way to Thailand. Plan B: It was our fallback, in case we encountered any obstruction and left later. We would find somewhere down river to hide and wait for a chance to head for the jungle.

We wouldn't be able to hide among Northerners, because the Northern and Southern accents were so different as to make discovery easy. The local people were very poor and looked forward to the reward for turning in escaped prisoners. They received rice, alcohol, and a reward certificate that allowed them days of exemption from village labour, and priority when food was distributed. Catching escaped prisoners was such a rewarding side-job for the locals that, upon hearing three gunshots reporting an escape, they competed to find the escapees. Some even had a bag ready for their rice reward.

Knowing all of this, we knew we had to hide in the jungle and avoid any human contact while we were still on our native soil. On the other hand, because most people had gardens in the jungle, it might be possible to find yams and cassava for our food. If we had to hide along the banks of the *Mã* River, there'd be fishermen to contend with. During the dry period, when the water level dropped, only a few fishermen were around. But after the rainy season fishermen would swarm to catch the shoals of surface-feeding *Mương*.

There were two months before our chosen D-Day. Every day I looked out through the window at the high wall, puzzling how all five of us could pass over it safely. When Father *Định* came near. I pretended I was standing there to breathe some fresh air. If it was just *Tiếp*, *Tiểu* and me, we might manage. But we had the aging *Thuyên* and especially *Lâm Thành Văn* with his stomach trouble. Before we could do anything else, we must find or make a rope ladder. The first was unlikely, especially as it would need to have a hook of some sort to hook it onto the metal pole supporting the barbed wire-on the top of the wall. We gazed longingly at the clothesline in our Flat House's yard, right in front of our room. Its two posts were four meters apart, with four lines stretched between. Some segments of line were nylon, some were electrical cable, but one was wire!

I was determined to steal this wire. But this job wasn't easy. We were never allowed to be in the yard without the guard's presence. I was frustrated until I hit upon a solution. Nobody paid attention to the state of the prisoners' clothesline, so it didn't matter what the lines were made of so long as there were always four strands. At the rubbish dump by the river, we searched for fragments of sacking. We unravelled the fibres and covertly plaited a cord, taking care to make it the same thickness as the wire. Then every time we passed the clothesline, one of us would loosen the wire strand a little. I was given the risky task of changing the line, as it had been my idea. I waited and worried.

On the chosen day, we hung our laundry as usual on the clotheslines. For some reason, the guards did not supervise us, and instead there were only two *Trật tự viên*. They waited for us to finish hanging our laundry and go back to the cell. While my four friends wrung out the clothes and held them up to shield me from the sight of *Trật tự viên*, I untied the wire strand and tied the replacement cord in place. Then, I quickly coiled the metal wire and hid it under my clothes. Once back inside, we twisted it into an S-shaped hook to go on the end of our rope ladder.

There was only one place in the cell where we could hide our illegal items: the water tank by the latrine. Rainwater collected on the flat roof drained through a hole into this tank. The tank's top edge reached the ceiling, but there was a 50cm.-square barred hole high up in the side that faced the latrine.

After routine evening roll call and before the cell door was locked, a guard or *Trật tự viên* would inspect the cell for any breaches in the walls, tapping them with a mallet. They never paid any attention to the water tank that was higher than a man to look inside, they would have had to stand on something and use a torch. We had learnt to tie each treasure to a length of string and poke it through the bars. Then, we could hook the string back when we wanted the object again.

Even a few days before Labour Day we weren't sure if our escape plans would pan out because we still had to suffer the customary a *Khám nội vụ* (Search of our individual possessions) that took place before every holiday. At these times, we had to lay out all the little things we had managed to acquire, then sit beside them waiting for the guards to go through them all, scattering everything into complete disorder.

In prison, everything was valuable, everything could be put to use, and everything had its own purpose, from a piece of newspaper, to a segment of nylon string, to a rusty tin can, to a torn piece of fabric, to a plastic box, a plastic bag…all salvaged from the dumpster. Now I worried did any of us have some small item that could lead to suspicion of our plans?

Certainly *Văn* did. Because of his gastric problem, he could not digest cassava and was given rice soup instead. For this reason, he received a small amount of salt which he had been saving for the escape. A search might uncover this tiny hoard and then questions would be asked. We also worried about the possibility of a cell change, which would ruin everything. Our plan depended on teamwork and we needed to stay together.

The inspection came and went without anything being found amiss and there was no cell change as well. We were told to go back to our respective rooms to celebrate Labour Day.

Now, it was time to make rope ladder. *Tiếp* and I split a length of bamboo for the rungs. We worked as quietly as we could in the latrine with the door closed, but still Father *Định's* suspicions were aroused. "What are you guys doing?"

He always addressed us as 'You people', as if to show us that he had no part in our affairs.

"We're cracking a bamboo to make light a fire for tobacco pipe spills, Sir!"

His voice came back as sharp as a butcher's knife, "All right; but you people be careful, ya hear?"

We stopped working and looked at each other. Were his words of advice or threat? I hoped and prayed that the first was true. We determined to be even more careful to avoid his attention.

We had the rungs, now for the rope. Someone suggested unravelling our clothes, but they were too ragged. In the end, we tore up our thin blankets, layered them for strength, and sewed them into strips. I'd acquired a nail, for some time, I'd been rubbing it against concrete to make one end flatter. Now, I bore a hole in, a hole just big enough for a single thread of the very strong fibres from a sandbag. Then, we hooked it over the strong frame of the water tank and took turns testing it with our very slight bodies. It seemed satisfactory. As well, we made a single rope for sliding down the other side of the wall.

We tried to estimate the time it would take to break through the wall, to pass through the tunnel, for every contingency. There wasn't a single issue we didn't consider. We paid special attention to our climb over the high wall. We would have to form ourselves a human ladder. *Trịnh Tiếu* and I would stand close together at the foot of the wall, *Đặng Văn Tiếp* would climb on our shoulders. *Tiếp* would hold a bamboo staff with the metal hook attached, hook the ladder onto the metal pole on the top of the wall. Then, he'd climb the ladder, let the single rope down on the other side, and slide down it. Next would be *Nguyễn Sỹ Thuyên,* following was *Lâm Thành Văn,* then *Trịnh Tiếu,* and I would be last. *Tiếp* was considered to have the most initiative, and *Văn* was weakest and might need support. I was to be last, responsible for pulling the incriminating ladder up after me. If anything went wrong, I would have to improvise.

But one still problem remaining, it was Father *Định,* who hopefully was still ignorant of our plans. As we were both priests, I was designated to break this news to him. On the last day of April, I asked him to hear my confession. What we were contemplating could lead to death and I wanted to be well prepared. After confession, I revealed our plans for the next day's escape. I knew that even if he didn't agree with our plans, he couldn't repeat my words to anyone; because of his oath to never reveal what was told him in confession. He was incredibly agitated and began to sob loudly while pacing up and down. "You people are so cruel! Why don't you just kill me? Why don't you just kill me?" he begged.

The five of us had sympathy for him in his fear and worry. At the same time, we worried that there might be guard outside to hear his outburst. As Father *Định's* shock slowly abated, *Nguyễn Sỹ Thuyên,* as the oldest person of the group, apologised and explained to him that our uncompromising stance and gave him a last chance to join us. But he resolutely declined. Then we told him what we had decided as the safest method of preventing his being suspected of aiding us in our escape: Before leaving the cell, we would bind and gag him so that he could not yell for the guard.

At last, we went to bed although I doubt that any of us slept; especially Father *Định,* who would also have tossed and turned all that troubled night.

On Labour Day, we were all given a small bowl of rice, another ration of soup and three small pieces of stewed pork. While we ate, we sat close and swore to help one another through what was to come. Then, we relaxed as much as we could. Realistically, I knew the probability of success was low. Father *Định's* face was drained of colour and his lips quivered constantly as he sat against the wall with his eyes shut. His meal was untouched, the pork fat congealed on the surface of his soup. I noticed some of the pig's hairs still sticking to the meat. His anxiety seemed to affect my own digestion, and my stomach churned.

My cellmates, shirtless and in shorts, radiated an odd sense of sadness. Everyone's hair was in a tangled and filthy and our bodies didn't have a scrap of flesh to cover our protruding ribs. The scene, combined with the plastic bowl of hairy stewed pork, made me sick and I rushed to the latrine.

I wanted to save my energy, for knowing that it would take everything I had to dig under the wall during our escape. *Đặng Văn Tiếp* sat cross-legged, yoga-style, in front of the window. *Lâm Thành Văn* sat rubbing his stomach. *Trịnh Tiểu* was busy with his clothes, perhaps choosing his escape outfit. *Nguyễn Sỹ Thuyên* carefully adjusted the lamp by the doorway. None of us had much to say.

I went to each person in turn, urging him to pray for tonight according to his own personal belief. Then, I sat facing Father *Định*. Whether our plan succeeded or failed, there was no stopping now. During the past four years, I'd planned to escape three times, each plan prevented by outside circumstances out of my control. Now, I was within minutes of entering a possible death trap, in order to find life once more.

Even though we'd planned so carefully in the past two months, I feared, in these last minutes, we still had too many loose ends. All I could do about it was sit against the wall with my arms crossed and wait. Our names had to be checked off for the night, and the guards would leave. With stretched nerves in the meantime, I listened for the sound of the *'Kleng'* for roll call. At the same time, I had wished the *'Kleng'* for roll call never sounded.

Eventually, the *'Kleng'* sounded. I shivered and my racing pulse seemed to miss a beat.

Father *Định* sat in his usual position for roll call. Keys' jingled and the outside door opened. Everything seemed normal. I prayed for God's protection. An unthinkable result could come from the smallest error. Nightly roll call always had a cadre and two *Trật tự viên* present. Tonight, the on-duty cadre was sergeant major *Hạ*. My cellmates all sat solemnly as two *Trật tự viên* ran into the courtyard, vigilant as usual. Whilst sergeant major *Hạ* stood outside observing, the two *Trật tự viên* used wooden mallets to hammer the outside walls, and examined the windows for signs of tampering.

As usual, they never looked a prisoner in the eye. Then, one came right inside our cell to inspect the latrine. I held my breath and hoped he wouldn't see that the hasp had been modified. The rope ladder I'd rolled into my pillow jabbed into my back. What if he should tell me to stand up? Surely he'd notice the strange contour of the pillow. I thought of every possible problem one after another.

But instead, they had not noticed anything amiss; then they left.

Chapter 12
The Gamble of Life and Death

As soon as Sergeant major *Hạ* and two *Trật Tự Viên* left, I stepped over and removed the hasp from the latrine door. In a hurry, I created a draught that snuffed out the flame of our lamp. This tiny lamp was made from a penicillin vial and its flame had never been blown out before. We looked at each other with dread. Was this an omen? I made myself think rationally, reminding me that I'd made the draught myself and so caused the mishap. But *Lâm Thành Văn* looked especially concerned as he whispered, "*Anh Lễ*, how are we going to dig if we can't see?"

In my time in prison, I'd acquired a number of skills, including a way of starting fire without matches. From my store, I extracted some wicks made from plaited lengths of string, and pierced disks from can lids. The idea was to twist the string, then pull it tight so that the discs would rotate quickly, as in the children's game. We caused the discs to grind against a broken ceramic bowl and create a spark. Our tinder was a small piece of charred cloth.

Normally, I could start a fire quickly. But this time, because of my stress, the more I tried, the more flustered I became. The string frayed and broke. When I threaded the last piece through the disc, my hands shook. Was this the end of all our work? But now the string held, the wick caught the tiny flame and began to burn. The others heaved sighs of relief as I relit the lamp.

Thuyên took the lamp, promising to guard its flame. To our relief, rain began to pelt down. Its sound would conceal any noise we made, and the guards were always slack during rainstorms, preferring to stay under shelter rather than stand outside our door.

Point of No Return

We wrapped layers of fabric around one end of the hasp to protect our hands. It wasn't a very effective digging tool but it was all we had. Before he started, *Tiếp* turned to me and said, "This is the knifepoint of fate, *Cậu Bảy*!"

I nodded my head and said, "Pray that God will have mercy on all of us." There was no way we could stop now. If the guards could see what we had been about to do, we would be punished whether we went on or not. At any rate, we were working for our freedom and were ready to pay the price. In the outside world, many of our Peoples were also trying to escape from the much greater confinement of Vietnam under Communist domination. As the minutes slipped by, I thought of the saying "Time is money". Better to say, "Time is life!"

We prepared to dig. As there was only room for one person at a time, *Tiếp* and I took turns digging. He forced the hasp between bricks while I poured on water in an attempt to soften the mortar. *Tiểu* and *Văn* drew more cans of water from the tank and passed them to me. *Thuyên* was on watch for guards, and sang loudly to hide any noise from the digging. *Tiếp's* hands seemed to be scrabbling as fast as a mouse's paws digging a tunnel. Fortunately, it was not yet 10.00 p.m., so we still had the light from the cell's one bulb. But soon, we would be reliant upon our tiny oil-lamp, and then our task would be harder.

As *Tiếp* passed me a brick, I noticed that it was bloodstained the blade had worked through the rags, cutting *Tiếp's* hand. He hadn't noticed.

"*Tiếp*," I whispered. "You're bleeding. Stop! I'll take over."

"What'd you say?"

"Your hand is bleeding, can't you see? Look at your hand."

He put down his tool and opened his palm to reveal raw flesh. "*Cậu Bảy*, give me some more rags." "I'll wrap it some more."

"Why don't you stop for a while?" I asked.

But he scolded me, "How can one stop? Bring me more cloth," and turned back to the bricks.

I had to yank at his shirt to get him to change places with me. He was a pitiful sight. Blood ran from his hand, mixed with sand and dirt. *Văn* gently rinsed it in a can of water. The digging was harder than we had expected. We had naively expected the mortar to be soft. Instead it was solid concrete. No amount of water would soften it. Also, the man digging was cramped into a narrow corner, unable to change his position. All four of us were soon taking turns at digging, all receiving lacerations to our hands.

We heard prisoners from other cells pounding the walls, which meant they could hear us. They were warning us to keep the noise down. But we couldn't stop doing so. The most important thing was to breach the wall the faster the better. If we could do this quickly, we'd survive, otherwise, we'd die. We tossed bricks into the cell where they lay mixed up with our belongings, scattered everywhere. But we weren't concerned about leaving a mess, just getting away. Father *Định* sat against the wall, eyes closed, lips moving constantly. I guessed he was praying, but for himself or for us? At that moment, I was too busy to pray.

We had counted on being out of the cell by midnight. But although we strained to the last of our energy, we took a long time to break the mortar. Even when it was removed, we found that the bricks in the corner were difficult to pry apart. They had settled into each other and the ground beneath. With a shock, we heard the first cockcrow. By now, we were supposed to be in the jungle, finding our way to the Laotian border. Instead, we were like trapped animals fighting to leave a cage. What if the guards were to come to inspect our cell and while we were still there, what then? I froze for a minute, but then told myself, "Where there's life there's hope". And pushed myself to work harder.

Then *Văn* was stricken with pain, probably from asking too much effort from his weakened stomach muscles. We told him to go back and rest so as to be refreshed for the breakout. Now, I began hallucinating, imagining the wall as the Grim Reaper, moving towards us with alarming speed. Finally, we made a hole just large enough to crawl through. The three of us dropped down into the sewer tunnel that was stinking and filled with baskets of excrement waiting to be carried out the next day. Beyond was a wooden door. We had planned to take the hinges off this door as quietly as possible. But now we were so much behind schedule that we resorted to all heaving ourselves at it. It crashed to the ground with a *"bang"*. We listened for a response from prisoners in the other cells, but there was none. The rain had masked the noise.

Now that we had assured our exit, we hurriedly crawled back through the tunnel to collect the rope ladder and other apparatus. However, the sewer was much lower than the hole through to our cell, so we had to help each other back up. In doing so, the skin on my abdomen was torn, but there was no time to care about that.

The Price of Freedom

Thuyên and *Văn* were ready to go, padded with all the clothes they had. Although we'd agreed to take only the absolute necessities, we understood we'd need to protect ourselves as we negotiated the barbed wire on top of the two walls. Essential objects were bound to our bodies, so that our hands would be free for climbing or swimming the *Mã* River. We bade farewell to Father *Định* who sat on the floor and wept profusely. Filled with pity, I knelt in front of him and gave him a bow, both as a goodbye and an apology. Then, I immediately bound and gagged him. I didn't know, whether or not, this would fool the guards. The other men crept through the wall and down the sewer to the outside. I soon caught up with them. It was so late that we heard the second cockcrow! I began to pray for the safety of the five of us, as well as for Father *Định*.

Đặng Văn Tiếp led the way, crawling close to the ground. Seeing nobody in the first yard, he motioned for the rest of us to follow him to the section wall. We helped each other up and over, rolling across the wire on top, then across the yard to the granite wall. It was the first time in nine months that we'd set foot in this outer yard. A watchtower stood at each corner, but at night they were empty. Instead, guards patrolled the entire prison on foot. We approached the final stage of our escape, also the most difficult. *Trịnh Tiếu* and I knelt for *Tiếp* to climb on our shoulders. He held the rope ladder and, manipulating a length of bamboo, hooked it onto the metal pole supporting the barbed wire.

Tiếp quickly climbed to the top and tied the single rope to the pole, so there was a way of sliding down the other side of the wall. *Thuyên* climbed on our shoulders, up the ladder, and got over with no trouble, joining *Tiếp*. But with *Lâm Thành Văn*, disaster struck!

When *Văn* was halfway to the top, the ladder broke. Fortunately, *Tiếu* and I caught him before he hit the ground. This was a misfortune beyond our expectations. This was a dreadful situation, three of us were still inside the wall; the upper part of the ladder beyond our reach and the other half lying at our feet. Even worse, we had no way of communicating with the two already outside.

We tried jumping for the dangling ladder, but with no success. I sat down for *Tiếu* to climb on to my shoulders, and *Văn* to climb on his, and then to tie the ends of the ladder. But I couldn't hold the weight of two men. It was hopeless. Then I looked at the horizon and saw a faint red glow dawn. For the first time, I felt that recapture was certain.

Nevertheless, I told the others to wait while I went back into the cell. I acted according to my survival instincts, now well beyond fear. No creeping across the yard this time I just focused on running. As luck would have it, no guards were patrolling the area. I scurried through the sewer faster than a squirrel. But the distance from the ground to the latrine floor was too great. I couldn't reach high enough to pull myself through. Previously, we'd helped each other up.

Then, I remembered the outside door we'd busted down and groped my way back to find some of its boards. I propped them against the bank. But they were slippery, making a foothold difficult. Many times, I slipped and fell into the basket of excrement, splattering the contents everywhere. It was completely dark and I could see nothing. After each unsuccessful attempt, I groped around to find the boards and try again. Finally, I got enough height, wormed through the hole, back to the cell. It looked like a battlefield.

The oil lamp still burned steadily. Father Định, lying on the floor, was surprised to see me back and struggled to sit up. I put all my focus on searching for my mosquito net. This was made of strong nylon net. Rolling it under my shirt, I retraced my steps through the wall, the sewer, over the first wall and back outside to my two waiting friends. By now, it was fully dawn. I pitched the net again and again until it caught on the barbed wire. We tested its hold and decided it was safe. I told *Văn* to climb while *Tiểu* and I hoisted him from below. But he was so weak he kept falling. Realising that he couldn't make it, he said in anguish, "I can't do it. You two go without me."

"No way, we swore to live or die together. How can we leave you to surrender?"

Văn waved his hands in protest. "*Tiểu*, you, and *Lễ* go on. I'm giving up! You two go right now. If you stay here, we all die!"

He grabbed our hands, squeezing them in farewell. Then he turned his back, and walked away. *Trịnh Tiểu* grabbed hold of the net and tried to climb. However, he couldn't do it either, even with my all-out support. He also turned away and followed in *Văn's* direction, leaving me alone at the foot of the wall. I was deeply saddened watching my two friends hand in hand walking away. I felt as though my innermost organs were torn to shreds. I could imagine what would happen when they met a guard. That thought reminded me of my own predicament: I must get out quickly.

I made a leap for the net and pulled myself up, trying to brace myself close to the wall. When I was almost at the top, part of the net was torn. I panicked and grabbed the barbed wire. The barb pierced the flesh of my palm and blood ran down my arm. This hand held the weight of my entire body. But when I thought of the likelihood of an armed guard below me, I was able to disregard any pain. With the greatest physical effort, I swung my body up on to the top of the wall.

Tiếp's rope was still tied to the pole my first piece of luck! Quickly, I grabbed it and slid to the ground. I didn't try to roll up the net hanging on the other side. It was much too late to try to hide any sign of our escaping. I couldn't have done so even if I'd wanted to, as it was tangled on the barbed wire.

A 'Touch' of Freedom!

As my feet touched the ground, I almost choked on the realisation that I was breathing free air! Even today, that sense of being a free person is impossible to describe. But then I remembered that *Tiếp* and *Thuyên* had been waiting for me for over two hours. An hour in those circumstances was longer than a millennium! I hurried to the buffalo stables where we'd arranged to meet. I'll never forget their joy at seeing me again. Even though there wasn't much chance of success, I still hung onto the hope that we'd be saved by some miracles.

I briefed them quickly on what had happened with *Tiểu* and *Văn*. Then we began running beside the camp wall, across the dirt road full of puddles from last night's storm, straight for the bushes by the riverbank. We quickly slipped into the water.

The river level was high because of the recent heavy rains and the current was strong. We swam in the direction of the flow, holding on to shrubbery on the bank to help us. Some distance along, we found a shallow cave in the rocky bank. A large tree grew above, its roots almost concealing the entrance.

The three of us ducked under the roots. There was just a small space inside. *Thuyên* stayed close to the entrance. We all held our breath and waited. Capture and death were probably close, but I felt no regret whatsoever. Many of my fellow peoples had paid the same price. If only I'd been able to bring a little freedom back to my people as I'd wished. After a while, we heard the three shots that signalled an escape from the Camp. The most terrifying moment had arrived.

Despite the danger, I still had hopes that we wouldn't be discovered. The cave was covered with grass above, and one had to dive under the roots to get inside. Although a fragile hope, I nurtured it. We were so quiet that the sound of the flowing water seemed like a roar. We hadn't got far from the Camp so it wasn't long before we heard running footsteps, men yelling, dogs barking, and more shots. The guards had brought dogs to track us. I closed my eyes, prayed, and entrusted my life to God.

The footsteps faded and I had a brief moment of silent celebration, thinking they'd gone on by. But soon the noise returned, the yelling and barking came closer and closer. *Thuyên* moved closer in, huddled against *Tiếp* and me. We hadn't said a word since entering the cave. Suddenly, *Tiếp* hugged me and whispered a request, "Would you baptise me?" In the time we'd been together, I had talked with him about my beliefs. *Tiếp* had expressed an interest in Christianity and of perhaps being baptised someday. Now, I splashed river water over him and said the words of the sacrament. Immediately he kissed me on the cheeks devoutly to express his joy. I didn't know it would be the last kiss he would ever give me. I was suddenly joyful too, so that at the end of my life *Tiếp*, my brother by oath, had become my brother in faith.

The sounds got closer. I wasn't sure where they were coming from, but it seemed that they were in front of us. Peering out through the grass, I saw Master Sergeant *Hoàn*, a handgun slung across his chest, standing in a small canoe. He was holding a small spear with one hand as he paddled his canoe with the other. He was poking bushes with the spear. Then a fisherwoman on the opposite side of the river yelled out, "They were just there!"

"Where?"

"In the bush of grass just in front of you. I saw them in that bush!"

Hoàn parted each clump of grass and shone a flashlight until he found us. Our escape was over!

The Price to Pay

It would be very difficult to describe how I felt at the time. I could imagine the consequences, for having witnessed others' treatment after attempting to escape they were treated worse than animals, some even beaten to death. I hugged *Tiếp* tightly and said, "We won't go out, let them shoot us in here." *Tiếp* hugged me even tighter. We could hear the voices of many men. They were like hunters, waiting for their prey to be killed. *Hoàn* was yelling at the top of his voice for us to come out. He sounded insane.

Nguyễn Sỹ Thuyên, hiding near the entrance, lost his nerve and swam out. *Tiếp* and I were still determined to stay in the cave. But *Hoàn* parted the overhanging grass and coldly drove the muzzle of his gun into my temple. "*Lễ*! Are you going to swim out? Or are you going to wait for me to shatter your skull?"

At that time, all I really wanted was for him to pull the trigger. I figured it was the best solution. But instead, he pointed the gun upwards and fired four shots to signal prisoner recovery. Then he stabbed his spear directly into the cave. Its sharp metal end pierced *Tiếp's* shoulder. The flashlight showed *Tiếp's* blood staining the water. No choice! *Tiếp* began to swim out, and I followed. A few dozen people, prison guards and civilians, stood and watched as I crawled up on to the shore. I felt like a convict on the way to execution.

On the bank, stood Lieutenant *Lăng*, the Camp Security Officer, with an AK-47. When I stood within his range, he swung the rifle stock into the middle of my chest, knocking me back into the water. From there, *Hoàn* speared me in the back and forced me back on shore again. I groped my way over bushes and on to the bank.

Lieutenant *Lăng* still stood waiting for me but this time, he grabbed my hair and yanked me up. Another guard came up and removed the cloth I'd tied around my waist. Wrapped in the cloth were my eyeglasses, which I never saw them again. Not far away, a pack of guards surrounded *Tiếp*, yelling and beating him relentlessly. The scene made me think of Jesus before he carried the cross to the hill of Golgotha, when a crowd of fierce soldiers surrounded and beat him. Then another group started on me and I suffered the same fate as *Tiếp*. I couldn't see what had happened to *Thuyên*.

The first hits and kicks produced excruciating pain, but soon my whole body became numb. With the ensuing beatings, I heard rather than felt the blows, like the sound of a ball being kicked against a wall. I lost awareness of my surroundings. In the midst of all the chaotic yells and insults, I heard one voice carry over the rest. "Enough! I tell you comrades, enough! I tell you comrades, enough!" But the pack didn't stop, instead, they punched and kicked me even more intensely. Having witnessed many cases of guards beating inmates in prison, I knew that orders to stop were actually a signal to beat prisoners even harder; people not in the know would think the Party was humane as their representative had called a stop to the torture!

When they got sick of beating, they pushed me in the direction of the Camp. It was then that I realised that *Tiếp* was nowhere to be seen. I approached the wooden bridge by the woodwork area. Here Warrant Officer *Khải*, the martial arts expert, was waiting for me. As soon as I was within range, he leaped into the air and smashed his heel into my face. I fell backwards off the bridge and into the shallow stream, bleeding freely from my nose and mouth. I must say, the kick was beautiful, perfectly executed, a textbook performance. Even then, I was even prouder to have taken this after the earlier beating from the guards who attacked me continually, nothing near the effect from that 'professional' kick from *Khải*. Lying in the shallow stream, I was still conscious, but then, I thought that if I pretended to be dead, they might stop beating me. A guard on the bank told me to get up, but I lay still. Others jumped into the stream and continued with their beating, while I continued to lie there like a corpse. Perhaps, this fooled them because they called the two *Trật tự viên* to fetch my body back to the Camp.

Bùi Đình Thi (Hereinafter BDT.) and *Trương Văn Phát* dragged me back to Camp, holding an arm each so that my back scraped on the stony path. Then they threw me face up on the concrete floor of the Camp hall. I passed out, and have no idea how long I was unconscious.

When I became conscious, BDT. was holding a bucket and pouring cold water on my face. Noticing my eyes open, he slammed the bucket down and grabbed my arm with both hands. As he pulled me up, he drove his heel sharply into my stomach. Foaming at the mouth, grinding his teeth and rolling his eyes, he said breathlessly: *"F*ck you Lễ! You rotten bastard! Don't you want to eat rice, but sh*t instead! You wanted to die, so I'll help you!"* Until the day I die, I will never forget these insulting words from BDT. because that was the first time I had ever heard a Catholic insult a priest that way. In the Confucian-inspired Vietnamese (Especially those who shared their faith), normally treated culture, seniors and priests with respect.

Tired of beating me, he left me lying there. It was afterwards, when I was chained with the others in the Disciplinary Section, that I found out that BDT. had paid a similar visit to *Tiếp* and *Thuyên*. I relapsed into unconsciousness. When I was again conscious, I found BDT. was dragging me by both legs up the stairs from the Camp Hall to the Flat House. My back and head banged agonisingly on the concrete steps. This pain had brought me back to consciousness; therefore, **I witnessed the murder of Major Đặng Văn Tiếp by Captain Bùi Đình Thi**. This scene is imprinted in my mind like a tattoo on one's skin, unable to be removed.

The Tale of Two Murders

Bùi Đình Thi dragged me back into room No.1 where we'd dug through the wall to escape the night before. I was certain that he thought I had died for he dragged me headfirst and left me facing the yard. In doing so, I was in a position to witness his most wicked crime. Had he known that I was still alive, he would have given me a 'coup de grace'.

After he had thrown me into the room, he hurried out the door and violently pushed *Tiếp* inside. I couldn't tell how long it had been since I had seen *Tiếp* beaten on the riverbank nor did I know how badly he was beaten. I only saw that he seemed better than I did at that moment. Although he was ragged and soaked, he was still able to walk upright. He was surrounded by a group of guards, and I heard the sound of women too; perhaps the guard's wives and their children.

I don't know who knocked *Tiếp* down, but I clearly saw *Bùi Đình Thi* jump over to grab his arm, using both hands. He used the same tactics he had used on me, holding *Tiếp's* arms to pull him up, while viciously digging his heel in *Tiếp's* belly. There was a chorus of savage cheers. I seemed to hear *Tiếp's* bowel gurgle and rupture under the grinding of *Bùi Đình Thi's* heel. There was no way *Tiếp* could take such a beating. I don't know how long the torture went on before I heard *Đặng Văn Tiếp's* loud scream: **"Oh my Mother! I'm dying now!"** They were the last words of *Đặng Văn Tiếp*.

This is how this politician and military hero was heartlessly murdered on that sombre morning, the 2nd of May 2, 1979, in *Thanh Cẩm* Prison Camp. He was just 46 years of age. **Captain Bùi Đình Thi was personally responsible for this brutal and savage killing. But his Communist masters were the real murderers because the way they encouraged one prisoner to kill another**. I knew I had to survive so that I could record this shameful tragedy.

Today, as I remember this event, my heart feels as if it is bleeding. I feel nauseated. Throughout my life, there has not been any other scene of such heart-rending sadness. The onlookers were like bloodthirsty spectators in the Roman Coliseum, madly cheering the animals attacking the Christians thrown to them. But unlike those early martyrs, *Tiếp* hadn't been sentenced to death. Instead, he'd been a Comrade-in-arms, a military Commander, and a fellow prisoner of the one who killed him. Every year on the anniversary of his death, I feel choked as I pray for him. I have never been as miserable as now in recording this tragedy, when I have to remember every detail.

Bùi Đình Thi threw *Tiếp's* body on top of me. The dead weight prevented my breathing and I felt I was about to die of suffocation. Fortunately, a guard came in. *Bùi Đình Thi* muttered, "The rascal *Tiếp* is dead!"

The guard grunted, "Get his body up!"

Tiếp's corpse was shoved up on the concrete platform where he used to sleep. Noticing I was still alive, with my knees tucked up against the wall, the guard took the crossbar off the door and hammered it on my left knee, forcing it down. I heard the high-pitched insults of the women outside the window as they pitched the bricks which we dug out so painfully the night before.

From where I lay on the floor, I could see *Tiếp's* muddied feet sticking over the edge of the platform. Some time ago, I had sewn a gold ring into the cuff of his pants. His brother had smuggled it in to him at *Hà Tây* Prison, in case he ever managed to escape. Would someone find it now?

Comatose

I drifted into a comatose state where I seemed to be walking aimlessly among white clouds, some of them crystallised into hard chunks of ice. It was completely silent. I began climbing up the clouds, not knowing where I was going. When one broke and I lost my balance, I clung to another cloud and climbed on. I realised now that I was having a near-death experience. This feeling of being on the borderline between life and death has taught me that death is gentle and comforting not monstrous, as popular opinion would have it. Suffering is reserved for the grieving survivors.

But if my loved ones had seen me on that gloomy morning in *Thanh Cẩm* Prison, as I lay motionless on the cell floor, they would have been horrified. My body was broken, bloodied, filthy, and apparently lifeless. They would have cried until they had no tears left. There was no way they could have imagined the contentment I was feeling a peace that I'd always lacked, in a place of utter silence and tranquillity. I don't think there is any possible way of achieving that kind of peace in this present life.

Of course, I hadn't actually died, but I believe I got to sample the experience a little. Although 'I' seemed to be in the clouds, I was still aware that my body was lying in the cell, and that I was reluctant to return to it.

My fate was not to die that day. However, if I had been rolled on my face I couldn't have moved my head, and so would have suffocated. Or just one more beating would have finished me off.

Descending to Hell

I don't know how long this coma lasted. I regained consciousness to find myself slung over *Bùi Đình Thi*'s shoulder. He held both my legs; my head and arms hung down his back. He took me into the newly built, extra secure, disciplinary Section.

I was shackled by one leg to the sleeping platform, where I lapsed into unconsciousness again. Time passed. It was pitch-dark when I was next aware of my surroundings. I could hear *Nguyễn Sỹ Thuyên*'s voice. He was shackled to the same platform, on the inside next to the wall. *Thuyên* told me that perhaps half the night had passed.

"This morning, when the rascal *Bùi Đình Thi* threw you in, you were in some sort of dream state. I called to you but you didn't respond. I thought you were gone, man. D'you know where *Tiếp* is?"

I whispered through bruised and swollen lips "*Tiếp* is already dead!"

"*Tiếp* is dead! Oh my God!"

"Yes, *Tiếp* is dead! That thug, *Bùi Đình Thi* beat *Tiếp* to death outside the door of our room. He threw his corpse on top of me."

Thuyên was silent for a considerable time before speaking again. "So *Tiếp* is dead! How about *Tiểu* and *Văn*?"

"I don't know". *Thuyên* didn't talk any more, but I heard him sobbing in the dark. I lay motionless, tears flowing down my face.

Then I began vomiting. I tried to turn my face to the floor but I was too weak doing so. The vomit ran over my neck. The smell was unbearable. Later, in the morning's light, I saw that I had vomited up nothing but fresh blood. During the day, I urinated and excreted blood also and became really frightened. Later on, I convinced myself that it was good to have this blood coming out, not putrefying inside. *Nguyễn Sỹ Thuyên*'s state was no better than mine. He had also been beaten and was bruised and raw all over. He too vomited up and excreted a substantial amount of blood.

Then he became very restless. It seemed he was groping for something. From the corner of my eye, I saw that he had a sharpened can lid and was trying to cut into the vein of his crotch. "*Thuyên*! What the hell are you doing?" I croaked.

Thuyên whispered desperately, "We're going to die anyway; better to kill myself now and be at ease."

I whispered back, "Come on, *Thuyên*, don't be silly! Don't act like that! It's better to let the Communists kill us, and then the world will know how savage they are. We don't have the right to take our own life, there's no sense in doing that!"

Thuyên gave up his idea of suicide. From that point on, we always comforted each other. On my part, I paid more attention to *Thuyên's* actions, even though I had taken away the blade. I found that his presence next to me was a great comfort; and I want to express to *Thuyên* my genuine brotherly love and honest appreciation. Every time I think of those terrible scenes from early May, 1979, I think that if *Thuyên* were not beside me during those first days, there is probably no way I could have survived. "Please, know in one-way or another, *Thuyên*, you are the one who saved my life".

In the days that followed, we saw so much blood still coming out of our bodies that we called to a guard to request medication. After insulting us, he brought the prisoner nurse who injected us with Vitamin K to stop the bleeding. This injection was our only favour from the 'Party' throughout that time. I tried different ways to purge the loose dead blood from my body.

When my urine began to clear, I drank a few teaspoons of it each day. I knew that urine contained salt that could dissolve the blood. The results were exactly as I'd hoped: Every time I took that "Medicine", I purged more blood. I continued to self-treat that way over several weeks, until my urine cleared. *Thuyên* followed my example. My body gradually got stronger. A week later, I could turn on my side to excrete on to the floor of the cell. No longer did I have to lie in my own bloody waste. However, it took about three weeks for me to be able to sit up.

I still remember struggling to sit up for the first time. *Thuyên* helped me by tying his shirt sleeves around my neck and pulling me up slowly. The effort was excessively painful, as if my bones were being torn out of their sockets. I persevered because I believed I would become paralysed if I lay down too long. During that time, I hated coughing or sneezing as these caused jerking movements that made me fear my bones would fly out through my broken skin. The pain was indescribable. Several days later, we found out that *Trịnh Tiếu* and *Lâm Thành Văn* had also been beaten, and was shackled in the old discipline block, the Black House.

The Second Murder

A week after our recapture, *Nguyễn Tiến Đạt*, our sanitary man, told us that *Lâm Thành Văn* had died that morning. We were both deeply upset that another brother had passed on. A month later, when the Black House was demolished, *Trịnh Tiếu* and Father *Nguyễn Công Định* were transferred into our cell. *Trịnh Tiếu* told us the details of *Văn's* death. When the three search shots went off to signal our escape, he and *Văn* were quickly seized. They were both taken for a beating session, although not as severely as three of us. However, *Tiếu* did have a broken rib. After that, they were shackled in the Black House.

During the following days, *Văn* gradually weakened. His stomach ulcers must have been aggravated by his injuries, and he didn't eat. Formerly, he had been given rice soup, in place of the cassava the rest of us received, plus an extra ration of salt. He had stored the latter for the escape attempt. But when we were caught, *Bùi Đình Thi* frisked us and found the salt. That did it for *Văn*. From then on, *Bùi Đình Thi* did not allow *Văn* to have any of his rice soup, instead, he kicked the bowl over. He tried to force *Văn* to eat cassava, which he couldn't digest. *Văn* pleaded for mercy at every meal, but the wicked *Trật tự viên* would always answer, "What? To give you rice soup so you can take the salt and escape from Camp? If you can't eat cassava, then you die."

During his final days, *Văn* had nothing he could eat and only water to drink. The night before he passed away, he raved deliriously and spoke only of food, asking about a dream of canned salted lemongrass from his younger sister. On his last morning, *Văn* called *Tiếu* to help him, as he was by now unable to sit by himself. With one leg shackled and the other bent, he sat with his head down and two arms circling his knee. *Tiếu* saw *Văn's* head limply fall to one side. He died gradually, like a lamp not enough oil that finally fizzles out. In death, he still had one leg shackled. *Lâm Thành Văn* left a wife and six young children.

The heartless deaths of *Đặng Văn Tiếp* and *Lâm Thành Văn* caused us great suffering. My grief still pours out like the smoke of incense, in remembrance of my two brothers with whom I shared the unfulfilled thirst for Freedom.

Chapter 13
"I Must Live! I Must Live! I Must Live!"

As for those who have died, they paid their debts in this life, *Đặng Văn Tiếp* and *Lâm Thành Văn* were out of the hell of *Thanh Cẩm* Camp. May they rest in peace. As for us, the three prisoners who survived the escape attempt, we still had to suffer the life of the disciplinary Section for several years. The disciplinary cell of *Thanh Cẩm* Prison was already Hell by itself. When it had the sadistic presence of *Bùi Đình Thi*, it went down many levels and turned into the Bottom of Hell.

It was right in this Bottom of Hell that man still faced his own fate. *Tiểu* and *Thuyên* were slightly more fortunate than me, they received less of his attention. I, on the other hand, could never escape the wicked hands of *Bùi Đình Thi*. Father *Định*, who did not participate in the escape, was not beaten, but all the same was locked in the disciplinary block. He now harboured great resentment against us, and when four of us were confined in the same cell, there were many regrettable incidents between Father *Định* and the three of us.

In the first week, both *Thuyên* and I had both feet shackled day and night. Neither one could turn his body, so we had to do our excreting and vomiting right on the cement platform where we lay, cleaning it off, as well as we could with our hands, and tearing our clothing into strips to rub our hands clean. We were supposed to use the bamboo tubes provided for our toilet purposes, but as we couldn't move, this was impossible. After a couple of days, the pile of faeces surrounding our bodies was growing higher and higher, and our set of clothes becoming smaller and smaller. We were, too, used to the stench to notice it, in contrast, every time the guards looked in through the window, they quickly covered their noses.

I worried about what we would use when our clothes were all torn up. We begged the guards to give us something to use, but they refused. Then *Thuyên* had a good idea. As soon as he was able to sit up, he took a piece of material, about twenty centimetres by ten, and tied a string to each corner around our hips and waist, rather like a 'bikini'. This type of bikini was very easy to put on. One had to tie the two front strings to the back and two back strings on either side around the waist. Though it looked a bit strange, it was tidy and very convenient. Untied, it served as a towel. *Nguyễn Sỹ Thuyên*, a math's teacher, had become a fashion designer! It was a pity that we had only one 'suit' each but there was insufficient cloth for a second one.

The First Fraternal Gift

After three weeks, we were unshackled for the first time and allowed to bathe and do laundry in the *Mã* River. There were twenty other disciplinary prisoners, among them were five priests. They all looked weak and fatigued as they lined up in pairs, each holding clothes and a container for water. *Thuyên* and I had no clothes to wash. When *Thuyên* and I stumbled out wearing our only 'bikini' bottoms, everyone turned to look. I don't know if they were looking at our strange dress or our walking skeletons, smeared with faeces and urine. Perhaps both of them.

I was blinded and disorientated by the light and didn't have enough strength to lift my feet. It was as though I was paralysed from lying flat for so long, and the guards had to tell two other prisoners to support me. *Thuyên* was doing better and could walk without help, but he looked so miserable, stumbling along with his feet wide apart. His still-bruised body was so hunched over that it seemed his head would touch the ground.

The river was only about a hundred meters away, but it seemed to take forever to go that far. As we passed the Camp hall, I shivered, recalling what had happened three weeks ago, and that unforgettable expression in the protruding eyes of *Bùi Đình Thi*, **"F**ck you Lễ! You rotten bastard! Don't you want to eat rice, but sh*t instead! You wanted to die, so I'll help you!"** Now, he was walking right behind me as I dragged along at the end of the row.

Everyone rushed into the river. The water so near the source was clean and relatively shallow, no more than neck-high. Once I'd immersed myself, I felt relaxed and wonderfully clean, having washed away so much dirt that had stuck to my body over the past three horrible weeks. I glanced around at the others, particularly my fellow priests, and found them looking at me with pity. No one dared to say a word, but their eyes spoke in sympathy. I was forbidden to have contact with any of the others; and I knew that there were eyes always watching me.

Even bathing for a short while left me out of breath. I stood looking down stream towards the cave where the three of us had taken shelter, where I had baptised *Tiếp* three weeks earlier…I dared not continue with my thoughts, but turned my attention to the shoal of little fish swimming among our legs. These finger-sized fish had learned that the filth we washed away could provide food for them.

Bùi Đình Thi signalled for us to return to our cells. Taking advantage of the crush as everyone pushed back on to the bank, Father *Trần Văn Nghị* discreetly passed me a clean face towel rolled into a ball. To me, it was a very valuable gift and I was deeply touched by his sympathy. Now, my possessions consisted of half a tattered mat, half a blanket, the 'bikini' bottoms that *Thuyên* made, and the towel. I thought to myself *"My life's not too bad"*. How mistaken I was!

Disaster Again!

Back at our cells, everyone was busy hanging his clothing to dry at the windows. I was almost exhausted but managed to shake out my rags and the precious towel and to put them out to dry. The towel was distinctive, white with a square marked in the centre. Suddenly, I heard a voice right behind me.

"*Lễ!* Where did you get this towel?" *Bùi Đình Thi* stood there, his hand pointing at the towel.

I was horrified because I knew that trouble was to follow, so I hurriedly lied. (May God forgive me!) "I picked it up down at the river. I don't know who dropped it, but I'll return it as soon as I find out."

"Unlikely you could come across that. Come on! Tell the truth, who gave it to you?"

I stood my ground but said more urgently, "I really did find it in the river…nobody gave it to me!"

Bùi Đình Thi hesitated, and then went away and I breathed a sigh of relief. The danger had gone. I hastened inside, climbing onto the platform as if it was a safe haven where I could avoid his reach.

Before I could regain my composure, *Bùi Đình Thi* came back along with the dark-skinned, slant-eyed guard. Without saying a word, BDT. leaped at me, grabbing my neck. The guard gave me a strong blow in the ribs, making me fold over. I was too feeble to bear such treatment. No longer able to control myself, I cried out, "Oh my God!" and tumbled off the platform on to the floor. They watched me writhing there for some minutes. Then the guard ordered: "Lock this dirty rascal up!" He spat on the floor as he left. BDT. grabbed me by my hair, pulled me up and shackled my feet. He screamed, "This will teach you not to associate with others! You are a barefaced liar. I will beat you until you quit lying."

Bùi Đình Thi asked the other prisoners who had given me the towel and finally sorted out the culprit. This was a pity, for Father *Nghị* was now in trouble because of his compassion. The duo took turns to beat Father *Nghị* black and blue, splitting his lips, bloodying his face. Then this Good Samaritan was shackled for seven days and nights and his food ration was reduced. Later, when I had a chance to apologise to him, Father *Nghị* laughed jovially, saying "What do you mean sorry, *Lễ*? I was happy to share a bit of your suffering. It really made me happy! What's more, when I tried to shield myself, I accidentally hit their fists. I know I hurt them because they got so mad they thrashed me more!" Again he laughed cheerfully.

I lay half dead for a few days after that thrashing. The beating three weeks before had been much worse, but at that time, I was still relatively healthy and able to bear it. However, this time it was different. My body was already seriously damaged and my crying out, "Oh my God!" was a natural reaction that I could not hold back. It was the only cry I ever made while being beaten, even in the dreadful torture that was to follow.

At the Brink of Death!

A few weeks after the towel event, the Black House was demolished and its customers were transferred to the new disciplinary building where we were. Father *Định* and *Trịnh Tiếu* were moved in with *Thuyên* and me.

It was a hot and muggy summer. At night, the door of our room was closed and there was no ventilation. We looked forward to mealtime when the door was opened and we could get some fresh air. Sometimes, I thought that if God gave me the ability to do miracles, my first would be to put a large hole in our roof, so the heat could escape and we'd have some fresh air to breathe. Many times at night, I had to lie with my face close to the floor to find the cooler air pressed down under the humidity above. The air seemed to have the consistency of condensed milk. I felt I had been ungrateful for not giving thanks to the Lord for all the time I had an abundance of fresh air to breathe. I made up my mind then, that if I survived, I would share this painful experience with others, to suggest, please don't take for granted the fresh air you're breathing.

Father *Định* still had a few clothes, but the rest of us didn't. When we went to the river we wore the 'bikini' pants, but in the room the three of us went naked. I continually asked for clothes but my requests went unheeded. One day, I saw an unfamiliar elderly guard pass outside the window. I called out to him loudly, "I have a request, Cadre."

He stopped some distance from the window's iron bars, and asked, "Who's calling, what's the matter?"

"Please, I beg you, either give me some clothes, or put a bullet in me. I'm a human being and not an animal to live naked! If I die by your hands in this jail, it won't matter. But if I survive, I'll find an opportunity to let the world know how inhumanely the Vietnamese Communist Regime treated the political prisoners! I think that there is no country in the world that would treat political prisoners so savagely."

Perhaps, it was because he was so surprised that he stood still for a long time without a word, and then he asked "What's your name?"

"Reporting to you, my name is *Nguyễn Hữu Lễ*!"

"What sort of prisoner group do you belong to?"

"I am a Catholic priest."

He smiled disdainfully. "Then you are of the priestly brood'?"

I answered indignantly, "I have said that I am a Catholic priest, cadre."

"What did you do to be disciplined?"

"I escaped."

"Escaped the Camp? Plenty of guts!"

I didn't answer and the Guard left.

I anxiously waited for the consequences of this dialogue. I was prepared to pay the price for what I said. But instead of punishment, BDT. was ordered to issue me with a pair of black trousers and a yellow shirt stamped with '*CẢI TẠO*' (Re-education) on the back. These were my clothes that were left behind when I escaped. A few days later, I had to tear off one leg of the trousers for toilet purposes. If I couldn't find any papers or rags in the rubbish tip, the shirt sleeves would soon follow.

Misfortunes Never Come Singly

The prisoner appointed to clean out the cells and empty the bamboo tubes was *Nguyễn Văn Hà*. One day, he saw me tearing up my clothes. He asked me to give him my yellow shirt that he could exchange for tobacco. When I told him that I needed it to clean myself, he said he'd find some rags for that purpose. So, without thinking, I gave him the yellow shirt.

In the following days, I forgot all about the shirt, and *Hà* didn't give me any rags. I could make do with the other trouser-leg until we next went to bathe. Then, I would wander over to the rubbish tip for some rags. We enjoyed our time at the river. As we washed ourselves clean, we surreptitiously talked with prisoners from other cells. And of course, we all examined the rubbish tip. One time, I was lucky enough to find a real 'treasure', a half-worn toothbrush. I brought it down to the river, cleaned it carefully and used it for nearly two years.

One morning, we lined up in pairs waiting for the signal to depart for the river. The slant-eyed guard, armed with a long rifle, escorted the group. There was no BDT. in sight, and we all felt quite at ease. Without the *Trật tự viên,* the rubbish tip was carefully targeted and more treasures collected. The morning was pleasantly warm and after the enforced rest of being locked up for more than two months, my physical condition had improved.

Walking back to the cell block, I turned my face towards the cloudless sky and inhaled a long breath of fresh air. How good life was! The tortures of the past few months had gone, forever I hoped. I recalled the popular saying: '*After a storm comes the calm.*' Surely, I'd paid all my debts. I forgot the dreariness of my present life and thought only of what I loved: life, the blue sky, nature, and human beings, including those who'd persecuted me even *Bùi Đình Thi*. I silently repeated the words of Jesus Christ as he hung on the cross between two criminals, "Father, forgive them for they do not know what they do." (Lk.23, 34)

I was surprised to find *Bùi Đình Thi* standing in front of our door, glaring at me. The slant-eyed guard stood next to him. I had a hunch on that. Immediately, my sixth sense warned me that something very serious was about to happen. I turned away to avoid BDT.'s eyes, which I'd always feared. I couldn't think of anything I'd done wrong. I told myself that it was just because I feared him so much that I became panic-stricken whenever he looked at me. But then BDT. came straight to me. In his left hand was a huge bunch of keys and his other hand pointed straight at my face, almost touching my forehead, and he asked in a menacing voice "*Lễ!* Where's your yellow shirt?"

Only then did I remember giving the yellow shirt to *Hà*. Obviously, the whole story had been discovered. I was petrified. I started sweating and felt I was losing control of my bowels.

So I told him another lie. (May God forgive me once more!) "I hung it in the window and someone took it by mistake a few days ago. I searched for it but couldn't find it. If you find it somewhere, please give it to me, *Anh Thi.*"

"Why did that rascal *Hà* say that you exchanged it with him?"

Warning bells rang when hearing the word exchange, because the Camp regulations prohibited this. Everyone involved would meet trouble; much worst for me.

I mumbled "It's not so, Anh *Thi*. I did not lie. Probably, he mistook my shirt for his. As I said, I didn't exchange it!"

I was hoping for his empathy. I hoped that he would forgive me because he found me so frightened and, especially, because of my poor physical condition. The guard seemed to be losing his patience. He stood still, but his fingers were continuously flexing. Suddenly, BDT. grabbed me roughly, saying, "Come to the front and hear what *Hà* has to say."

The guard led us swiftly along the narrow corridor that led to the front cells. Evidently, the reason BDT. hadn't come to the river was that he could search all the rooms. He had found the shirt and *Hà* had told him everything. However, I still had one last glimmer of hope. If *Hà* said he'd stolen the shirt, he would be given a few slaps, and that would be all. But if *Bùi Đình Thi* discovered that I'd given the shirt to *Hà*, it would provide an excuse to unleash his deep resentment towards me.

Keeping this in mind, when I was still in some distance from *Hà's* room, "I cried out "*Hà! Hà!* Why did you take my shirt as it was drying in the window? I've been looking for it for days. Brother *Thi* said you have it, so please give it back to me, *Hà!*"

I hoped he would support my story but he either didn't understand my signal, or he was afraid of being beaten. He called out "I did not take your shirt! You exchanged it with me!"

Oh! My Lord Jesus Christ! That was the answer I most dreaded, but the one that *Bùi Đình Thi* and the guard expected. For me, it was the moment of terror.

Suddenly, a felt like a mountain has fallen on my back. It was in fact a strong punch from *Bùi Đình Thi* on my back, making me fall forwards. Then the guard seized me, punching in my belly, making me fall backwards. BDT. punched me forwards again, and so they continued like two soccer players using me as a ball. I wanted to run for my life but the narrow corridor was blocked at both ends. Besides, I didn't have the strength to run. This torment went on for quite a while, each person taking ten or more hits on my back and abdomen. My legs were too weak to run away and I reeled to the ground mumbling, ***"Lord Jesus, I commit my soul in your hands!"*** I closed my eyes.

Images of Death appeared in my mind, but I thought to myself I can't possibly die this way! Then, I concentrated all my strength into my throat, all the desire of a living creature to protect its very life. I gave the loudest roar of my entire life. It was the maximum that my throat could sustain without bursting its blood vessels. I yelled three times in increasing volume:

"I MUST L…I…V…E!
I MUST L…I…V…E!
I MUST L…I…V…E!"

But in actual fact, I was waiting to die.

Suddenly, my survival instincts kicked in. I felt a surge of strength flow into my body, like a deflated balloon suddenly pumped to firmness. My bony frame had turned to iron and my legs became as sturdy as bridge supports. My mind was telling me, "Run! Run! Run at any cost, if you don't run, you'll die!"

I whipped around and charged into *Bùi Đình Thi*. This was so unexpected; he lost his balance and fell backwards on to the ground. I ran like an arrow back to the cell. BDT. climbed to his feet and chased me, right on my heels. I knew that if he caught me he'd kill me. I truly believe this would have happened. Dashing into the room, I jumped up on the bunk platform and seized the free horseshoe-shaped iron shackle waiting for me. It weighed about one and a half kilos. I held it high and stood waiting, gasping for breath. BDT. stopped at the threshold. How wise he was!

With the shackle in my right hand, I challenged him, "Come on! *Bùi Đình Thi*, just the two of us! I'll give up my life for yours! You've pushed me to the dead end. Step inside if you want. Come on, *Bùi Đình Thi*! Come on. Come on!"

Bùi Đình Thi went crazy because he'd failed to finish off his wounded prey. Eyes aflame, foam speckling his lips and gnashing his teeth, he pointed his shaking finger at me, screaming in anger *"F*ck you Lễ, you bastard! I will k-i-i-i-l-l you!"*

Hearing the way he ground out the word '*K-i-i-i-l-l*', I understood that only the iron shackle had saved me. The guard arrived and looked very pleased to see two prisoners about to kill each other. Had he known that one was a Catholic and the other was a Catholic priest, he would probably have been happier still. He ordered BDT. to lock me up.

But I yelled, "Guard! I mustn't be shackled. If I were, BDT. will beat me to death."

"I said you are going to be shackled." The Guard commanded.

"But do you, Guard, guarantee that BDT. will not beat me?"

"I guarantee it. Now you'd better be shackled." With the guard's guarantee, I sat down and offered my leg to be put in the horseshoe-shaped iron lock and for BDT. to insert the iron bar. The whole scene had taken place in front of my three roommates, all stunned and watching in trepidation.

In the Stage of Madness

When the duo locked the door and left, I lay down exhausted. My blood was spurting out from my mouth and my nose. *Bùi Đình Thi* beat me so viciously that I couldn't breathe. I could no longer contain myself and was not aware of those around me. I started cursing. Half out of my mind, I rolled over and over, crying loudly: "*Bùi Đình Thi*, you murderer! I swear to you, if I live through this, I'll try every way I can to get you and your poisonous brood. I'll tear out your guts! I'll put them on the altar of *Đặng Văn Tiếp* and *Lâm Thành Văn*! Only then will I be satisfied! *Bùi Đình Thi! Bùi Đình Thi! Bùi Đình Thiii !*"

Later, I felt terrible remorse for saying such things. I had believed I was able to control myself, but now I knew I was a very weak person. Now, I would like to take the opportunity to apologise to *Trịnh Tiếu, Nguyễn Sỹ Thuyên* and Father *Nguyễn Công Định*, those who witnessed the scene and heard my wicked words.

After I was beaten by BDT. to near death, *Nguyễn Tiến Đạt*, a young Catholic, from the next room called over to comfort me and asked, "What do you think, Uncle *Bảy*? If later on BDT. repented and wanted to confess, would God forgive him?"

At the time, I was so enraged with anger that I blurted out, "That bastard! If God's feet hadn't been nailed to the Cross, He would have given him a hard kick on his head, let alone forgive him!"

Many years had gone by I always regretted saying those blasphemous words. In my insanity, I had stated such an indignant expression. It should never come from the mouth of a priest. This would cause a bad example for my inmates. Instead, I should have said, "If later on, *Bùi Đình Thi* genuinely shows remorse, God will forgive him definitely. For the mercy of God always overcomes the sins of a repentant person."

Bùi Đình Thi continued to hold the post of *Trật tự viên* in *Thanh Cẩm* Camp for almost another year, causing many more catastrophes for his fellow prisoners. No one seemed to know why he later lost his position and was downgraded to a building-group chief.

In early 1981, he was released, if my recollection is correct. The day *Bùi Đình Thi* lost his position as *Trật tự viên* was one of the two happiest occasions of my thirteen prison years, second only to my transfer from 'Gateway to Heaven'.

Chapter 14
The Pits of Hell

The Punishment Section of *Thanh Cẩm C*amp, in which we were incarcerated was only three years old. Because I lived there for a long time, I was able to observe how carefully it had been designed to maximise the results of sadistic punishment. A high wall topped with barbed wire separated this section from the rest of the camp. The rectangular flat-roofed house was built of reinforced concrete. It was made up of six cells. The three at the front faced a large yard while the back three were adjacent to a narrow path that led to the section wall. Each cell was three square meters with a metal door and a barred fifty centimetre-square window. Between each pair of cells was an auxiliary cell, a meter and a half wide. This auxiliary cell held the end of the metal rod that went through the shackle that held the prisoner's foot. That way the prisoner and the padlock were in a separate cell. This prevented any tampering with the lock.

It also meant that in order to enter one's cell, one had to go through two doors; the first wooden door to this auxiliary cell and then the second metal one to the confinement cell. This made escape doubly difficult. Another result of the two-cell arrangement was that air circulation was almost completely blocked. Two cells were exceptions to this rule, numbers One and Six were both at the corners of the building. Each of these was fronted by a concrete terrace and had only one door.

I realised that I was rotated among all six cells. Some of my companions had been in the Punishment Section for years, while others stayed for months, weeks or even just days before going back to the 'Village' (Collective Section). Some went down to the Village for a while before being returned to the Punishment Section. I never was given such a vacation. Each cell had a platform with a shackle on each side of a central aisle. The platforms were eighty centimetres above the floor and were uncomfortably narrow for two men, too wide for one.

The room was designed for four customers, but sometimes it would accommodate an extra prisoner. This prisoner would lie in a cell's aisle and wouldn't be shackled, which was a real blessing. Although I was in this building for precisely one thousand and twenty days (1.020 days), I never had this privilege, not even for a single night. Normally, it was only those who were shackled with a long-term sentence. For the first three months, such prisoners would be shackled all day and all night, followed by a period of night-only shackles from 5.00 p.m. to about 7.00 a.m. Those sent for a short, sharp punishment were shackled all day and night for a few weeks.

The cell was dark except for a small amount of light from the window. Our eyes soon adjusted to this so we were accustomed to the dimness. But anyone trying to look in from outside couldn't see well at all. Especially on sunny days, they would have to take a long and hard look to see how many people were in the cell. The ceiling was low and almost within reach of any one standing on the platform. A single light bulb, turned off at 10.00 p.m., provided a flickering glow in the evening.

The 'Socialism' Toilets

There were no toilets. Instead, we were given hollow bamboo segments or 'the movable toilets'. Using these was not simple, even for unshackled prisoners. Newcomers required instructions and often encountered difficulty using them the first few times. A prisoner needed to grasp two bamboo tubes, one in each hand at the same time, a narrow one for urine held in front and a wide-mouthed one, of course, at the rear. He then stood slightly bent, as in a martial arts fighting stance. While defecating, one had to reach an arm back to hold the tube in place. It was often heavy and therefore, difficult to hold, making it easy to spill the contents. Before meals, any resultant mess would be cleaned away by the sanitary man.

Those of us who had been confined in this section for some time had ankles no thicker than a cycle pump, and so were able to move our legs inside the shackle and contort our bodies into the needed position. But newcomers usually had some flesh still on their ankles. They found the shackles much tighter, here for more constricting. We tried to evacuate our bowels at night, after one leg was shackled, partly out of consideration for others and partly for our own privacy. However, in cases where we couldn't wait, nobody complained.

Furthermore, because we were used to these close living conditions, we got used to the offensive smell. We each minded our own business. While one person defecated, others could be eating, doing physical exercises, standing at the window, sitting to pray, playing chess, sewing…The designated prisoner (Sanitary man) collected each cell's bamboo tubes twice a day before distributing food and dumped the contents into a pit in front of the building. After the bamboo tube was emptied, he dipped his smeared hand inside a small water tank sitting at the corner of the house. The pit had no cover and became a happy breeding ground for green flies.

In the Human 'Baking Oven'

In summer the extremely hot Laotian winds blew into Central Vietnam. The more wind, the hotter the day. Even so, there was very little air movement in our cramped cell. The sun's heat baked the roof which in turn radiated its heat at night, squeezing every last drop of moisture out of our frail bodies. To make the night a bit more comfortable, each person set aside a bowl of water from his rations. He would soak a cloth in this water, sponge himself, and then squeeze the water back into the bowl. We went naked all day and night except for meal times, because sweat-soaked clothing would plaster itself onto our skin. The long-term residents like me had little left to wear anyway. Our pants were all torn off at the knee, shirts had sleeves torn out, and we would save our clothes for the occasions when we had to leave the cell.

I recalled those summer nights which I endured in the correctional cell of *Thanh Cẩm* Prison. It felt as if I was inside a closed iron box with dial turned on maximum temperature available. There were some suffocating nights when I could no longer breathe in that burning air. We had no choice but to shout out at the top of our hoarse voice to the guard to open the cell door as there were prisoners dying of suffocation. When a prison guard opened the door, the air, which rushed in made me feel so happy.

For me, it was one of the happiest moments in my life! However, when the cell door was slammed shut again; the wretched and naked inmates with their feet in shackles had to relive the nightmare as before. At that moment, I realised that nothing in life was more valuable than the fresh air we could breathe into our lungs.

During our time in the Punishment Section, we officially got to bathe in the river once every two weeks. However, if the guards were busy the wait stretched to three weeks. When this happened, we'd yell and holler in complaint until they would allow us to have our bath to avoid the noise. More important than the actual dip in the river was the chance to investigate the contents of the dumpster by the roadside. Every time we passed the dumpster, I searched for rags to use as toilet paper, plastic bags to store tinder and fuel, or even better, discarded paper bags that I could use for writing on.

The Chinese Inmates

When I'd been in the Punishment Section for three months, fifteen Chinese prisoners were transferred from another section of the camp. Living with men of a different culture was a new experience to me. These men all looked dirty, and like all the Chinese I'd ever seen were encumbered with a number of seemingly worthless possessions. A few were tall but most were tiny. They went into different cells to live among us, the Vietnamese; some of them had served over ten years already and had experience of other camps before being transferred here. All were charged with spying for the Chinese.

I gradually learned that some had been petty traders and cross our border to sell medicine, watches, or lengths of fabric. However, as soon as they were caught, they were imprisoned as spies. Some, due to their political leanings, had to leave their own country and live hidden among our ethnic minorities, changing their names and adapting to a new culture. Some had been Red Guards for Mao Tse-Tung and when he changed his program, they became persecuted and had to run. The majority spoke Mandarin, while a few spoke Cantonese, and some knew some basic Vietnamese language. A few of them were kind and gentle, but the others came from a tough background of banditry and often revealed their violent natures.

Being constantly hungry and shackled in such heat did nothing to improve their natures. Those who had previously lived in gangs, stealing goods and murdering people, now formed powerful alliances and became much feared. They had only one goal, to survive. To do this, they found ways of getting sufficient food, even in this prison where many died from starvation. They were willing to become slaves of other prisoners in exchange for food. They were willing also to attack, even kill to get another man's food. A man on his own acted like a puppy, but a group in alliance was like a pack of hungry wolves. Those who were gentle served as storage facilities just a pair of hands to receive and hold the food until the bully was ready to take every bite of it.

Vietnamese prisoners in general were more fortunate than the Chinese. Even in the North, families short of food for themselves, the families were forbidden to visit us, but they posted us food and medicine. Although we could not receive more than 5kg of food every three months, that amount helped prolong our lives. The situation improved after a policy change in 1979 that allowed family members to visit their imprisoned relatives at the *Thanh Cẩm* Prison. We were told that this was a favour from the Government, but significantly the change happened at a time when the entire country was close to a famine and the Government was no longer able to feed its prisoners.

When groups of visitors began to arrive, so did money and goods. This resulted in a clear demarcation of social classes. Earlier, the prison had been egalitarian. But now those with goods, almost all Southerners, became the masters. Prisoners without visitors or gifts from visitors had to serve those who had. They were effectively demoted to servants, and most of the skilled servants were the Chinese.

At the beginning of 1980, my second year in shackles, I lived with two Chinese and a Southerner named *Lê Thiên Bảo*. His presence prevented the Chinese from persecuting me. *Bảo* was my age. Prior to his capture, he'd been a Tae Kwon Do martial arts instructor in the National Police Headquarters in Saigon. In prison, he lived with a number of priests and was struck by their kindness and generosity. He told me that he wanted to find out why they were like this. I gradually told him about the Christian faith and its ideals. After a while, he asked to be baptised. Many respected *Lê Thiên Bảo's* good nature and self-discipline as a martial artist. He was also skilled in languages; speaking Vietnamese, Mandarin and Cantonese. Day after day, in our cell, he spoke Mandarin to the two Chinese and Vietnamese to me.

At that time, I was unable to speak a word of Mandarin and while listening to their conversation, I thought, the human brain is really something, to make them able to speak and understand such a bizarre language!

One of the two Chinese named *Lý Đức Nghĩa* was originally from Hunan, and a former member of Mao Tse-Tung's Red Guard. When Mao achieved power in China he executed former comrades who could threaten his leadership. Then he used students as his Red Guards in an effort to destroy China's ancient culture. When these young people got out of control, Mao used the Red Army to eliminate the Red Guards. It was at this time that *Lý Đức Nghĩa* left China and headed for Vietnam where he lived as a thief.

Lý Đức Nghĩa still worshipped Mao and was contemptuous of the Vietnamese Communists, claiming they had treacherously turned against their master. He was held for 10 years under the charge of Chinese espionage. Although he'd lived in Vietnam for many years, he couldn't speak our language.

He was a tall man with unusual eyes, clear and narrow-set, and he was able to glance through their slit corners. I thought an artist would delight in using their vicious expression. *Lý Đức Nghĩa* had many *'mosts'* among the Chinese prisoners. He spoke Mandarin with the most accurate accent. Most skilled with his hands, you could give him a piece of fabric to unravel and in an hour he'd hand you back a roll of thread that looked as though it had been formed on a machine. He was also the dirtiest among the Chinese. He'd never used a toothbrush in all his life. As a result his teeth looked like rotten wood. I once asked, "*Nghĩa*, I can't understand why you don't brush your teeth."

He answered, "Chairman Mao never brushed his teeth, but still managed to be chairman of gigantic China, to rule over a billion people!" Of course, *Lý Đức Nghĩa* was also the most vicious of the group.

Learning Mandarin

I decided to use this opportunity to learn Mandarin. I began on 1 January 1980. My first sentence was "My sister from Saigon comes to visit me." I found it very difficult at first, but *Lý Đức Nghĩa* helped me with the pronunciation. Every night, while we all lay with one foot in shackles, we told each other stories. *Nghĩa* told us about the Red Guard, and *Lê Thiên Bảo* translated his words into Vietnamese. But at the same time I listened to each sound from *Nghĩa*. Occasionally I asked him to stop so that I could practice the correct Mandarin pronunciation.

Thanks to *Lý Đức Nghĩa* and *Lê Thiên Bảo* I learned the language spoken by over a billion people. When I had enough vocabulary, I told them Bible stories, asking them to correct me if I made a mistake. After two years of always living with one Chinese prisoner or another, I began to speak Mandarin with ease slang, idioms and obscenities too! Later I learned to read and write the language. I used charcoal to write the characters on the floor. Later on, with more easy-going guards, I could ask for a pencil, and on bath day could pick up paper bags from the dumpster to use as paper. I am grateful to all those who helped me.

Learning Mandarin was one of my better achievements during my lost years in Communist concentration camps. Some of the Chinese were shot for attempting to escape. Others, despite their best efforts to get food died of disease or starvation.

The Hungry Wild Beasts

At the end of 1981, our *Trật tự viên* was *Nguyễn Văn Bảy*. But we called him *Bảy Chà* (Indian *Bảy*) because of his dark skin colouring. Perhaps, he was appointed to this post for his intimidating appearance as he was tall and large-framed. If anyone who didn't know him any better might fear him. But if *Bùi Đình Thi* was our tyrant, *Bảy Chà* was our saviour.

At that time, I was in cell No.4 in the rear of the building. In the next cell, there were three Chinese, *Chu Vạn Hồi*, a bandit; *Lý Đức Nghĩa*, previously a Red Guard and *Lưu Tùng*, a poor trader arrested for doing business on the border. He was older than the two others and as thin as a reed. I had shared a cell with *Nghĩa* and *Hồi* many times and thought I knew what was happening. So, on one bath day, I privately asked *Lưu Tùng* if the other two stole his food. He didn't dare answer, but his eyes darted back and forth and with one hand he made a sawing motion on his neck. I told *Bảy Chà* that I believed the other two routinely confiscated nearly all of *Lưu Tùng's* food allocation, but that he didn't dare speak up. *Bảy Chà* promised to report this to the guard.

One day cell No. 5 received a new prisoner, a visiting criminal to be shackled day and night. Because they were with us for just a short time, we never took much notice of these visitors. But on his first night, shortly after lights out, I suddenly heard the terrible sound of a blow *"BOOOM"* from next door, followed by a yell *"Reporting to you guard, reporting to you guard! They're trying to kill me; they're trying to kill me! Save me! Reporting to you guard! They're trying to kill me! Save me...!"* The blood curdling screams of a man sure that he was about to be killed disturbed us all. We called out to know what was going on. The yelling persisted. The guards came running. I heard the sound of a cell door opening, the guards shouting at the Chinese...and then their footsteps as they took the new prisoner away.

To the disciplinary prisoners, fighting, yelling...became common events. I myself had to fight with *Lý Đức Nghĩa* when he robbed food from an elderly prisoner. But this time, when I heard the criminal yelling in great fear in the next cell, I knew it wasn't an ordinary fight. It must be that something very serious happened. A few days later, the on-duty Officer *Thanh* filed me into cell No. 5 with three Chinese, including *Lý Đức Nghĩa*. I reminded the guard that I had punished *Lý Đức Nghĩa* previously to protect an old man, if I were made to share his cell, he would surely take revenge. I was prepared to go into any of the other cells. Guard *Thanh* looked at me thoughtfully for some time then put me in cell No. 2 at the opposite end of the Section. I didn't realise it at that time, but that providential decision probably saved my life, as I will tell later the 'Horrifying Story' in Chapter 15 of this book.

Out-of-Season Shower!

There is a Vietnamese saying *'Live long and you will gain a high rank'*. I appeared to have the highest ranking in 1982, after almost three years in shackles, I automatically became 'Big Brother' to others. Because of my contact with many groups of prisoners, politicians as well as criminals, I was being regarded as the elder of high rank. If this status of high rank had no special meaning for the political prisoners, then it meant a difference between life and death for the criminals, where the respect for big brothers had become an unwritten law. Anyone who disregarded this rule ended up paying very dearly.

For four years, I lived among criminals in the 'Gateway to Heaven' and *Thanh Cẩm* Camps, so I had the opportunity to witness how such debts were paid. According to the severity of the offence, the violator would be assigned a punishment from the big brother. That old hands would bully the newcomers was taken for granted in prison. As soon as new prisoners entered the cell, the residents would beat them into submission. If any new prisoner had enough courage and wit, he would later find his own place to stand and take a leadership position.

The business of working oneself up the ladder was played out in many forms, but all had the common thread of mercilessness-only one man survived as *'Đại Ca'* (Big brother). Therefore, excluding the notorious well-known prisoners who had followers everywhere, most men went to sleep with only one eye shut. They had learned to be constantly alert. I had observed this behaviour among the ordinary criminals but didn't think I had a place in the hierarchy.

Then one morning a guard pushed in a young criminal in his twenties through the open door of our cell. The cell had four shackle stations at the time, with only three being occupied by two Chinese inmates and me. So there was room for this newcomer. Our new companion, blinded by the contrast between the brightness outside and the dimness of the cell, stood motionless in the middle of the cell while he adjusted to the oven-like heat and foul smell.

He clutched a rolled-up sleeping mat with his clothes and a blanket inside. In his other hand was a lidded metal bowl. His arm gripped a long-stemmed smoking pipe with an aluminium water can hanging off its end. While he was still blinking, the three of us spoke in Mandarin to make him think we were all Chinese. The guard worked quickly to shackle him and get out of the stinking heat. Seeing that, he was very frightened, I said in Vietnamese, "Can you see clearly yet?"

He seemed to relax slightly before politely saying, "Greetings, older brother! Are you *Anh Lễ?*"

"How do you know my name?" I asked.

"Some of our band came back from the Punishment Section speaking highly of you. They say you are very kind!" I laughed at that.

"What's your name?"

"Brother, my name is *Huống* (Thereafter H.), I stole some peanuts from a guard, he found out, and I was sent to be shackled."

He came close, holding out his bowl.

"I invite you to enjoy a bowl of rice!"

He uncovered it and carefully placed it beside me. Looking at the rice, the two Chinese appeared very animated. White rice was equivalent to a feast in a punishment cell where hunger was a constant companion. On looking at the three, I felt empathy for them. The tortured prison life had metamorphosed them from their true selves. This new prisoner had just sacrificed his own portion in exchange for safety. The two Chinese inmates were totally focused on the bowl of rice.

"Where'd you get rice?" I inquired.

"I made smoking pipes to trade for it. They call me 'Smoking Pipe *Huống*.'"

"If you give me the rice, what will you eat?" I said.

"I'm not hungry, brother!"

It pained me to hear him say that, because who wouldn't be hungry in this prison?

"*Huống*! Don't think I'm a criminal mafia boss. Lick (Eat) your rice, man. Who in this hell isn't hungry?"

He was surprised at my response but still didn't dare eat. I had to encourage him several times before he picked up the bowl, saying, "With your permission!" He scoffed it quickly and still looked hungry.

That night, H. and I lay parallel on the same platform. I was next to the wall, our leg shackles locked with the same metal rod. When it was almost time for the light to go off, he complained of a bellyache. Feeling we were about to have trouble, I hurriedly instructed him to turn his body away and put his unshackled foot down on the floor. He struggled to follow my directions, but couldn't twist around. Worse still, the bamboo tube had already been used twice, making it heavy.

In desperation, H. called out, "*Anh Lễ*! Help me! Hurry please! My bellyache is so severe!"

He stood looming above me. I answered quickly, "You've got to try to solve your own problem. Get down! Damnit, how are you going to go while standing up so straight? Why not just take off your pants? Are you embarrassed?" I turned to ask the Chinese man on the edge of the other bunk to demonstrate the technique. He quickly placed one foot on the floor, grabbed a bamboo tube and skilfully demonstrated the method of defecating into it. H. tried his best to copy, complaining of pain as the shackle cut into his leg. His shin was thicker than ours, still having some flesh, while the shackle was small.

Seeing that H. could not stand on the floor while shackled, I asked, "Can you try to wait for morning?"

"Oh, no, no, no! I really have to go now! It's leaking into my pants!"

"Can you do it while standing on the platform?"

"I'll try my best! I have such a terrible urge! Please hand me the tubes!"

"What'd you eat this morning to cause the bellyache?"

"Raw peanuts and I drank cold water! Poor me!"

I was irked but amused as I yelled cheerfully, "Poor you? No, poor me!"

He thought I was yelling at him in anger. "Please, please help me!"

With 1 free leg, I stepped down from the platform and picked up the tubes.

"Now stand on the platform, "I said, "Drop your pants, legs apart, bend your knees like a dog defecating! Have you ever seen a dog defecate?"

H. answered hurriedly, "Yes, yes!"

"Remember to hold it close to your butt. Which hand are you more comfortable with?"

"I'm right-handed!"

"So, use your right hand at the back, since that tube's heavier. Remember to hold it firmly."

Poor H.! He had a terrible time before he could hold the tubes in the right position. And all the while his urge got stronger. I lay down again, feeling nervous, the bamboo tube was right above my face. All of a sudden, I felt a warm sensation flow over my face, followed by a gust of wind "*Phuuuffff*"! I instinctively raised my arms to protect my face, but too late. His excrement had covered my face, neck and chest. H. yelled, "Oh my God! Oh my God!" as the pipe fell and spilled all over our sleeping mats. It happened too quickly for any of us to move out of the way. The other two Chinese inmates fiercely cursed him in Mandarin. H. began crying brokenly, "I plead with you to forgive me! Forgive me!" It was a very severe crime in prison to sh*t in the face of the 'Big brother' and it called for the death penalty.

H. fearfully unbuttoned his shirt and started to clean me. Then he prostrated himself, shaking and quivering, "Please forgive me…! Please forgive me…! Please forgive me!" I felt compassion for him. He hadn't intended this to happen.

To distract him from his fear, I decided to try some humour, which amazed the Chinese. "I really must thank you, *Huống*, in this section, we bathe only twice a month. Today you've given me my third bath!" I slapped his shoulder and continued, "Don't be afraid *Huống*. It was an accident. You didn't mean this to happen. It's just the situation we have to live in."

H. still sounded as if he might cry. "I thank you, Big brother, thank you for your compassion!" He continued trying to clean me with his shirt, and I let him do so to prove I wasn't angry with him. Only a smile and generosity of mind could rescue us at this time.

Strangely enough, although I had human faeces all over my face, hair and bedding, I didn't notice any smell. This made me realise the miraculous quality of the sense of smell. Luckily, we only had to wait for five more days to bathe in the river. If this accident had happened after a bath day, I would have had to wait fourteen stressful days.

After the bath five days later, I felt myself refreshed again although some others may disagree as the following account will prove. One morning our group from the Punishment Section joined prisoners from other sections of the Camp while the guards checked our records individually. We had been confined so long that we were very happy to see the other prisoners again. Immediately, I ran over to sit beside Father *Cao Đức Thuận*, whom I'd lived closely with in the 'Gateway to Heaven'. He, however, moved away from me. The closer I approached, the more he avoided me.

I didn't understand how such a kind person could change so much. Had life in prison changed him? Perhaps, he was afraid of the guards. It was only much later, when I'd been transferred back to the Flat House, (The solitary confinement) that I received an explanation. While welcoming me to his group, Father *Thuận* said, "Do you remember the day we were outside for record checks? I was thrilled to see you, but when you sat next to me I felt so nauseous I almost threw up on the spot. I had to turn my face away. It wasn't appropriate for me to tell you then. But oh gosh! Your body stank like a bucket of sh*t! I couldn't withstand the stench from your body!"

As for me, the smell was no longer a problem. Often our cell was smeared with excrement, especially if the food delivery was late; therefore, the waste wasn't removed on time and so overflowed into the aisle. The prisoner who emptied the tubes also distributed our food, and often didn't wash his hands in between. Sometimes, the soup had faeces floating on its surface. We used our spoons to remove them before sipping. There was nothing else to eat, and we had to eat to survive. Our punishment was multifaceted, but the most severe punishment was to the stomach. In the situation of permanent hunger, the prisoners tried to toss into their stomach anything that could be edible. Rats and lizards were truly a festival. Some criminals were poisoned to death by eating cockroaches, spiders and fire-bellied toads…

Madness for Sugar Craving

I discovered that when really hungry one craves sweets and fats the most, particularly sweets. I remember one particularly sad incident. One day, an inmate's family brought him some food. Because he was shackled, he was unable to go to the guest room to meet his relative, who had brought him ten kilograms of food. This was received on his behalf by the on-duty guard, who stored the bulk of it in the auxiliary room adjoining our cell. Only some fruit and a packet of lump sugar were given to him at that time. He generously shared with us the fruit and quite a large chunk of sugar. I was deeply touched and mumbled my thanks, asking God to bless this man who had such a kind heart. Then, I slowly nibbled the lump of sugar and felt it strengthen both my spirit and body. When it had all gone, I sucked my sticky finger tips to savour every last piece. What added to the occasion was that our whole group had shared the wonderful experience, which our friend could have kept to himself.

Out of consideration for our feelings, he didn't eat the rest of his treat in front of us, but waited until night to quietly enjoy it. I lay next to him and could hear him bite into the chunk. The sound nearly sent me crazy! My craving made me shake like a malaria victim. It was all I could do to resist asking him for more. I used two fingers to plug my ears to block that munching sound.

Although the food in the auxiliary cell was legally his, every day at mealtime he had to beg a guard for a small portion of it. One day, two *Trật tự viên Bùi Đình Thi* and *Trương Văn Phát* stole some. They put it in a lidded pot and carried it away in front of our eyes. The rightful owner was about to yell; "Thieves!" but I stopped him. I knew that those tyrants would take terrible retribution if he caused them to be punished. Then some mice found the food. They ate most of it and left their waste sprinkled in the rest. We didn't know this, and on succeeding days our friend continued to plead. *Bùi Đình Thi* ended his complaint with the curt response, "Mice have eaten it all!" I will always remember my friend's pained expression. He was the first victim of the new, malicious rule that gifts of food must be stored in the auxiliary cells. As a result, many mice were well fattened, while the owner's food went hungry.

And so, the lives of inmates in the Punishment Section became even more miserable, realising that, their relatives had deprived themselves, had travelled long distances in dangerous conditions to bring them food only to have it stolen by vermin, men or mice. Our hunger was continuous and left us only skin and bones. At that time, my thighs were half the width of my knees, all my ribs protruded and my belly was perennially sucked in. I could encircle an ankle with my thumb and middle finger. While lying with my spine on the mat, I had to cushion my hips with both hands. We were given whatever food was seasonally available, mostly corn, sweet potatoes or cassava. Rice was seldom served. Sometimes, we were given the bean husks that were a by-product of processing soy into tofu, but there was no way we could ram that down our throats, despite the unceasing hunger.

The Cat's Tongues!

One evening, the *Trật tự viên* brought our meal in a large pot normally used for cassava. There were five of us in the cell at the time. When we looked into the pot, we saw a grey piece of boiled dough no bigger than a cigarette packet. Glancing at one another we asked, "What's this supposed to mean?"

We thought the kitchen must have mixed up the portions, giving us one share instead of five. We lifted out the dough but didn't divide it up instead, waiting for roll call to complain to the guard. Several hours later, the guard approached the cell.

I yelled, "Reporting to you, Guard, I have a question."

"What's up?"

"Reporting to you, Guard, this cell was not given the correct amount of rations."

"How is that? What do you mean?"

"Reporting to you, Guard, this cell has five people but we were only given one portion. We kept it sitting here for you to see!"

"Let me see!" he requested.

I quickly put my free foot on the floor and lunged towards the window, my left leg stretched back to the shackle. I held the metal bowl in my hand and the dough lay neatly in the middle. The Guard glanced at it and said, "You guys are funny! This is the ration for five people! Why do you think there's a mistake?"

"Reporting to you, Guard, but…"

"But what? It's the same amount of dough. Baking makes it bigger. Boiling makes it smaller. Don't you understand?"

I was too stunned to speak. He put his hand through the bars as if to take the dough.

"So are you guys gonna eat this or not?"

I quickly pulled the bowl back inside the bars, away from him.

"Reporting to you, Guard, yes…yes…yes! We'll eat it!"

With a smirk, the Guard walked away.

A Heartfelt Sharing with My Readers

On recounting this episode, I would like to share with my dear and respected readers, "Don't you know that you are living in paradise? I would like to talk to you: Please never complain." I have reason for those bold statements. I am, Father Andrew *Nguyễn*, who had been stuffed in a cold closet for eight months in the 'Gateway to Heaven', I am Father Andrew *Nguyễn*, who had literally been shackled for three years in a baking hot cell (I repeat, a baking hot cell) of *Thanh Cẩm* Prison. I, Father Andrew *Nguyễn*, had been beaten until blood spattered on my skinny body.

I had been tortured to death and was revived to endure the torture again and again. I had had inmates' corpses piled on me. I had multiple injuries. I went totally mad as the environment was utterly unbearable for human beings. My feet were shackled, my body was naked, my throat was dry and my stomach was empty and craving for food. I crawled around like an animal in the hot baking oven of the punishment cell.

If you will, please for just a moment stop and think about the personal sufferings related above. Then consider how lucky you are. Consider if your sufferings are beyond your strength to endure. Are you luckier than Father Andrew *Nguyễn*? I have returned from the bottom of Hell! I am sharing all my experiences with you, my dear readers. I sincerely would like to ask you to pause and consider if your situation justifies complaining? Perhaps, you might find strength if you focus on your blessings. This might mitigate your sufferings and help you carry on.

Please also be grateful to God who has given us the blessing we enjoying.

In the morning, when I get up and breathe fresh air, I say, "Thank God, you have given me fresh air to breathe." When I hold up a glass of water, I say, "Thank God, you have given me fresh water to drink." When I hold up a bowl of rice, I say, "Thank God, you have given me rice to eat." I am living in Paradise at present. Yes, I am living in Paradise, indeed because ***I have the three most valuable things in life which are: Fresh air to breathe, Water to drink and Food to eat.***

I feel and conscientiously know that I am lucky. I am lucky because I have survived whereas many friends of mine have perished in the intolerable concentration camps of the Communist regime.

*I am lucky because I lost only one eye when I left prison, luckier than those who lost both of their eyes and had to spend the rest of their lives in darkness.
*I am lucky because I had only one leg paralysed when I left prison, luckier than those who had both their legs amputated due to illness or accidents.

*I am lucky because I had one lung left with which to breathe for the rest of my life.

*I always thank God for all my present good fortune and happiness that I am enjoying. I know a lot of people who are not lucky and happy as I am.

*I would love to share all my feelings and emotions with all my dear and respected readers who have read *"I MUST LIVE!"* I would like to see the readers, after reading, this memoir of my life from the beginning to the end, close the book and say: ***"I am the luckiest and most fortunate person in this world."***

The Occasional Visitors

During my three years in *Thanh Cẩm's* Punishment Section, I seemed to play the role of the butler, receiving many Vietnamese as well as Chinese inmates. As we were routinely shuffled among the six cells, I had the chance to get to know many of them. It also meant that I was also able to keep track of activities in the Camp and to send messages back to friends. Occasionally, short-term visitors brought food for the prisoners, some hot peppers or a bit of tobacco, but what we needed most was clothing and bedding. But when *Bùi Đình Thi* was *Trật tự viên*, there was no chance of our keeping any of the clothing. Even though the guards never paid attention to this, he would take it on himself to beat anyone he discovered with anything extra. Although I lived naked, everyone knew not to leave me anything, or I would be punished severely.

When *Bùi Đình Thi* lost his *Trật tự viên* position, my life improved significantly. It was especially pleasing to be able to wear clothes again. When *Bảy Chà (Indian Bảy)* took over that position in 1981, my life became far more comfortable. It was a pity he got this job so late in my stay. So, my life began to get better, despite I am still having one leg shackled.

Chapter 15
'Bình Thanh', The Notorious Bandit

One morning in late 1981, my third year in shackles, I looked out through the window to see a guard and *Trật tự viên* leading a group to the Punishment Section. They all looked relatively young and healthy and their clothing was better than ours, so I knew they must be criminals. Each person carried only a backpack. Most were short and of small build. They walked silently and without a word or smile, but didn't seem as miserable as most prisoners did on their arrivals.

I noticed that the man at the end of the line seemed to have a different attitude from the others. He looked to be in his early thirties, strongly built, and with the healthy complexion of a student, and the trousers he wore made him look like a soccer player. The group stared at our building while they waited in the yard for the *Trật tự viên* to unlock the back cells.

"Hello! Greetings to you mates. What camp have you transferred from?" I called through my barred window.

They looked to my direction, squinting through the bars, but couldn't make out anything in the dark cell. Then the tall and handsome man stepped closer and called in, "Greetings mates! We're from the Department of the Interior Prison in Hanoi, transferred here. You come from the South? I recognised the accent. How long have you been in this section?"

"I've been here in shackles for over two years now!"

"Why so long? What are you in for?"

I answered in one word: "Escaping!"

He gave me a delighted smile, saying, "You're number one! That's the way. While you were still in the South, what did you do?"

"Priest!"

"I couldn't hear. What did you say you were before?"

"I was a Catholic priest, a religious Father!"

"Ah! I understand now. You worked in a church, right? Defending the rights of the poor against the Government. *Anh Cha Đạo* (Religious Father) put in prison, but escaped! You're wonderful! You're number one! I'm *Bình Thanh* (Hereinafter BT.) and I'd really like to get to know you. What's your name?"

As he spoke he put his hand over mine on the metal bar. "I'd like that, BT. My name is *Nguyễn Hữu Lễ*. You can call me *Anh Út*" (Brother *Út*)."

"Thank you, *Anh Út*!"

The approach of a guard prevented any more conversation. The newcomers were put into their respective cells and I noticed that BT. entered cell No.3 next door to mine. Two new guys came into my cell. They both spoke with thick Northern accents. Most unusually, they were very polite to me from the moment they entered. They both took off their shirts, revealing a number of tattoos. The young one was tattooed on the back, belly, both thighs and both arms. He was called *Bình*, nicknamed *Bình Bưởi*. The other was *Tiến*, nicknamed *Tiến Ngựa*". No criminal was without a nickname. Although *Bình Bưởi* was younger, he was of higher rank in the criminal hierarchy. They told me that their group came from a prison in Hanoi. More of the group was in the "Village" (Collective Section). They also told me that BT. was the Big Brother of the group.

I'd lived with criminals at the 'Gateway to Heaven' and I understood their language and rules. *Anh* (Big brother) had a very important position, while *anh em* (Brothers) referred to group members and equals. Although these two men didn't yet know me, I sensed they already respected me. When we were allowed into the yard at lunchtime, I saw BT. dart around among the group. While the rest of us were skinny and sickly looking, he radiated strength and health. On seeing me, BT. ran over to take both my hands and say, "*Anh Út*, please wait a moment, I'm going in to see how my little boys are doing; I'll be right back with you!"

Then he ran inside to check on those of his group who were cleaning the cells. A few minutes later, he was again shaking my hand, saying, "*Anh Út*, the guys in my cell respect you very much and say you're great. I ask you to accept me as your fraternal brother."

I found this very moving. He seemed a very sensible person. Although his eyes were beautiful, hiding in their depths I sensed the tiger's wild spirit.

However, I squeezed his hand reassuringly, "From now on you're my younger brother."

I pulled him into a hug, and *Bình Thanh* squeezed me like a bear in return. I felt surprised that we had accepted each other so quickly. I knew he must be a *lưu manh* (Bandit), but a man of courage and dignity as well.

During the period that *Bảy Chà* (Indian *Bảy*) was our *Trật tự viên*, our conditions were considerably more comfortable. If the guards weren't about, he'd open the doors so that we could move around between the cells. Now that BT. had joined us, I saw something special for the first time of my three years in the Punishment Section. Although BT. was shackled like the rest of us, he received gifts of food and tobacco from criminals in the 'Village'. His followers sneaked over the section wall to bring them to him, passing the gifts through his barred window or if Indian *Bảy* was on duty, being delivered by him.

Bình Bưởi and the others told me about BT.'s life and accomplishments. In his circle, all respected him. Any recently captured prisoner could be spared the initiation ritual from the head honchos when they mentioned his name. BT. was not a typical headman because he didn't bully the weak for food, instead, he protected the lower rank. If necessary he'd go hungry himself so that his younger brothers could have their fill. He was a Robin Hood and sided with the socially oppressed. In that prison, he really was a social phenomenon.

The Rules of an Outlaw

Of course, the outlaws' world had its own rules, and as leader BT. would ruthlessly punish anyone who disobeyed them. Criminals had clear ranks, consisting of brothers, outsiders, underlings, and enemies. Once sworn in as brothers, they would live and die for one another. Outsiders could sit with them to share a meal, but not take part in any counsels. The underlings had to obey their superiors unconditionally, but ideally the superiors cared for their underlings. Enemies were those who had to be eliminated at any cost. In this group, only *Bình Bưởi* was BT.'s sworn brother. This weak and frail twenty-five-year-old guy had been in prison since he was twelve and received special consideration from BT. The rest were either outsiders or underlings, except for one was the enemy.

According to the principles of this criminal world, all gifts were to be offered to BT. with the words, "Brother BT., I invite you to share these gifts from my family." In response, BT. would laugh and say, "F*ck, it was your folks who brought the stuff, so you 'lick' it! If you have any tobacco, a few beads will be enough for us, brothers" (In their slang: 'Lick' meant eat).

Shortly after BT.'s group arrived, a criminal named *Thụ* from a back cell received gifts from his family. He didn't make the customary offering to his leader before eating some himself. Later that evening *Thụ* took a very small portion of this food, some sauce, and some tea, to BT. I heard the Big Brother shout angrily: "F*ck you, what are you afraid of? I'm not starving to death. You disgrace me. Take your f*cking stuff back to your cell!"

He wouldn't accept anything. In the following days, *Thụ* continued to look frightened. Unluckily for him, a cell shuffle put him in BT.'s cell a few days later. *Thụ* stood outside the cell wailing, determined not to go in, but finally the guard pushed him in and locked the door.

Being aware of the man's fear, I called out from my cell to ask BT. to have pity for him. BT. answered, "I hear you *Anh Út*. I won't do anything to him!" And BT. did leave him alone, making no more mention of the incident. However, that evening when the *Trật tự viên* unlocked the cell for mealtime, *Thụ* ran to the Camp gate and asked the guard for a different cell. He fabricated a story that BT. stole his food!

The guard disregarded his pleas and marched him right back into the cell, he reprimanded BT. not to steal food from *Thụ*, then he locked the door and left. *Thụ* had again brought punishment on himself.

From my side of the wall, I listened to BT.'s anger. He'd been insulted, accused of stealing another's food, something so foreign to his nature, it was below his status and beyond his imagination and tolerance. Now, he intended to kill *Thụ*. As BT. beat *Thụ*, who wept and pleaded for his life to be spared, I yelled as loudly as I could from my cell, saying that *Thụ* had lied out of fear. Such a beating is enough for him to know his mistake.

BT. answered, "But he lied! He dared say I took his food! Because of your request, I'll spare his life. Instead, I'll have to ask him for his set of tusks! (Teeth)."

Next, I heard BT. say more quietly, "Well, you useless lump of sh*t! My Big brother told me to spare your life. But you'll have to lose all your teeth. Will you knock them out yourself or do you want me to do it?"

With no way out, *Thụ* knocked out every one of his own teeth. Only then would BT. let him go. Interestingly, after that *Thụ* became BT.'s obedient shadow.

A Tale of 'Lame Sửu'

During the time that *Bảy Chà* was *Trật tự viên*, our life in the Punishment Section was more comfortable. When the guards weren't noticing, he'd open the doors for us to move around between cells and also helped us receive gifts from the 'Village'. It was like living in a dream.

When I was transferred from the front into cell No. 4 at the back, BT. remained in cell No. 3 with two others from his group. One afternoon, the guard brought in a Southerner named *Nguyễn Đức Khuân*, who'd been punished for writing a song in which he'd called *Hồ Chí Minh* a 'Red Devil'. *Khuân* was beaten in the walkway, and then shackled in BT.'s cell. I already knew *Khuân* and regarded him as a good friend, so I called to BT. "*Khuân* is a close friend of mine. Think of him as me." *Khuân* was a charming fellow and very musical. He liked to sing and tell stories. BT. always wanted to learn, especially about the South, so the two complemented each other. BT. respected *Khuân* as an older brother, but this made the third cellmate jealous. This man *Sửu* (Nicknamed *Lame Sửu*) had been in conflict with BT. in the past, although BT. hadn't referred to it.

One humid afternoon, while *Khuân* was telling BT. stories of the South, *Sửu* couldn't control his jealousy and shouted, "F*ck off! You're just telling lies!"

Khuân stopped talking. BT. burned with anger because *Sửu* dared disrespect *Khuân* whom he had accepted as a brother. This was an intolerable crime. Secondly, he didn't like to have his listening interrupted. So, BT. jumped up, pulled out the knife hidden in his pack, held it to *Sửu's* neck, and threatened to stab him. *Khuân* had to pull him off. The cell's atmosphere was heavy with anger and fear. *Sửu* stupidly chose this moment to say "Brother BT., look into my eyes. I am not a malicious person, so why do you treat me as though I am?"

This was not the apology that BT. expected. In his anger, he remembered the conflict from their earlier days. He pushed *Sửu* down and began to poke out one of his eyes. *Sửu's* screaming could be heard throughout the whole section.

As the guards pounded down the corridor in response, BT. made a deep cut in his own arm to draw blood. Then, he went back to work on *Sửu's* eyes. When the guards arrived, one of *Sửu's* eyeballs already lay on the floor.

BT. held out the knife and showed the cut in his arm as proof, he said, "Reporting to you, Guard! When he came in here, *Sửu* hid a knife in his smoking pipe. Just now, I was sleeping soundly when he stabbed me for no reason. Luckily, I defended myself and only got this cut in my arm. I'm still bleeding, you see!"

Tiến, the fourth cell member, to ingratiate himself with BT., added maliciously, "Reporting to you, Guard! *Sửu* has been threatening to kill BT. For a long time. If I hadn't yelled, he would have stabbed BT. in the heart!"

Hearing this, the Guard yelled at *Sửu* to quiet down, confiscated his knife, and took him to the infirmary to have his wounds treated. The guard didn't punish BT. as he was a victim defending himself. The story didn't end there.

When *Sửu* was in the infirmary, BT. instructed his minions, *Tuấn Béo (Chubby Tuấn)*, to eliminate *Sửu*. One night about three weeks later, *Sửu* returned to 'Village'. While *Sửu* sat on the floor drinking tea, *Tuấn Béo* struck him with a wood chopping knife, split his head into two. *Sửu* died immediately. That night, *Tuấn* was brought to the Punishment Section in a separate cell next to mine. Later on, a trial was held in the Camp, sentencing him to 18 years.

Sửu's death caused a cell shuffle, which would have put me into cell No. 5 with the three Chinese *Lý Đức Nghĩa*, *Chu Vạn Hồi* and *Lưu Tùng*. I knew there'd been an incident in this room a few days before, but didn't know how serious it had been. These Chinese had beaten a criminal and cracked his skull, causing it to bleed. Even without this knowledge, I asked the guards to put me into a different cell because I had caused *Lý Đức Nghĩa* to be punished for stealing a rice cake from an elderly prisoner. I knew that if we were to be in the same cell, I'd be in trouble. It sounded reasonable to the guard, so to my great joy he put me in the front Cell No. 2 with BT.

Although BT. had been in the section for over a month, we only saw each other at mealtime and on bath days in the *Mã* River. But we were used to calling out to each other. As I waited for the guard to unlock the cell door, I recalled that I'd stayed in each cell at least once, and each cell had its special memories, but I'd never before entered in such a happy state of mind. Before I had a chance to put my stuff down, BT. gave me a hug and kissed my forehead. *Bình Bưởi* also hugged me as a brother. BT. turned to the other two men, saying "*Thịnh* and *Trọng*, this is *Anh Út*, my Big Brother! Treat him accordingly! Okay?" I thought it was just a simple introduction and didn't realise that it was a very strict order, as I will now relate.

They already had four shackled men in the cell, so *Trọng* got to lie on the floor, unshackled. *Trọng* was a few years older than BT., but this didn't bring him any respect as he was classified as an underling and couldn't dine with the brothers. The other man was called *Thịnh*. He was classified as an outsider who did eat with the brothers, though he had no real connection with them. I lay on the same platform as BT., nearer to the wall.

I felt tired from the hassle of moving. Although I was getting better gradually, the long-term shackling left me with a near-paralysed leg, and the life-style wore me down. So I lay down to rest, musing on my strange life. Here I was, a Catholic priest, confined with a notorious Northern bandit whom I especially loved. I watched BT. busily organising everything in the cell. It was the first time I'd seen him without a shirt. He had more tattoos than anyone I'd ever seen. On his arms were a torch and a sword. The front of his chest showed a picture of two dragons fighting for a pearl. A Buddha's image above a smoking incense-burner covered his back, and below were the words:

"*Life, C'est la vie!*
"*When I die who will build my tomb?*
Who will cry and farewell my coffin?"

When the doors opened for mealtime, I'd go outside and run around while *Trọng* cleaned the cell. *Bình Thanh* always divided up the food into five equal portions. Then he'd pass two portions to *Trọng*, saying, "You do much, you eat more!" We, other four tried to apportion the rest evenly. But BT. would take only a small amount saying, "You and *Bình Bưởi 'Lick'* the rest. I won't die of starvation."

My sister from the South came to visit me while I was living with BT. I got to see her for fifteen minutes during that particular visit and told her about B.T., my younger brother by oath. I also said I was sure that someday B.T. would find his way to visit her in disguise. As usual, I'd been plotting an escape plan, this time with B.T. as my willing partner.

I returned to the cell with her gifts of food and gave it to BT. He saved enough for each of us to have a meal, and distributed the rest among the other cells. Going to each cell, he said, "This is from my Big Brother. My Southern sister brought it. Now let's all enjoy it together!" I also sent some of this food to the priests living in the nearby Flat House. I was very pleased with what BT. was doing, agreeing that as we suffered together, we should also comfort and celebrate when we could. I understood that he was also seeking to have others admire me.

Character of a Big Brother

As an underling, *Trong* did all the cell chores such as cleaning the floor, bringing water, doing our laundry in the shallow well out the back, and drying the clothes. He was always paying attention to BT., checking for any displeasure. If BT. corrected him, he'd shake and go pale. I hadn't realised how tough BT. was on *Trong,* until on one occasion, I unintentionally caused something I regretted. *Trong* knew that B.T. respected me very much, and that he was to treat me the same.

One day at mealtime, I was going out the back to wash my shirt. Suddenly, BT. called me over to introduce me to a friend from the 'Village' who had just climbed over the Punishment Section wall to meet me. I said to *Trong*, already busy carrying water, "Please wash this shirt for me, then hang it on the line. Okay?" Without waiting for his response, I joined BT.

Back in the cell, as BT. divided the food, I looked out the window but didn't see my shirt hanging on the line. "*Trong*, I asked you for a favour wash my shirt. Where did you hang it? I don't see it."

Suddenly *Trong* answered, "Couldn't you see I was too busy getting water?"

This unexpected response made me angry. I never used food to control him. I empathised too much with his position of powerlessness. I knew he had a wife and two kids, and having no status in prison he had to play by the rules of malicious outlaws. Normally, I did whatever I could for myself and didn't order *Trong* about as the other cellmates did. So, now I said: "*Trong*, why did you answer me like that? If you weren't going to help me, you could have said so. Because you didn't say anything, I thought you'd accepted my request. If you were busy, of course, I could do it myself some other time!"

Suddenly, BT. sprang up, grabbed his pack and drew out his knife. He stormed at *Trong*: "F*ck you, you f*cking bastard, you're excessive! F*ck you, if you don't respect my brother then how can you respect me? A dog like you doesn't deserve to live."

He grabbed *Trọng* by his shirt and slammed him on his back on the platform, the knife raised high and ready to stab. We other three leapt over and tried to hold BT.'s arms, but he was too strong. He pushed the other two away, but I still hung on, trying to pry the knife out of his hand. "*Bình Thanh! Bình Thanh*! Forgive him. Listen to me; if you do this, I will get the blame!"

Despite his crazy spell, he let me take the knife out of his hand and then helped *Trọng* up. Then he yelled into the man's face, "F*ck you, if it wasn't for my brother, I would have killed you! Do you understand? Do you understand?"

It was the first time I'd personally witnessed BT.'s full-scale anger. *Trọng* was like a reed in his hands. BT. repeatedly shoved him away and yanked him back, his elbow hitting him in mid-chest. I heard what I thought was the sound of a breaking rib and saw fresh blood spurt from *Trọng's* mouth on to the cell floor. BT. shoved *Trọng* on to the puddle of blood. This was how malicious outlaws punished each other in prison!

I helped *Trọng* back on to the platform, wiping the blood from his body and applying oil. The terror had passed. *Trọng* tried to open his eyes to look at me. "Thank you, brother!" I felt both remorse and distress.

"*Trọng*, I am so sorry. Please don't be angry with me."

He gently shook his head and shut his eyes.

That night, I told BT. that I thought he'd been too heavy-handed with *Trọng*. BT.'s reply was "You are a priest, so you're always speaking of love for others. We're outlaws, so our life is different. This is the first time I've ever taken my knife out and put it back without it being bloodied. It was for you that I broke the rule. But this S.O.B. *Trọng* disrespected you and that's why I punished him that way."

Days earlier I'd told B.T. the story of my experiences with *Bùi Đình Thi*. Now B.T. said, "As for the f*cking *Bùi Đình Thi*, his fate is worse! I'd love to have him still in this camp, or with me in any other. But I wouldn't kill him; it'd dirty my hands. I'd just take his *headlights* and *chopsticks*. (Both eyes and two arms.) To *cắt* (Kill) him would be the easy way out for him."

I answered, "The *Bùi Đình Thi* business was three years ago. Right after the beating, I certainly foamed with rage, but now I've calmed down. I've forgiven him, because forgiveness lightens the spirit."

"With a crime like that, how could you forgive him?"

"I'm a priest. I'm the person who teaches the love and forgiveness that Jesus Christ taught and modelled."

BT. laughed in my face as he heard that. "*Anh Út!* What a funny God you have. He's definitely not my God."

I spoke seriously, "*Bình Thanh!* I don't want you to make fun of this matter. Religion is a great issue for mankind. I want you to have a respectful attitude when speaking of religion. We have to respect each and every religion. You say you respect me, so why do you offend the Heavenly God who is worthy of my worship? You've saddened me."

BT. put his arms around me "*Anh Út!* I was just kidding, just kidding for fun. I didn't intend to offend the Higher Power. What you said of your forgiveness for *Bùi Đình Thi* was just so hard for me to understand. Hearing you tell me about the evil way he behaved and his torture of you, just hearing it drives me mad! The day you came into this cell, when I felt how you're just skin and bones, it reminded me of *Bùi Đình Thi's* beating and made my blood boil. Now, you speak of forgiveness for that slaughterer. Really, it's hard for me to understand. I am an outlaw, not a religious father like you!"

"But you are my younger brother."

"You're right. Because I am your younger brother, I have to do my duty."

"What duty?" I said.

"The duty of getting vengeance for you."

I saw that BT. still hedged around this issue. "I said I forgive him, so, what need is there for vengeance? Besides, vengeance only calls for more of the same. What good does it do?"

BT. still argued, "Forgiveness is your business, but life's Karma is the law of my life. I'm an outlaw."

"So you don't think that love and forgiveness bring happiness to people? Yet you know the Karma rule of outlaws can only create more hatred and bring us suffering?"

He shot back sarcastically, "*Anh Út!* You're preaching to me, eh?"

"Right! Yes! I am preaching to you. If I don't preach to you then to whom will I preach? I try to tell you what I believe is right because I love you very much!"

Bình Thanh thought for a moment before saying, "*Anh Út*, you can't preach to me yet. I was born to be an outlaw, not a child of God. You say that to be a child of God you have to forgive. I can't possibly do that."

"Many people have said that, but then God's mercy changed their hearts and they did become children of God."

He mumbled quietly, "I hope that day will come to me."

I took my outlaw brother's hands and said, "I'll pray for that too."

BT. kept his hands in mine for a long time. Then he gave me a grin. "I never thought I'd have a brother who was a Catholic priest!"

"And I never thought I'd have a bandit as a brother."

We were quiet for a while until B.T. sighed and said, "Life, C'est la vie!"

I laughed. "Where'd you learn that French phrase?"

"You didn't see those words tattooed on my back?" Only then did I recall that the tattoos on his back included the words *"Life, C'est la vie!"* And below that was "When I die, who will build my tomb? Who will be mourners, following my coffin, weeping and saying their farewells forever to me?"

Trọng lay motionless for a few days and concerned BT. looked after him.

The Beauty and the Bandit

During the time of being shackled together, BT. told me much about himself. His real name was *Đỗ Thanh Bình*; he was aged thirty-three and originally came from *Hưng Yên* Province in North Vietnam. His family was comparatively rich. His father was a Major Police Officer and his mother was an elementary teacher. BT. had been an intelligent student, a skilled writer and very artistic. He developed a strong physique, was always ready to defend the weak, but had a tendency towards violence.

Once, before he was twenty, he had intervened when a guard stopped a car to demand bribe. Without thinking of the consequences to himself, he beat the guard to a bloody mess, and was arrested and taken to the Police station. His father came to bail him out, but BT. had already escaped after knocking out the guard. BT. didn't return to his home since then. Instead, he lived on the streets and formed a gang for the elimination of all oppressors and the protection of the minority.

He was admired by many gangsters and soon became well known in the outlaw world of the North. His gangs were sometimes disguised as Communist soldiers. Sometimes, they were even disguised as guards and thanks to his artistic talents the group soon had all the necessary documents, looking more realistic than the Army's own issue. BT., who checked their papers and sent them back to their military unit, apprehended many servicemen absent-without-leave. No amount of pleading could get around 'First Lieutenant B.T.'. His gang of bandits tended to 'borrow' (to rob) storage facilities and their contents, and the military vehicles needed to transport them. When they weren't able to get supplies in this way, they reluctantly became pickpockets on trains.

It was during his time of impersonating a First Lieutenant that BT. met and fell in love with a beauty named *Hương* (Rose) from a music and dance group. The story began one morning when BT. along with another serviceman went into a café in the city of *Hà Tĩnh*, in the Centre of Vietnam, to order some food. He noticed some pretty ladies having drinks, the most beautiful one among them aged about twenty. Incidentally, a group of legitimate servicemen pulled up chairs to sit at the ladies' table. Perhaps, as they were locals, they knew the women. Furthermore, there were enough of them to block the aisles and prevent the First Lieutenant (BT.) and his friend coming near.

Bình Thanh and the other outlaw didn't say a word. They just beat up the other men who were taken by surprise and not ready to defend themselves. Soon the café was a mess. The girls ran out the back, but peeped through to see what would happen next.

Bình Thanh bled freely from a split lip, which he wiped with his arm. Then he whipped out a large sum of cash and placed it on the table as payment for the café's damaged furniture. Stooping over and picking up his helmet lying on the floor, he proceeded to bow in farewell to the pretty dove-eyed lady who had first caught his attention.

As he put on his helmet, she called out, "The star's the wrong way!" BT. turned, not understanding what she was saying. The girl giggled and pointed to B.T.'s helmet. "The star is the wrong way! You're wearing your helmet backwards! The star is turned towards the back, see? The star is backwards, see?" The words from the pretty lady in the café, 'The star is the wrong way', became the first words to a very beautiful but tearful ballad.

Their relationship quickly grew. Many times BT. took *Hương* out to Hanoi, a city she had never visited. They went to the cinema, theatre, and circus, and this made *Hương* very happy. He gave her gifts, clothing, and jewellery. Life was rosy for the girl from the dancing group. Many times her parents suggested a wedding, but he would always find a way to gently delay it. Nor did *Hương* see the need for a wedding, partly because of her profession and also because she was satisfied with her life as a lover. The business of organising a wedding would come, of course, but not yet. *Hương* lived with her lover for nearly two years without knowing that BT. was an outlaw. She truly believed he was an officer in the transportation corps. She always saw soldiers with him.

One moonlit night B.T. and his friends went to bathe in the river while she prepared a late meal. When it was ready, *Hường* went down to the river to call him. Coming ashore, B.T. quickly slipped into shorts and T-shirt, but not before she'd seen the tattoos on his chest. Previously, he had always been careful to hide them and had never let *Hường* see him shirtless.

Hường was extremely surprised. She knew that tattoos were not allowed in the Army. So, she pressed him for answers and eventually BT. had to tell the truth; that he was a bandit masquerading as an officer. *Hường* cried herself tearless. BT. knelt before her and asked for forgiveness. "It was because I love you so much that I didn't dare tell the truth. I was afraid of losing you!"

Although very upset, *Hường* gradually came to accept that she was the lover of a bandit. But she didn't tell her family or friends.

Two years later, when BT. was twenty-eight years old, after a botched raid, he was arrested and sentenced to ten years confinement at a prison camp in the *Quảng Ninh* Province not far from the Chinese border. *Hường* trekked North from the Central region to visit him. After less than a year, he escaped from that prison camp. Police were watching him and knew he had a lover in *Hà Tĩnh*, and eventually *Hường* innocently led them to B.T. He resisted capture, was beaten, grabbed a gun and took off. A policeman fired at him as he ran away. BT. fired back to retaliate, and killed the policeman. Afterward, he was caught by the militia. His previous prison term was replaced with a sentence of fifteen years.

Over the years *Bình Thanh* successfully escaped from prison camp five times. However, he was always recaptured because he'd always look up his old friends especially *Hường*. When transferred to the *Thanh Cẩm* Prison, BT. still carried a 15-year sentence, as time had been added after each escape. "A sentence is a sentence, but no prison can confine me, *Anh Út!*" B.T. boasted.

I felt compassion for the beautiful lady *Hường*. Even though I didn't know her personally, our vow as brothers had made *Hường* as my sister-in-law. Fate had lured her into the café. If *Hường* were to learn of the last chapter of BT.'s life, who knows how much she would suffer?

When I refused to go into Cell No. 5, the big wrestler-like *Phi Tàu* (Chinese *Phi*), entered in my place. He was formidable but was not as vicious as *Lý Đức Nghĩa*. All the same, his presence made life difficult for *Lưu Tùng*.

This frail fellow began to look frailer. I noticed that the other Chinese kept him on a short leash, afraid he would report them. One day, when the door was unlocked during mealtime, I saw *Lưu Tùng* sitting all by himself.

I asked him in Mandarin, "*Lưu Tùng*, are your meals being stolen?"

He clutched my arm and spoke quickly, "Please, *Anh Lễ*, save me!"

He told me that he now ate one meal every two days the other three meals were shared by his cellmate. I told this to *Trật tự viên 'Bảy Chà'* who said he'd already reported the situation to a guard. But the guards didn't care much about business among the prisoners and seldom acted on reports.

I went back to my cell and told BT. and the others what I'd found out. During the last three years, I'd come to understand the cruelty of those three Chinese. We discussed our plan. Then we told the *Trật tự viên* that to avoid getting into trouble, he should go elsewhere for about 15 minutes as soon as he'd unlocked the cells. I noticed that my own cellmates had all taken care to dress appropriately. BT. put on his tennis shoes and carefully placed rocks in his hand held socks.

That evening when *Bảy Chà* opened the doors, the four of them quickly invaded cell No. 5. One stood watching while the other three attacked *Lý Đức Nghĩa, Phi Tàu* and *Chu Vạn Hồi*. BT. used his socks to whack *Phi* and *Nghĩa* until their blood splattered the walls. A short time later, *Trật tự viên* discovered *Phi* and *Nghĩa* lying motionless. *Chu Vạn Hồi* was still able to walk. That very evening, everybody in cell No. 5 was separated into different cells, an event which added several years to *Lưu Tùng's* life.

Bình Thanh and I shared that cell for a considerably long time, until 1982 when we were placed in cell No.1 at the building's corner. This cell had only one door to the outside, instead of two like other cells. *Thịnh* and *Minh Lùn* (*Dwarf Minh*) also shared the cell. Of course, we surveyed this new cell for possibilities of escape, hoping to use the opportunity before *Tết*. (Lunar New Year). If we escaped successfully, I would stay up North for a while with BT. before going South and finally leaving the country.

I felt more secure this time as B.T. had already had five successful escapes and knew his way around the North very well. We had prepared forged ID's with stamps and signatures. I admired B.T.'s cleverness in his creation of these fake papers and also his ability to mould a fake, but very realistic-looking, shackle out of cassava dough. Other prison camps are many times more strongly built than this one. "This camp will be a piece of cake! Get out of here with me and you won't have to worry about anything," he promised.

I dreamed of escaping with *Bình Thanh*. Then one morning, just ten days before our planned breakout, I was called to leave the Punishment Section. I had been there, in shackles most days and every night, from May, 1979 to February, 1982. I was sad to say farewell to BT. The guards escorted me back to cell No. 4 of the Flat House, a solitary confinement without shackles, to live with some other priests. B.T. missed me, so whenever the door was unlocked, he'd climb the fence to visit me in my cell. The *Trật tự viên* watched without interfering, knowing they couldn't make any difference. The other priests were very surprised at the special bond between us.

It was only later that I found out the circumstances of my release from cell No.1 of the Punishment Section. Father *Nguyễn Huy Chương's* niece from Saigon had left him a large number of gifts. He was a compassionate man and gave some of the gifts to an On-duty guard saying, "Reporting to you, Guard! Poor Mr *Lễ* has been shackled for three years. For this *Tết* (Lunar New Year) please let him live here with us." Fr. *Chương* thought he was doing me a favour. I regretted that I hadn't had the chance to escape with B.T. It was only later that I could appreciate that this was also part of God's plan for me.

Ten days later, B.T. climbed over the fence to the Flat House. He kissed me and said, "I came to say goodbye, perhaps forever! I'm leaving tonight, please pray for me, *Anh Út*." We both cried. The other cellmates watched in surprise, not knowing what was happening. But I didn't dare explain. I had carefully instructed BT. not to make any contact with his lover, *Hường*. He would have to leave the North as quickly as he could. He promised to go to the Mekong Delta and see my Sister first. I knew that she would give him advice and arrange to help him see *Hường* in a safe way.

That night, I didn't sleep a wink. I prayed that God and Our Lady Mary would protect BT. By midnight, I had not heard any warning shots; so I knew that BT. had probably got away safely. I silently thanked God. At morning roll, I looked out through the cell window to see a panic-stricken *Bảy Chà* running to report to guards that prisoners had escaped. Three warning shots rang out in the bright morning. Now, I could pray aloud "Thanks be to God!"

That evening, I was disturbed to hear sounds of beating and screaming from the Punishment Section. Later *Bảy Chà* told me that *Dwarf Minh* had been recaptured and taken back to the camp to be beaten to death. As for B.T. and *Thịnh*, there was no news. Surely they were free!

Over a month later, I received a coded letter from my sister. After telling me about family matters she wrote, "I forgot to tell you that *Hường* (BT.'s code name) stopped by to visit me on the way to take care of duties." The sight of three armed strangers frightened me, but I was very happy to recognise her! She is a First Lieutenant now. It had been so long since she was here last that others had to guide her to my house. The three of them had a meal and then left. I was thrilled with the news.

A few months later I received a second coded letter from a female officer in the Communist Army named *Hường*. It was sent from Saigon. *Hường* (B.T.'s code name) spoke about the visit to my Sister in *Vĩnh Long*, unfortunately giving her a scare. The letter continued, "Perhaps, I will go to Cambodia for a while. I will write to you, Uncle, when it is convenient." I was overjoyed. That was the first and also the last letter. I didn't hear any more of B.T. and this alarmed me very much. If he didn't keep in touch with me, at least, he could contact my Sister; but there was absolutely no more news.

Six years later in 1988, when I left *Thanh Cẩm* for *Nam Hà*, I still hadn't heard a single word from *Bình Thanh*.

(Please read Supplement 1: Death of *Bình Thanh*)

Part Three
From Small Concentration camps to a Huge One

Chapter 16
Last Leg of the Journey

Towards January of 1988, I had entered my twelfth year in prison, through eleven of which I was dragged across the contrasting Northern climate of different prison camps. By now, there weren't many Southern prisoners left scattered in Northern concentration camps. Excluding those who'd died of hardship, sickens and starvation, the large number had been released and other groups were transferred to the camps in the South. Some went home rather early, starting in 1980. From then, every year saw a cycle of releases, many at times and few at others, but always some releases. I was still in *Thanh Cẩm* at the time. This camp released a large number of prisoners, some transferring to *Hàm Tân* Camp in the South. Political prisoners in *Thanh Cẩm* numbered no more than two hundred, among them were twenty-nine priests. Compared to its most crowded times in 1979, the recent count was less than one-third of the original.

The priests lived in the newly built Solitary Confinement Section facing the prison gate. According to regulations, this section was to be a no trespassing zone, but in reality, things weren't quite so strict. Chinese prisoners lived in the Flat House where we had dug the wall to escape in 1979. At first, there were a large number of them but after more than 15 years of confinement, the number gradually dropped due to death of disease or starvation. Others were shot dead after attempting to escape. Now, they were down to ten. After political prisoners had been moved to the South, criminals were added so that the total number of camp prisoners remained roughly four hundred.

On 27 January, 1988, we were unexpectedly transferred to another camp. In my case, I was six months shy of my 10-year mark at *Thanh Cẩm* Camp. During this transfer, all political and Chinese prisoners were moved to *Nam Hà*

Camp. For others it was a new place, but to me it seemed I was just moving in a circle.

I'd been there in 1977 when first shipped from the South, then to the 'Gateway to Heaven', before being transferred to the pit of hell in *Thanh Cẩm*. Now, I was back again. But whereas I remembered *Nam Hà* as being well ordered, now it was cluttered and slovenly. Outside all the cell blocks were containers of pots, pans, and china, with overhead awnings like stalls in a fish market. Apparently *Nam Hà* Camp had turned into a storage facility.

I'd left *Nam Hà* as a healthy 34-year-old. Now, I was middle-aged, with salt-and-pepper hair, and every part of my body had been injured. Worse, I had become tired of life! Only a handful of my former friends in *Nam Hà* remained. They too were now much changed from the privations they'd suffered. We were glad to be reunited and talk about old times.

The majorities of our previous number had died mostly of starvation and were buried in the cemetery by the camp wall. This cemetery hadn't existed when I was here in 1977. A few Generals from the former Southern Army were now in the Camp. Also a few former Army Chaplains transferred from other camps, some of whom were friends from my Seminary days. But I missed my old cellmates.

By chance, I was put into my old cell, No. 6. It wasn't happiness to return there, since imprisonment in one cell is the same as another. Entering that old room, I had intentions of getting dibs on my old spot in the front corner. Looking at the wall, I could still see the nail that I'd driven into the wall eleven years ago. The nail remained but the head was worn down to a sleek shine. In fact, the only difference seemed to be that different cellmates, aged and fatigued like myself, had replaced my old friends. On the first night, drifting in and out of sleep, I kept thinking it was the night of Christmas Eve, December 24, 1977 that I was sure I'd soon be called to climb on to a truck.

During the first few days, we were given time to reorganise our personal belongings before these were inspected and to have health checks. By this time, most prisoners had money, as it had become easier for their families to transfer funds. Camp rules required us to deposit all our cash into a camp bank supervised by a Finance Officer. We were really surprised to find that *Nam Hà* had an open, bustling market. In fact, a few prisoners were such successful entrepreneurs that they became wealthier than most citizens outside. In a strange reversal, some sent business profits home to their families.

The Mid-Summer Breeze

Another surprise was finding that *Nam Hà* had a female Financial Officer. This young woman looked at each of us in this motley collection and laughingly commented, "*You guys have an awful lot of stuff!*" As I waited my turn to verify my entry in her book, I studied the first female Finance Officer I'd seen in years. Whereas my mother and sisters, like other women of my childhood, had worn their long hair in a braid down their back, this woman's hair was cut in a short but feminine style. Instead of the beautiful traditional *Áo dài* (Long white dresses) or the horribly unflattering uniform of the police, she was dressed in a white chemise, long black pants, and high-heeled sandals. It was wonderfully refreshing to note her poise and grace and frequent smiles. After all the years of gruff, barked commands, I appreciated her gentle voice. Her favourite word seemed to be '*a-w-ful*', mostly in a positive context.

Soon after our arrival, an announcement was made of the releases for *Tết* 1988, the year of the Dragon. Apparently, all the Southern prisoners had been gathered in this one camp to make their departure easier to arrange. The Government orchestrated a much-publicised ceremony, with officers from the Central Committee. Released prisoners numbered almost a thousand, including all the Southern priests except Father *Nguyễn Bình Tĩnh* from *Ban Mê Thuột* Diocese, and myself.

Because journalists were everywhere during the release ceremony, those of us still being detained were hidden out in the fields or put in cells with all the windows covered. To rub in our continuing misfortune, the camp officials were so busy that they forgot to feed us until the ceremony was over and all visitors had left. So we got our breakfast in the late afternoon!

On that day, *Nam Hà* Camp was more animated than I'd ever seen it before. Excited men walked in and out of cells, wishing one another luck for the future. All the pots and pans that had been carefully gathered over the past dozen years now lay scattered. Food and drink, firewood anything that could be useful, was offered to those remaining. Anything unnecessary was trashed. The mess overflowed out of doors into the courtyard.

I sat with my back against the wall, watching others make their farewells. Although I was pleased that so many were able to leave, I was overcome by an insurmountable sadness at being left behind. It was particularly hard to be separated from my fellow priests, those who had lived with me for years. These 28 men had helped me so much when I was released from the Punishment

Section with my frayed body and trampled soul. Although our cell was overcrowded and lacking in amenities, causing occasional friction, we never let any conflict last more than a day. Being isolated from other prisoners, we were able to say Mass daily, using wine and bread brought in by family visitors.

These priests were gentle, tolerant and compassionate towards prisoners and guards alike, true witnesses to God's love. The majority had been imprisoned for working as chaplains to the Southern Army. A few shared my crimes of criticising Communism and standing up for the rights of ordinary people. Although I was the youngest, I felt very much a part of that family and very proud to have belonged to. Now I wept. They silently looked at me, wanting to comfort me but unable to find the right words.

Ever since my capture I'd thought about being free. In every camp, I'd plotted to escape. But my history of organising the attempted hijack of the *SÔNG HƯƠNG*, the thwarted plan from 'Gateway to Heaven' and the botched escape from *Thanh Cẩm* Camp when my friends, *Đặng Văn Tiếp* and *Lâm Thành Văn* were killed, had made it unlikely that I'd ever be released. But things were changing.

There were less than a hundred political prisoners left imprisoned, and these included ten Chinese held for more than fifteen years. With so many others being freed, my hopes were rekindled. I'd been told that a re-education term lasted only three years. I'd done three of those terms. So, I clung to a fragile hope, focusing all my energy on receiving my freedom again. I tried to remember all the happy occasions in my life, passing school exams and being ordained a priest comparing such times with the greater joy that must come soon of release.

Recognising God's Will

The night after their departure I lay tossing and turning, pained by my disappointment. At last, I sat up and prayed the Lord's Prayer, concentrating on the phrase "Thy will be done." Then, I continued in my own words: "Lord, let me know what your will is for me. I've had to endure so much misery already, more than those who've gone home. Do I have to continue in these conditions? You have said you are the light and the way. Please show me the way I have to follow." As I finished praying, I seemed to hear the words, "I want you to continue being here, to be with the suffering prisoners who are left. To love, comfort and share your life with them. Perhaps to die with them."

Suddenly, happiness flooded my soul, a joy more intense than I'd ever felt before. My life did have meaning. I wasn't forgotten but was chosen to bring God's love to everyone, especially the most miserable. I no longer wanted to be released. From now on, prison would be my accepted environment, the other prisoners my brothers to love and comfort. Even the guards seemed different in this new light: "I would show them the way of faith and hope."

The next morning I felt like a new person. I wrote to my Sister in the South, telling her not to send any more gifts because I had sufficient. I knew that in the past the family had gone without to be able to give me food. But now, I was rich with the food and clothes left by the released men.

Then I set about forming a support group. I gave these friends the task of distributing goods to those who needed them most. My closest friends at this time were the Chinese and the others who'd lived with me long-term in *Thanh Cẩm's* Punishment Section. These were the men I trained to be my helpers. With their backgrounds, they would have been natural for them to hold on to everything in case of future need. But, as they shared my work, they gradually came to accept that this was a better way to live.

Two months later, there was an exodus of Southern prisoners to a camp in the South. Now only three prisoners from the South were to stay: Father *Nguyễn Bình Tĩnh*, Mr *Nguyễn Đức Khuân*, and myself. *Nam Hà* Camp began to feel deserted. Again, my departed friends gave me all their food and goods. I felt I was like a tycoon. Remembering ironically the times when I went naked, close to starvation, owning no bowl to hold my rice ration, not even a can to collect water. Now, I had abundance of items that most needed in prison; my cell was crammed with boxes, cups and bowls, sacks, clothing, medicine…At the same time, our Supportive Community had grown, so that we were well able to have share-out these new items. This time, I was content to be left behind. My place was here.

I joined the group of Northern political prisoners in digging irrigation trenches. Next I moved so as to share a cell with the Chinese men. Using Mandarin, in which I was now fluent, I began to teach those who were interested about Christianity, and celebrated Mass at night in our room. Two of the Chinese men asked me for them to be baptised. One thirty-year-old *Chu Vạn Hồi* couldn't speak more than a few garbled phrases of Vietnamese. He had been living in deep depression and I spent a lot of time with him, assuring him that God helps those who go astray but repent of their mistakes. He asked me to be his Godfather. As I performed the ceremony of baptism the entire room fell silent.

A Horrifying Story

However, after being baptised *Chu Vạn Hồi* surprised me by slumping against me and sobbing profusely. I wondered what could possibly make a tough bandit act so out of character.

"*Chu Vạn Hồi*, what's up with you?" I consoled him.

He only sobbed harder, his tears soaking my shirt, his shoulders shaking. Realising this was serious, I stayed silent and just patted him on his skinny shoulders.

After a while, he said through his tears, "Papa! Once I almost killed you. I tried to kill you so that I could eat some meat! Our cellmates had already been starving." Fortunately, he was speaking in Mandarin and so they couldn't understand this outlandish statement.

I continued to support him as I asked, "What? What are you saying? Kill me? I don't understand!"

"How could you understand when *Lý Đức Nghĩa* and I kept this secret in our hearts for many years? *Lưu Tùng* is now dead, only *Lý Đức Nghĩa* and I are left. He must also apologise to you." He called *Nghĩa* from the other end of the room.

When we were all sitting against the wall, with me in the middle, *Chu Vạn Hồi* began his story, "Tonight I am a child of God, and your godson. You have told us that we must confess our sins and ask for forgiveness. So, now I have to tell you what happened back in *Thanh Cẩm*." Looking rather bewildered, *Nghĩa* said quietly to *Chu Vạn Hồi*.

"This matter has been long finished. Why are you bringing it up?" *Nghĩa* asked.

"Even though it's been a long time, I won't have any peace of mind until I confess to the person I now call Papa." He settled more firmly against the wall. "It was eight years ago, but I'm sure you still remember the night we beat up a criminal in cell No. 5 of *Thanh Cẩm* Punishment Section, he yelled and screamed so that the guards took him to the infirmary?"

"Yes" I answered, "I remember that night very clearly. I was in the cell next door, and I heard a very loud screaming. A guard had to take him out of the cell. But why do you bring that up now? What's its significance?"

"Because it has to do with you. If you weren't my Godfather, I wouldn't tell you. But now I must, no matter how long it's been."

Nghĩa had been sitting still with a bowed head. Realising *Hồi* was going to tell the whole story, he turned to me and said quietly in Mandarin, "*Anh Lễ*! I apologise!"

I stared at them, from one to the other. "I don't understand a single thing. Tell me what's up!"

Chu Vạn Hồi stared upward the ceiling, his voice little more than a whisper. "At that time, *Lý Đức Nghĩa* and I were absolutely desperate for food. We'd endured ten years of miserable hunger and thirst. No matter which camp we were in, we were always kept in punishment. We wanted to die. But we wanted our deaths to mean something. To show that we were forced to do so by the barbarity of the Vietnamese Communist regime. We decided to become famous by murdering and cannibalising the next Vietnamese prisoner who came into our cell. We planned to kill him, whoever he was, and eat his internal organs first; leaving the corpse covered in blankets to look as if he was just asleep. Then we'd gradually strip away his meat until we were discovered.

We knew we'd be shot, but we wanted this barbaric act to highlight the cruelty of the Vietnamese Communist prison camps. At that point, we no longer wanted to live. *Lưu Tùng* was also in our cell, but since he was Chinese like us, we wouldn't kill him. He was as thin and weak as a reed; so, we could have killed him at any time! Instead, we took most of his food ration and left him just enough to live."

Chu Vạn Hồi paused to drink some water. Then he continued, "That evening, guards brought a Vietnamese criminal into our cell. Our chance had arrived. As soon as he was shackled, he rolled over and went to sleep, making it even easier for us to carry out our plan. He was on the same sleeping platform as *Lưu Tùng*, but nearer to the edge. We three spoke Mandarin so he couldn't have understood what we were saying.

When the lights went out, and while he slept soundly, I put one foot down on the ground and reached over to empty a urine bamboo pipe. This pipe was really heavy. I used my full strength to give him a hard whack '*BOOOM!*' on the head. I expected he'd die instantly, but no! The pipe broke into pieces, blood splattered everywhere, and he screamed, *'Reporting to Officer! Reporting to Officer! They're killing me! Reporting to Officer! Reporting to*

Officer! They're killing me'. Then I squeezed both my hands around his neck. Here, I'll show you."

He demonstrated by placing his both hands on the back of my neck, with two steel fingers pushing into the front. Although he did this gently, I still felt that my throat would burst and I had to tug his hands away.

"You see, I've squeezed gently and you can't stand it. I can't understand why, when I used all my strength, he didn't die. God must love me, because if he had died, then I wouldn't be here today. When the guards heard the screaming, they ran up. I was trying to use my body to block the window so that they wouldn't see inside. Then the guard stuck a bayonet through the bars. I instinctively dodged to one side and the bayonet went to the other. If I'd dodged in the other direction he'd have struck me in the heart! Now I understand that God saved me."

Chu Vạn Hồi stopped, crossed his arms and looked up as though offering a prayer of thanks. Then he continued, "The guards took the man to the infirmary. Straight away, *Nghĩa* and I squeezed every last drop of blood from the guy's blanket. It nearly filled a bowl. We used a bit of the shattered bamboo pipe for a fire to heat up the blood. Then we drank it, human blood, half each, ignoring the smell. We weren't in the least disgusted by what we'd done. Instead, we had a craving for more."

I felt chilled at this story of the two people for whom I'd learned to care for very much. After some minutes I asked, "You said you meant to kill me. When?"

"Do you remember the cell change a few days later, when Guard *Thanh* was going to put you into our cell?"

"I remembered that clearly. Yes, but I wouldn't go in. I asked the guard for another cell because I'd previously helped beat *Lý Đức Nghĩa*. I thought he'd beat me in return. You mean that if I'd gone in…" *Chu Vạn Hồi* stole my words.

"Exactly! We were waiting for our next victim, and then the guard brought you. By then, we could think of nothing else, only human blood. We were determined to kill and eat the first Vietnamese who came in. Knowing it was you made us even happier, because you were a well-known and respected political prisoner, and murdering a celebrity would mean even more fame for us after our deaths. Moreover, *Lý Đức Nghĩa* wanted revenge. He said you beat him during *Tết* because he stole a rice cake from an old man."

He continued, "We had to make our plan quickly while you were still outside because you'd have understood our Mandarin. We threatened *Lưu Tùng* that if he signalled you in any way, he would die. But then you asked the guard not to put you in with us, and he put Chinese *Phi Tàu* in your place. We were so frustrated! If you'd come into cell No. 5, we really would have killed you."

"As it was, when *Phi Tàu* joined us, we became strong enough to cannibalise any Vietnamese. But we never got the chance. That bandit *Bình Thanh* and his guys came and beat *Phi Tàu* and *Nghĩa* black and blue. They were paralysed for over a month. They beat me too but less severely. The guards put us all into separate cells that very evening." *Hồi* paused to kiss my hand and say, "Papa, please forgive me!"

The whole time, *Nghĩa* had been sitting with his head down. He spoke up the second time, "*Anh Lễ*, I apologise!"

I sat still, my eyes closed. I couldn't believe that such a thing could have happened. Taking the hands of these friends, these truly miserable people who'd shared a part of their lives with me, I held them for a long time as my tears flowed. *Chu Vạn Hồi* also cried. *Nghĩa* bowed his head and mumbled again "I'm sorry, *Anh Lễ*, I'm so sorry." I shivered with cold while thinking of the years I had endured in the punishment cell at *Thanh Cẩm* Prison. I couldn't believe there were such things that happened in my life.

Seeing that, I was sitting still and with tears streaming down my cheeks, *Chu Vạn Hồi* turned around to embrace me, and then the two of us burst into tears. We cried out loudly. At that moment, *Nghĩa* bowed his head mumbling a few words in Mandarin, a language that he had taught me: "I am sorry, Older Brother *Lễ*, I am sorry."

At that moment I realised that the hand of God had undoubtedly touched my life.

On that morning, if I had walked into the cell No.5 my blood and flesh would have been blended in the body of the two Chinese inmates. They would have been certainly convicted of murder because they had killed an inmate for meat. I raised my two hands to cover my face and burst into tears, and shouted out in Mandarin: ***"Dear God! Dear God! You had saved me from death in the hands of Bùi Đình Thi. Now You have saved me from a horrifying death, a***

death without a complete corpse, in the hands of the two Chinese inmates!"
That night I could hardly sleep at all. I have cheated death twice in my life!

God Spoke Through Me

The next day, I was called to the camp Supervisor's office on account of saying Mass openly in the cell. When I tried to speak, he browbeat me and told me to shut up, threatening to put me in shackles. I answered bluntly, "I am a priest. Therefore, I have to act as a priest wherever I am. My actions don't affect camp security. Your threats don't frighten me. I'm used to being shackled. Either you will have to shoot me, or let me do my duty as a priest." And I repeated the words of Saint Peter "It's better for us to obey God rather than men!" (Acts 5:29).

Seeing he couldn't make me change, he passed me on to the Education Officer. He, in turn, lectured me about saying Mass and teaching publicly. Finally he said: "*Anh Lễ*, if you don't care about yourself, then at least, care about me and my family. If you continue doing this, I will be the first to get into trouble."

I answered, "Thank you, Officer, for speaking so honestly. For your sake, I won't say Mass in public anymore but I will do it privately."

From then on, in free time, our group clustered outside and shared God's Word among ourselves quietly. At first, the group members were all Chinese and I spoke only Mandarin, but as Vietnamese joined we had bilingual meetings. More and more people joined us. I shared with them what I believed and prepared to baptise three more people.

Later, I was named quarry team leader. In this new role, I found myself associating more with the guards. Our group was transferred to the quarry, to break rock from the mountains which surrounded *Nam Hà*. This work was heavy and dangerous. There were many stories about prisoners who'd lost their lives or become maimed. I felt responsible for our group and took precautions to protect my prison mates. If prisoners didn't care for prisoners, then who would?

A Lovely Memory

Then I contracted dysentery. I became very ill, probably because my physique was so enfeebled. I had only a little chance of survival. But thanks to the medicine my fellow prisoners left me before they transferred to the South, I gradually improved. I was still too weak to be able to supervise my team, so I rested and helped with cleaning our cell.

One morning I sat reading **'War and Peace'** by Leo Tolstoy. A released friend left this valuable book to me. The camp security Officer, First Lieutenant T. came in. Noticing the title of the novel, he sat down beside me to discuss it. Then we discussed various Western and Chinese classics. I'd read most of them and we had a harmonious discussion. I formed the impression that although an avid reader, he couldn't always comprehend the context very well probably from lack of academic training.

After that morning's conversation he often stopped by to talk. He also arranged for me to act as a role of an interpreter for a prisoner named *Zheng Ming-Hua*, previously a physician in China and famed as a diagnostician. Many guards and their families came to *Ming-Hua* for a consultation.

In time, I recovered and went back to quarry team supervision. Then one day the same Security officer called me up 'To work'. This always took priority over labouring jobs. It had been five months since my arrival at *Nam Hà*, but this was the first time I'd been called 'To work'. There wasn't much left for them to exploit, after thirteen years of probing my memory. So, I wasn't worried.

When I entered his office, Lieutenant T. welcomed me with a smile. I sat at a small table set with tea and a pack of tobacco. Next to the tobacco was a folder, which I guessed, was my dossier. After pouring tea and offering me a smoke, he told me he'd greatly enjoyed our previous conversations. We began to discuss literature, and then went on to European history. He asked me about the fall of the Roman Empire and the French Revolution in 1789, subjects he didn't understand very well.

Then he lowered his voice to a whisper "*Anh Lê*, I think you understand how I'm thinking. Now, I want to hear you speak your mind. What do you honestly think of Communism?"

The officer before had never asked me this, but I didn't think it was a trap. After some thought, I answered, "Sir, I don't think you really want to learn my ideology."

He laughed lightly; but I sensed his grief that I didn't yet trust him despite his being so open. "*Anh Lê*, I've read your file very carefully, and I called you up here for a private conversation because I understand you. What else is there to investigate?" With that he flipped open the cover of my file to show the comment stamped in black ink: ***"With disposition that cannot be re-educated."***

It was the first time I'd seen this statement. Sadly, I answered, "Sir, I had to answer because you asked. Even if you're going to shackle me, I'm certainly not afraid to speak my mind - and this is my genuine belief I think the Communist regime cannot survive, Sir!"

Lieutenant T. sat still, gently nodding his head. "What do you base that on?"

"Communism goes against the natural human instinct of private ownership. This is a very important basic human right. Any regime, that tries to ignore it, is going against our natural tendency and therefore cannot survive. In reality, have you been able to get rid of private ownership? You are the Party member; you'll know this issue much better than me."

He pondered my answer, then said very softly, "*Anh Lễ*, please keep your thoughts to yourself. Don't speak out, it will only hurt you. I admire you, and don't want to see you hurt." I was moved and was about to take his hand, but suddenly remembered there was a wall between the two of us that for now could not be breached. I admired him very much and had compassion for his situation. He was obviously questioning the philosophy on which his career and possibly his life was based. From then on, we sincerely respected each other. We were divided by status, but inside, we were friends. He asked the re-education warden to exempt me from labour. He requested me to teach him English.

The Supportive Community

During that time, our Brotherhood Community was developing strongly. This example of sharing, of sincerely caring for all those in prison, was an extraordinary experience for most. We were offering an ideal way of living, in contrast to abuse, deception, and deprivation, even of killing. Men who'd almost lost their humanity were learning to care for others. I could clearly see God's hand. Every day I appreciated being able to participate in this rebirth. Why hadn't I acted this way before? Perhaps, I'd been distracted by my hopes for my own freedom.

Some nights I told inmates about Bible stories. Many had never heard them before and were happy to listen. A number had accepted the Regime's anti-Christian propaganda and thought that Catholicism was something unclean, to be distrusted. Some told me, "If I hadn't met you, Father, I wouldn't understand that people need love and forgiveness." These observations comforted me. I'd never before seen such impact of my efforts as a priest. I felt that now I was completely living my vocation.

I had ceased to see the guards as frightening. I knew that most were not comfortable in their jobs. In the early years, they had too much power without guidance. Some had been sadistic and should never have been appointed. Now, as I got to know them better, I could see they were deserving of pity rather than blame. Those who'd been here a long time had formed friendships with Southern prisoners. Lieutenant T. occasionally brought his tiny daughter to visit.

The ideological boundaries were fading. I didn't find this surprising. My long incarceration had given me the opportunity to refine my thoughts. I'd decided that it would be wrong to annihilate people, including those who serve the Communist regime. What we had to do was exterminate the inhumane communist structure. There were many who doubted, even among those who served the Party, but once their feet were caught in the trap, they had no exit. It was those who used the Party system for their own advantages, trampling on others' basic rights, feeding corruption, and stealing our resources, they were the criminals. Most of the lower-ranking guards were victims rather than perpetrators. These thoughts comforted me in the present condition of my existence. I consider every Vietnamese individual as my family member in a great nation.

A Prairie Flower

About this time, I had the chance to socialise with KT., the female Financial Officer, who had accompanied a group of prisoners to the South. After the propaganda she had always been fed, this was an eye-opening experience for her. One day, she asked me which province I came from. I told her I came from *Vĩnh Long*, in the Mekong Delta. I spoke briefly of the beautiful scenery and the riches of that region. She listened intently but didn't seem to understand much, since she hadn't left her city. Then she asked, "Were you familiar with *Hồ Chí Minh* City?" I found myself uncomfortable and had a reaction against anyone who calls Saigon by this political name.

So, I annoyingly answered, "I don't know anything about the city you mention, but I know Saigon very well."

She was surprised at my answer, "*Anh Lễ*! You're just '*awful!*' Come on; don't spoil the fun. I just want to know more about *Hồ*…oh! No…Saigon. Some of the guys asked me to visit their families in that city. They treated me very warmly and gave me gifts and toys for my son."

She spoke of places she had visited, and then asked if I knew the Interior Security Department where she stayed during the trip. I told her I'd been confined there when first captured, and that I had an aunt who lived across the street.

After that, KT. often visited me in the mornings when the others had gone to labour. She always brought along her book of financial records, but often it wasn't used. She'd tell me stories about her visit the South, thinking they'd make me less homesick!

There were times she wore her full uniform, and I once told her humorously: "I don't know why, it terrifies me when you're in full uniform."

"Why are you afraid?" She asked in all seriousness.

"I don't know why! Maybe my 'blood type', just doesn't go well with the colour." KT. made no comment, was quiet for a moment and gave me a sympathetic look, as if she knew my miserable history in prison.

She later asked, "*Anh Lễ*, I've heard that you escaped *Thanh Cẩm* Camp and were tortured severely, weren't you? How long did you stay at that camp?"

"From 1978 to 1988," I continued, "Ms. KT. what did you do and where did you live in 1978?"

"I hadn't started my career at that time; I was living in the rural area in this province."

For a long time, she showed a special sympathy towards me, expressed in her behaviour and manner.

In early June of 1988, all the remaining Chinese prisoners were transferred to another location. I was saddened to say goodbye to them, having lived with them and shared so much of the sufferings during our years in *Thanh Cẩm's* Punishment Section. These men wouldn't have survived without our support during their sixteen years in Vietnamese camps. In return, they helped me become fluent in Mandarin. I'd baptised five of them and considered them the mainstay of our community, sharing and caring for others. Now, I hoped they would sow the seed of faith among people in their motherland, China. Their departure left me saddened for a long time. I've never heard from them ever again.

I often had free time now. During the mornings I helped the sanitary man with his cleaning duties and distributing hot water. Then, I sat in the mess hall preparing my English lesson for the evening class. Usually only First Lieutenant T. came but sometimes other guards would join in.

There had been rumours of an upcoming mass release. I didn't hope to go home and didn't pay much attention to it. Then I had a letter from a friend, saying there were negotiations going on between President Reagan's special envoy and Vietnamese authorities to normalise diplomatic relations between the two nations. One of the proposed U.S. conditions was the release of all imprisoned religious leaders. Fellow inmates also told me that I had hopes of going home. Also, some prisoners previously released to America had asked for Amnesty International's intervention on my behalf. I listened but was not much interested, no longer seeing much point in it.

Then there was another sign. A visiting medical team from Hanoi asked about my medical condition and how long I'd been in camps. Ironically, the doctor questioned on topics not related to the medical issue. Finding that I was a priest, he asked how I felt about the canonisation of the one hundred and seventeen Vietnamese Martyrs that would occur on 19 June that year.

At that time, it was a controversial issue because the Vietnamese Government was strongly opposed to Rome's declaration. I answered, "I'm in prison, so I can't get enough information to form an opinion. But I will say that while my body is under the jurisdiction of the Vietnamese government, as a priest, my soul is under the guidance of the Pope." He asked nothing further.

When I came back to the room, fellow prisoners visited to let me know that whenever that medical team called someone, that person was released.

One morning, First Lieutenant T. came to visit me. We greeted each other in English and chatted for a few minutes. Then he said he wouldn't be around for a while, and wished me well. When I mentioned our English lessons, he fell silent and said we would take a temporary break. Then he continued, "If for whatever reason, I don't see you again, remember my advice about keeping your thoughts to yourself."

I was puzzled by the difference in his manner. If he were only taking leave for a few days, as in previous times, why would he say that? Surprised, I asked, "Mr T., are you transferring elsewhere?"

He responded casually, "I don't think so, but how are we to know about tomorrow?"

I said courteously, "Please pass along my greetings to your family."

He nodded. "Thank you, *Anh Lễ*. Stay well."

The next intimation of my release was from a prisoner who worked in the Administration Office. He told me, "I hear your name's on the release list." That was the first time in thirteen years that I'd heard of a possible release. But it came after I'd stopped wishing it. For I had come to the realisation that I would be transferring from a small prison to a larger one where I wouldn't be able to be my true self. If I lived according to my beliefs, I wouldn't be safe in my own country.

The next morning KT. came to me, without her familiar notebook, only a piece of white paper rolled into a tube in her hands. I was pleased to see her as always. Then she said, "*Anh Lễ*, let's have a party."

I faked a calm response. "We have a party with every one of your visits. We drink tea, eat sweets."

Thinking I didn't understand, she said softly, "*Anh Lễ*, your name is on the release list."

That cemented it. But now I received it with indifference. However, I tried not to disappoint the news bearer, pretending incredulity. "I can't believe it."

"*Anh Lễ*, I'll show you something." And she unrolled the paper, "You can look at it, but you have to keep it a secret until the official announcement. If you say anything, they'll shackle us both!" It was a carbon copy of the typewritten Release Permit, the words just legible. There were fourteen names with mine at the very end. Included were Father *Nguyễn Bình Tĩnh*, Mr *Nguyễn Đức Khuân* and Brother *Kỳ*, a former seminarian from the North. I studied it for a long-time, not really reading it, because I was in such a strange state of mind. I read my name over and over, but it didn't seem to register. At last, KT. took the list from me. "*Anh Lễ*! You'll be released, why do you look so sad?"

I shook my head without a word. There was no way I could explain my mood. I recalled Lieutenant T.'s cryptic farewell yesterday. He knew I was going home, but couldn't tell me, and I had incorrectly made my own conclusion. Instead of his transferring, I would be released during his leave of absence. I guessed he was just as cheerless as me.

The Emotional Farewell

The very last night, I went to say goodbye to my prisoner brothers. Our tears flowed. I had baptised some of them, they are my children in faith. I hugged each person as if to transfer strength to those who were still new to the faith.

The next day we heard the official announcement, and those of us to be released had our fingers printed and received our signed release documents. On it were the words "Person must present himself to local authorities within thirty days of signature date." Folding it into quarters, I tucked the release paper into the inside pocket of my shirt, carefully securing it with a safety pin to foil pick-pocketing attempts. I visited KT.'s office to take care of some financial matters. A number of money orders from my family were still being held. I gave them to her as a gift to her child.

Then I slung my backpack on my shoulder and walked out of the office. KT. walked with me along the long hallway to the front of the building towards the main road. She was no longer my guard, but a good friend. Knowing we'd never meet again, I said quietly, "Well this is it, KT.! I wish you and your family much good fortune. Thank you for your consideration and help."

"*Anh Lễ,* go in peace. I hope you build a bright future."

I gently squeezed her hand saying, "All the best!"

I turned away, springing towards the main road to catch the bus to *Phủ Lý* Ferry, and from there to Hanoi.

I turned for one last look at *Nam Hà* Camp, looking deserted and desolate. Among the innumerable Southern prisoners taken to the North in the past decade, I was the last one to step out of a Northern prison. I found myself saying: "Yet time passed so quickly! One foggy cold night, I was fresh here on a bus from *Hải Phòng*; that was over eleven years ago! A man's life is like a dream…"

A bus was approaching. I raised a hand and went to catch my ride.

Part Four
Release from Prison

Chapter 17
Thinking of the Road Ahead

A streetlight still softly sang its weak notes into the room and the late-night chirps of insects call their companions home. Somewhere nearby was the rustling sound of the wind, loosening autumn leaves to a soft and carefree fall. I rolled over, switched on the light, and saw the clock displaying nearly 2.00 a.m. Sleepless- and dizzy- I brought my hands up to rub my eyes, and then pushed my fingers through bed-tangled hair-the result of so much tossing and turning. The Hanoi Diocesan Centre was peacefully silent with only the occasional click of a house lizard watching for prey. Images of the past danced in my mind, one image blending in with the next, at times woven tightly and clustered together like a long dramatic play. I felt my head faintly heat up, as if from a machine running incessantly for many hours.

Switching on the bathroom light revealed the unimaginable tidy setting when contrasted with the *Thanh Cẩm* Prison disciplinary cell: so amazingly clean with towel rails, large bath towels and facecloths carefully folded into quarters, a running water faucet and small tray holding the ordinary toiletries everyone takes for granted. As I used the W.C. facilities, I smiled as I remembered the two bamboo pipes provided by *Thanh Cẩm* Prison. After washing my face, combing my hair, and drying off with a detergent-fresh facecloth, I took another look in the mirror and smiled. "Not bad!" I thought to myself. I knew that washing my face would make it harder to go back to sleep. However, my body felt so tired, that I absolutely had to wash as a way to feel comfortable. And truly, washing my face did make me feel more upbeat and look more visibly refreshed.

I did not return to the bed, but went out on to the balcony and looked down on the silent sleeping city. One would have to wait awhile to hear an automobile or to see the silhouette of a cyclist biking through the main street. It was only yesterday afternoon that the 'Three of us out-of-place wise guys' stepped into this Diocesan Centre. Across the street, where last night young people danced, there was not a single soul.

A Release Permit

Not even twenty-four hours had passed since I put in my pocket the brown Release Permit, a dark brown colour, thin like a butterfly's wing and ripped around the edges, made of the poorest quality material I had ever seen. Since walking out of the prison camp Headquarters of *Nam Hà* to catch a ride to Hanoi the previous morning, my wandering thoughts always returned to the 'Release Permit' sitting deep in my inside shirt pocket, pinned twice so that I could always feel its existence on my chest.

What a contrast between the Release Permit's physical appearance and its actual meaning. When the cadre put the 'Release Permit' on the table and told me to sign it, I was stunned by their disrespect. I bent over and scribbled a worm-like line across the space designated for a signature on a piece of paper that did not deserve my signature. I considered it an insult that camp Headquarters would provide an enduring legal document of such value in the form of a dirty blackened piece of paper, worse than the paper for bagging cement, the edges frayed and ripped like the blade of a saw. I thought to myself, "Good heavens! My life has become blackened and torn with thirteen years of imprisonment. But this piece of paper is even more blackened and torn than my own state of being!" I looked on the bright side, "…but at least its lines of typed text give it value!"

From *Nam Hà* Prison to the *Phủ Lý* Ferry and then to Hanoi, was a dream-like trip, unreal, lacking awareness. In a very spaced-out state of mind and very tired, I closed my eyes and leaned against the seat throughout the entire ride. However, from the time I planted my feet in Hanoi, and especially after entering the Hanoi Diocesan Centre, I had captured many images and thoughts fuelled by Cardinal *Trịnh Văn Căn*, Bishop *Nguyễn Văn Sang*, the as-like-as-two-peas twin brothers, *Trác* and *Trạc*, the seminarians and priests I met in the dining hall yesterday evening. The very setting of the Hanoi Diocesan Centre with its classic architecture and hierarchical system of activities from top to bottom was all a strange experience to me.

I stood up straight, thrust out my chest, and took a long and deep breath. The pure air in the capital city of Hanoi that early dewy morning got me feeling invigorated. "Thanks God for giving me this pure and refreshing air to breathe," I spoke quietly. I recalled the summer nights in the disciplinary cell of the *Thanh Cẩm* Camp, no different than being shackled in a sealed metal container, heated to high temperatures. There were nights I almost suffocated, not being able to inhale the hot air. There was no other way; we, prisoners had to scream for our lives until hoarse. When the guard came up and had the iron cell door opened, the air flooded in from outside, giving temporary relief and left me thinking there was no greater happiness in this life.

It was getting close to 3.00 a.m. and even after yesterday's weary travel, I still didn't feel sleepy. The pure air, my state of mind, and the very first night of freedom after years in jail all combined to keep me awake. I love my life. I love this life wholeheartedly. I committed myself to actively pursue a fairy-like life, unique to my own existence.

I was aware of many challenges on the road ahead, but I did not want future anxieties and sorrows to diminish this extraordinary enjoyment of the present. Standing for any length of time made my feet ache, and so I went inside and flopped into what I would say the most luxurious chair I have sat on for years. I leaned my head back, had my arms wide open, stretched out my legs, and observed the scenery as things went in and out of visibility, through the streetlights of Hanoi. I looked passively, not noticing any single detail, wanting to make the most of my relaxation time at the moment.

Happenings from the past ten plus years appeared consistently in my mind like a movie in slow motion. While sitting comfortably, I closed my eyes and asked myself, "The 13-years taken out of my life and the pleasant and unpleasant experiences I had overcame, what value it holds for me and for others?" I sat still and tried to answer that question. That part of life, especially when the human condition is reduced to sheer survival, has given me a substantial understanding. Regarding Political Institutions, the trust for power, wealth and prestige clouds integrity to the extreme! Winning at any cost is the focus no matter the cost to human life or property destruction.

The Lesson from Life

First of all, from a religious perspective, in that miserable setting, I perceived the role of a priest as crucial to bring love and hope to places where both were scarce, if not lacking altogether. It is the love and hope of Truth from the Gospel that has given me a supportive foundation. I shared God's mercy with the fellow prisoners I'd had a chance to live with. I think in that hellish prison environment, I lived my priesthood ministry with more results than in the six years before being imprisoned. Moreover, I have come to realise that what seemed to be accidental events or coincidence are in fact the Providence of the Almighty God. **I always believe that each single situation bears the fingerprint of the Hand of God-protecting me, later revealing the true meaning and objective of my life.**

What's the worth of speaking of the Communist regime's prison policies? We entered a prison with the attractive title, *'Concentration and Re-education Camp'*, bearing a promise that "Successful re-education warrants a return home." Therefore, our rights to hope were stripped off! Hope is the reason people rely on to live and move forward for a meaningful life of great purpose.

The slogan "Successful re-education warrants a return home" encouraged division and betrayal among Southern political prisoners. Speaking of the hopeless mindset at the time, after entering the camp, I recalled reading some lines of poetry from Dante Alighieri's Inferno, describing Hell this way. Inscriptions on the Gate of Hell include the following lines:

"Only eternal things are older than I [the gate]; and I will forever endure. Abandon every hope, you who enter."

Living blindly in a hopeless state of mind, I had always thought, that if I were sentenced to five years, ten years, fifteen or twenty years, or longer…, I would be happier with the definite sentence. With nothing definite, there was no knowing. There is nothing more miserable and frustrating than a human being living in despair. It is the style of dangling a carrot in front of a donkey pulling a cart, by rationalising, "You are all playing soccer, and we are nearing the end of the second half, only a few last minutes until the whistle blows signalling the end of the game! Try harder!"

We exhausted our hearing of the Communist lecturer's style of speaking. This kind of "Soccer game" exists in every camp. But oh! How terrible, the last few minutes of the match, like a high quality rubber band, one that could be stretched eternally.

In those circumstances, the vague promise of "Successful re-education warrants a return home" seduced a number of weak-willed people who tried hard to be 'Re-educated' or 'Reformed'. There were some who wanted to be

'Well-reformed'! For them, the best way was to forget their own identity, forget the identities of those in prison uniforms, and also betray others in the same circumstances.

That vague promise, in my opinion, was the wicked policy of the Communist regime prison system. It tortured our minds and did so much damage, making some ignorant people believe in the empty promises in order to inflict pain upon their prison brothers. As I've said the pain, suffering, and humiliation I had to endure for thirteen years in Communist concentration camps was not only the physical ordeal alone such as torture, shackling, beatings, hunger and thirst, nakedness, suffocation, verbal abuse, as I remembered, but also all the physical abuse has a profound impact on mental and psychological life. **The crucial point was the hopeless state of mind and particularly, witnessing the betrayal among the prisoners which was not only tolerated but encouraged.**

Stemming from that experience, I gained a better understanding of the human heart. When a human being is put under a limited and pressured setting, no longer covered by uniforms, by labels, by ranks and former titles, he is fully exposed as a simply human being. Living in crowded conditions in miserable settings, hungry and thirsty with no hope, for a long period of over ten years, allowed me to extract a bitter lesson: *The kindness and compassion of the human heart has its limits. However, the evil of human nature is boundless and beyond one's imagination, especially when evil is nurtured by immoral regimes.*

Good and Evil

My 13-yearlong imprisonment, especially the three years (1979-1982) under lock and key, writhing in the bottom of the disciplinary Hell of *Thanh Cẩm* Camp, gives me a well-founded stance for saying that: in each person there are equal parts of good and evil, developing according to the living conditions. If a person is living in an environment of righteousness and morality, and ruled by law, then the good portion will develop to suppress the evil part. In contrast, if a person falls into an environment of immorality, hostility, and lawlessness, then the evil segment will perk up and dominate.

In prison, I witnessed and endured the cruel and malicious actions of a number of prison guards, as well as those of treacherous fellow prisoners. I know that it was partly due to their cruel nature. **However, if there were no**

nurturing and encouragement by the Communist regime, then those actions would not have occurred, or if they did they would not have reached such degrees of extreme cruelty. From that perspective, I conclude: "Never condemn a human being, never hate a human being, never destroy a human being; but at any cost, wipe out any repulsive regime that encourages and nurtures hostility among humans. Replace it with a healthy society so that humans get to develop their righteousness and integrity."

The years in prison also provided me with the opportunity to share and live with the peoples' pain and suffering. If I had not experienced that, perhaps, I would not know, or would have but a shallow knowledge of the sorrowful fate of the peoples of Vietnam. Through that road, I love and bond with my Peoples all the more.

I also think, later on, I will have an obligation to share my life's knowledge and understanding with all others, with my beloved peoples and especially with the younger generations that was not affected by a ravaging war caused by conflicting ideologies. I want to leave a heartfelt message for future generations: *Never blindly worship any foreign doctrine and forget the love for your Vietnamese peoples, so that mutual destructive war will not occur. Political regimes will pass, kingdoms will collapse, and only the nation's peoples will remain through time.* History has proven that the more cruel and oppressive the regime, the faster the collapse of the system. No regime can use the gun and the prison to rule, and still stand fast. Only the love of humanity can persuade and win people's hearts.

The Un-Finished War

While deep in thought on this matter, I recalled a story from long ago. In 1966, during my first year of theology at the Saigon Seminary, Father *Gérard Gagnon*, a Canadian Redemptorist who lived in Vietnam for more than three decades and speaks Vietnamese fluently, paid a visit and gave a talk to the seminarians. During that talk, he told a story of his riding a motorcycle from Dalat to Saigon. He was stopped by *Vietcong* (Communist) at a desolate area and taken into the jungle for propaganda.

"What do you think?" asked the propaganda agent. "Your Catholic Church has been operating for almost two thousand years, but has only a few hundred million followers. Communism, on the other hand, was born only 50 years ago but dominates a third of the human world. Therefore, between your religion and our Communist theory, which one is better?"

"I don't know", replied the Redemptorist "We have to wait until Communism comes up to two thousand years old, like Christianity, then I will be able to answer your question."

Now in Hanoi Diocesan Centre, steeped in thought, the seed for this book was planted. I decided that when the time was right, I would record all the details occurring in prison, and my thoughts during those radical changes. I write about it, not to complain and rant about life, and not to blame people. Instead, I wanted to share my experience with all, express gratitude to those who were virtuous, among my prison mates and even a few prison guards, and remember those who lived with me and those who died in prison. This memoir is written as a historical lesson for my beloved peoples of Vietnam, especially those among the younger generations. This memoir does not distinguish between my peoples from the North or the South, inland or overseas, religious beliefs, present or past political affiliations in the destructive war on our homeland.

My heartfelt messages are as follows: "My beloved peoples of Vietnam, enough Vietnamese blood have been shed. The painful scars still remain on the body during the remaining years of life, and in the mind and spirit of wounded veterans on both sides of a destructive war. It has inflicted enough pain and anguish. The suffering of innocent Vietnamese peoples has been too excessive. The insanity of worshipping a foreign doctrine killed and harmed enough of our fellow peoples. Weapons and ammunition from foreign countries have ploughed and ravaged the body of our Motherland, Vietnam. Suspicion among factions and among religions has damaged the peoples' unity far too much. The boundless greed of those in power, through the eras, resembles a wild beast let loose from its restraints, wreaking havoc and assaulting the unfortunate and voiceless in society. Remember that any political system will pass, only the Peoples stand firm through time."

Also, I want to send my heartfelt sympathies to the younger generations of Vietnam. "My beloved friends of the younger generations, our peoples have experienced a phase of sadness, full of blood and tears. Those from the previous generations, despite much effort, have not brought love and cultural unity. I have faith that love and cultural unity will be achieved in your lifetime. Do not be bound by sorrowful historical events. Instead, use history as a lesson to avoid the reoccurrence of events that proved traumatic for our people. Let the dead rest in peace. Respect the heroes but do not live for them. National history is a continuous journey, and each era will produce new heroes. To me, genuine Vietnamese heroes are actually those with courage to think outside the square, not tied up by the past, but looking forward to the future with the spirit of knowledge and tolerance. Do not sit and lament history, grumbling about people; but use history like a beacon of light that brightens our road ahead.

Looking back on recent times, I see the destructive war is full of blood and tears, dragging on for many decades. In the hearts and minds of the peoples of Vietnam, the war is not over. **The absurd reality is that the war has no winner, only losers, and the losers are clearly the Peoples of Vietnam.** Leave the past behind and look forward to a bright future for our country. Let the shadow pass, and let us direct ourselves to the light source to a new dawn for the Vietnamese race."

The following day there would be many things to do and among the first would be to find *Bình Bưởi* and make enquiries about my sworn brother *Bình Thanh*, whom I had not heard of for over six years.

With that in mind and determined to get some sleep, I climbed back into bed, talking to myself. "Forget everything! I must sleep well to restore energy for tomorrow's journey. Not like the first night after release from *Thanh Cẩm* disciplinary cell six years ago." While recalling that night, my mind was even more tense and reflective. There was no way I could get to sleep despite this being my first night of free legs after three years of being shackled.

That night Fr. *Lê Đức Triệu*, the musician who set to music the only poem I wrote in prison, kept me company. In the memory of him, I include here a section of the poem with the romantic title 'Counting Raindrops' written on a cold wet night at *Phan Đăng Lưu* Prison while in solitary confinement in remembering my *La Mã* parish.

The cell was empty and cold that night,
Outside, the rain pours and increases melancholy.
I am away from you, away for a long time,
Tonight I send my love and sadness to whom?
Missing you, I miss you day and night.

So many white nights, bitter and waiting hopelessly.
The sad music of crickets chirping!
Dear cricket! You don't sleep, who are you calling?
Or is your heart and mind also bitter,
Borrowing love and crying for two lives?
Silently watching and counting raindrops,
As many raindrops as there is affection.

Waking Up!

Here in Hanoi Diocesan Centre, Fr. *Lê Đức Triệu*'s music of Counting Raindrops lulled me to sleep, a deep sleep perhaps, because when woken by a loud door knocking I was startled, thinking I was still in prison. "Oh, gosh! I over-slept! The prison guard had to wake me! The unit guard must be announcing time to go out for labour." I exclaimed.

But no! It was not the familiar world of prison; it was the entirely new world of freedom. In a daze, I slid off the bed and stumbled to the door.

"Good morning, Father!" The man said, "Perhaps, yesterday you had an exhausting journey so you slept well. I have been knocking several times. Sorry to wake you up, Father. The Cardinal invites you to breakfast."

I did not look at the clock but quietly answered, "Hello Brother!" and mumbled a few words that I didn't remember.

However, as I hurried to the bathroom, I do remember asking myself, "Good heavens! Was this gentleman *Trác* or *Trạc*?"

AUTUMN OF 2003, THE 60th BIRTHDAY OF THE AUTHOR

Epilogue
In the Pursuit of Freedom Again

Supplement 1
Death of Bình Thanh

After getting out of prison, I stayed in North Vietnam for half a month. At this time, I searched the *Bưởi* Village to enquire about *Bình Bưởi* for the news of *Bình Thanh*, my efforts were fruitless. Some people said *Bình Bưởi* got caught again and was put in prison. My direct line to the news about *Bình Thanh* (Hereinafter BT.) ended.

While I was in the North, I visited a number of attractions in Hanoi City and some Catholic Dioceses. In addition to visiting Bishops and priests, I wanted to learn about the stability and growth of the Church in the North. I also visited some of the former prison inmates who were released before me. Having decided later on if I was to record the changes in the North, I asked a friend of mine to take me to see the mummy of *Hồ Chí Minh* to observe how the Communists worshipped his decomposing corpse as yet not buried.

After two weeks in Hanoi, I took the train to Saigon on a late evening of 27 July 1988. Setting foot on *Gò Vấp* railway station in the early morning on 1 August 1988, I took a ride on a motorised cyclo to Saigon and I found myself very much like an alien from another planet. I was 45years old then and had been a priest for nearly two decades. It was less than 12 years since I left Saigon and yet everything had become so unfamiliar.

After 13 years in the small prison, constrained by the conditions of my release from prison, I was once again back in the big prison. The condition of my probation was, to report my activities every two weeks. The names of the people with whom I had been in contact, the places I had visited and details of my conversations they were all part of my report.

Stepping into a Huge Prison!

Prior to my release, my biological sister had warned me about threatening words from the local authorities. When hearing about my pending release, they had said, *that guy deserves to be chopped up and feed the fish, why did they release him?*

Hearing how the local authorities felt about me, and knowing my Release Permit would have me back at my home village, I knew something had to be done. My home village was not safe and I knew I could not return. I approached the Bishop of *Vĩnh Long* to ask for help to find a temporary place in the Diocesan Centre House. He said, "The Diocese is burdened with too many predicaments from the local authorities. If you go there, the Diocese would have more trouble!"

I was at a dead end. I had no choice but to write to Ms. KT., the Financial Officer who I knew in *Nam Hà* Camp. She helped reissue me a second Release Permit with the new address in Saigon as I had requested. That was my life-saving amulet at the time.

My Aunty gave me temporary shelter in Saigon. A group of very kind-hearted parishioners, who used to send gifts to the imprisoned priests, helped me financially with some pocket money. An acquaintance gave me a bike, a cousin gave me some clothes and a friend from Canada sent me a box full of gifts. Despite many kind deeds and acts of charity, I still felt like a stranger in a strange land. I had no personal legal document at that time other than the Release Permit. I felt like an outcast, there was no room for me in my own homeland.

Years ago, while in prison, I had learned Mandarin from a group of Chinese inmates. Mr *Phùng Thiên Bình* was a fellow inmate of mine; he was released sometime before me, and was living in the city of *Hải Phòng* in the North. After my release, he introduced me to his relatives in *Chợ Lớn*. They were very kind and gave me a job in their shop that sold iron chains, cutlery, nuts, locks, pipes and other hardware.

Every day, I sat at the stall in front of the house selling iron and steel accessories. In my free time, I would refresh my skill in English. Every morning, I started the day saying Mass at my Auntie's home with the neighbours attending. After Mass, I cycled to *Chợ Lớn* to continue my duties there. That was my routine for a while.

I could not keep living in an unusual situation for long. I decided to find my way to escape overseas, and let fate decide the future consequence of this ultimate decision. I no longer worried about where to go or how to get new place to live, I just knew I must leave this country. Again, I decided to play a game of life and death, putting my own life at stake. This was a game of 'All or Nothing'!

Recalling nine years ago in *Thanh Cầm* Prison, I also played a game like this. Along with 4 inmates, we plotted a plan to escape the prison on May 1st, 1979. At that time, we drew a 'Black card', it costed the lives of our two dearest friends, *Đặng Văn Tiếp* and *Lâm Thành Văn*.

By God's grace, I survived. In return, I had to pay a price beyond imagination (Please read Chapters 12, 13 of this book). I knew my life was at stake. I could not lose this gamble. Yet it was still better than dragging my 'half-alive-and-half-dead' body while living this nightmarish situation in Saigon.

My luck began to improve when I met a benefactor, Mrs. *Đinh Thị Thập*, a parishioner in *Bắc Hải* Parish. Mrs. *Đinh Thị Thập* and a group of ladies in the Parish regularly supplied food, medicines, and clothes to the priests in prison in the North, even though they never knew who the imprisoned priests were.

When I went back to Saigon, I found out that my Sister and Mrs. *Thập* knew each other well. I regarded her as my foster Sister. Meeting her was the beginning of hope. She was warm and loving. She cared for me like an older sister taking care of her younger sibling.

Mrs. *Đinh Thị Thập* started researching different channels of crossing borders and even acted as a guarantor to pay the fees for border crossing. This act of kindness gave me hope and changed my future forever. It was the spark of light in the dark days of my life. I will never forget her good deed and will always treasure her kindness every day of my life. This blessing will be kept until I go to my grave.

One night, I travelled back to *Vĩnh Long*, my hometown 150 kilometres from Saigon, and sneaked into the graveyard at night to visit my Mother's grave. She had passed away 11 years ago when I was still in prison. During this visit I said prayers for my late Parents, I lit an incense stick and knelt and prostrated myself in front of the graves, asking for my Parents' blessings for my upcoming destiny trip.

I could not visit my family home during the day-time, for fear that local authorities would imprison me at any time. In a bigger city like Saigon, it was easier to live and move around. I was in a difficult situation, my right of citizenship had been withdrawn from me, I had no residential document, and was unable to resume my role as a priest.

Since returning to Saigon, I did my own research on the different ways to cross the border. I had heard that the ultimate price was a horrendous death for attempting to escape out of the country. However, there were also success stories of people who arrived safely at Thai Refugee Camps. They sent letters and photos about the camps where they were staying to their family members in Saigon. It made me more determined to attempt this escape. Eventually, Mrs. *Thập* found a connection through her neighbour. She introduced me to the organiser and acted as a guarantor to pay the fees for me.

A Gamble of Life and Death

On the late evening of January 10, 1989, after five months in Saigon, I caught the bus from Saigon to the border city *Châu Đốc* heading to Thailand. I had hibernated in Saigon for five months after saying goodbye to the small prison. Now as an exile from my homeland, I was making my way towards an unknown future. I was much like an exhausted albatross which took to the sky again after months of hovering over her destroyed nest.

From the time the car started the engine and rolled out, the second gamble of my life began! I crossed the border to Cambodia. From there, I went to Thailand by a fishing boat and to *Banthat* Refugee Camp in January 1989. I stayed in the house with two young biological brothers, *Bùi Anh Văn* and *Bùi Văn Võ* whom I first met in this *Banthat* Refugee Camp in Southern Thailand.

One afternoon, when we were in the house, a stranger, about 40 years old with heavily tattooed arms, wearing a white T-shirt and trousers walked in. I did not have a very good impression of this tattooed stranger. At that time, *Banthat* Camp was very crowded with refugees. He was from another area that was not Catholic, so I had never met him before.

When he entered the house, before I could stand up to welcome him, he asked, "Excuse me, are you Father *Lễ* from *Bưng Trường* village?"

I was startled by this stranger's question. He seemed to know so much about me. I replied, "Yes, I'm Father *Lễ* in *Bưng Trường*. How do you know me?"

The man's face was expressionless, still keeping a straight face, he replied, "So, you must know *Bình Thanh*?"

Hearing the name *Bình Thanh* (BT.) was like an electric current running through me. I hurried over and grabbed his shoulders, "What did you say? What did you say? You know who? Heavens! I have been waiting for news from him, for the last seven years now. You must tell me where he is now, where is my good brother?"

I asked a string of questions without waiting for his responses. He stood still like a statue, not answering my questions directly. He just said, "Please come over to my place tomorrow morning, about nine o'clock, we will talk then."

He gave me his shelter number and the Section of the site where he was staying. The two flatmates and I were in disbelief as he left our place. I had even forgotten to ask what his name was. The attitude of this stranger made me more anxious and worried. I was itching for news about B.T. for the last seven years.

That night, I tossed and turned, unable to go to sleep. The attitude of the stranger was disturbing. It made me worried about the possibility of receiving bad news about my brother. Nevertheless, I had to be mentally prepared to receive the news when it came.

The next morning, I came to his house on time and found him alone inside the house. He had a 3-year-old child. The child was playing in the yard when I arrived. When I came inside, he asked me to sit on a chair behind the creaking table. He sat opposite and offered me a cup of hot tea. I offered him cigarettes in return. He pulled out one cigarette, left it in his mouth and lit my cigarette first. He made these actions slowly in the awkwardness of silence. There was no hurry, nor was there any expression in receiving a stranger in his home. Although I was very impatient, I kept still knowing my reason for coming here.

I noticed something odd about his mannerism in purposefully procrastinating before getting to the subject of my visit. After pulling off the first puff of cigarette, he picked up the tea cup briefly then lowered it down to the table again. My guess was he had something very difficult to express, this thought made me even more distressed. He put the cup of tea back on the table, just rotated the cup with his fingers, looked straight at me and blurted: "*Anh Út!* (Brother Út!)"

Bình Thanh Is Dead!

I was startled, only *Bình Thanh* called me by this name. Nobody knew this name unless BT. had spoken to him about me. Noticing my reaction, he continued, "*Anh Út! Bình Thanh* is dead!" He went on longer but I could not hear anything.

There is a saying in Vietnamese, "*Sét đánh ngang tai*" (Which roughly translates to "*struck by lightning in the head*"). His words struck me like lightning. I was numb.

Unconsciously, I removed the cigarette from my lips, put it on the ash tray and buried my face in my palms. Tears streamed down my cheeks. I fumbled for a handkerchief in my side pocket but could not find any. I pulled up the flap of my shirt, after removing the pair of glasses and put them on the table, and used the flap to wipe away the tears. I sat there, with my face in my hands and sobbed.

When there were no more tears to cry, I stood up and staggered outside. Reaching the front yard, I leaned against a tree trunk, and again, I sobbed uncontrollably like a child. I had not heard yet about the time and the cause of his death, but I could guess that my brother died in an unusual circumstance.

I started having flash back of BT., especially during his happier time. He once said to me: "I will never die in bed from illness." Now I understood why yesterday, this man did not announce the news in my shelter, instead he invited me over to his, when there were no people around.

A long time elapsed, he walked out to the front yard where I was still standing and invited me back inside the house. This stranger suddenly became the only person in this world who could share the sudden pain of losing my beloved brother forever.

The moment he sat down on a chair, he started to speak without waiting for me to ask him anything. "*Anh Út*, my name is *Đạo*, a friend of BT. The moment BT. arrived in South Vietnam, we went to *Bưng Trường* to visit *Chị Hai* (Eldest Sister). At the time, we were disguised as a group of soldiers. *Chị Hai* was extremely afraid the moment we stepped inside your family home. Did *Chị Hai* tell you about us?"

I nodded guessing that was the case. I continued, "I knew if BT. was still alive, he would send news of his whereabouts to me or to *Chị Hai* during these last seven years."

Đạo said, "We became acquainted during his time in the North. A month after he escaped from prison, we went to the South to visit your sister. He was determined to go to *Vĩnh Long* to visit *Chị Hai*, whom he regarded as his own Eldest Sister from the day you and he swore to be Brothers for life. B.T. spoke to me about you with highest regard, full of respect and special affection. I could never have guessed one day we would meet here, at a refugee camp, in Thailand."

After that, *Đạo* recounted the time he was in Saigon, when B.T. went to *Hố Nai* alone, "For a special mission", he said.

Only I knew the reason why he went.

Đạo continued, at that time, B.T. had a plan awaiting you in South Vietnam, together we would cross the border to another country. He also knew it was difficult for you to get out of prison sometime soon, he actually hatched a plan to go back up to the North, storm the prison and free you, for he knew all the schedules in and out of *Thanh Cẩm* Prison. However, this plan required a lot of financial investment for him to work on it. That was the reason why the gang went over to Cambodia. We drove over in a military truck.

Đạo took a sip of water and said, "*Phnom Penh*, at the time, was crowded with many active gangs, from both Vietnamese and Cambodian backgrounds. They had to compete with one another for a space to survive and to lead the herd. Unfortunately, in a standoff with another gang members, *Bình Thanh* was critically injured and died the next day, surrounded by all his gang brothers."

"He died a couple of months after visiting your sister. We buried him near a pagoda on the outskirts of the capital city of *Phnom Penh*. Shortly afterwards, we disbanded, and pulled back to Vietnam. I stayed back in the South, met my wife and we had a son together, he was the child you saw playing in the front yard. Our family then crossed the border to Thailand, and here we are, I did not expect to meet you here."

My heart sank as I listened to *Đạo* retell the story of B.T.'s death. I asked him about *Hường* (*Bình Thanh's* girlfriend).

Đạo said, "B.T. told me that *Anh Út* instructed him never go directly to see her in any part of the country for fear that the police would follow her to get to him. Instead, *Chị Hai* would arrange for them to meet. As a result, B.T. only sent *Hường* messages letting her know she must be ready for them to cross the border." However, this was depending on the timing of my getting out of jail. "After the death of B.T., no one dared to give *Hường* the bad news for they feared she would be devastated and might hurt herself in the midst of her mourning." I enquired from Đạo a few more details about B.T. Right before I left his shelter, Đạo stood up and asked me, "Anh Út, do you believe the soul of B.T. set up a chance for us to meet each other here?"

I stood still for a while, reached out my hand to shake his and spoke in place of answering his question directly, "*Bình Thanh* is very serious about friendship or any relationship. He loves deeply and cares deeply."

That night, in a little hut of the refugee camp where I was staying, I sat alone in the study room while the two brothers *Văn* and *Võ* were already deep in their sleep. These two young men arrived in the refugee camp some time before me. The three of us, like father with his two sons, were assigned to this hut. We bonded like a family unit, and became protective of one another. I sat alone quietly lighting one cigarette after another, but only had one puff and put it down in the ash tray.

The news about B.T.'s death devastated me, I was emotionally exhausted. I reminisced about the time when we were inmates, we hatched a plan for the future to leave this country and cross the border. We must go overseas. B.T. would give up the life of a gang leader, which was caused by the political situation in this country, and would start a new life. At this moment, I had already crossed the border to Thailand, standing in front of the threshold of the free world and my beloved brother, the one I loved the most no longer existed!

Recollecting Souvenirs

I sat quietly late into the night to recollect each and every memory of B.T. I recalled the phrase tattooed on his back. It says: "When I die who would build my grave. Behind my coffin who would shed farewell tears!" Underneath this phrase was an image of a censer filled with incense smoke, and right above the smoke was the image of Buddha.

Bình Thanh, although well-known as a notorious bandit who may have been hated and cursed by people, to me was one of the people I loved most in this world. He was not just a bandit, but a chivalrous one. His highly emotional quotient had given me a rosy sky in the midst of the darkest nights of hell inside the disciplinary prison of *Thanh Cẩm*. B.T. was a bandit who may have acted in cruelty to some. But the cruelty was caused by the circumstances, and not by his character. On the contrary, I witnessed and was a victim of a few people who bore high titles and roles in society. Yet, when in jail, they acted horrendously beyond beastly nature. Their actions were not just driven by circumstances but by their actual character. If I would put the quality of human traits on a scale, these guys would be placed on the scale a hundred thousand times lower than that of B.T., the notorious bandit!

I stood up, went to my bedroom and opened a bag looking for a small nail clipper, already rusty by oxidation. That was a gift from B.T. He gave it to me one late afternoon right before he escaped from the prison. Since then, this nail clipper stayed with me everywhere I went, even when I escaped from the country. Now, it became the only souvenir I had from my beloved brother. I went back to the chair, staring intently at this souvenir and recalling every little detail of that late afternoon we last saw each other.

That evening, during feeding time, B.T. climbed over the wall standing between the two disciplinary Sections to see me. He said that night would be the night, and asked me to say a prayer for him. That afternoon, we shed many tears. B.T. gave me a hug, and kissed me on the forehead and said, "This is my goodbye and probably my farewell kiss to you, my brother for life."

I had a feeling that was the last time we would see each other in this life. Unfortunately, the feeling I worried the most about had come true!

I remembered there was another souvenir from B.T. I stuck out my left foot closer to the lamp. There was a very small tattoo closer to the ankle. The letter *'H'* about the size of a fingertip, which B.T. had tattooed for me when we were locked up in Room No. 2 of the *Thanh Cầm* disciplinary cell back in 1982.

Bình Thanh had said, "I tattooed this mark on your left foot. It is in the most visible spot when your feet are in the shackles. In the future, if you get a chance to wear shoes again, whenever you put your shoes on, you will see the letter *'H'*. It stands for 'Hatred'. It would remind you of this time in the disciplinary cell."

The tattoo is still on my left foot and will follow me to the grave, but its meaning has changed significantly. The *'H'* no longer means 'Hatred'. Today it stands for '**HOPE**'.

Through all the traumatic experiences and struggles I had endured, I would continue to fight and hope for a brighter future for the peoples of Vietnam. I would not let hatred caused by circumstances in the history to dictate the rest of my life.

It was getting past midnight. There was the sound of footsteps behind me. I turned to see *Võ* approaching, he stood beside me and asked quietly, "It is so late at night, you did not go to sleep? Let me arrange the canvas bed for you, Father."

Between the two brothers, *Võ*, the younger one was closer to me. He took great care of me in everything. I loved him the most and yet he also got reprimanded the most from me. Whilst asking, *Võ* rearranged my study desk so he could get closer to the wall. He hooked up the mosquito net onto the wall.

In his distinctively slow voice *Võ* asked, "I noticed since this morning, there was something bothering you. Did you have some sad news, Father?"

I shook my head and replied, "It is getting late now, I will tell you tomorrow morning."

Looking at *Võ*, suddenly he reminded me of B.T. Destiny had taken me into prison to meet B.T. and the circumstances that had pushed me to Thai refugee camp to meet *Võ*. During the time living in Thailand, I loved *Võ* so much, like the love of a Father for his own son. I knew our lives would intertwine in the future for as long as the memory of the bandit *Bình Thanh* was still fresh in my mind.

Supplement 2
Pristine Land Beckons Birds

I returned to Saigon on 1 August 1988 after 13 years in prison. As I was unable to live in peace in the big prison of Saigon; so, I decided to find a way to cross the border.

In the evening of January 10, 1988, I took a passenger car heading for *Châu Đốc*, a city situated near the Cambodia border. So, after returning to the big prison for 5 months, I began to leave again into the uncertain future. The second gamble of my life began, from the moment the wheels of the car started to roll and left Saigon in the dark to flee to the West. My target was to reach a refugee camp in Thailand that I had "Painted in my mind" through photos sent by people from that camp to their families. This time, my heart really sank.

Once again, I had to leave my beloved Saigon. When I turned to look at Saigon fading away in the night, I wondered if I would ever have the opportunity to see Saigon again? Was this the last time in my life I that I would see my beloved Saigon?

In a sudden but intense emotion, tears streamed down my cheeks, which I couldn't control. A female passenger sitting across from me turned away when she saw me crying. I pulled out a handkerchief to wipe away my tears, and buried my face into my palms. She probably knew that I had some sorrow and turned away because she respected my suffering. This mood I experienced once 12 years ago, when I was handcuffed, along with 350 other prisoners in *Gia-Ray* Camp to board the *SÔNG HƯƠNG* ship to the North on a night of April 1977. When I climbed onto the deck and stood in line waiting for the entrance to the cargo chamber, I turned my head looking back at Saigon one last time, tears also rolling down my cheeks.

The car quietly plunged into the night along Highway 4 towards *Vĩnh Long* in Mekong Delta. There were about 15 passengers or so in the car, most of them were females. As I learned about this trip, it seemed obvious that they were petty traders in Cambodia. They carried bags fully loaded. Nobody talked much, so after a while most of them dozed off. My heart was in a complete tumult because this was a fateful trip. I didn't know what awaited me ahead. Sitting still for a while, I dreamily remembered the last year I spent at *Nam Hà* Camp. At that time, the relationship between Camp officials and prisoners became close and comfortable. Gone were those harsh and dogmatic conditions in the early years when I was first interred as a prisoner.

Even though I was in prison, I felt comfortable and safe. On the contrary, military surveillance had turned Saigon into a big prison. Tonight, I was sitting in a car darting into the…uncertainty, I did not know where I was going. What would happen? What was waiting for me ahead?

Although the target was some remote refugee camp in Thailand, how could I know what would happen to me along this completely unfamiliar road? As far as I knew, this car would take me to *Châu Đốc* and from there I would cross the Cambodian border at night by boat. Once again, I embarked on an uncertain future with the mood of someone who had nothing to lose.

I sat stiffly, thinking ceaselessly. I remembered my late parents. My Father died in 1975, a few months before I was in prison, my Mother died in 1977 when I was imprisoned in the North for one year. When I returned to the South and before I left the country, I sneaked back to my hometown once at night to see my Mother's grave for the first time after 11 years of her death. I had to sneak home at night because if I had gone during daytime, there would have been many unfortunate incidents.

Many memories and emotions switched through my mind as the car plunged into darkness as the journey continued. That night there was a new moon. By the time the car stopped at a location next to the river bank, it was already late. In the river, there were some *Tác ráng* waiting. (*Tác ráng* was a long and narrow boat equipped with a motor at the rear, which was very common in this river and canal area.) Some of the passengers were familiar with this scene. I stepped on to the *Tác ráng* and carried only a light back bag, while the ladies had all sorts of big and small bags that seemed heavy and bulky. The boat operated quite quickly and smoothly in the canal between the two reedy banks.

About midnight, the *Tác ráng* tried to enter a pier, next to a few fish cages. We went ashore and entered a fairly large, poorly built house. More like a pavilion than a house, there were only bamboo stalls on either side, in the middle was the aisle, and no walls. It looked like this was on an islet, because at night I couldn't see it clearly. That night, people talked to each other very comfortably. I didn't know anyone; so, I lay down and pretended to sleep, but I could not sleep for my mind was fully occupied with anxieties and confusion.

Crossing the Border

The next morning, we boarded a sizable motorboat to a busy market location with many boats in the wharf. I knew this was part of Cambodia, because there was a checkpoint manned by Cambodian soldiers. Whoever passed by must produce a pack of HERO cigarettes. I didn't know where this place was, just followed people wherever they went and *"When in Rome do as the Romans do."*

With a HERO cigarette pack serving as my papers, I passed through the checkpoint without issue. When we got ashore, we travelled about three kilometres by horse cart to a bus stop where there were numerous old cars. I was surprised to see none of the cars had number plates, and passengers were crammed beyond what I thought was possible. A vehicle that could carry 10 people would cram in 20 or more.

One of those tightly packed cars took me to *Phnom Penh* at dusk. That night I slept in a hostel with bamboo flooring, overlooking the capital of Cambodia, *Phnom Penh*, dotted with sparkling lights.

The next morning, our overstuffed, unregistered, vehicle headed to *Kampong Som*, also known as *Sihanoukville*. It was a port province in southern Cambodia. Along the way, the driver's assistant sat on the hood of the vehicle, securely clenching the headlights between his thighs so we would not fall.

Occasionally, armed Cambodian soldiers would wave us over to the side of the road. The driver would slow the vehicle just enough for the assistant to discretely pass something into their hands. This scene was repeated many times on the road from *Phnom Penh* to *Kampong Som*.

I was hiding in this province for ten days waiting to contact the Thai fishing boat. Those ten days were filled with so many incidents that I wish I could share them with you if I had time and space. Perhaps in another supplement.

Eventually the boat arrived, and after three days and nights in the bottom of a Thai fishing boat compartment, I was thrown onto a beach in Thailand. It was midnight. I was dropped ashore with 31 other people, including women and children. Fortunately, we met with Representative from the UNHCR (United Nations High Commissioner for Refugees) that very afternoon.

From that moment, my life received an upgrade. It had only been six weeks since I left Saigon. In such a short time, there were many unfortunate incidents which I survived! As the saying goes, "After the rain the sun shines."

Refugee Camps in Thailand

I lived and worked at *Banthat* and *Panat Nikhom* Refugee Camps for two years, and was made The Administrator of The Vietnamese Catholic Community by the Thai Bishop of *Chonbury* Diocese. At that time, Father *Trần Xuân Lãm* assisted me. In addition, there were also a few foreign priests who came in to help refugees. Father Peter *Namwong*, who was Thai, also loved refugees very much and helped our people with compassion. At that time, the Catholic community accounted for 5,000 people out of a total of 16,000 refugees in *Panat Nikhom* Camp in 1989.

Life in a Refugee Camp was very complicated. With 16,000 people crammed into such a small camp, so many problems occurred. At one point I thought, life in the Refugee Camp was much grimmer and more complex than the life in prison which I had just left six months ago.

At that time, I was both the Administrator of the Catholic Community and at the same time representing the *Les Enfants Du Mékong Association* (The Children of the *Cửu Long* River), a charity Association from France that donated money to the refugees who didn't have families and relatives abroad.

I was also in charge of the investigation, and compilation of documents of those who need help and sending the reports to the General Director's office in France. This was a very hard role with a lot of pressure and very dangerous to my safety in this brash and bustling society. The amount of the Association's assistance was limited ($ 25,000 USD a month) while the number of people was very large and everyone wanted to receive assistance. How did I satisfy everyone's needs? Otherwise, I could be harmed! Of course, we had special techniques and the General Director from France flew over to meet me to discuss ways to help keep me safe. We agreed on a special code that I approved for each application in front of the applicant, and sent it to France.

At that time, there were some well-off people in the Refugee Camp, either because they brought money or gold with them when they crossed the border, or their families or relatives in a third country sent them money; so they lived very comfortably. Thai people seriously exploited this case. They set up a money exchange agency, restaurants, pubs, grocery stores, and all the other ways and services to reap money.

The hottest topic in the Refugee Camp at that time was how to resettle in a third country? Most of the refugees hoped and dreamed of going to the United States. When would a delegation from foreign countries come to interview people acceptable for re-settlement in their country? Which delegations have priority? Who has relatives in which country? These topics were discussed and talked about everywhere in the Camp. There were many countries that accepted refugees, but everyone wanted to go to the United States, and was not keen enough to go to…France!

Going to the U.S. was a big dream. Everyone wanted to go to the U.S. at all costs, so much so that a young man hung himself because of a rejection from the American delegation.

Those who wanted to be accepted by the U.S. must have met requirements such as: having worked for the U.S., having relatives in the U.S., having been in prison, or having some form of contact in the U.S. So, everyone tried to prove that they somehow had some contact in the U.S., one way or another.

At that time, two other Vietnamese priests, who arrived in the Refugee Camp after me, were waiting to be seen by the U.S. delegation. My case was much simpler. After being accepted by the American delegation, there was a Vietnamese Catholic Community in Canada that needed a priest, and I was about to go to Canada. Suddenly, Bishop Denis Browne of Auckland Diocese, in New Zealand sent a letter to all three priests but invited only one priest to New Zealand to be a Chaplain for the Vietnamese Catholic Community in his Diocese.

In his letter, he said: "Monsignor *Trần Văn Hoài*, Director of Overseas Pastoral Office from Rome informed me that there were 3 Vietnamese priests at *Panat Nikhom* Camp, I sent this letter to you all to invite only one to Auckland, New Zealand, to be in charge of the Vietnamese Catholic Community in the Auckland Diocese".

The other two priests were waiting to be interviewed by the U.S. delegation. I said, "Yes!" So, I asked the U.S. delegation to transfer my file to New Zealand. Although I didn't know anything about this country right then. I accepted the invitation easily and quickly because I realised that wherever there was an invitation, that was my place. A few days later I went to the library to borrow books about New Zealand to learn more about this country.

In March 1990, the foreign priests helping in the Camp asked me to postpone my leaving for a year because the work of the *'Les Enfants Du Mékong'* needed a person who was familiar and experienced in administration. I answered them that I was willing to stay for another year but that I had to have the consent of Bishop Denis Browne of Auckland. The priests then asked the Apostolic Nuncio in Bangkok to send a letter to Bishop Denis Browne, who answered: "If the Refugee Camp needs Father Andrew (Fr. *Hữu Lễ Nguyễn*), the Auckland Diocese needs him too. Please allow Fr. Andrew to travel to New Zealand within the time limit discussed and decided". So, in early June 1990, I left the *Panat Nikhom* Refugee Camp to fly over and resettle in Auckland, New Zealand.

First Step to Heaven!

On a clear and frosty morning of June 6, 1990, an AIR NEW ZEALAND plane landed at Auckland Airport. I followed in the footsteps of the people leaving the plane. As soon as my foot touched the ground of the airport, I said: "Dear God, I thank You for leading me to the country of FREEDOM. From now on, I will accept this place as my second homeland." I was 47 years old at the time.

For me, New Zealand (Kiwi) is a wonderful country and Bishop Denis Browne of Auckland Diocese is an unparalleled Bishop. To express our gratitude to him, every year on New Year's Day, the Vietnamese Catholic Community in Auckland and I visit the now retired Bishop to celebrate his kindness. This habit we have kept for decades.

Choosing to resettle in New Zealand was one of the best and most important decisions of my life. In the end, the saying "Pristine Land Beckons Birds" was so right for me, after I had done everything but found no place in my homeland. In the end, the albatross with tired wings found a good place for a safe landing.

When I first arrived in New Zealand, a reporter from a major newspaper interviewed me, "Please tell me your feelings after 13 years in prison, and how you felt when you came to New Zealand?"

At that time, I said, **"In short, I would like to say, after getting out of prison and recalling those horrifying 13 years, I see clearly that God's**

Hand always touches my life. As for resettling down in New Zealand, I feel that New Zealand is my first step to Heaven!"

Hearing those remarks, the reporter laughed out loud. Probably, at that time he thought that I was just joking. He did not know that it was a most true and accurate words from bottom of my heart! If he had known that I was subsequently could not find a place in my homeland, that I had to risk my life again to cross the border into Thailand for freedom, he would have gasped marvelling how I had survived to relate first-hand statements being a living eyewitness to the inhumane atrocities of Communism, he would not have laughed. Maybe he would quietly sit and watch me for a long time with his…tearful eyes!

Supplement 3
Thankful for the Can of Water

Of all the guards I met during my thirteen years in prison, the majority of them gave me the impression that they did this job only as a way of earning a living. However, they all had a strong influence over our everyday activities. Guards were trained to carry out the policy of the Party, especially towards political prisoners. They were to treat us like their enemies.

Conversely, there were those who were gentle and likeable in their behaviour. These particular guards left me with a sense of fondness and appreciation. During my time at *Thanh Cẩm*, there were guards who gave me goosebumps at the very sound of their names, but there were also people like Master Sergeant *Hạ* to whom I would like to express my appreciation. I owed a deep gratitude in my mind and heart to him as I recalled those sad days of my life in the Bottom of Hell in *Thanh Cẩm* Prison.

Master Sergeant *Hạ* was the guard on duty the night we dug through the wall for our escape. He was, therefore, technically responsible, so I especially feared him the most after we were caught, expecting him to exact revenge. But I don't recall any sight of Guard *Hạ* among those who beat us after our recapture. Even a month later he was nowhere to be seen. I was glad and prayed he would go elsewhere, never coming near me again.

Then one afternoon, we were ordered to bring out all "*nội vụ*" (Belongings) for inspection. We were frightened out of our wits when we saw Guard *Hạ* standing in the shade at the building's end. He seemed to glare straight at me, making me even more afraid. I bowed my head and carried my possessions to a corner far from where he stood. When I turned around, I still saw him looking at me and I thought the time for retribution had come.

Master Sergeant *Hạ* walked slowly towards me. My heartbeat rapidly as I waited. I said, "Greetings, Cadre!" following the prison camp rules.

He nodded slightly but said nothing. Then stepping closer, he looked straight into my face and said just loud enough for me to hear, "*Anh Lễ*, you have made me lose everything!"

I replied sincerely, "I honestly apologise to you, Cadre, but please understand my situation."

That was our only conversation. I hadn't realised that he had such a kind heart. After that, Master Sergeant *Hạ* would sometimes come to take roll call with *Bùi Đình Thi.* Since our meeting, he had said nothing to me, until one day, almost two months after we were first shackled, we had an incident in our cell.

The *Thanh Hóa* summer climate was blazingly hot, making the disciplinary building like an oven in use. At that time, *Thuyên* and I were shackled in cell No. 5. Every day, we received our shared water ration of two aluminium 750ml. cans, one in the morning, one in the evening. This was all we had for drinking, washing, bathing, laundering, and wiping off sweat at night. We decided that, at any cost, we would always have to save one can for overnight when unimaginable heat radiated from the flat concrete roof, and we needed water to ease our resulting thirst.

Our food ration was yams and *Mắm chượp* (Salted fermented fish sauce). *Mắm chượp* had a terrible stench, but in our hunger we had a craving for anything, fishy smelling or not. Our combined ration twice a day was three yams, each being slightly bigger than one's big toe. One and a half pieces of yam per person was too little to satisfy us. I had the idea of splitting all three of them lengthwise so that it seemed as though we each had…three yams. My intention was to fool our eyes, but perhaps it fooled our stomach as well, because I felt fuller after dividing the yams the new way. *Thuyên* admired my insight very much. Every meal, we split the unpeeled yams, put them in a bowl of *Mắm chượp*, added a bit of water, and stirred well. But after eating the salty fish sauce, we were endlessly thirsty, not only for the moment, but throughout the entire night. It was imperative always to save some water.

One day *Thuyên*, who was addicted to nicotine, asked our cleaner, *Đạt,* if he could to get him some tobacco. That evening while collecting the 'movable' toilets, *Đạt* slipped him a bean-sized wad of rustic tobacco and a matchstick paper-wrapped in paper. To *Thuyên,* this was a priceless treasure.

That evening, after *Bùi Đình Thi* shackled us in for the night, *Thuyên* asked me to help organise everything on the platform, because he knew that after so long without any tobacco he would possibly get incredibly high.

As he had no pipe, he had to curl paper into a cone and wedged this between his lips. Before smoking, he instructed me that if he became too drugged, I was to push down on his chest to restore his breathing. We'd both heard of people who'd got so high on our strong locally grown tobacco that they stopped breathing and died. I helped him get a flame going, fired up a small piece of fabric and lite his paper cone. He "*ffffup...fffup... fffuped*" with all his strength. Perhaps, throughout his entire life, *Thuyên* had never been so delighted as when he tipped his head back towards the ceiling and exhaled puffs of smoke.

Then all of a sudden, he fell back. Coughing, eyes rolling, arms waving frantically in the air while his unshackled leg kicked wildly, he yelled, "*Anh Lễ...! Anh Lễ...! Help...! Help...! Anh Lễ...!*" I was frightened that he might die as I tried to pound his chest. But he turned away, pushing my hands aside and scratching himself all over as if hornets were stinging him. In this overdosed state, *Thuyên's* arm knocked over the last, precious can of water. I had carefully placed this in a corner, at the extremity of my arm's reach, thinking that, there it would be safe.

When *Thuyên* eventually quieted down, he was frightened by the water he spilled. It was only four p.m. in the afternoon and we would have to wait nineteen hours for the next distribution of water. Worse still, I had already begun to be thirsty and *Thuyên* was probably even thirstier after his ordeal. There was nothing we could do but wait for roll call when we could ask for water. Of course, if *Bùi Đình Thi* was on duty alone, we were unlikely to get any.

By roll call at 6.00 p.m., our throats burned with thirst and we were pleased to hear the jingle of the keys until we saw *Bùi Đình Thi*. As he inspected our shackles I asked for water, explaining we'd spilled our ration for the night. *Bùi Đình Thi*'s voice held a note of triumph as he replied, "You guys spilled plenty of water when you dug through the wall. So don't be asking for anymore!" He went out and locked the cell.

Then I saw Guard *Hạ* outside the window. I called out loudly to request water to replace what we'd spilled, saying our throats burned with thirst. *Bùi Đình Thi* repeated his previous reasoning. Upon hearing *Bùi Đình Thi*'s reasoning, Guard *Hạ* hesitated as if he wanted to say no.

I called out more eagerly again, "Please have compassion on us. We're so thirsty now, if we don't have water for tonight, we'll probably die!" I squeezed my aluminium can almost flat and slipped it through the window bars.

Guard *Hạ* still hesitated, then ordered, "*Bùi Đình Thi*, get these guys a can of water!" He had no option but to follow the Guard's orders. But when he passed me the filled can, he slammed it down so hard that nearly half of the water splashed out.

Bùi Đình Thi had got the water from the shallow tank where we did laundry and washed our hands, especially after emptying the bamboo toilet tubes. **According to my reasoning, despite the water was so dirty, however all the germs in that water tank would have been… poisoned to death, and could not cause us any harm!**

I will never forget my appreciation to Guard *Hạ* for his humanity to help us have a can of water. This can of water in fact a life-saving gift. Without it, we could sure die of thirst in the baking oven that night. (Please read Chapter 14: The Pits of Hell, The Human Baking Oven)

Shortly afterwards Master Sergeant *Hạ* left the Camp, not returning until 1986, a gap of seven years. I had been transferred back to the Solitary Confinement Section with twenty-eight other priests, and Guard *Hạ* came to visit us. By then, the relationship between the prisoners and the guards had grown a bit closer. During that visit, I reminded him of the water can incident. He answered, "I don't remember any more!". I said in all sincerity, "But I still remember and will always remember that I was grateful to you for the can of water."

Guard *Hạ* looked at me and smiled, something rare on his usually grave face. That was the last time I saw him, the Guard who showed humanity in a Communist prison.

Supplement 4
Meeting Bùi Đình Thi Again 15 Years Later

People who have read *"I MUST LIVE!"* are sure to recognise the role and the evil deeds of *Bùi Đình Thi* (Hereinafter BDT.), a prisoner Enforcer assigned by the Communists to *Thanh Cẩm* Prison. As for me, the person and the name *Bùi Đình Thi* (Hereinafter BDT.), have carved on my heart the embodiment of an evil devil and a horrid monster. It has stayed with me like a large and darkened tattoo which nothing can erase.

In the role of a prisoner Enforcer, BDT. himself murdered two of his fellow inmates, *Đặng Văn Tiếp* and *Lâm Thành Văn*. This was the same devil who tortured me until the end and pushed me to the brink of losing my mind. He tried every possible way to kill me but fate spared me from his murderous hands; however, he has left numerous wounds on my body. In Chapter 13 of this book, I wrote: **The disciplinary cell of *Thanh Cẩm* Prison was already Hell by itself. When it had the sadistic presence of *Bùi Đình Thi*, it went down many levels and turned into the Bottom of Hell.**

Fortunately, BDT.'s position as a prisoner Enforcer ended in 1981. The day he lost his position was one of the two happiest occasions of my thirteen prison years, second only to my transfer from *Quyết Tiến* Camp nicknamed '**Gateway to Heaven**' in August 1978. From that time, I was determined to shake off his name and image from my mind.

After getting out of prison in 1988, I escaped to Thailand, and eventually resettled in New Zealand in 1990. My new life in this democratic country, I decided to leave behind all the incidents of blood and tears that had filled my past, especially the thirteen years I had spent in communist prisons. In subsequent years, I travelled extensively to United States and other countries around the world in the role of a Chairman for the Committee of Human Rights and Religious Freedom for Vietnam.

A Flashback Memory

Unexpectedly, one day in September 1996, a former inmate in *Thanh Cẩm* prison, whom I had been close to, Mr *Lê Sơn*, told me that BDT. had arrived in the USA in 1994, in accordance with the H.O. Program. (Humanitarian Operation Program to accept South Vietnamese Army officers who spent at least 3 years in Communist prison). He had been seen at a Shopping Mall in South California. The person who saw him had also managed to get his address and phone number.

This news that BDT. had arrived in the USA really alarmed me because for the previous fifteen years his name had been erased from my mind. For a long time, I had always imagined that BDT. would have spent the rest of his life in Vietnam under the protection of the Communist regime, as a way of repaying his fervid service to a regime which had abetted him in the torturing and killing of the South Vietnamese political prisoners whom they wanted to get rid of.

Now suddenly, the news that he had shown up in California shocked me to the core. The entire picture of that 'Hell on Earth' with the sadistic image of BDT., suddenly came flooding back vividly to my mind. The memories of the beatings that he dealt me, the way he tormented me to the limit of my endurance, and pushing me to the realm of madness as I described in Chapter 13 of this book always imprinted markedly on my mind, despite the fact that it had happened 15 years earlier.

In addition to that, there was a scene where *Đặng Văn Tiếp* was lying on the floor, curled up and frozen in fear, under the heels of BDT., who kept stomping madly on his chest and his stomach. Then the loud scream, "Oh, Mother, Mother, I'm dying, I'm dying!" Those were the last words from *Đặng Văn Tiếp*. He died under the heels of BDT... I also retain the image of *Lâm Thành Văn* whom the evil devil had starve to death in a disciplinary cell at *Thanh Cẩm* Prison. Those morbid and gruesome images were still dancing in my head. (Please read Chapter 12: The Gamble of Life and Death)

A Problem of Conscience

I could not understand why *Bùi Đình Thi* had chosen to go to the USA, and worse than that, had decided to settle in California where many former inmates from *Thanh Cẩm* Prison were living, and every one of them was very aware of his heinous crimes. With this news that BDT. was now in the USA, I began to ask myself: "What should I do? What do I have to do?" I had a feeling that the lost souls of my two brothers who had been murdered by BDT. after our failed escape from prison on the 1st of May 1979, had returned to beg me to hold the murderer to account. Former inmates from *Thanh Cẩm* Prison, who knew very well the horrible crimes committed by BDT., at the time, urged me to take action. Some of the former inmates were even considering taking his life.

After a few days racking my brain, and asking God for help in these unusual circumstances, I opened the Bible to seek solace and guidance. I read those verses about forgiveness towards one's enemies especially in Luke, Chapter 6, and Verse 27: 'Love your enemies, do good to those who hate you.' I pondered this verse for many days, mentally tortured by it. I realised then that there was a big gap between reading God's words and practicing God's words. It was really easy to read God's words, but practicing God's words was certainly not easy at all, especially when God taught us to forgive enemies, and particularly in this case, that the enemy is the evil monster *Bùi Đình Thi*. He was the person who gave me a strong reason to write this sentence in Chapter 17: *"The kindness and compassion of the human heart has its limits. However, the evil of human nature is boundless and beyond one's imagination, especially when evil is nurtured by immoral regimes."*

It was a very difficult time for me. I prayed so much at that time. I prayed continually. Eventually I decided to forgive him because I thought that under the circumstances, only a complete and unconditional forgiveness could solve this problem deep within my consciousness. I discussed my decision to forgive BDT. completely with two former Catholic inmates at *Thanh Cẩm* Prison: *Lê Sơn* and *Nguyễn Tiến Đạt*.

A Hard Decision

On the evening of 8 September 1996, *Nguyễn Tiến Đạt* was at *Lê Sơn's* house in Fullerston, California. We decided to go ahead with that decision to forgive. *Đạt* telephoned BDT., and after an exchange of courtesies *Đạt* said, "*Anh Thi*, (Brother Thi) there is someone here who wants to talk to you," and passed the phone to me.

I held the phone and started, "Hello *Anh Thi*, bastard *Nguyễn Hữu Lễ previously in Thanh Cẩm* Prison is here!"

There was a complete silence at the end of the line, then I heard: "Is that you, Father *Lễ*?"

I was surprised by the way BDT. addressed me. His answer made me cry and tears rolled down from my eyes because I always thought I would never hear the word "Father" from BDT.'s mouth again. After that phone call, I was more determined than ever to forgive BDT... I said I would come to see him and he said he would like me to come at 6.00 p.m. the following day.

The next day, September 9, 1996, I went with *Lê Sơn* and *Nguyễn Tiến Đạt* to meet BDT... I wanted to have a witness to this encounter. Moreover, I felt that I needed to be supported by these two close friends in order to feel safe in the presence of BDT. who I still feared. The fear and horror I had experienced during those years at *Thanh Cẩm* Prison have always haunted me. In those days, whenever BDT. called me up for interrogation I would often urinate or defecate in my pants.

Bùi Đình Thi was living in a communal building block. There were a few blocks running parallel with each other. There were walking corridors in between, not wide enough for parking a car. Therefore, we had to park along the street and walk to his apartment.

When we came to his apartment, it was getting dark. From afar, we saw BDT. squatting on the pavement waiting for us. I was somewhat apprehensive, so I asked *Lê Sơn* and *Nguyễn Tiến Đạt* to walk close to me in case something bad happened. When approaching BDT., I noticed that he was wearing a white T-shirt and a pair of black pants. The T-shirt was tucked inside the pants. He now looked much older. His face looked austere but visibly fierce. Probably he had been waiting too long for us, so he had had to sit down. That was the first time I had met my 'Old friend' for fifteen years.

I was afraid that in this position BDT. might do something desperate. Who would know? He might have been hiding a knife in his hand or any other weapon to murder people without any evidence. At that moment, I could only have blamed myself for being too naïve and trusting. I shouldn't have made an appointment to see him. To be on the safe side, I should have come unannounced, as a person like BDT. who easily commit any evil act if he had a mind to.

When BDT. saw us approaching, he stood up. I glanced quickly at his hands. He held no weapons; so I felt assured to hold out my hand to shake his. As soon as BDT. grasped my hand, I experienced a sudden and unusual feeling.

A Frightened Allusion

I felt as if I was being electrocuted, I became dizzy! I could not see things clearly and everything was moving around me in a circle. I saw BDT.'s hand covered in blood. The blood flowed from his elbow down to his hand, and then trickled down to the concrete he was squatting on drop by drop…It was all fresh blood. It was my blood! It was my blood which was spurting out from my mouth and my nose when BDT. tortured me so viciously, a beating that was due to fact that I had given a fellow inmate a yellow shirt in the disciplinary cell at *Thanh Cẩm* Prison in 1979.

I suddenly lost my balance and then passed out, slumping down on the lane. *Lê Sơn* and *Nguyễn Tiến Đạt* hurriedly lifted me up. I stood still, holding *Lê Sơn's* shoulders, and after a while recovered my composure completely. I pulled out a handkerchief to wipe off the sweat on my face and my shirt.

Bùi Đình Thi took us to a small and narrow house. It seemed strange that it was dark inside the house, there was only one light in the kitchen. As I was afraid of the dark, I asked him to turn the light on in the living room. BDT. then told his wife to bring us three glasses of Coke. We sat down at a table in the middle of the house. I was facing BDT., *Lê Sơn* sat between us, and *Nguyễn Tiến Đạt* was busy taking photos. BDT. sat quietly, his hands clasped together and his head looking down. He never looked up straight to my face.

This was the first time I had sat face to face with BDT., having a chance to observe his features and other characteristics showing on the body of this evil person. His hair was thin, his face was long, gaunt, and darkened. His chin was almost pointed. His cheeks were protruding above an ugly mouth. His lips didn't seem to close properly and were always wet with saliva. Occasionally, he licked the corners of his mouth with his tongue. He put his two long hands on the table. They were rugged and full of veins. The nails were long and dirty.

I still remembered the hands with long, sickening and ugly-shaped fingers, which had been covered by the blood of many inmates in *Thanh Cẩm* Prison, perhaps, mostly with my blood. This was the typical image of the hand of a murderer. This was the person I feared most in my whole life, and he was now sitting in front of me, with his head facing downwards. At that moment, BDT.'s wife came to stand behind him.

As there was nothing much to say I started right away: "Brother *Thi*, I came here today to forgive you. However, there was one thing I would like to ask you. This was a big question which had been haunting me for many years.

Could you tell me why you resolutely wanted to kill me, after you had killed *Tiếp* and *Văn*? I thought you would have gained enough merits for your role in prison. We had had no hatred between us, we hadn't known each other before, I was a Catholic priest, and you were a Catholic, so why were you determined to kill me?"

Bùi Đình Thi sat in silence, his head bent downwards. After a while, he looked up, but not at me, and muttered: "Father, I found it hard to say."

I replied, "If you can't tell me, I don't want to force you. But this matter will stay with me until the day I die." Then I told BDT. he had to kneel in front of the altar where *Đặng Văn Tiếp's* photo was displayed to ask for forgiveness. As well, I gave him the phone number of *Đặng Văn Thụ*, a younger brother of *Đặng Văn Tiếp*, who was living in Maryland. Later I learned that BDT. did call *Thụ* to ask for permission to go to his house, but *Thụ* declined, saying: "Please let my brother's soul rest in peace."

After about fifteen minutes, I stood up to leave. The three glasses of Coke had not been touched. *Nguyễn Tiến Đạt* had taken photos as I wanted to have a record of the meeting and in one photograph, one of my hands was shaking BDT.'s hand, and my other hand was around his neck. For other people, this photo was very normal, but for me it is the most historic photo of my life. After the visit to forgive BDT. unconditionally, I felt totally relieved.

While remembering this episode, I would like to share with you, my dear and respected readers, the following idea: The story of my meeting with BDT. after 15 years when the circumstances had changed completely and the positions of the players had also changed, brings to mind a common saying we often hear, that is '**What goes around comes around**'.

As the earth is round, people with power and wealth at present have to act towards other people, especially those people who are powerless, in such a way that when circumstances change, they are able to face those people without shame. I just hope that what happened to me would be a lesson to other people, especially to those who have followed my memoir, "*I MUST LIVE!*"

Auckland, New Zealand

The 50th Anniversary of my Priesthood (1970–2020)
Father Andrew Huu Le Nguyen (Fr. Andrew Nguyen), Author of "*I MUST LIVE!*"